The Great Transformation of China

China's Economic Transformation, Innovation and Development

Series Editor

Fulin Chi, China Institute for Reform and Development, Haikou, Hainan, China

China is facing unprecedented challenges in its continued modernization process. This series brings together government insiders, academics, and policymakers in articulating specific social and political issues that China is trying to resolve, offering scholars around the world insights into what China's leadership see as the biggest challenges facing the nation and how best to resolve them. The series publishes monographs and edited volumes with contributions on a global basis dedicated to ground-breaking research on the Chinese modernization process.

More information about this series at
https://link.springer.com/bookseries/15346

Qingyou Guan · Weigang Gao

Internet Finance

Concepts, Factors and Ecology

ZHEJIANG UNIVERSITY PRESS
浙江大学出版社

palgrave
macmillan

Qingyou Guan
Reality Institute of Advanced Finance
Beijing, China

Weigang Gao
PSBC Wealth Management
Corporation Limited
Beijing, China

Translated by Fan Fang, Wantian Hu and Yueyu Chen

ISSN 2509-6001 ISSN 2509-601X (electronic)
The Great Transformation of China
ISBN 978-981-16-4739-0 ISBN 978-981-16-4740-6 (eBook)
https://doi.org/10.1007/978-981-16-4740-6

Jointly published with Zhejiang University Press
The print edition is not for sale in China Mainland. Customers from China Mainland please order the print book from Zhejiang University Press.
ISBN of the China edition: 9787308152457

This Palgrave Macmillan imprint is published by the registered company Springer Nature Singapore Pte Ltd.
The registered company address is: 152 Beach Road, #21-01/04 Gateway East, Singapore 189721, Singapore

Series Editor's Preface

The Year 2020: A Historic Choice of Economic Transformation and Upgrading

A great nation with 13 billion people is facing a changing situation it has not ever faced for a thousand years. Change, transformation and innovation feature the main melody of the era. In this era of high integration of growth, transformation and reform, "great transformation" is exactly what decides the destiny of China. In other words, not only will "toxic assets" left in the traditional system have to be eliminated completely but also the new way for further growth needs to be paved quickly while letting loose the new motive force of development.

The major transformation in China's "13th Five-Year Plan" (FYP) is historically decisive. With the economic transformation as the focal point, both social transformation and government transformation are in the crucial period of transition in which innumerable thorny problems have to be tackled. Our general judgment is that the year 2020 is like a "gorge" we have to jump over. Specifically, by the end of 2020 we will have eliminated the pressure on short-term growth and changed the way for economic development while achieving a comparatively prosperous society in an all-round way and becoming one of the high-income countries in the world. If we plan well enough to make the best use of 2020, a mid-term period in the 13th FYP, we can lay a solid foundation for the medium-to-long-term peaceful and sustainable growth. If we fail to grasp the historical opportunity of 2020, we will lose the initiative of "great transformation", thus resulting in multiple systemic economic risks.

The significant breakthrough for achieving the economic transformation and upgrading in the 13th FYP period is how to cope with "four threes". Firstly, three major trends: one for industrial transformation and upgrading from "made in China" to "intellectually made in China"; one for urbanized transformation and upgrading from scale to population; and one for consumption pattern upgrading from material to service. Secondly, three major challenges: one for achieving a major breakthrough in structural reform by enhancing the structural adjustment despite the economic downturn; one for "corner overtaking" by responding to the global new round of scientific and technological revolution and increasing the ability to innovate; and one for a real and down-to-earth reform. At present, the transformation depends more on the all-round breakthrough in reform. It couldn't move forward at all without the change in systematic structure. And the growth would suffer big pressures. Thirdly, three major goals: one for industry, namely forming the service-dominated industrial structure by accelerating the process of service in manufacture; one for a major motive force, namely forming a consumption-oriented new pattern of economic growth, in which consumption guides investment and domestic consumption becomes a main force that spurs economic growth; and one for opening-up, namely forming a new open pattern dominated by service trade so as to redouble service trade in scale. Finally, three major relationships to be handled properly: one between the short term and the medium-to-long term in which the best job should be done for 2020 (the mid-term period) while resolving contradictions in the short term, basing ourselves on the mid-term and keeping our eyes on the long term; one between speed and structure which requires accelerating the structural adjustment while maintaining an increase by 7% or so; and one between policy and system in which the key is to gain a policy advantage in achieving institutional innovation under the economic pressure.

The past 40 years of reform and opening-up have left us numerable valuable assets. The most valuable one is that the more complex the situation may be and the more fundamental the change in environment, the more determined we will be in carrying out the reform and pushing through the transformation. All these require that the "great transformation" need overall arrangement and ambitious planning, need a significant breakthrough in the reform of industrial structure, urban–rural structure, regional structure, ownership pattern, open structure and administrative power structure, and need prospective planning in green sustainable development and "internet plus" development trends.

By judging the transformational reform in the 13th FYP period, China (Hainan) Institute for Reform and Development (CIRD) and Zhejiang University Press have jointly designed and published this set of series entitled *The Great Nation in Great Transformation—Economic Transformation and Innovative Development in China*. The book series has paid attention to readability based on being strategic, prospective and academic. It is our expectation that the series will offer enlightenment to readers who are closely watching the transformational reform in China while playing an active role in promoting the transformational reform in the 13th FYP period.

The authors of the series are mostly well-known scholars in their own subject areas, who wrote their respective books in their spare-time. As the director of the editorial board of the series, I wish, first and foremost, to extend my sincere thanks to the consultants, editorial board members, authors, and the leadership and editors of the press.

Last but not least, this set of series covers a wide range of subject areas, each volume representing its author's own research conclusions and academic opinions. The set does not require consistency in terms of viewpoints. Any criticism and correction from readers are truly welcome.

September 2015 Fulin Chi

Preface

The first time I received the invitation to writing this book is in August 2014. CIRD specially convened a forum to listen to our opinions on "Series of Big Transformation of the Great Power—Economic Transformation and Innovation Development of China". At that time, the Internet finance was born one year, and there were a plenty of views on Internet finance in the industry. It can be said that there were many different opinions and it is unable to decide which one was right. Under such circumstance, it is exactly the right time to discuss the big transformation of the great power, because the reform of the financial industry under the new normal background is an important factor which determines the structural transformation of China's economy. As an important force in China's economic and financial fields in the future, Internet finance has already received the approval of the top government official. Where will Internet finance march toward? What impact will the Internet finance have on China's financial system in the future? These are all issues that deserve our in-depth discussion. But firstly, we should make clear several issues: What exactly is Internet finance? What are the core factors of Internet finance? What kind of ecosystem does Internet finance have? I think these should be answered first. If even the concepts are not clarified, the explorations of the future development trend and the impact on the financial system will like a blind man feeling an elephant.

Besides, when I received the invitation, some important strategic concepts such as the new economic normality, Industry 4.0 and the

"Internet+" action plan were just proposed or not yet proposed, which led us not to think about the "past and present" of Internet finance from a more macro or profound level. It can be seen that the core of Industry 4.0 and that of the "Internet+" action plan both emphasize on the digitalization of future economic components and economic driving forces, or datamation. A series of data-centered processes such as data transmission, interaction and matching will become the source power of future economic development. If Industry 4.0 and the "Internet+" action plan put forward the requirements for the "Internet + Finance" datamation from the perspective of economic development, then the emergence of Internet finance is to reverse this process. Since Internet finance is the use of big data to achieve a series of processes such as credit assessment, default probability and risk pricing which cannot be achieved or are not worth achieving by the traditional finance. It can be said that Internet finance itself emphasizes datamation. In this respect, the thoughts on Industry 4.0, "Internet+" action plan and Internet finance are consistent, which can be said to be "coincidental". Therefore, if the emergence and development of Internet finance are studied on the basis of Industry 4.0 and the "Internet+" action plan, it may be easier to understand why Internet finance has been quickly recognized as soon as it emerged, and has made great achievements in a short time.

In the context of structural transformation of China's economy, this book attempts to answer the three questions including what is Internet finance, what are the core factors of Internet finance, and how the ecosystem of Internet finance is structured; and this book intends to explain to you various modes of Internet finance, their basic features and why they belong to Internet finance based on the core factors of Internet finance. Actually, these questions are mostly neglected by existing researches. In the author's view, without a deep study on each business model, the direct analysis of these modes is lack of preciseness. Now that the domain of Internet finance is uncertain, such as P2P and crowd funding, why are these models included in the scope of Internet finance? It seems that no one is concerned about such a question, and no one can answer it. As a book which systematically introduces Internet finance, it is necessary to study these questions carefully.

Internet finance in a narrow sense refers to the behavior of Internet enterprises using IT technology and accumulated mass data to finish customers' credit assessment and risk pricing through technology and method innovation, so as to provide financial services to customers bypassing the traditional financial institutions. Big data, low transaction costs and a convenient user experience are the three pillars supporting Internet finance. In particular, the use of big data is the core factor and key force supporting all business models of Internet finance. The complete ecosystem of Internet finance includes seven models, including credit reporting, searching, online financial management, big data finance, P2P, crowd funding and third-party payment, wherein credit reporting is the foundation and premise of Internet finance. Without the guarantee of credit reporting, some financial activities will be out of the question. The emergence of Internet finance is exactly because traditional financial institutions are unable to complete the credit reporting of the grass-roots economy. Search is the flow entrance of the Internet financial system. Users can realize product matching through search. Online financial management, big data finance, P2P and crowd funding are the investment and financing models of Internet finance, responsible for product design and sales. Lastly, the third-party payment is the fund expressway of Internet finance in the way that all fund transfers are completed through the third-party payment. These seven models have constituted an integrated ecosphere of Internet finance, none of which is dispensable. However, we will emphasize herein that although Internet finance has a great improvement compared with traditional finance, the positioning of Internet finance is still the supplement to existing financial systems at present.

The most important core parts of the Internet financial system are four investment and financing modes including online financial management, big data finance, P2P and crowd funding. As a kind of finance, Internet finance also provides the investment and financing service of funds. It realizes the financing of funds through online financial management, big data finance, P2P and crowd funding. It should be specially explained that the three core factors of Internet finance are fully reflected in the above the four investment and financing models, especially big data. The application of big data in Internet finance is the most praiseworthy aspect of Internet finance. The effects of big data are mainly reflected in credit assessment, risk pricing and risk control. In online financial management products, big data should be used for liquidity risk prediction and assessment. In big data finance, P2P and crowd funding products, big data should be used for credit assessment. Certainly, in other models, the application of big data is equally important.

This book comprehensively and profoundly introduces Internet finance, containing ten chapters. Chapter 1 introduces the great power economy in the transformation; Chapter 2 introduces the ecosystem of Internet finance; Chapters 3–9, respectively, discuss the main models of Internet finance, focusing on the big data which is the fundamental innovation of Internet finance; and Chapter 10 is a reflection on the development of Internet finance.

Internet finance is a broad, profound and complex financial ecology. For such a topic which is still in the process of constant evolution, the difficulty to give it a comprehensive, complete, objective and detailed description can be imagined. Only with an evolutionary perspective and sustained attention can we look into its wonderful essence. In addition, since the author is limited, various problems will inevitably occur in this process. Please don't hesitate to let me know if there is any mistake.

Beijing, China

Qingyou Guan
Weigang Gao

Contents

List of Figures

Chapter 1

Chapter 2

Chapter 3

Chapter 4

Chapter 5

Chapter 6

Chapter 7

Chapter 8

Chapter 9

List of Tables

Chapter 4

Chapter 5

Chapter 6

Chapter 7

Chapter 8

Chapter 9

CHAPTER 1

New Thinking on Dangerous Situation: A Great Power in the Transformation

Over the past 30 years, the relatively balanced international economic structure and the stable domestic environment have molded the China model and China speed with Chinese characteristics. But the outbreak of the subprime mortgage crisis has broken this delicate balance, marking the collapse of the world economic structure. Based on this, China model and China speed that have been proud of in the past start to come down, and their aftermath has gradually emerged—high debt, real estate bubble and overcapacity. Unavoidably, we must start a new round of reform. Transformation and upgrading are effective methods for reform. The process of integration and optimization centered on transformation and upgrading of our economy is called the new economic normality. The transformation from traditional manufacturing industry to high-end manufacturing industry, from secondary industry to tertiary industry and from investment-and-export-driven economy to consumption-driven economy still relies on small and micro economies ultimately, which are the decisive factors of China's economy. To invigorate them, the most important thing is to restructure our financing system. Fortunately, Industry 4.0 and "Internet+ " have provided us with new ideas: digitalization can solve the financing difficulties that have perplexed us for a long time.

For decades, China's economy has always been one of the topics which are most frequently talked about in China and even in the world. Speaking

Q. Guan and W. Gao, *Internet Finance*,
The Great Transformation of China,
https://doi.org/10.1007/978-981-16-4740-6_1

of China's economy, it will inevitably refer to reform and opening up. Normally, we will regard reform and opening up as the starting point for the economic take-off of new China. Since the implementation of reform and opening up in China, great improvements have shown in economic growth, income, taxation, production and other aspects. Many people are asking, what is the reason for the success of China's economy? What does reform and opening up bring to China? What changes has China made? In fact, these are very complicated issues. We may see different reasons from different perspectives and levels. However, in our view, the great success of China's economy gained in the past 30 years may be because that the reform and opening up helps China find a development model that conforms to the trend of world economic development and meanwhile corresponds to China's national conditions. This model helps China find the role and positioning suitable for its own development in the world economic system. It complies with the general trend of the world economic development and China's economic development and effectively connects China's development demands with the objective changes of the world economy, thus forming a mode of economic development with Chinese characteristics and China speed, becoming an oriental color in the world economy in the past period.

However, we should remember, as exhorted by Marx, that things are constantly changing. The economic models built relying on past world conditions and national conditions are not necessarily tenable in a changing world. Under the general background of the new world economy and China's development, it is necessary to change the past models, otherwise China's economy will have no way out.

1 Formation of China Model

Looking back on the 37-year development of China's economy, the most amazing achievements are the huge scale of China's economy and the incredible China speed. The total scale of China's economy in 1978 was only 0.37 trillion yuan, less than the odd of present scale. Perhaps the Chinese themselves might not realize that they would achieve such rapid development at that time. Several climaxes once appeared in China's economy throughout the 1980s and 1990s, but the overall growth was unstable, and the characteristic of sharp fluctuations in economic growth was prominent. The real highly stable growth began in 1999 when China took the lead in getting out of the predicament of the Asian financial crisis, and China's economy quickly bottomed out. In 2000, the scale of China's economy reached 9.98 trillion yuan, with a year-on-year growth of 8.4%. China's accession to the WTO in 2001 has become a powerful driving force to support China's economic take-off. After then, China's economy has maintained rapid growth for seven consecutive years. As of 2007, the scale of China's economy reached 26.8 trillion yuan, with a growth rate of 14.2%. China officially surpassed Germany and became the world's third largest economic entity. Even under the impact of the financial tsunami, China still maintained relatively high economic growth, and its economic aggregate had increased steadily. In 2010, China surpassed Japan and became the world's second largest economic entity with a total scale of 40.89 trillion yuan. Although China's economic growth had declined slightly since then, by the end of 2014, China's economic aggregate had reached 63.65 trillion yuan. According to the estimation of the World Bank based on purchasing power parity, China had surpassed the United States and became the world's largest economic entity on September 29, 2014. Although the National Bureau of Statistics is doubtful about this, China's continuously enhanced economic influence is unquestionable (Fig. 1).

China model and China speed are both high-profile worldwide. It should be known that there are only 13 economic entities which maintain a high growth rate over 7% for continuous 25 years after the World War

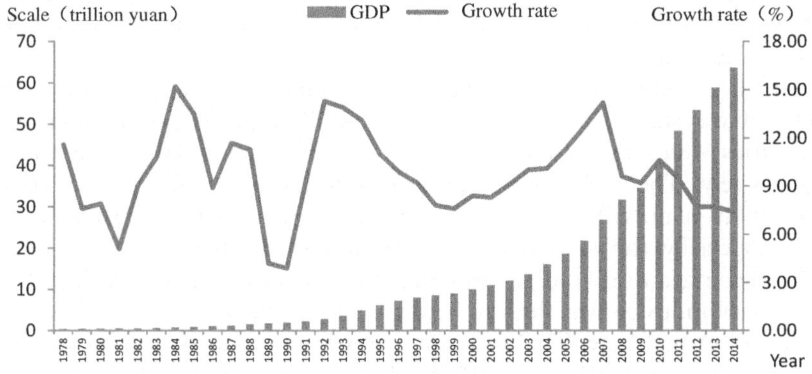

Fig. 1 Scale and growth rate of China's GDP from 1978 to 2014 (*Data source* Wind Database)

II, wherein 10 of them started to slow down from the third decade. Only Taiwan of China keeps the growth rate over 7% in the fourth decade, and the rest economic entities have fallen below 4%. At present, China has entered into the fourth decade of high growth. What does the high growth of China's economy benefit from? What factors have contributed to the high growth of China's economy?

China's Industrial Structure

For a long time, the features of China's industrial model dominated by the secondary industry are obvious. Especially, the development of the manufacturing industry is in line with the development strategy of China's industrialization. From the perspective of China's industrial structure, among the three industries, the secondary industry has always been in a dominant position, which is followed by the tertiary industry. The primary industry is the last. The establishment of a country based on industry is a basic strategy based on national conditions. In the initial stage of reform and opening up, the basic situation of China's economy was the contradiction between backward productivity and the productive relations with huge demand, mainly reflected in the shortage of product supply, especially the supply of manufactured goods. To achieve the development of national economy, a powerful manufacturing industry is necessary. Therefore, within quite a long time, we have been expanding the supply of manufactured products by vigorously developing the secondary industry. Thus the secondary industry has maintained a relatively rapid growth rate and a large scale.

At the beginning of reform and opening up, the scale of each industry was still relatively small. The scales of the primary and secondary industries were relatively large, 100 billion yuan and 170 billion yuan, respectively. The scale of the tertiary industry was the smallest, only 90 billion yuan. After that, each industry kept a relatively fast growth rate, especially the secondary industry and the tertiary industry, basically keeping a double-digit growth rate. It is not hard to see that the secondary industry was slightly better than the tertiary industry both in scale and growth rate. The first climax of China's industrial development occurred between 1978 and 1988, during which each industry maintained a relatively high growth rate. During this period, the growth rate of the tertiary industry exceeded that of the secondary industry, and its gap with the secondary industry was also shrunk constantly. Even the primary industry had maintained a double-digit growth rate. As of the end of 1988, the scale of each industry had realized exponential growth than in 1978. The second development climax occurred between 1991 and 1997. During this stage, the secondary industry realized ultra-convention development and far exceeded the tertiary industry both in development speed and scale. The industrial model that the secondary industry drove economic growth was basically formed. By the end of 1997, the scale of the secondary industry had reached 3.74 trillion, which was 1.35 times of the tertiary industry and 2.62 times of the primary industry. Also at this stage, the development of the primary and tertiary industries was relatively stable, the fluctuation of the growth rate was small and the gap between the primary and tertiary industry and the secondary industry was significantly enlarged. The third stage of industrial development is from 1998 to 2012. The most obvious feature of this stage is that the growth rate of the secondary industry and that of the tertiary industry tended to be the same, the gap between the two industries was gradually shrunk, and the trend from the secondary industry in the dominant position to the common development of the secondary and tertiary industry began to show. In general, the industrial model dominated by the secondary industry in the development history of the past 30 years is undoubted (Figs. 2 and 3).

The composition of China's industrial structure can be clearly demonstrated through the proportion of each industry in GDP. In the composition of GDP, the secondary industry has always ranked the first place, with an average of 45.04%. Especially since 1991, the secondary industry has risen steadily. The proportion of the tertiary industry shows a trend of slow rising, from around 20 to 45%, which is basically the same as the secondary industry. In recent years, the tertiary industry has surpassed the secondary industry. The secondary industry shows a trend of constant decrease. At present, the proportion of the primary industry in GDP has dropped to below 10%.

From the perspective of the contribution rate of each industry to GDP growth, the growth of the three major industries before 1990 was not stable, the industrial model of China did not take shape, and the contribution rate of each industry to economic growth also fluctuated. But in general, the contribution rate of the secondary industry is the largest, and the contribution rate of the primary industry and that of the tertiary industry are equivalent. However, since 1991, with the formation of China's secondary-industry-dominated industrial model, the contribution

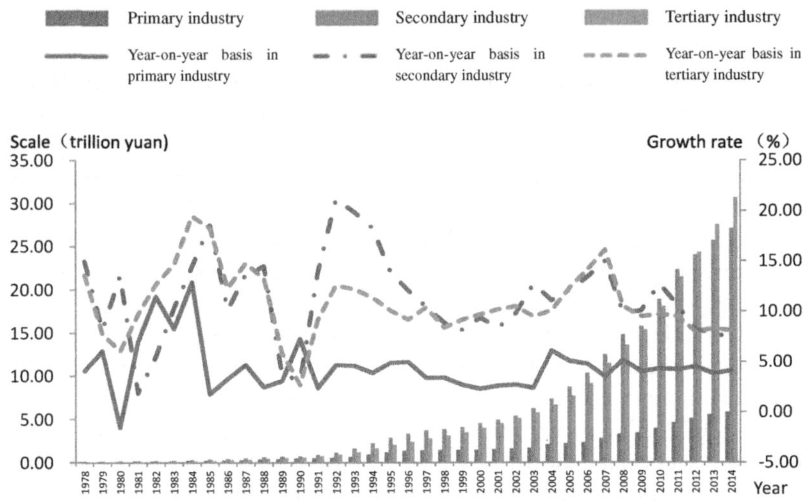

Fig. 2 Scale and growth rate of each industry in China from 1978 to 2014 (*Data source* Wind Database)

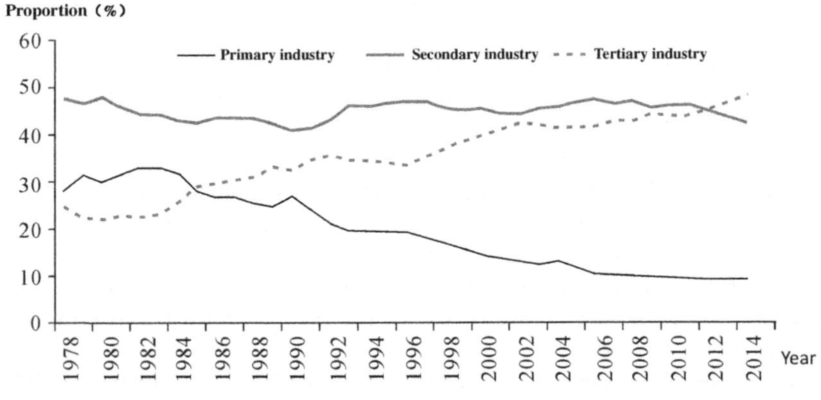

Fig. 3 GDP ratio of each industry in China from 1978 to 2014 (*Data source* Wind Database)

of the secondary industry to economic growth had begun to emerge. Since the early 1990s, the contribution rate of the secondary industry had maintained in a high level of about 60%. Meanwhile, the contribution rate of the tertiary industry was only 30%, and that of the primary industry was less than 10%. After 2000, the contribution rate of the secondary industry began to level off and remained at about 50%. At the same time, the contribution rate of the tertiary industry increased slightly, which was about 45%, and that of the primary industry further dropped to about 5% (Figs. 4 and 5).

From the perspective of the pulling rate to economic growth, the effects of each industry are different. The pulling rate of the secondary industry to economic growth is the largest, with an average of about 6%, especially before 2000, its pulling effect on economy is quite obvious. After 2000, the pulling effects of the secondary industry and the tertiary industry on economy tended to be equivalent. The pulling rate of the tertiary industry to economy was in an average of 4%, but the pulling effect had been gradually enhanced after 2000. The pulling rate of the primary industry to the economy gradually decreased, which is below 1% at present.

According to the analysis on China's industrial structure, especially the five indexes of each industry, including scale, growth rate, proportion,

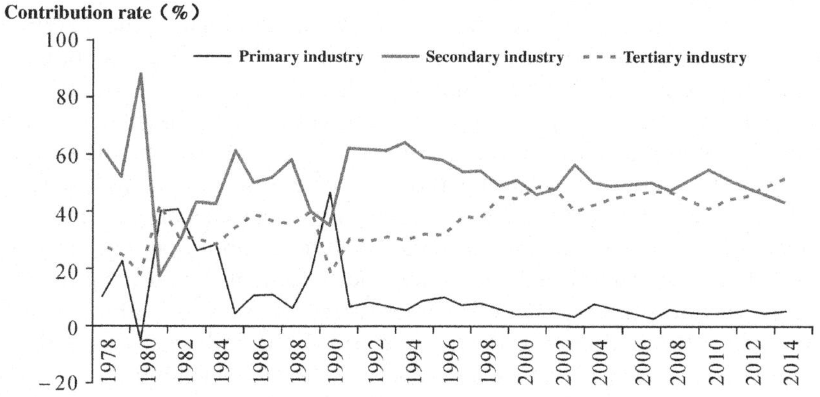

Fig. 4 Contribution rate of each industry to economic growth from 1978 to 2014 (*Data source* Wind Database)

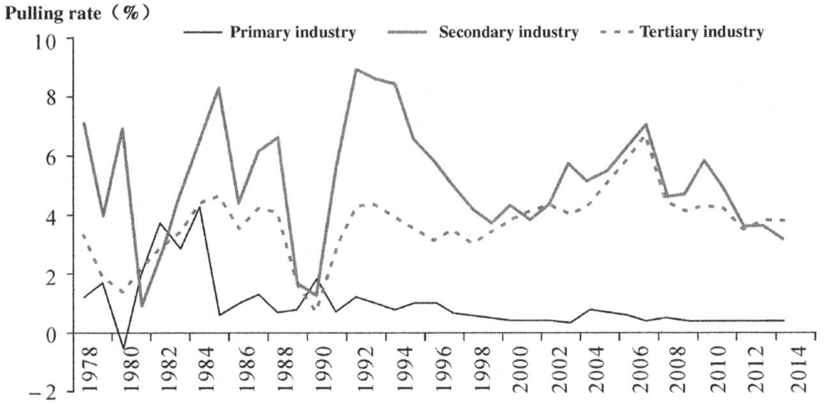

Fig. 5 Pulling rate of each industry to economic growth from 1978 to 2014 (*Data source* Wind Database)

contribution rate and pulling rate, China's economy has gradually established a secondary-industry-oriented economic development structure through reform and opening up. That is, to satisfy domestic demands, improve industrial structure and improve international competitiveness by vigorously developing industries, especially manufacturing industry. From 1990s to the beginning of twenty-first century and even before the financial crisis, the secondary industry has dominated the development of China's economy, and the importance of the secondary industry on economic growth can be seen from scale proportion, contribution rate and pulling rate. This kind of economic growth model is based on current situation of commodity shortage in China. It can realize the increase of commodity supply by enlarging the scale of the secondary industry, so as to further improve the competitiveness of China's secondary industry. Facts prove that at the initial stage of reform and opening up, the way of driving the overall economic development by developing the secondary industry especially manufacturing industry is correct, which not only satisfies domestic demand, expands the industrial strength of China, but also makes China's economy finds its role in the world economic system and successfully integrates into the system, becoming a member of the world economic system. In the previous development, the secondary-industry-centered economic model is effective.

China's Demand Structure

From the perspective of demand structure, China's economy has formed a fixed model. According to the quantity required, the scale of consumption is the largest, that of investment is in the second place, while the scale of export is the smallest. However, from the perspective of development speed, the growth rate of export and that of investment are higher than that of consumption all the time, especially export, its growth rate has always been at the leading position. This model of driving economic growth led by high growth in export and investment has continued throughout most of the period after the reform and opening up until the outbreak of the financial crisis in 2007. The result of China's economic development led by this model is the expansion of investment and export scale and relative reduction of consumption scale (Fig. 6).

At the initial stage of reform and opening up, the scales of consumption, investment and export were very small. The scale of consumption was 220 billion yuan, and that of investment was only 140 billion yuan. The growth rate of consumption was slightly higher than that of investment at the beginning. In 1980, export had increased in a rate higher than consumption and investment. In 1983, the growth rate of investment started to exceed that of consumption, and such growth rate has been maintained in the subsequent 20 years. At this point, the model

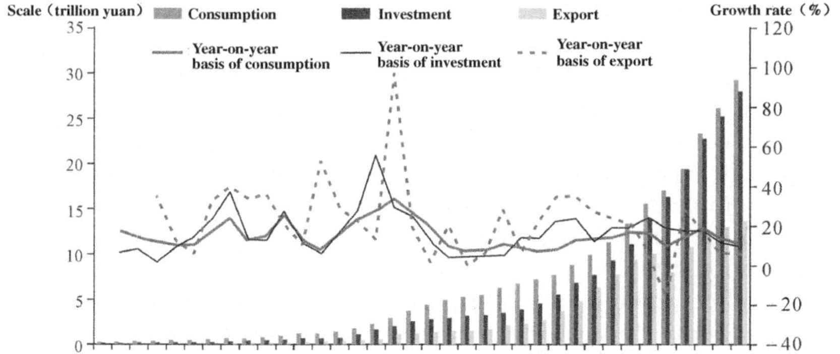

Fig. 6 Scale and growth rate of China's three major demands from 1978 to 2013 (*Data source* Wind Database)

that economic growth is driven by export, investment and consumption had been basically formed: the growth rate of export ranks the first, followed by that of investment and last is that of consumption. At this stage, the growth rate of the three had changed a lot, especially the export, reflecting that the demand structure was still immature. Since 2001, this model has truly matured: export has continued to expand at a stable growth rate, and investment has expanded constantly. In contrast, the growth rate of consumption has declined significantly. China's model of stimulating economic growth by export and investment took shape. Under this model, China's economy had achieved continuous high growth. Before 2007, export maintained a growth rate of over 27%, and the growth rate of investment reached more than 20%, while that of consumption was only about 13%.

Under the model that economic growth is driven by export and investment, the most obvious feature is that the proportions of export and investment in GDP have constantly increased, and meanwhile the proportion of consumption starts to decline. In 1980s, the proportion of consumption in GDP was over 60%, which even once reached 67% at the initial stage. However, the proportion of consumption had been slowly declining since then, and this downward trend was particularly evident after 2000. By 2010, the proportion of consumption had dropped to around 48%, which was basically the same as investment. The proportion of investment had been rising slowly, and the upward trend began to accelerate after 2001. By 2010, its proportion had risen to 48%. The growth rate of export was higher than that of investment, which had kept high since 1980. In 2007, the proportion of export rose to 35%, and declined to some extent after then (Figs. 7 and 8).

From the perspective of the contribution rate to GDP, the effect of investment significantly exceeds consumption, especially after 2001. The contribution rate of investment to GDP has reached more than half. The contribution rate of consumption is about 40%. When calculating the contribution rate of export, we have considered the influence of import which offsets some effects of export, thus the contribution rate of net export is relatively small. In fact, the contribution rate of export is far beyond this number (Fig. 9).

From the perspective of the pulling rate to GDP, the pulling effect of investment on economy also exceeds consumption and export. The pulling effect of investment is more obvious especially in the periods of

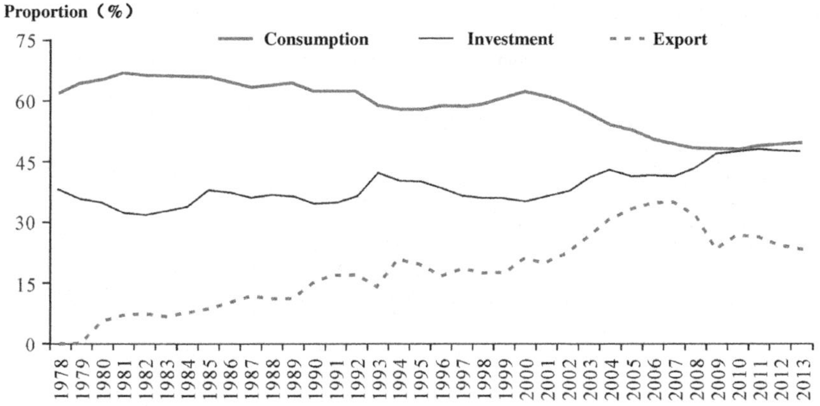

Fig. 7 Proportions of China's three major demands in GDP from 1978 to 2013 (*Data source* Wind Database)

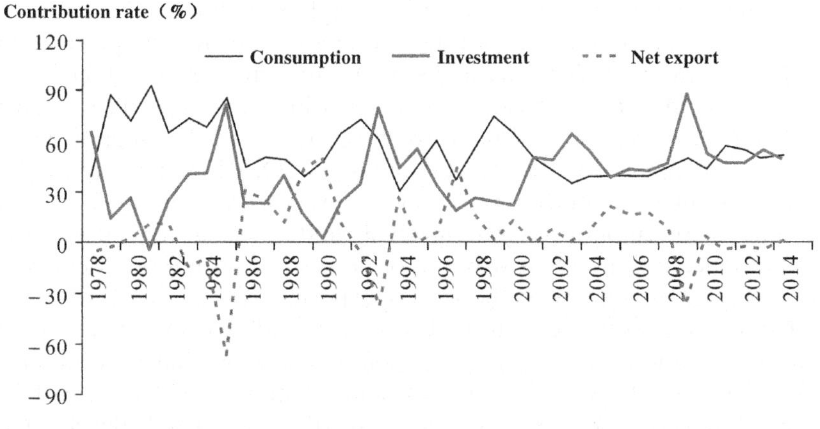

Fig. 8 Contribution rate of demands to economic growth from 1978 to 2014 (*Data source* Wind Database)

realizing large-scale stimulation. The pulling effect of consumption has always been mild, and the pulling rate keeps in about 5%.

It can be seen from the demand structure of economy that China has formed the model that investment and export are the main forces to stimulate economic growth for a long time. Relative to consumption,

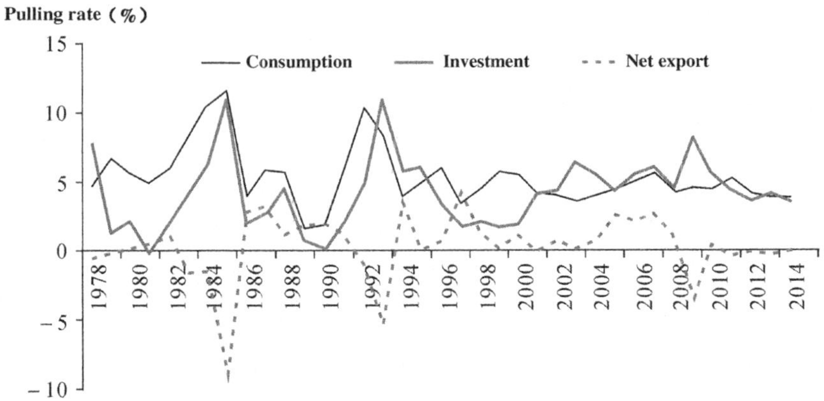

Fig. 9 Pulling rate of demands to economic growth from 1978 to 2014 (*Data source* Wind Database)

investment and export have maintained a high growth rate. The enlarged investment can expand the industrial scale and improve the production capacity of the manufacturing industry on one hand; on the other hand, it has been put into the construction industry including real estate, airport and railway, expressway and infrastructure, so as to further support rapid rising of economy. In addition, by joining WTO, China has exported a large amount of manufactured goods to overseas markets by means of advantages of labor force, raw materials and exchange rate under the circumstance of limited growth rate of domestic consumption demands, which has greatly increased the scale of export.

Combining with the industrial structure and demand structure of China's economy, we can see the basic features of China's economic growth in the 30 years since reform and opening up. That is, to take investment as the impetus of economic growth, to vigorously develop the secondary industry including manufacturing and construction, to improve production capacity of enterprises through large-scale industrial expansion and to improve economic growth rate through large-scale investment in construction industry, including construction of real estate and infrastructure. Due to expansion of the industrial production capacity, some products are used to satisfy the growth of limited consumption demands, and the other are mainly exported to the world market. This growth

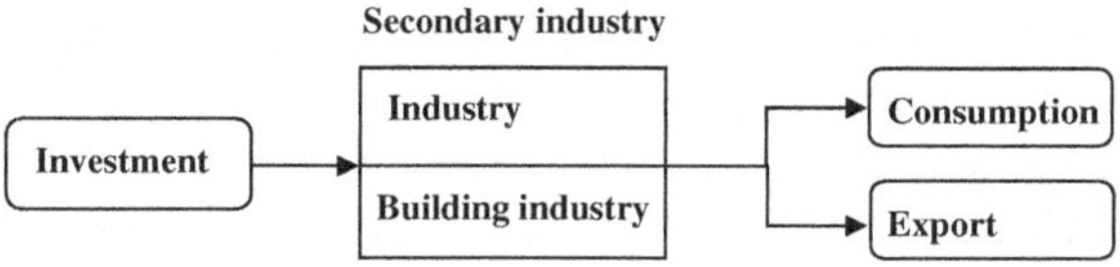

Fig. 10 China's economic growth model

model can not only effectively adapt to the change of external environment, but also have great economic adjustment function. When external demand is enlarged, the production scale can be enlarged and the export can be increased by reinforcing investment, so as to realize the pulling effect of investment and export on economy; when external demand is shrunk, the deficiencies of economic growth rate can be made up by reinforcing the investment in the construction industry, and the pulling effect of investment on economy will be more prominent. But anyway, the role of investment is indispensable to economic growth. In fact, the high growth of China in the past 30 years is built on this growth model (Fig. 10).[1]

Except pulling economic growth of China, this growth model has also exerted an influence on China's economy in three aspects: firstly, it enhances the scale and competitiveness of China's industrial sectors and helps China realize the objective of industrialization; secondly, China's economy has found its role and positioning in the international economic system by being integrated in the international economic system through export; thirdly, it has improved the hard environment of economic development.

Exactly under such circumstances, we have formed the so-called economic growth model with Chinese characteristics. In over 30 years of development, we have maintained a high economic growth rate. However, we must clearly know that this growth model is not impeccable. To play its role, China model needs the following preconditions: The first is adding leverage by government and enterprises. Realizing the increase of investment scale through large scale of liabilities will certainly

[1] Certainly, this wording may be not rigorous, since it neglects the primary industry and the tertiary industry. In consideration of the leading role of the secondary industry in industrial development, the economic growth model, as a matter of fact, realizes the adjustment on macro economy through the adjustment among different sectors of the secondary industry.

increase the debt ratio of the government and enterprises. The second is advantages of production cost, including advantage of labor cost, cheap raw materials and fast-growing rate of technical progress. Once these advantages are lost, the advantages of exported products will disappear. However, with constant and rapid growth of economy, the increase of labor cost, the demand for raw materials exceeding the supply and slowing down of technical progress are inevitable, which will necessarily reduce the market competitiveness of the products. The third is strong external demands. Department of residents in developed countries must add leverage on a large scale to meet their growing consumption demand. Once developed countries deleverage, external demand will decrease. The externality of demand will directly affect the stability and sustainability of growth.

Fortunately, in over 30 years of development, these external conditions have hardly changed, which enable us to maintain over 30 years of high growth and create the so-called China speed; but unfortunately, these changeless external conditions do not bring us enough impetus for reform and innovation, so that we are not prepared yet when this growth model is unsustainable due to change of external conditions. Perhaps, this is the worst thing.

2 When China Model Encounters Financial Crisis

In fact, China's model of stimulating economic growth through investment and export is quite effective, especially under the circumstance that Western countries add leverage on a large scale. The consumption-led economic growth model in the West has two characteristics, one is hollowness of manufacturing industry, and another is high leverage ratio. Developed countries satisfy domestic consumption demands through a great deal of imports, which undoubtedly brings a broad development space for China's manufacturing industry. China enlarges the production scale of the manufacturing industry through investment, which on one hand can satisfy limited domestic consumption demands; and on the other hand will export a plenty of residual products to developed countries to earn foreign exchange through exports. People's Bank of China will get a large amount of foreign exchange earnings, then it will put domestic currency into circulation for supporting further investment, then it will use foreign currencies to purchase bonds of developed countries and the foreign currencies will flow into developed countries again… Exactly through this kind of economic model, China has constantly strengthened its economic connection with the world and formed its own development model (Fig. 11).

Through this model, we must see the following facts: firstly, China is responsible for production, and the United States is responsible for consumption; secondly, China sustains surplus, and the United States sustains deficit; thirdly, China continues to lend money to the United States for consumption; fourthly, China continues to increase domestic investment and expand the production scale for export. The development of this model will result in the continuous expansion of China's production scale and the continuous increase of foreign exchange reserves, while resulting in the constant accumulation of debt scale of the United States. Broadly speaking, this is the economic model that has supported China's rapid economic growth for more than 30 years since the reform and opening up. It now appears that this model is unsustainable, but at that time, there were few voices of doubt until the outbreak of the financial crisis. If there was no financial crisis, perhaps China's economy is still maintaining rapid growth, and there will be no problems such as rising unemployment rate and increasing pressure of economic downturn. Unfortunately, there are no ifs. What will happen when China model encounters financial crisis? In fact, this is a good question, because the problems of a mature growth model can be found only in the test of a crisis. Can the high growth model formed by China's reform and opening up over the past 30 years withstand the test of the crisis? Can we still maintain the outstanding China speed in the face of a crisis? This is also

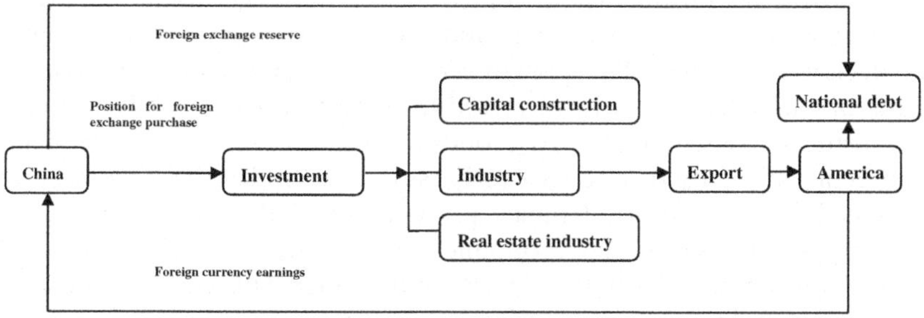

Fig. 11 Economic and trade relations between China and the United States

a simple question because China's economic growth model is so fragile behind its seemingly powerful economy.

Looking back on the past, the influence of outbreak of the financial crisis on China's economic growth seems like "a fire on the city gate brings disaster to the fish in the moat". But dialectically, it is the best out of the worst, because it is unsustainable relying on investment and export, which are economic growth model not endogenous. Once external conditions change, stagnation of China's economy will occur. Financial crisis is just a fact that another external condition has caused the change of external conditions supporting China's economic growth. But everything came too sudden and too fast.

There are many researches on subprime crisis, and the reasons will not be explained herein. The main result brought by the subprime crisis is that the Western countries also start to rethink whether the model of economic growth driven by consumption is correct. The direct result is the active deleveraging and the proposal of re-industrialization, American Recovery and Reinvestment Act and Industry 4.0 Plan of Germany are both representatives. The primary and most important influence brought to China is the rapid shrinking of export. In 2007 when the crisis broke out, the growth rate of China's exports did not decline in a large scale, but its rising trend had been influenced. From November 2008, export started to drop dramatically, and it started to recover its growth until December 2009. Even so, the general trend of growth rate reduction of export is quite obvious, which is mainly the demand decline caused by deleveraging of the Western countries. The strike is obvious for China whose economic growth is stimulated by investment and export.

With constant shrinking of export, to maintain economic growth rate, macroscopic readjustment and control have to enlarge money supply to support the increase of investment and offset the economic decline caused by decline in exports. The growth rate of currency issuance by People's Bank of China has gradually increased from 15 to 30%, which is doubled. "Transfusion" is conducted to economy through credit so as to maintain economic growth rate. It can be seen that under the circumstance of speed loss of export, China's growth model driven by investment and export still keeps the economic growth rate through increase of currency insurance by the People's Bank of China. This currency issuance model is exactly the same as "drainage". Thus it can be seen that the endogenousness of China's economy is questionable (Figs. 12 and 13).

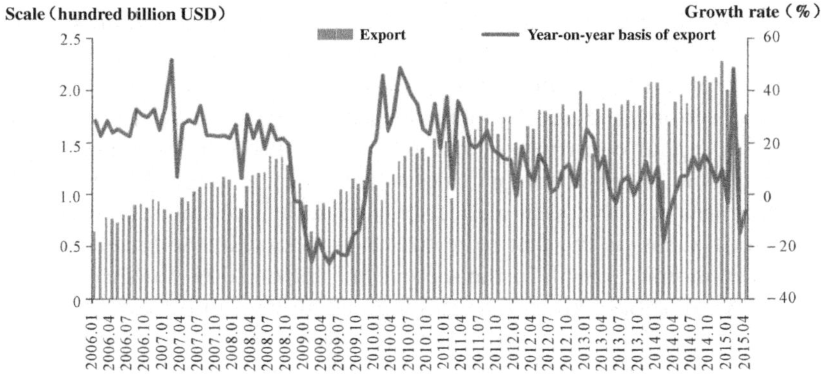

Fig. 12 China's export scale and growth rate from January 2006 to April 2015 (*Data source* Wind Database)

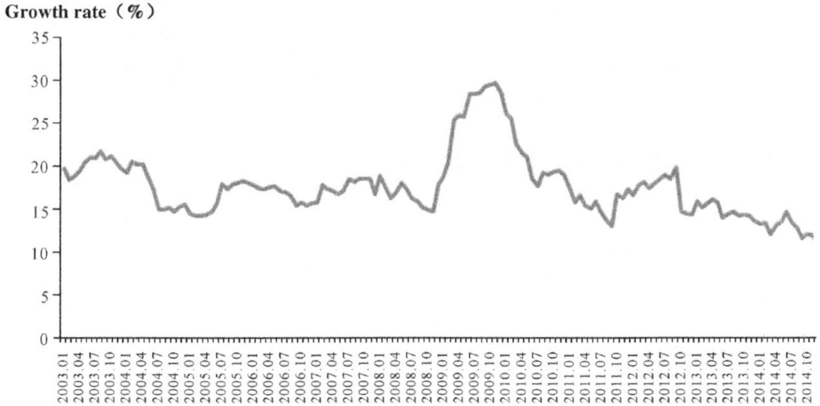

Fig. 13 Year-on-year growth rate of M2 from January 2003 to October 2014 (*Data source* Wind Database)

The orientations of investment increased by the government mainly comprise three, namely, real estate, capital construction and manufacturing industry. The main idea of government bailout is still to stimulate the growth of the entire economy by enlarging construction of real estate and infrastructure and to realize quantitative increase by enlarging the scale of the manufacturing industry. This bailout model is closely related to the growth model. In fact, the two hands of China's economic growth model are, respectively, investment and export, enlarging production scale and promoting export through investment. When export encounters obstructions, the development of each industry will be stimulated by enlarging capital construction and real estate through investment. This model is time-tested in the practices of past decades (Figs. 14 and 15).

As it turns out, the pulling effect of large-scale investment on economy is obvious. China is the first to realize the rebound in the financial crisis, and its economic growth in the second quarter of 2009 was increased to 8.4%. But we should know that although economy can be saved through this kind of bailout in a short time to avoid striking the bottom, the disadvantages of this model will appear as time passes.

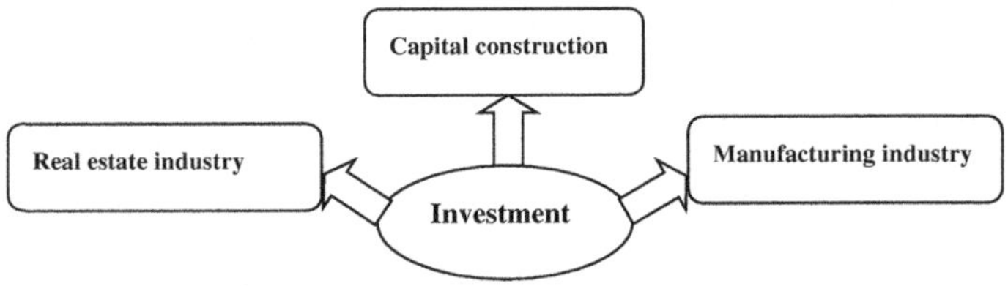

Fig. 14 Large-scale investment's flow direction

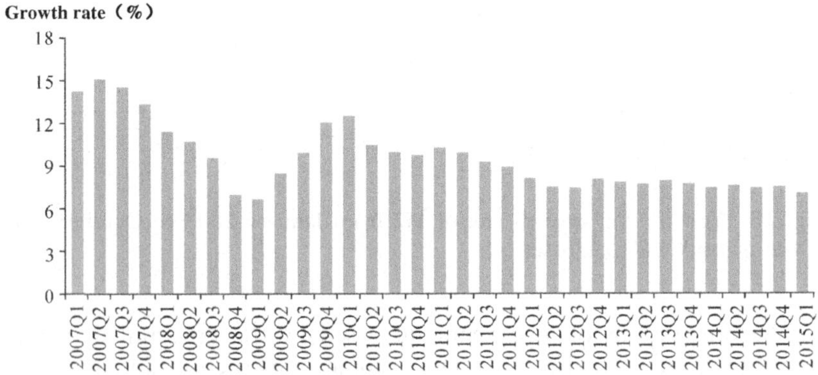

Fig. 15 China's GDP growth rate from the first quarter of 2007 to the first quarter of 2015 (*Data source* Wind Database)

Disadvantages brought by China's economic stimulation model are mainly reflected in three aspects: rise of debts, real estate bubble and excess production capacity. The three aspects are caused by the long-term influences of investment and export expansion. With constant deepening of the crisis, these influences have gradually appeared (Fig. 16).

First is the rise of debt level. Money supply had been enlarged blindly, and transfusion had been conducted to economy through loans, thus China's M2 stock had reached 122.8 trillion yuan by the end of 2014. China has become the country with the most money stock worldwide. However, the GDP was only 63.65 trillion yuan. After the financial crisis, the money utilization ratio of China's economy had constantly declined due to the fact that economic growth was stimulated through issuance of a large sum of money. China's M2/GDP in 2008 was 1.5, but by the end of 2014, such ratio had risen to 1.93. It can be seen that the marginal growth rate of economy driven by a large sum of money had decreased constantly.

Driven by currencies, the debt ratio of the government and enterprises had increased rapidly. As of December 2012, the debt scale of China's government had reached 27.77 trillion yuan, wherein the debt of government's liability for repayment was 19.07 trillion yuan, the debt of government's liability for guarantee was 2.77 trillion yuan, and the debt of government's liability for rescue was 5.93 trillion yuan. As of June

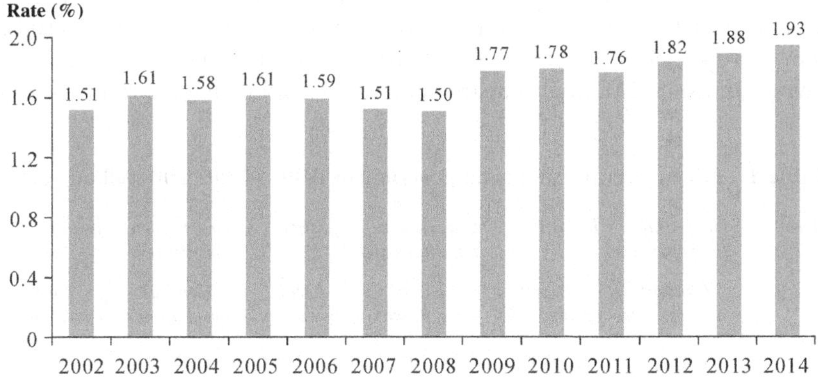

Fig. 16 M2/GDP (*Data source* Data on stocks of M2 comes from People's Bank of China; GDP data comes from Wind Database)

of 2013, the total scale of government's liabilities had risen to 30.28 trillion yuan, wherein the debt of government's liability for repayment was 20.7 trillion yuan, the debt of government's liability for guarantee was 2.93 trillion yuan, and the debt of government's liability for rescue was 6.65 trillion yuan. According to the statistics, the total debt ratio of national governments had reached 113.41%, and the debt ratio of liability for repayment reached 105.66%. It can be seen that the debt burden of the government is quite heavy. The delayed effect of investment expansion on stimulating economic growth is insufficient (Table 1).

In addition, the debt level of enterprises had also increased constantly. At the beginning of 2006, the debt scale of industrial enterprises above designated size was about 13.93 trillion yuan; the debt scale of large- and medium-sized industrial enterprises was 9.9 trillion yuan, and such scale had increased at a growth rate of 20% since then. In February 2008, the debt scale of industrial enterprises above designated size reached 20.19 trillion yuan, and such scale reached 30.45 trillion yuan in May 2010; and the debt scale of large- and medium-sized industrial enterprises reached 21.66 trillion yuan. In May 2014, the debt scale of industrial enterprises above designated size exceeded 50 trillion yuan. As of February 2015, the debt scale of industrial enterprises above designated size had reached 52.16 trillion yuan, and the debt scale of large- and medium-sized industrial enterprises had reached 37.47 trillion yuan (Fig. 17).

It can be seen from the trend of enterprises' debt ratio that there was an obvious process of adding leverage by the enterprises after the financial crisis, especially by large- and medium-sized state-owned enterprises since they were easier to get the support from loans. The debt ratio of state-owned and state-holding industrial enterprises suddenly rose to 60% from

Table 1 Scale of central and local government debts (Unit: 100 million yuan)

Debt	*Government's liability for repayment*		*Government's liability for guarantee*		*Government's liability for rescue*	
	Central government	*Local government*	*Central government*	*Local government*	*Central government*	*Local government*
2012.12	94,376.72	96,281.87	2835.71	24,871.29	21,621.16	37,705.16
2013.06	98,129.48	108,859.17	2600.72	26,655.77	23,110.84	43,393.72

(*Data source* iFinD Database)

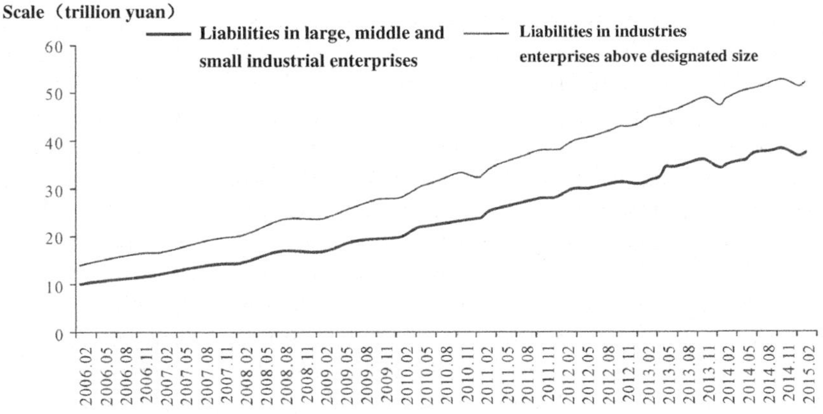

Fig. 17 Debt scale of large- and medium-sized industrial enterprises and industrial enterprises above designated size from February 2006 to February 2015 (*Data source* iFinD Database)

56%, which were still increasing by years. Confronting with the crisis, enterprises had to maintain their productions through loans (Fig. 18).

According to the statistics, the leverage ratio of China's substantial economic sectors had risen to 215% in 2013 from 170% in 2008. The

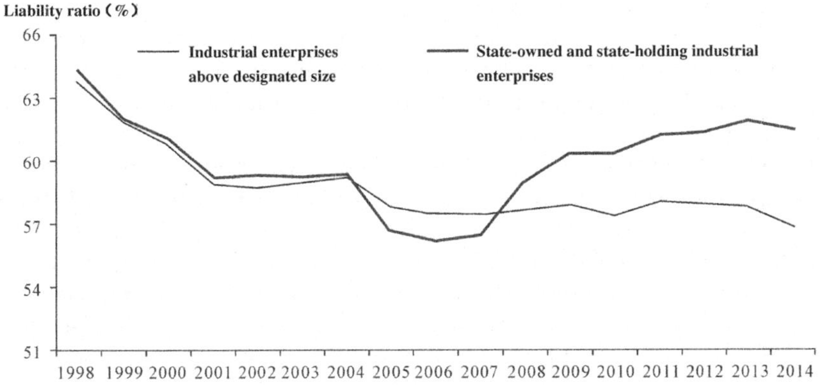

Fig. 18 Debt ratio of industrial enterprises above designated size and state-owned and state-holding industrial enterprises from 1998 to 2014 (*Data source* iFinD Database)

total debt scale of non-financial sectors of China's economy was 118.47 trillion yuan, which was 197% of the GDP of that year, wherein the resident's debt ratio was 31%, the government's debt ratio was 53%, the debt ratio of non-financial enterprises was 113%, exceeding Canada, France, Germany, Italy, Japan, the United Kingdom and the United States, and also exceeding 90% of the international warning lines.[2] A certain economic growth rate can be maintained by adding leverage largely in a short time, but it is the overdraft of long-term growth behind this. The high debt ratio of the government and enterprises had worsened their financial conditions and restricted their capacities of further growth. Therefore, this model of adding leverage is ultimately unsustainable.

Second is real estate bubble. A large amount of capital invested by the government had flowed into the field of real estate, and the planned total investment scale of real estate had surged to new highs again and again. The planned investment scale of real estate was only 3.82 trillion yuan in 2003, which was still only 8.1 trillion yuan in 2006. But since 2008, to cope with the pressure of economic downturn, the investment scale of real estate had increased rapidly, which reached 14 trillion yuan in that year. In 2010, such scale exceeded 20 trillion yuan, approximately 30 trillion yuan in 2011, and 43 trillion yuan in 2013. The growth rate of actual investment completed had also increased rapidly, which reached 30.2% in 2007, declined after then, but rose to 33.16% again in 2010. In the face of export stagnation, real estate investment is a very important aspect in the newly increased investments (Fig. 19).

A large amount of funds flowed into the real estate industry, pushing up the cost of land acquisition and raising housing prices. The consequence is the acceleration of the bubble in the real estate industry. The most important manifestation is the rapid rise in housing prices. In 2006, the average selling prices of commercial houses and residential houses nationwide were, respectively, on 3366.79 yuan/m^2 and 3119.25 yuan/m^2. The prices had risen rapidly since 2008, which, respectively, reached 4681 yuan/m^2 and 4459 yuan/m^2 in 2009. In 2010, 2011 and 2012, the prices continuously rose in a high speed, which, respectively, rose to 6237 yuan/m^2 and 5850 yuan/m^2 in 2013, nearly doubled than in 2006. It can be seen that bubblization of real estate was very serious.

[2] Data source: http://www.lyjkq.gov.cnnewsmeitijujiao/20141203/6002.html.

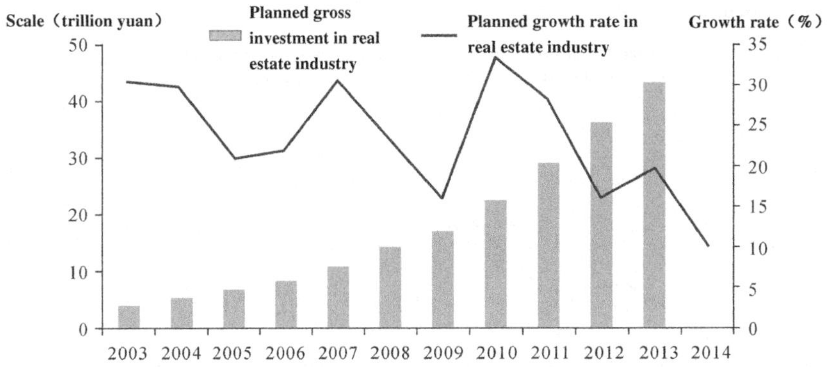

Fig. 19 Scale of total planned investment in real estate and growth rate of complete investment from 2003 to 2014 (*Data source* iFinD Database)

In fact, at the time of the bubblization of real estate, more and more funds flowed into the real estate industry, which eventually led to an imbalance between supply and demand in the real estate industry, overstock of commercial houses and high vacancy rate. Influence by this, the growth rate of investment in real estate started to decline rapidly. In 2014, the actual investment completed of real estate only had a year-on-year growth of 10.5%, which was the minimum value in recent ten years. The growth rate of the prices of commercial houses also stagnated, and the average selling price in 2014 was 6323 yuan/m^2, which was basically equal to that in 2013. Besides, according to the indexes such as sales area of commercial houses, sales area of residential houses, area of newly built houses, area of newly built residential houses and sales volume, the real estate industry started to decline in 2014. The real estate bubble caused by heavy investment eventually evolved into severe excess and even recession, marking that the model of stimulating economic growth by investing in real estate is inadvisable. The model itself has violated the supply and demand rule of the market, which is not endogenous, and therefore its failure is inevitable (Fig. 20 and Table 2).

Third is the generation of a large number of excess production capacities. A large amount of investment in the manufacturing industry especially mid-low end manufacturing industry will inevitably cause excess production capacity, particularly under the background that the pressure of economic downturn is increased, and the growth rate of real

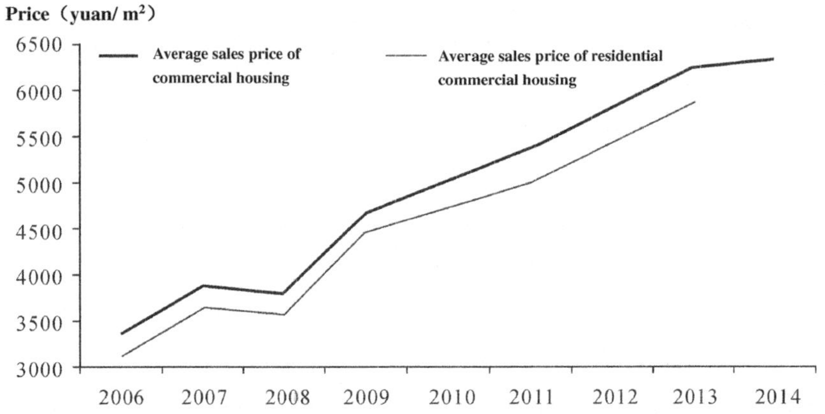

Fig. 20 China's real estate price from 2006 to 2014 (*Data source* National Bureau of Statistics)

Table 2 Overview on new commencement of work and sales of real estate from 2006 to 2014

Category	*Sales area of commercial houses (100 million m²)*	*Sales area of residential houses (100 million m²)*	*Area of newly built houses (100 million m²)*	*Area of newly built residential houses (100 million m²)*	*Sales volume of commercial houses (trillion yuan)*	*Sales volume of residential houses (trillion yuan)*
2006	6.19	5.54	7.93	6.44	2.08	1.73
2007	7.74	7.01	9.54	7.88	2.99	2.56
2008	6.60	5.93	10.26	8.36	2.51	2.12
2009	9.48	8.62	11.64	9.33	4.44	3.84
2010	10.48	9.34	16.36	12.94	5.27	4.41
2011	10.94	9.65	19.12	14.72	5.86	4.82
2012	11.13	9.85	17.73	13.07	6.45	5.35
2013	13.06	11.57	20.12	14.58	8.14	6.77
2014	12.06	10.52	17.96	12.49	7.63	6.24

Data source iFinD Database

estate slows down. Through several years of large-scale investment and construction, the problem of excess production capacity has been gradually exposed. The rate of capacity utilization of the industries such as coal, steel, cement, plate glass, electrolytic aluminum, ship, calcium carbide, crude steel and paper making has maintained at below 80% for a long time.

The problem of excess production capacity is formed by one-sided increase of investment and expansion of production scale as time passes. Fundamentally this is the disadvantage brought by unreasonable growth model, and the shackle of the economic model itself. For this reason, MIIT of China published the list of three batches of industries and enterprises with excess production capacity in 2014. MIIT of China clearly pointed out that 16 industries including iron making, steel making, coking, iron alloy, calcium carbide, electrolytic aluminum, copper (including secondary copper) smelting, lead (including secondary lead) smelting, cement (clinker and mill), plate glass, paper making, leather making, printing and dyeing, chemical fiber, lead storage battery (polar plate and assembly) and rare earth were industries with excess production capacity. MIIT clearly required cutting down the excess industrial capacities. But now, even if the excess production capacities need to be digested, it cannot be completed overnight, and it must undergo a long selling period (Fig. 21).

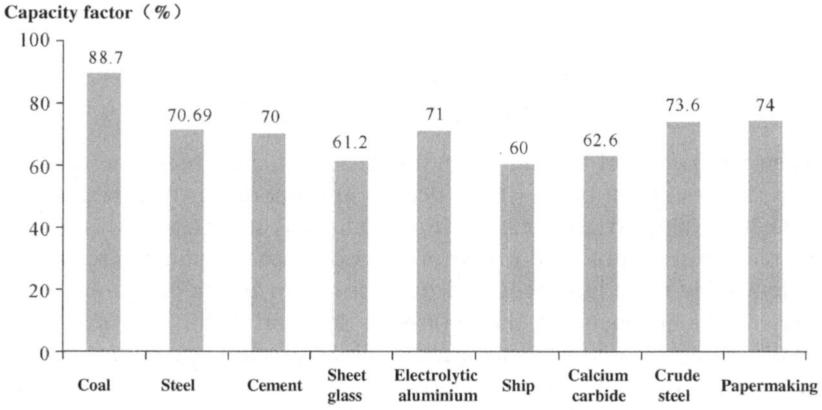

Fig. 21 Rate of capacity utilization of some industries with excess production capacity (*Data source* Collected from network data)

Investment and export constitute the "capable assistants" of China model. When foreign demands increase, export supply will increase; when foreign demands shrink, the investment will be enlarged. When China model encounters financial crisis, export will be turned to investment. Although it can stimulate rapid rebound of economy in a short time, the aftereffects of investment will appear as time passes. Enterprises with high debt ratio, real estate bubble and excess production capacity are three crises of China's economy at present, which are the inevitable consequences of the development of the unreasonable economic growth model. The lack of endogenousness of investment and export-determined economies determines the unsustainability of the economic growth model. To achieve sustained economic growth, it is inevitable to expand the investment to stimulate the economy, which will lead to high debts and excess production capacity. Therefore, the problem of China's economy is seemingly the problem of excess supply and insufficient effective demand, but at a deeper level is the problem of excess demand and insufficient supply—too much ineffective demand and insufficient effective supply. What is ineffective demand? What is effective supply? What is represented by investment is ineffective demand, which is largely filled in economic activities, not only resulting in wasting of resources but also squeezing the effective demand out; what is represented by high-end manufacturing industry and service industry is effective supply, which does not realize rapid growth, resulting in the imbalance of the industrial structure.

3 Transformation from Old Model to New Economy

When China model lacking of endogenousness encounters the financial crisis, the result will be inevitably decline in economic growth rate; excess ineffective demand and imbalance of industrial structure have brought the real estate bubble and excess production capacity, and the result will be inevitably the adjustment and transformation of the economic structure. The adjustment of the economic structure ultimately needs the transformation from scale and speed-oriented extensive growth to quality and efficiency-oriented intensive growth, behind which is the transformation of growth impetus from driven by factor to driven by innovation. To break the shackles of the China model, transformation from the old model to the new economy is required. The most fundamental thing is to conduct the transformation of the economic structure, in which we must solve the problem of endogenous driving. It is necessary to abandon the mode of expanding the scale through the expansion of production factors, but to achieve new development through innovation. Supply management should be conducted through innovation, so as to drive consumer demand, form stable economic endogenousness and shape China's new economic model. This is the way out for the future China's economy. From this point, decline in economic growth rate is not a short-term process, but a long-term process existed along with reshaping of the economic structure.

In May 2014, the General Secretary Xi Jinping pointed out during his investigation in Henan that "China's development is still in a period of strategic opportunity. We must enhance our confidence, start from the periodical characteristics of China's economic development at present, adapt to the new normality and maintain normal mentality strategically".[3] This is the first time that the central government proposed the concept of new normality. On November 9, 2014, Chairman Xi Jinping made a speech entitled Pursue Sustainable Development and Jointly Build Asia-Pacific Dream in APEC CEO Summit and systematically interpreted new normality for the first time. The new economic normality mainly includes three characteristics: firstly, it has changed from high-speed growth to medium-high-speed growth. Secondly, the economic structure has been continuously optimized and upgraded; the tertiary industry and the consumer demand have gradually become the mainstay; the gap between urban and rural areas has gradually narrowed; the resident income ratio has increased; and the development results have benefited the wider public. Thirdly, factor-driven model and investment-driven model are turned to innovation-driven model.[4] At the Central Economic Working Conference held in December 2014, the new normality was comprehensively interpreted from nine aspects, including consumption, investment, export and international balance of payments, production capacity and industrial organization form, production factors, market competition, environmental constraint, accumulation and solution of risks, resource

[3] Data source: http://news.cntv.cn—08/10/ARTI1407636275712964.shtml.

[4] Data source: http://politics.people.com.cn/n-1110/c1024-26000531.html.

allocation and macro control.[5] At the consumption level, the imitative wave-type consumption in the past has ended, while individualized and diversified consumption has gradually become the mainstream. At the investment level, traditional industries are relatively saturated, but investment opportunities for infrastructure interconnection and new technologies, new products, new formats and new business models have largely emerged. At the export level, the low-cost advantage has changed. At the level of production and organization, the industrial structure must be optimized and upgraded, the roles of emerging industries, the service industry and small and micro enterprises are more prominent, and production miniaturization, intelligentization and professionalization will become new features. At the level of market competition, the quantity and price competition are transformed to diversified competition. At the level of risk solution, various risks such as high leverage and bubblization should be dissolved.

The statement of the central government on new economic normality is relatively corresponding to the development status of China's economy. The model of stimulating economic growth by investment and export was indeed beneficial to China's economic development at the initial stage, including improvement of income level, capital formation, technical progress and management improvement. This model is fundamentally a kind of demand management but not supply management. With the continuous expansion of the scale of China's export and investment, the marginal effect of this demand management is gradually declining. Faced with this situation, the correct way is to reduce factor input, reduce demand, turn to industrial structure upgrade, strengthen supply management, improve product supply and form new consumer demand. It is a pity that we have not adopted this way of sacrificing short-term benefits in exchange for long-term benefits. Instead, we have adopted a way that currently seems to be more eager for immediate success, that is, one-sided expansion of production scale to stimulate economic growth. This method is beneficial to stimulating the economy in a short term, but it is at the expense of abandoning the supply management of upgrading and transformation of the industrial structure. The results of demand management are large-scale debts, asset price bubbles, low industrial structure and excess production capacity. Therefore, we begin to realize

[5] Data source: http://finance.sina.com.cn/china/20141211/185221054526.shtml.

that we need to abandon the economic control method based on demand management, strengthen economic supply management and realize health economic development by new industries and new tools.

The current stage is a period of transition from the old economy to the new economy. This transition period can be called the new economic normality. The characteristics of the new normality are manifested in three aspects, respectively, economic growth rate shift, industrial structure adjustment pain and early stimulus policy digestion. In the case of a potential slowdown in economic growth, it is necessary to undergo a process of deep adjustment of the industrial structure, realize the transformation from the manufacturing industry to the service industry, from the low-end industry to the high-end industry and realize the transformation of economic driving forces from the factor scale to the technological innovation. Meanwhile, it is necessary to deal with the problems such as high debts, asset bubbles and excess production capacity left over by the old economy. All these economic performances can be collectively referred to as the new normality. The leading mission under the new economic normality is the optimization and upgrading of the economic structure. From the perspective of the industrial structure, China's industrial structure should be transformed from the low-end manufacturing industry to the high-end manufacturing industry. From the perspective of demand structure, it should be transformed from investment and export-driven type to consumption-driven type.

In the past, China's industrial structure was mostly the low-end traditional manufacturing industry, mainly relying on labor-intensive industries and resource-intensive industries, with low technical content and poor market competitiveness. The massive investment has caused severe excess production capacity in the industries which were previously less competitive. On the one hand, the development of these industries with excess production capacities should be strictly controlled to digest the excess capacities; on the other hand, the industries should be transformed and upgraded toward high-end manufacturing industry and service industry. In the future, China will focus on the development of ten emerging fields, including the new generation of information technology, high-grade CNC machine and robot, aerospace equipment, ocean engineering equipment and high-tech ships, advanced railway transportation equipment, energy-saving and new energy automobile, electronic equipment, agricultural machinery equipment, new materials, biological medicine and high-performance medical apparatus and instruments. It is necessary to accelerate the coordinated development of manufacturing and services, promote business model innovation and format innovation and promote the transformation of production-oriented manufacturing to service-oriented manufacturing. We should vigorously develop the producer services closely related to the manufacturing industry, and promote the construction of service function areas and service platforms.[6] In August 2014, the State Council introduced the Guiding Opinions on Accelerating the Development of Producer Services to Promote Adjustment and Upgrading of the Industrial Structure, initially making a comprehensive planning on the development of the producer services and specifying that the producer services mainly comprised transportation industry, modern logistics industry, financial service industry, information service industry, high-tech service industry, commercial service industry and the like. Under the new normality, the high-end manufacturing industry and the service industry will become the dominant force in the industrial composition. In fact, as early as 2012, the proportion of the tertiary industry in GDP had been equal to that of the secondary industry, exceeding the secondary industry in 2013. From the perspective of the contribution rate and pulling rate to GDP, the tertiary industry has officially exceeded the secondary industry, indicating that China is undergoing the transformation from the manufacturing power to the service power. Such trend is gradually accelerating. Similarly, the development of the high and new technology industry and the equipment manufacturing industry is also rapid. Their growth rate in the first three quarters of 2014, respectively, reached 12.3 and 11.1%, obviously exceeding the average growth rate of the industries. It indicates that the compositions of China's industrial structure have been continuously optimized, and the supply structure has been obviously improved.

Consumer demand has been growing slowly in China's demand structure. This has both internal and external reasons. Without the support of consumption, it is infeasible to form an endogenous economic growth model. The Central Economic Work Conference of 2014 also proposed to give play to the fundamental role of consumption and to form an economic growth model centered on consumption growth. In the past, due to the shortage of commodities and the characteristics of consumer demand such as imitation and wave type, consumers have relatively simple

[6] Data source: http://news.china.com/domestic/945/20150519/19710486_all.html#page_2.

requirements for the characteristics and performance of commodities. Manufacturers can meet the demands of consumers through large-scale volume production. With constant change of consumer's demand, large-scale production can no longer satisfy the consumer demand. Within a period in the future, individualization and diversification will become the new features of consumption, which require miniaturization, intelligentization and professionalization of production. Small and micro enterprises in the future will become the subjects of the market. Since 2012, the proportion of consumption in GDP had gradually increased. In 2014, the contribution rate and pulling rate of consumption to GDP exceeded investment for the first time, indicating that China had been moving toward consumption-driven economy. Even so, we still cannot ignore the pulling effect of investment on economy. Particularly, a large amount of investment opportunities exist in the infrastructure of interconnection. The key role of investment still needs to be exerted under the new normality.

From the perspective of China's new economy developed in the future, with the continuous optimization and adjustment of industrial structure and demand structure, an economic model dominated by service industry, high-end manufacturing industry and consumer demand is taking shape. In the future, the traditional market competition will be broken, and products with the characteristics of differentiation, diversification and individualization will become the mainstream of consumption. This makes the industrial organization form more miniaturized in the future. The market position and function of the small- and medium-sized enterprises will be more prominent in the future, which will be the main feature of service-oriented economy. In other words, China's market economy in the future will center on the small- and medium-sized enterprises and consumers. On the one hand, we should enhance the market vitality and competitiveness of the small- and medium-sized enterprises; on the other hand, we should cultivate the consumption consciousness of the consumers, improve consumer demand and strengthen the consumption ability. Lastly, it is necessary to form a new economic model with endogenousness dominated by the service industry and taking consumption as the main approach by adjusting the industrial structure at the supply end and adjusting the demand structure at the demand end. This will be the main direction of China's economic development in the future.

4 Dilemma of the Financing System

The future economic pattern under the new normality can be summarized by demand individualization, production miniaturization and competition differentiation. In the future economic development, medium-, small- and micro-sized enterprises will constitute the subjects of economic development. This will be a very obvious microscopic feature that is different from the old economy. Among the newly registered enterprises of each place in 2013, the proportion of enterprises of service industry reaches up to 2/3. In the service industry, the small- and medium-sized enterprises account for over 70%. In the original economic structure, the pulling effects on economic scale are usually realized through large enterprises, large projects and large platforms; but in the future new economy, with constant strengthening of the leading position of the tertiary industry, the promoting effect of small- and medium-sized enterprises on economy will be more obvious. It thus can be seen that the economic model that growth is driven by small and medium-sized enterprises will be formed in the future.

The key to the transformation and development of small- and medium-sized enterprises is financial support. Whether it is diversified, differentiated, personalized product supply, or innovation, transformation, upgrading and other industrial development needs, it is inseparable from the financial support. From the perspective of sources of funding, the strength of small- and medium-sized enterprises is relatively weak. They seldom rely on endogenous financing, but mostly rely on debt financing and equity financing, especially external borrowing. It thus can be seen that the problem of financing constraints of small- and medium-sized enterprises is the fundamental reason for restricting the development of small- and medium-sized enterprises. Solving the financing problem of small- and medium-sized enterprises is the decisive factor for spanning the new economic normality and realizing the transformation and upgrading of the economic structure in China.

Features of Existing Financing System

For a long time, both China and other countries have indirect financing models represented by banks and direct financing models represented by securities. The funds enter the bank in the form of savings. The bank lends the funds to the borrowers through lending, or directly invests in the borrowers in the form of stocks through the exchange, or the bank conducts investment instead of the customers through the exchange. This mode has the following characteristics: firstly, there are financial intermediaries. The depositors only need to deliver their funds to the financial intermediaries who will take the place of customers to complete the investment. In this way, the limitations of customers such as insufficient investment experiences and deficiencies in energy can be avoided, and meanwhile the funds of the customers have certain insurance guarantee (especially under the circumstance of indirect financing of the bank). This is quite important for investors, especially under the conditions of limited assets and short of funds. Secondly, under the condition of incomplete marketization of interest rates, financial intermediaries have the monopoly advantage of obtaining spreads. For a long time, due to the lack of funds, China's interest rate has not been liberalized, and banks just get benefits from the difference between the upper limit of the deposit interest rate and the lower limit of the loan interest rate. The borrowers' financing cost is high, the depositors' yield is low, while the abundant capital difference is obtained by the financial intermediary, and therefore the upstream and downstream participants have not obtained the capital convenience. Thirdly, the financial intermediaries have high threshold. In consideration of the protection of the investors' interests, financial intermediaries have strict requirements on the qualifications of borrowers. Banks normally have requirements on the assets, mortgage and guarantee of the borrowers. The exchange is only open to enterprises with certain conditions, which is "unreachable" for individuals and small and micro enterprises. In general, the existing financial system has three characteristics including intermediation, high cost and high threshold (Fig. 22).

According to China's social financing structure at present, indirect financing represented by bank loans still accounts for the majority. In China's social financing structure from 2006 to 2014, the proportion of yuan loans is between 50 and 70%. It has slightly declined, but still accounting for the majority. The scale of direct financing such as enterprise bond and domestic equity financing of non-financial business has constantly extended, although its proportion is still small, which is less than 20%. The proportions of entrusted loans, credit loans and undiscounted banker's acceptance are still limited (Tables 3 and 4).

According to the regional financing structure of 2013, among the three areas, the proportion of direct financing of the enterprises in eastern

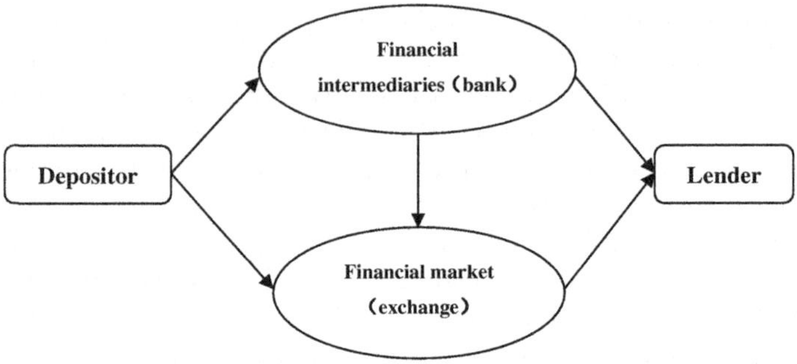

Fig. 22 Situations of traditional financial intermediaries and market (*Data source* Xie Ping, Zou Chuanwei and Liu Haier, *Manual of Internet Finance*, China Renmin University Press, 2014)

Table 3 China's social financing structure from 2006 to 2014

Year	*RMB loan (%)*	*Corporate bond (%)*	*Trust loan (%)*	*Entrusted loan (%)*	*Undiscounted banker's acceptance (%)*	*Foreign currency loan (%)*	*Domestic equity financing of non-financial business (%)*	*Other (%)*
2006	73.8	5.4	1.9	6.3	3.5	3.4	3.6	2.1
2007	60.9	3.8	2.9	5.7	11.2	6.5	7.3	1.7
2008	70.3	7.9	4.5	6.1	1.5	2.8	4.8	2.1
2009	69.0	8.9	3.1	4.9	3.3	6.7	2.4	1.7
2010	56.7	7.9	2.8	6.2	16.7	3.5	4.1	2.1
2011	58.2	10.6	1.6	10.1	8	4.5	3.4	3.6
2012	53.8	14.8	8.4	8.4	6.9	6	1.6	0.1
2013	51.4	10.4	10.7	14.7	4.5	3.4	1.3	3.6
2014e	61.7	15.7	2.1	13.9	1.3	2.1	2.5	0.7

Data source China Reward-based Crowdfunding Market Research Report of 2015

China is the largest, but is only 3.5%, and the proportion of RMB loans is 49.8%. Compared with the eastern China, central China's and western China's degree of dependence on bank loans is higher, and their scale proportions of RMB loans are, respectively, 52.4 and 53.6%; the proportion of direct financing (including enterprise bond and domestic equity financing of non-financial business) is low, which is only 3.6%.

Table 4 Social financing structure in the eastern, central and western part of China in 2013

Area	*RMB loan (%)*	*Corporate bond (%)*	*Trust loan (%)*	*Entrusted loan (%)*	*Undiscounted bankers' acceptance (%)*	*Foreign currency loan (%)*	*Domestic equity financing of non-financial business (%)*	*Other (%)*
Eastern part	49.8	3.5	16	8.7	5	12.4	1	3.9
Central part	52.4	1.6	12	12.8	5	10.3	2	3.9
Western part	53.6	1.8	13.3	12.5	4	8.3	1.8	4.8

Note The eastern part of China comprises Beijing, Tianjin, Hebei, Liaoning, Shanghai, Jiangsu, Zhejiang, Fujian, Shandong, Guangdong, Guangxi and Hainan; the central part of China comprises Shanxi, Inner Mongolia, Jilin, Heilongjiang, Anhui, Jiangxi, Henan, Hubei and Hunan; the western part of China comprises Sichuan, Chongqing, Guizhou, Yunnan, Tibet, Shaanxi, Gansu, Ningxia, Qinghai and Xinjiang

Data source Chinese Equity Crowdfinancing Market Research Report in 2015

It can be seen that China's overall financing structure still relies on indirect financing such as bank loans, while the proportion of direct financing is relatively low. In addition, the proportion of indirect financing in the central and western China is higher than that in the eastern China. Especially, the western China's degree of dependence on loans is the largest. Excessive dependence on loans can only result in the increase of the financing constraints, especially on private enterprises and medium-, small- and micro-sized enterprises. The increase in demand for loans from a large number of state-owned enterprises and large-scale projects has led to "financing squeezing" for the private economy and medium-, small- and micro-sized enterprises.

Financial "Inhibition" of Small and Micro Economy

Acquisition of sufficient financial support by small- and medium-sized enterprises, as the main force of economic growth under the new economic model in the future, is the fundamental guarantee to support their innovation and development. Regrettably, under the existing investment and financing system, the problem of financing constraints on small- and medium-sized enterprises has always been a "long-standing, big and difficult problem" that restricts the development of small- and medium-sized enterprises.

According to the statistics, by the end of 2013, there were a total of 11,698,700 small and micro enterprises and 44,362,900 individual businesses in China, accounting for 94.15%. Newly increase in employments provided by small and micro enterprises had reached more than 90%. They had accommodated over 80% of newly increased employments and completed 65% of patents for invention. Their GDP accounted for more than 60%, and the taxes they paid accounted for more than 50% of the enterprises nationwide. However, the reality is that less than 10% of small and micro enterprises that contribute greatly to the national economy can obtain loans from banks, and their availability is extremely low. According to the statistics, by the end of 2014, the balance of small and micro enterprise loans accounted for only 30.4% of the balance of overall enterprise loans.[7] Besides, the loan interest rate of small and micro enterprises usually floats upward by 30–45%. The ultimate average financing cost is between 12 and 15%. The "two financing" problems including difficult financing and expensive financing have always perplexed the development of small and medium-sized enterprises and have not been effectively solved.

Besides, fund use of small and micro enterprises has the characteristics of being "short, small, frequent and urgent". Bank credit normally needs complicated procedures such as offline investigation and cross validation, which is time-consuming and too slow. Small and micro enterprises usually will miss the best opportunity. 90% of the small and micro enterprises have to obtain the high-price funds with an interest rate of about 25% through small-amount loans and private lending.[8] According to the statistics, the scale of private lending has reached approximately 2 trillion yuan, which account for 10% of the total loan.[9]

The financing problem of the small- and medium-sized enterprises is not the problem of monetary aggregate, but the problem of monetary

[7] Data source: http://news.cntv.cn/2014/08/14/ARTI1408013735972668.shtml.

[8] Gu Shengzu: Relieving the Financing Difficulties of Small and Micro Enterprises both Superficially and thoroughly, *Finance and Economics, 2015: Prediction and Strategy*, 70–73.

[9] China E-business Research Center: Research Report on China's Internet Finance Development Trend from 2015 to 2018.

structure, and ultimately the problems of economic structure imbalance. At the industrial level, depending too much on real estate and manufacturing industry has caused that a large amount of funds flow into real estate and low-end manufacturing industry, forming the real estate bubble and excess production capacity, squeezing the financing space for small- and medium-sized enterprises; from the perspective of economic subject, economic subjects represented by state-owned enterprises and local government financing platforms are lacking in the soft budget constraint, which are not sensitive to the capital interest rate. They have borrowed a large sum of high-price funds, thus pushing up the financing costs of the small- and medium-sized enterprises.

Actually, the problem of economic structure is one aspect resulting in the financing difficulties of the small- and medium-sized enterprises. The other aspect is the risk control problem of the financing. Since the small- and medium-sized enterprises are generally lacking of asset pledge and financing guarantee, in traditional indirect financing, financial institutions cannot use traditional risk control methods to conduct risk pricing to small and medium-sized enterprises, nor can they conduct risk control. Faced with this situation, financial institutions can only focus on large-scale state-owned enterprises with strong strength.

It thus can be said that under the model of the old economy, the economic structure at the macro level and the risk control at the micro level have jointly resulted in the problem of financing constraints on the small- and medium-sized enterprises. At present, under the background of the new normality, the "two financing" problems including difficult financing and expensive financing of grass-roots economy during the transformation of the economy to the service industry are the major problems restricting China's economic transformation and upgrading. With constant deepening of the post-subprime crisis, the rebalancing of the global economy and the entry of China's economy into the new normality, how to break the financing constraints on small- and medium-sized enterprises is directly related to the reshaping of the economic model and the success of the transformation and development under the transitional background of the new normality. This is why Internet finance has emerged and rapidly developed as a life-saving straw for the grass-roots economy.

5 Digitized New Thinking

In April 2013, Germany's "Industry 4.0 working Group" released Guarantee the Future of Germany's Manufacturing Industry: Opinions on Implementing the Strategy of Industry 4.0, officially proposing the strategy of Industry 4.0. Two years later, Premier of the State Council Li Keqiang proposed the "Internet+ " action plan on the Twelfth National People's Congress. The background, contents and objectives of the two plans are different. But behind the two seemingly unrelated plans, there is one important thing in common, that is, digitization. It can be seen from these two plans that among numerous forces guiding future economic development, it is not technology, not innovation, not thinking, not factor, but a clearer force, that is, digitalization—the combination of thinking, technology, factor and innovation.

The purpose of proposing Industry 4.0 by Germany is to improve the level of Germany's manufacturing industry through this strategy. The core of Industry 4.0 is to establish a digital intelligent manufacturing model through information technology and connect the products, equipment and resources with the consumers. Data sharing in each production step can be realized through digitalization of each link on the value chain. Therefore, the data of the consumers can be acquired from design and the production links, so as to realize individualized and customized production. It can be seen that the key step of this strategy is to realize the digitalization of each link, so that the data "sharing" can be realized.

China's "Internet+ " action plan is to push the combination of mobile Internet, cloud computing, big data and Internet of things with modern manufacturing industry. This plan intends to transform modern manufacturing industry by utilizing Internet and IT technology and realize optimization and upgrading of modern manufacturing industry. The specific method is to carry out digitalized partition to each link of the value chain. Digitalization is necessary in each link such as acquisition, production, sales and logistics, so that the coordination among the links can be realized.

It can be seen from the two plans that the future productivity revolution may occur in the field of digitalization. In the field of production, instead of simple information exchange, the entire production link can be efficiently completed by digitalizing each production link and then conducting digital exchange and digital matching. Therefore digitalization will be the key factor in the future. Some researches consider that we are entering into the era of digital economy. Such digital economy is even called data economy in the researches of Alibaba. No matter how it changes, use of digits or data for economic activities seems to be a big trend in the future. This kind of data is achieved through uniform digital transformation of a mass of unstructured data, including all kinds of information such as pictures, languages, photos and emotions. Besides, such data economy will not be limited to the manufacturing industry, but will spread to the entire economic system in the future. It can be imagined that the future economy will be "Internet+ agriculture", "Internet+ manufacturing industry" and "Internet+ service industry"... data will play an irreplaceable role. So what if digital thinking is introduced into the field of finance? Whether it can help solve the problem of financing constraints on small- and medium-sized enterprises? This may become a crucial part in the transformation of the great power.

CHAPTER 2

Uncover the Truth: Ecosystem of Internet Finance

Though the Internet finance is still newborn, it has attracted great attraction within a short time. It's worth noting that its influence is beyond expectation. However, most people cannot be strategically situated to capture the essence of the Internet finance. Both "the Internet + finance" and "finance + the Internet" are the presentation of the Internet finance spirit. What is the Internet finance? It cannot be summarized according to its literal meaning or from the perspective of business models. We must carry out in-depth analysis to understand the essence of the Internet finance. Only in this way can we really master the secret of the Internet finance. On this basis, we can integrate all models that can be called as Internet finance into a unified organism. That's what we stress, the concept of the ecosystem of the Internet finance. In fact, models, such as third-party payment, money management, P2P, crowd funding and credit investigation, are interdependent and in harmony with one another, and they form the ecosystem of the Internet finance together.

Since the Internet finance started to prevail in 2013, various researches and articles about the Internet finance have come in great numbers. Many scholars and experts have studied the Internet finance from different perspectives. However, all of these researches lack the core. In other words, all of these researches focus on different models of the Internet finance, but ignore the most important questions: why these models belong to the category of Internet finance; and what characteristics of

Q. Guan and W. Gao, *Internet Finance*,
The Great Transformation of China,
https://doi.org/10.1007/978-981-16-4740-6_2

Internet finance can be seen from these models. To answer these questions, we should first figure out what Internet finance is. However, most of existing studies are disconnected and only focus on one model, but ignore establishment of the overall ecosystem of the Internet finance. Hence, in the eyes of the author, these studies are of limitations. According to current primary researches, no research has studied the Internet finance on the whole; pointed out what Internet finance is; what the core of Internet finance is; and what the ecosystem of the Internet finance is like, which is the foothold of this book.

1 The Origin of Internet Finance

In fact, when Industry 4.0 and Internet plus are in the ascendant, a financial model is growing up rapidly. We can call it a meeting between finance and the Internet. As early as 2012, Xie Ping has put forward the Internet finance, the third type of financial model which is new and different from indirect bank financing and direct securities financing. Though he predicted that it had to take twenty years to develop the Internet finance in China, which was quite optimistic at that time, the Internet finance has developed as if it is a single spark that can start a prairie fire. Since the birth of Yu'E Bao in June, 2013, people across the country discussed "Baobao" and argued about Internet finance all of a sudden. Even now Internet finance is still one of the hottest terms. Though the present development of Internet finance is different from the planning of Internet finance proposed by Xie Ping, we think, according to the present development, the Internet finance has developed a closed ecosystem of the Internet finance in China. Why does the Internet finance has grown up in China?

For a long time, the financial system of China mainly serves upper circles of the social pyramid. As these clients have great property, mortgage assets and guarantee, financial institutions usually prefer to provide financial services for them. Though most people are at the bottom of society, involving the widest scope, and make the largest economic contributions, financial institutions usually exclude them from their services because of their lack of property, mortgage assets and guarantee and high risks. As a result, these people have the strongest financing restriction, the biggest fund demand and the strongest will to reform. However, due to lack of reform motivation and will, the financial reform of China is stagnant for a long time (Fig. 1).

Fig. 1 Social pyramid hierarchical structure

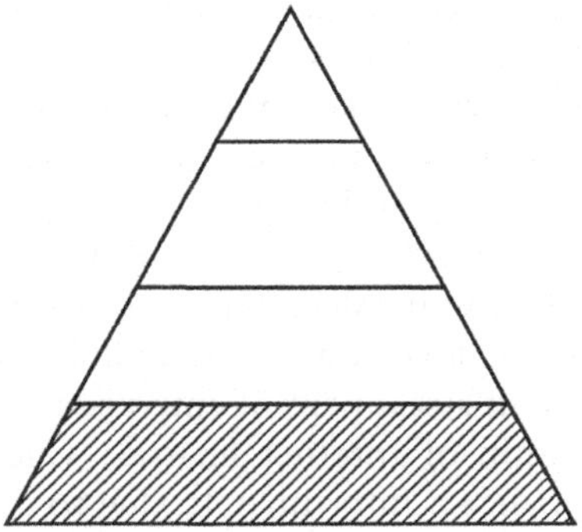

We usually regard the year of 2013 as the first year of the Internet finance. First, the birth of Yu'E Bao gathered much popularity in a short time, impacting the financial system and resulted in certain "financial panic". Second, due to the effect of Yu'E Bao, both the industry and the regulatory authority started to face the Internet finance squarely. However, it is undeniable that, even putting aside Alipay, the attempt of Internet finance can be traced back to as early as 2007.

According to data published by Ali Finance, the general financing amount required by small and micro enterprises on the Alibaba platform is below five hundred thousand. However, only 12% of these enterprises obtain bank loans, while the other 88% have no chance to obtain loans because of lack of guarantee or complicated bank procedures.[1] How dose Ali, who always claims to help enterprises start a business, deal with financing of enterprises on its platform? It can make banks to provide a loan for these enterprises or provide a loan for these enterprises by itself. In fact, Ali have tried both ways successfully to some extent. Initially, Ali wanted to cooperate with banks and provide loans for enterprises via banks. However, this method requires certain qualifications of enterprises, namely enterprise credit. As enterprises on the platform are too small to meet requirements of banks without mortgage or guarantee, they cannot meet requirements of risk assessment conducted by banks. That is to say, they cannot show their credit to banks. Ali must solve this problem, but

[1] Data source: http://opinion.hexun.com/2013-08-21/157286980.html.

how? It does not depend on bank requirements, but on what Ali has. Well, what dose Ali have? Ali has payment data from Alipay, platform transaction data and comments of consumers, etc. Ali hopes to work out credit, prospect, default probability and risk pricing of enterprises by analyzing and mining these mass data, so that it can fully reveal operating conditions of these enterprises to banks, leading to proper loans of banks. As a result, Ali cooperated with Industrial and Commercial Bank of China and China Construction Bank in May, 2007, where Ali was responsible for credit assessment of enterprises and banks for loans. This is a typical application of Internet finance, which fully reflects the thinking of Internet finance. Unfortunately, due to different ideas of Ali and banks, the cooperation above came to an end in April, 2011. In addition, Ali also tried the second method. In June, 2010, Ali founded Zhejiang Alibaba Small-loan Limited Company with Fosun Group, Yintai Group and Wanxiang Group. Ali directly provided loans for platform enterprises by establishing a small-loan company. Due to the success of this method, Ali founded Chongxing Alibaba Small-loan Limited Company later.

Thus, we can understand why the Internet finance originated and exerted such an enormous influence in China. Ultimately, the financial system of China cannot meet financing demands of much grass-roots economy at the bottom of society. The Internet finance attempts to realize function of financial intermediaries, such as banks, by other ways based on IT technology and advantages of the Internet industry to release lots of investing and financing needs.

The appearance of Yu'E Bao initiated the Internet finance. It has attracted a large number of investors via the entrance of the Internet and greatly impacted traditional financial institutions represented by banks. The concept of Internet finance started to enjoy popular support. Since then, everything is out of control……

However, what's Internet finance and what's the core composition of Internet finance? In fact, it began to take shape since the cooperation between Ali and the China Construction Bank and the foundation of the Alibaba Small-loan Limited Company. Internet enterprises attempted to pass credit assessment, evaluation of default probability and risk pricing through mass data relating to enterprise economy that they have, so that they could avoid their deficiencies in respect of assets, mortgage and guarantee and complete financing. In this process, mass data is the key supporting the Internet finance. If there's no mass data, there would be no Internet finance. As Internet finance is based on mass data, the future development tendency of Internet finance is also digitized, which happens to hold the same view with Industry 4.0 and Internet plus. However, Internet finance is just a special application of Internet plus to the field of finance.

2 The Concept of Internet Finance

Though there are various concepts of Internet finance, there's no official one because of multiple factors. The Internet finance is a financial form of constant evolution whose boundary has not been defined yet. As a result, it has no unified concept. In this book, the author doesn't intend to pay much attention to this issue, but state the meaning of the concept.

The concept of Internet finance should be defined in both a narrow sense and a broad sense. Information technology enterprises represented by Internet enterprises attempted to bypass traditional financial intermediaries through IT technology and mass data to complete credit assessment and risk pricing of clients through technology and method innovation, leading to financial services for clients, which formed the original model of Internet finance. Therefore, the narrow sense of the Internet finance refers to the behavior of Internet enterprises to be engaged in financial services in the field of finance. As Internet enterprises invaded in the field of financial institutions, financial institutions also started to step into this field, where both sides started to fight hand to hand with each other. Therefore, in a board sense, the prevision of financial services based on the Internet thinking by financial institutions also belongs to the field of Internet finance. The Internet finance involved in this book without special instructions refers to narrow-sense Internet finance.

It should be pointed out that the essence of the Internet finance is finance. The Internet is only a new form to provide financial services. However, its financial services and duty to conduct risk management should not be ignored. The Internet is just a tool to carry out risk management and offer accommodation of funds.

In addition, it should be specially noted that according to development experience of foreign Internet finance and the positioning of Internet finance defined by supervision departments, the Internet finance is only a supplement to traditional finance. At present, many researches describe a promising prospect of Internet finance, which cannot be denied. However, whether there are overoptimistic thought and exaggeration is worth discussing. Clear positioning of Internet finance is in favor of rational judgment on the Internet finance, especially when we pay close attention to various models of the Internet finance.

3 The Core Elements of Internet Finance

As the essence of the Internet finance is still finance, problems relating to finance still need to be solved. In the process of accommodation of funds, finance is confronted with two issues, namely information asymmetry and transaction cost. The information asymmetry involves two aspects: (1) credit assessment and risk pricing; and (2) information matching. The former corresponds to credit investigation, while the latter to information search. The transaction cost also involves two aspects, namely search for transaction objects and transaction concluding. The Internet finance uses Internet thinking and network resources to solve problems of information asymmetry and transaction cost.

What elements constitute the Internet finance? What's the pillar of the Internet finance? Xie Ping holds that payment, information processing and resource allocation are three pillars of the Internet finance, but not all models involve these three aspects. The author thinks that these three aspects are not enough to summarize the principle of financial activity of the Internet finance. What's the logic of financial activity of the Internet finance? We can get inspiration from the Alibaba small-load mode. The cause for its appearance is that Internet enterprises attempt to realize their credit assessment and risk pricing through data accumulation to create a precondition for financing. This model involves three aspects: first, an enterprise must have sufficient data that can reflect user information and carry out effective and reasonable analysis and mining; second, data application and capital transactions must be quick and low cost; and third, financial service must be convenient and efficient online service, or in other words, the customer experience must be good. Only when these three conditions are met at the same time can problems about information asymmetry and high transaction cost in the Internet finance be solved with good customer experience. Hence, the core elements, namely the three pillars, of the Internet finance, in the author's opinion, are big data, low (transaction) cost and convenient and efficient customer experience (Fig. 2).

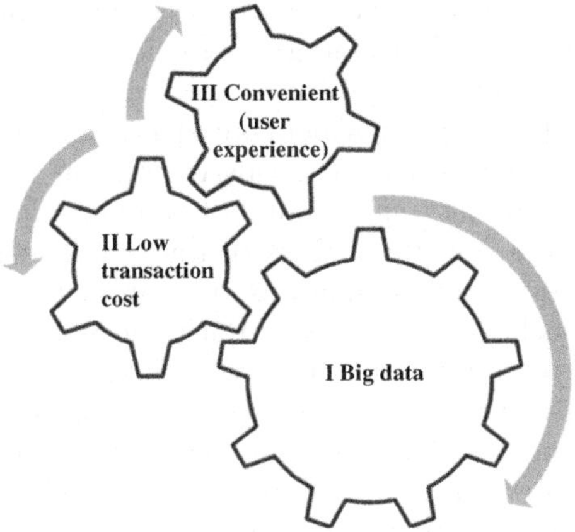

Fig. 2 Core elements of the Internet finance

Big Data

Now we can see that various industries are discussing big data and applying big data to various functions and targets. However, it seems that no one can clearly explain what on earth big data is. What is big data? The author thinks that the concept of big data includes two meanings: a noun and a verb. When big data is regarded as a noun, it means that data are of various types and in great amount. When it is used as a verb, it refers to modes of data processing, including search, analysis and mining. Through cooperation between them, targets of financial activity relating to credit assessment and risk pricing are achieved.

Big data are of numerous types and each company utilizes different types of big data. For example, Ant Financial mainly uses payment data and transaction data; Tencent applies social data; and Baidu employs search data. How many types of big data should be applied to Internet finance? The author summarized current big data in the industry. In general, the current big data can be summarized as "1+7".

Where "1" refers to basic data of individuals, including age, occupation, education and income etc., which can be obtained by enterprises through collection of information submitted by users and social investigations, etc. The other "7" types of data include payment data, transaction data, behavior data, social data, credit data, communication data and search data.

Payment data refers to capital flow data of users via third-party payment, including transaction amount, frequency and objects, etc. Through analysis of payment data, we can figure out cash flow of users. Third-party payment companies, such as Alipay, have payment data. Transaction data means transaction records on e-commerce platforms, including types, number, money amount and frequency of transactions etc. By analysis of transaction data, we can obtain operating and consuming conditions of customers. Usually, e-commerce enterprises, such as Taobao, have transaction data. Behavior data refers to unlawful conditions, violation and infringement of users, including driving under the influence, default of utilities payment, breach of taxi taking contract and receiving court summons, etc. Through analysis of these data, we can work out characteristics of users' daily work and life. Generally speaking, public departments, such as courts and traffic management bureaus, have behavior data. Social data refers to social chatting and social interaction of users. Through analysis of Moments and friend interaction of users, we can understand their circles of friends and evaluation by their friends. Social network companies, such as Tencent, usually have social data. Credit data refers to loan data of users, including money amount, term, usage and breach of contract, etc. Credit data is the most important data to judge credit of users. General financial institutions, such as banks, have loan data. Communication data refers to places, time and objects, etc. of users' communication by telephone. Through analysis of communication data, we can obtain home address and unit address of users. Telephone companies, such as China Mobile, have communication data of users. Search data refers to search contents, frequency and time, etc. of users. We can figure out focuses and characteristics of users by analyzing search data. Search giants, such as Baidu, have huge search data (Table 1).

The Internet finance means that Internet giants carry out credit analysis of users on the basis of big data that they have, usually of some type or several types, to figure out credit and probability of default of users, so that they can conduct risk pricing. Credit assessment and risk pricing are the precondition and basis of accommodation of funds conducted by users. Financial institutions usually set up certain thresholds for property, mortgage and guarantee of users. Though small and micro enterprises, private business and individuals fail to reach these thresholds, they can get a loan through Internet finance, where means, such as cloud computing,

Table 1 Types and functions of big data

Data type	*Data content*	*Function*	*Type of business*	*Representative companies*
Basic data	Occupation, diploma, income	Acquire basic conditions throughout analysis on basic personal information	Public departments	Public security bureau
Payment data	User payroll, sum, object, frequency	Acquire corporate or personal cash flow throughout analysis on payment data	Payment companies	Alipay
Transaction data	Transaction records, type, quantity, sum	Acquire corporate business conditions throughout analysis on transaction records	E-commerce	Taobao
Behavioral data	Violation of laws, violation of regulations, arrears, violation of contract	Acquire personal behavioral characteristics throughout analysis on user daily work, and life behaviors	Public departments	Court
Social contact data	QQ, Wechat friends, friend circle	Analyze the circle and friends' assessment according to users' friend circle and interaction with friends	Social giants	Tencent

(continued)

Table 1 (continued)

Data type	*Data content*	*Function*	*Type of business*	*Representative companies*
Credit data	Credit data, sum, term, purpose, violation of contract	Analyze personal historical credit throughout analysis on credit history	Financial institutions	BOC
Communication data	Communication site, length, object	Judge the residence and working unit according to users' GPS positioning	Telecommunication companies	China Mobile
Search data	Search content, frequency, time	Conclude users' hot spots and characteristics throughout analysis on users' search data	Search giants	Baidu

are adopted to evaluate their credit by analyzing big data, such as operating conditions and behavior conditions of enterprises. Thus, it can make up for and replace function of financial institutions.

When big data is used to solve problems about information asymmetry, information matching is another application, which also requires big data. After individual analysis based on big data, the other party of capital is matched to find out the optimal combination for both sides. Vertical financial search is a typical representative of big data application. However, the application of big data concentrates upon credit assessment in Internet finance.

Low-cost Transaction

The transaction cost also involves two aspects, namely search for transaction objects and transaction concluding. In traditional finance, search for transaction objects is of high cost, where financial institution must find out proper transaction objects, match transaction objects and finally consider cost for a successful transaction. However, these problems can be easily solved in Internet finance. Through big data analysis, problems about information asymmetry of objects, including credit assessment and information matching, can be solved easily. As a result, it can find out proper transaction objects easily with low cost, which only includes cost for data analysis and data search matching. During a transaction, all capital transfers are conducted via the Internet, which fully removes restrictions caused by physical boundaries. That is to say, big data expands the possible scope of transactions from an area to the entire region; from online to offline, so that both sides break limits of interpersonal relationships and geographical areas and realize free capital flow on the Internet. Low transaction cost can ensure effective financial service provided by the Internet finance.

Convenient and Efficient Customer Experience

Main clients of Internet finance are at the bottom of society and Internet finance is a supplement of traditional finance. Financial demands of grassroots economy are fragmentary, frequent, of a large number, urgent and small, etc. Therefore, service of Internet finance should be convenient and efficient, so that clients can enjoy financial service in time and at any time. Good customer experience is an important basis of existence of Internet finance. If the Internet finance is the same as traditional finance, its existence is not necessary. Internet finance can provide clients with timely and efficient service and meet their financing demands via online media. For example, Alipay allowed its users to transfer at any time with daily settlement of interest. However, now Alipay has changed daily settlement of interest into settlement of interest in two to three days. As a result, clients can achieve their financial management target easily and their payment needs won't be affected, leading to achievement of fragmented financial management targets. Clients can enjoy good experience by combining payment with financial management. On the basis of traditional financial service, the Internet finance should further provide good experience for clients.

4 The Ecosystem of Internet Finance

Models of Internet finance are not disconnected, but constitute a complete ecosystem. The ecosystem of the Internet finance includes credit investigation, search, third-party payment, online financial management, big data finance, P2P and crowd funding, which constitute the Internet finance and cannot exist independently. It's worth noting that all of these seven parts contain the three core elements of Internet finance.

Credit investigation is the precondition and basis of the Internet finance. Without credit assessment of investors and financiers, risk pricing cannot be conducted and investment and finance also cannot be conducted. Ye Daqing holds that the Internet finance starts from search. The author thinks that this point of view is not comprehensive. In fact, the Internet finance starts from credit investigation, the precondition of all financial activities, instead of search. Search is the entrance of Internet finance. From the angle of participants, Internet finance starts from search. Indeed, investors enter into the system of Internet finance from search as an entrance. Online financial management, big data finance, P2P and crowd funding form the financial platform of Internet finance, where all financial activities happen. The third-party payment is the "investment highway" of Internet finance and responsible for transfer and flow of capital.

The ecology of Internet finance faces with investors and financiers, both of whom provide their data to from the big-data system. Credit of investors and financiers is evaluated through cloud computing and Internet technology to figure out their credit and risk pricing, which is the process of credit investigation. Investors and financiers propose their financial demands via platforms of online financial management, big data finance, P2P and crowd funding and these platforms design proper financial products according to their demands (Fig. 3).

Then, investors and financiers can search for proper financial products via the platform of vertical financial search. After they come to an agreement, investors will transfer capital to financiers via third-party payment. In this process, the Internet finance is a pure infomediary which does not involve in the transaction or touch the capital.

From the perspective of development of Internet finance, third-party payment first appears with the largest scale and most mature model. Big data finance and P2P also appear early with basically developed models, which still require further adjustment and evolution. Online financial management appears late with rapid development and mature fund products. However, its other products are still under development. Though crowd funding appears early, it develops slowly. It was not until 2014 that crowd funding met with its opportunity period. Now the industry

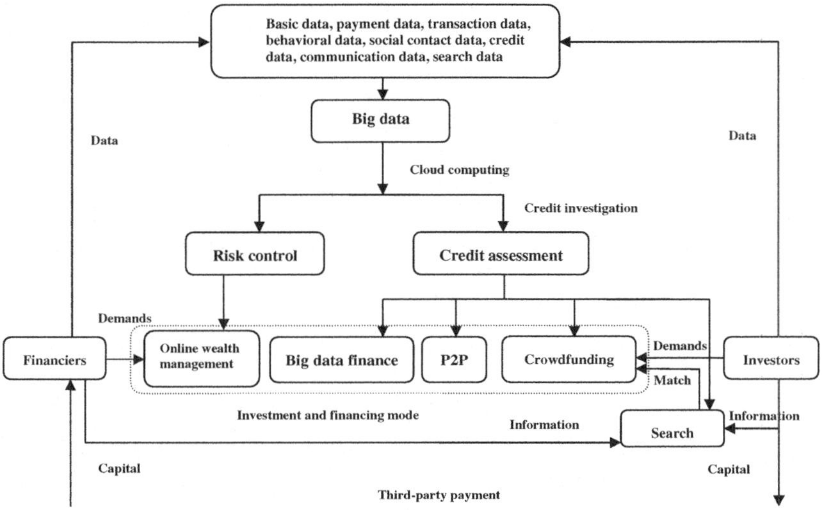

Fig. 3 Internet finance ecology

is during a period of rapid development. Search and credit investigation appear late with great market potential and immature development opportunities (Table 2).

5 The Influences of Internet Finance on Traditional Financial System

Though Internet finance is a supplement to traditional finance, it cannot be denied that Internet finance impacts traditional finance unavoidably in this process. Sometimes, the impact is great. According to the present development, Internet finance has impacted banks, securities, insurance, funds, small-loan companies and PE/VC, etc. (Fig. 4).

Present financial products, such as Yu'E Bao, are typical money market funds. People can buy currency fund products via the Internet any time and any place, which clearly impacts the traditional fund industry. Internet banks have received approval. Pure Internet banks will appear in the future and they are of lower cost and more effective than traditional banks. Internet securities are also launched. In future, online account opening, online purchase of financial products and online financing can

Table 2 Development status of various models of Internet finance

Mode	*Sub-division*	*Generation time*	*Scale*	*Development stage*	*Big data application*
Third-party payment		October 2003	9.22 trillion	Maturation period	
Online wealth management		June 2013	600 billion	Development stage	Risk control
Big data finance	Platform finance	May 2007	500 billion	Development stage	Credit assessment
	Supply chain finance	January 2012			
	Consumer finance	February 2014			
P2P		June 2007	100 billion	Development stage	Credit assessment
Crowdfunding	Commodity crowdfunding	July 2011	10 billion	Growing stage	Credit assessment
	Equity crowdfunding	November 2011			
Search		January 2012		Budding stage	Credit assessment Information match
Credit investigation		June 2014		Budding stage	Credit assessment

Note Scale data come from 2015 to 2018 Research Report of China's Internet Finance Development

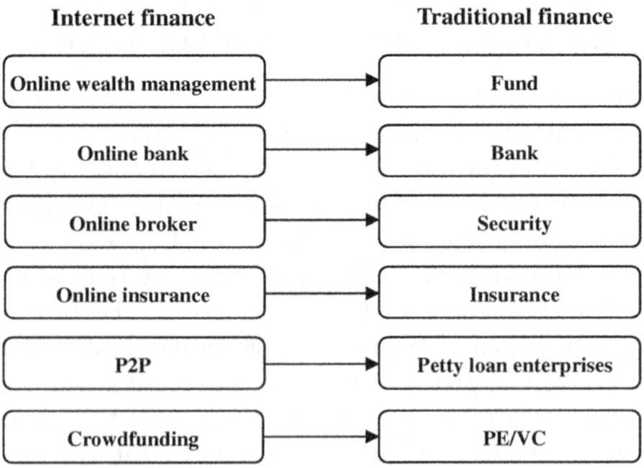

Fig. 4 Internet finance impacts traditional

be realized, impacting traditional security business. Internet insurances have appeared to seize businesses of offline insurances. The appearance of P2P severely squeeze the market share of small-loan companies. The application of crowd funding challenges monopoly of PE/VC. We have to admit that Internet finance has brought about unprecedented impacts on traditional finance, so that some people even think Internet finance will completely overturn the present financial system (Fig. 5).

Though the theory of subversion is exaggerated, impacts brought about by Internet finance should not be overlooked. So far, the most obvious victim impacted by Internet finance is commercial banks. Impacts of Internet finance on commercial banks are mainly reflected in the asset end, the debt end and intermediate business. At the asset end of commercial banks, commercial banks compete with big data finance, P2P and crowd funding. As a result, both clients and return on assets of commercial banks reduce. At the debt end, online financial products absorb a large amount of current deposit, which return to banks later in the form of agreement deposit, increasing debt costs of banks. The dual influences of the asset end and the debt end reduce interest spreads of deposit and loan

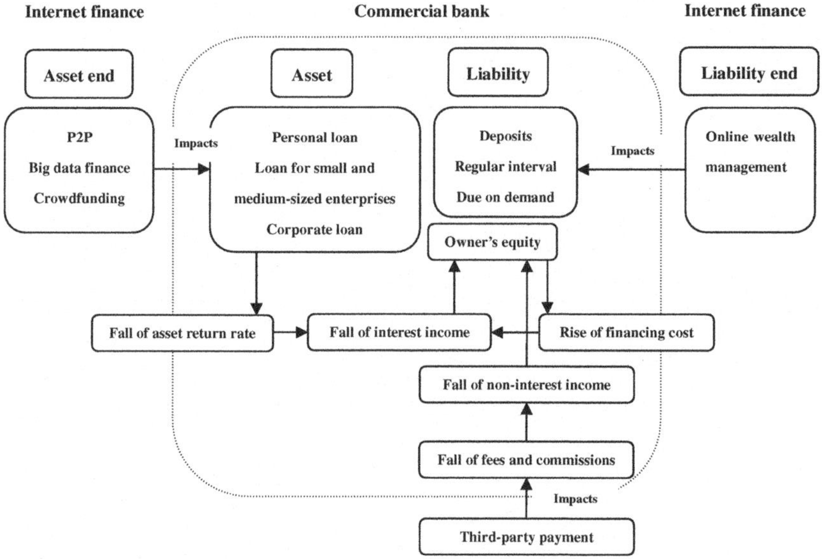

Fig. 5 Impacts of Internet finance on commercial banking business

and interest income of banks. In terms of intermediate business, Alipay and online marketing platforms replace transfer and marketing functions of banks and reduce bank income from fees and commissions. To sum up, banks are confronted with impacts of Internet finance in respect of deposit, loans and transfer and their businesses are affected.

CHAPTER 3

Vanguard of Internet Finance: Third-Party Payment

Third-party payment is credited as the "vanguard" of Internet finance. Though third-party payment is not invented specifically for Internet finance, it should be acknowledged that third-party payment has become an indispensable part of Internet finance. For instance, the well-known Yu'E Bao is exactly based on Alipay. If there is no Alipay, there will be no Yu'E Bao. To be sure, it is never possible for the public to familiarize with Tianhong Asset Management. In the world of Internet finance, third-party payment is more than a payment instrument, but also a flow entrance and data accumulation platform which bears too many functions. At present, third-party payment also turns to be the focus of contention. In particular, mobile payment illustrates the main current in the future and also rests in the key to the success or failure in the future. But in the initial start-up stage, what counts most in third-party payment is data accumulation as usual. Market entities' behavioral characteristics can only be comprehended with substantial accumulated authentic and reliable data. Correspondingly, it lays the foundation of credit investigation and expansion of business.

The reason why third-party payment is referred to as the "vanguard" of Internet finance is third-party payment gradually becomes the basis of Internet finance in the process of development. As third-party payment makes sustained progress and data accumulation, it forms a development

Q. Guan and W. Gao, *Internet Finance*,
The Great Transformation of China,
https://doi.org/10.1007/978-981-16-4740-6_3

foundation different from traditional finance on which Internet finance depends. Therefore, for understanding the main form of Internet finance, the discussion should begin with third-party payment.

1 The Definition of Third-Party Payment

Many articles and opinions view third-party payment and mobile payment as a major part of Internet finance, and even one of its backbones. We don't go into the role of third-party payment here, which will be explained later. This section focuses on the definition of third-party payment. This simple problem is usually overlooked by the public, even including scholars and experts, for many articles hold dissents about third-party payment, and some of these opinions are totally contradictory. Therefore, we are about to define the concept and scope of third-party payment in the first place.

Actually, there is no great difference in third-party payment mentioned in this book and other articles at all. We just try to give a brief explanation for its normative concept and implication. According to *Management Measures for Non-Financial Institution Payment Services* enacted by People's Bank of China on June 14, 2010, non-financial institutions' payment service means partial or whole monetary capital transfer services provided by non-financial institutions between payers and receivers in the capacity of the intermediary, including Internet payment, issue and acceptance of prepaid card, bank card acquiring service and other payment services prescribed by People's Bank of China. Non-financial institution payment service here indicates the service provided by third-party payment institutions. In practical operation, a great many scholars confuse third-party payment with electronic payment, online payment, network payment and online banking. As a result, ambiguity and nonsense expressions prevail in the literature. It is essential to rationally state third-party payment concept in Internet finance so as to differentiate it from other similar concepts.

E-payment (electronic payment) means that users directly or indirectly send payment orders to pay or transfer capital via electronic terminals. Applicable instruments here include bank card, e-cash, e-cheque or smart card. Different from traditional means of payment in which users directly pay to sellers or indirectly pay to sellers via banks, e-payment allows users to send electronic orders via terminal and entrust the bank to pay to sellers via network. E-payment specifically includes online payment, phone payment, mobile payment, POS payment and ATM payment. It can be easily seen that e-payment is more concerned about e-channel instead of any physical channel. Moreover, online payment is mainly composed of online bank and third-party payment. It is the reason why third-party payment is known as third-party online payment.

If we go deeply into this matter, we may find that there exists a slight difference between online payment and third-party payment. As a sort of e-payment, online payment stresses the online channel by which Internet transfers capital from users' bank account to sellers' bank account. While third-party payment focuses more on the platform intermediary and solves information asymmetry between users and sellers to ensure the smoothness of transaction. In this sense, online payment is a pattern conducive to third-party payment (Fig. 1).

Management Measures for Non-financial Institution Payment Services clearly stipulate the composition of third-party payment, including Internet payment, bank card acquiring service and prepaid card. We, here, place emphasis on Internet payment. Many people equate third-party payment to network payment, or equate network payment to Internet payment and mix these concepts. In analysis, they often do not differentiate these concepts. Actually, such practice is not rigorous. Comparing with bank card acquiring service and prepaid card, network payment is more concerned about the online operation of third-party payment, and it is therefore mainly made up of Internet payment, mobile payment

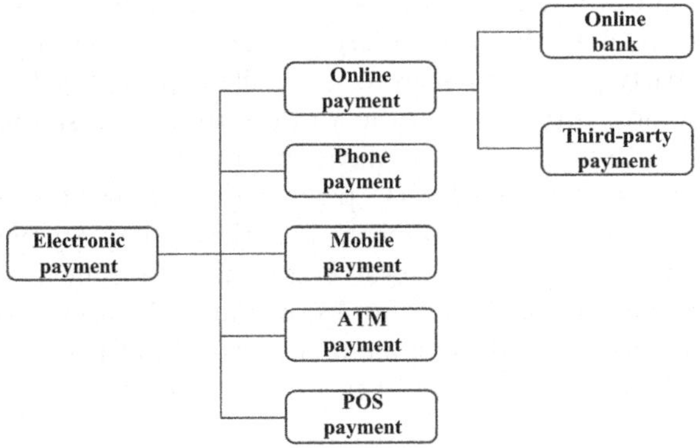

Fig. 1 Composition of electronic payment

and phone payment. Due to the small proportion of mobile payment and phone payment, many articles equate Internet payment to network payment in discussion. However, together with the prompt development of mobile payment in recent years, mobile payment scale and proportion have been on the rise. In such circumstances, it is improper to equate Internet payment to network payment with no distinction. Mobile payment is primarily composed of mobile Internet payment, message payment and near-end payment. Accompanied by the fast development of mobile payment, the composition of mobile payment also experiences fast changes which will be discussed in subsequent chapters.

Once the composition of third-party payment has been clarified, it is much easier to further the discussion.

2 The Development History of Third-Party Payment

As it is, third-party payment comes into being with Internet, especially the growth of network economy. Throughout the development history of worldwide third-party payment, it is better to judge that third-party payment witnesses the development of worldwide e-commerce.

America is the birthplace of the first third-party payment company in the world. It is followed by a group of third-party companies represented by PayPal. At first, the third-party payment companies were established to solve payment problems in e-commerce business because then commercial banks couldn't totally cover personal payment business. When PayPal was acquired by eBay, the world's largest C2C online trading platform in 2002, third-party payment began to gradually expose its advantages, and PayPal, therefore, turned to be the world's third largest third-payment platform until it was replaced by Alipay in July 2009.

The development of third-party payment in China bears much similarity to that in America, which means that third-party payment in China was also created to promote local e-commerce business at first, and then entered the explosive stage until government's macroscopic control in 2010. Therefore, the development history of third-party payment in China generally falls into three stages.

Gateway Payment Pattern Stage in 1998–2002

At present, Internet finance in narrow sense usually means the transition of Internet company to traditional finance industry, and uses Internet thinking to transact financial business. But as a matter of fact, the industry that takes the lead to popularize Internet is exactly banking industry. In a rather long period of time, the banking industry has been always one of the few industries with supreme networked degree. Early in 1997, CMBC released its Netcom business and became the first commercial bank with online business. Afterward, CCB and CITIC Bank successively followed the trend to open online channel. At the same time, in 1999, e-commerce companies represented by ebay and Dangdang sprang up, indicating the entry of e-commerce age in China. In the same year, the foundation of Shanghai IPS and Beijing Capital indicated the sprout of third-party payment in China. Till then, three roles involved in the third-party payment industry—commercial bank, e-commerce platform and third-party payment company converged.

Characteristics of the third-party payment industry in this stage may be represented by "gateway". The cause is that on the one hand, limited by bank system security construction, hardware facility and other technical causes, online bank business is so single to support online payment functions and can only offer simple information services like account inquiry. Then network is nothing but a convenient channel of information display. On the other hand, as bank systems are independent from each other, it is impossible to fulfill inter-bank liquidation. In response to the requirements of e-commerce payment, third-party payment companies can only integrate the gateway ports of different banks. When users make payment, they just need to enter the bank payment interface maintained by third-party payment via third-party payment platform, and input bank accounts and passwords to conclude the transaction (Fig. 2).

Third-party payment companies are not engaged in third-party payment business, but just play the role of e-bank port which creates convenience for users. Consequently, third-party payment in this stage does not engage in payment business yet. This decides that third-party payment in this stage remains in the budding stage.

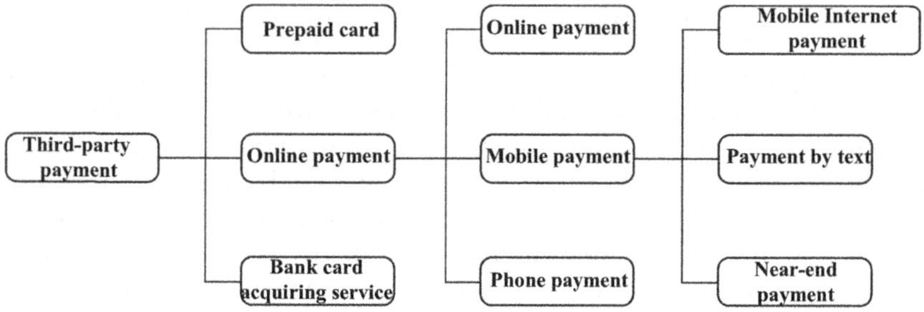

Fig. 2 Third-party payment flow of gateway mode

Great Leap Stage of Third-Party Payment in 2003–2009

Marked by the rise of Alipay's "secured transaction" pattern in October 2003, third-party payment industry in China starts to transit from gateway pattern to third-party payment. From then on, Chinese third-party payment enters the super-normal fast lane.

Alipay discovers the bottleneck hindering Chinese e-commerce development since its foundation. The fundamental cause of e-commerce's slow development should be ascribed to the pending bother in transaction–information asymmetry. In reality, information asymmetry does not simply means constraint on e-commerce. After all, information asymmetry obstacles exist in all industries. But in the field of e-commerce, this problem is more prominent.

This is mainly based on the characteristics of e-commerce: trading parties do not have to know each other nor respective identity, but just need to communicate about trading details via the network. Such business pattern invisibly increases bilateral information asymmetry while improving communication efficiency and lowering communication cost. As a result, the parties hold suspicious attitudes toward the trading. The buyer worries about product quality or refuses to make prepayment because of uncertain date of product delivery, while the seller worries about timely receivables and refuses to make a delivery first. It is exactly such information asymmetry that fundamentally restricts the development of e-commerce. As it is, for ensuring the success of online trading, the first step is to solve information asymmetry problem, especially payment.

Aiming at such a payment dilemma, Taobao comes up with "secured transaction" pattern and intervenes the trading process in the capacity of the third-party judge responsible for bilateral information asymmetry and smooth payment. To be specific, the buyer shall transfer capital to third-party platform for custody after placing an order to ensure that capital will be sent to the seller upon product delivery. At the same time, the seller can only receive the capital after products reaching the buyer and obtaining quality acceptance. In this way, capital custody on third-party payment platform is able to effectively solve bilateral information asymmetry and promote the smooth progress of trading.

The rise of "secured transaction" presents an excellent solution for information asymmetry. After that, the successive release of "secured transaction" pattern in leading third-party payment companies greatly facilitates the development of e-commerce in China, which in turn boosts the sustained progress of third-party payment. In this period, there are new changes in the third-party payment pattern as platform-dependent payment pattern derives independent third-party pattern. Likewise, payment means also extends from online to offline means. The realization of bank card acquiring service makes full coverage from online to offline means possible. The business pattern of third-party payment also starts to expand in the integrated and vertical direction, thus greatly enriching the business category of third-party payment.

On the whole, in this period, "secured transaction" pattern successfully solves the biggest trading barrier of information asymmetry so that it better caters to trading requirements. From then on, third-party payment enters the fast lane of development. The main characteristics include continuous growth of third-party payment companies and payment scale, new breakthroughs in platform pattern, new sort of payment means and innovated business pattern. As a consequence, third-party payment in this stage witnesses the leap development.

Stage of the Coexistence of Normative Development and New Business Type Since 2010

Following seven-year fast and disorderly development, government departments began to perform normative management on third-party payment in 2010 and expected to reorganize chaos in third-party payment market and propel the healthy development of third-party payment. In reality, since People's Bank of China's enactment of No. 7 Document as of April 16, 2009, government departments had relaxed control on third-party payment. No. 7 Document primarily determined the connotation of payment liquidation, and the scope of non-financial institutions qualified for payment settlement business, requested the registration and filing of third-party companies and confirmed the mainstream status of the Central Bank in supervision work. *Management Practices for Non-financial Institution Payment Service* and execution rules on June 2010 further clarified the attitude, mode and measures taken by government departments toward third-party payment normative management and supervision. As a result, the issue of management practices marks that domestic third-party payment transits from disorderly development stage to orderly development stage. In 2011, the Central Bank began to issue first batch of business license to non-financial institutions, and in 2012, fund license was issued. In the following years, management practices for prepaid card, bank card acquiring service, Internet payment, mobile payment and excess reserves have been successively formulated, indicating that government departments have made clear management provisions for all sorts of third-party payment means and corresponding precipitation capital on the whole, and gradually developed a sound supervision system to make sure of its healthy development. In addition, considering the new forms, trends and characteristics of third-party payment, relevant supervision policies for third-party payment will be continually improved (Table 1).

Despite government efforts in continuous specification of third-party payment, we must notice that in recent years, third-party payment begins to gradually deviate from primitive inherent pattern, and derives some new trends in the payment industry. These new trends demonstrate some new changes spontaneously occurring in the payment industry.

First of all, throughout long-term industry development, all companies' market shares in the third-party payment field turn stable, and some large payment institutions standing out from market competition have gained overwhelming competitive advantages in one or few fields. With a large consumer base and strong viscosity, these institutions can generate scale effects, such as Alipay and TenPay. In consequence, corresponding admission threshold will be promoted and new companies encounter more difficulties in market exploitation.

Secondly, the influence of third-party payment products is on the decline. The homogenization of third-party payment makes sure all parties do not exploit the market by products. How to attract and improve consumer viscosity turns to be the key to the success of

Table 1 Third-party payment supervision policy

Object	*Time*	*Document*
Third-party payment	June 2010	Payment Service Management Practices for Non-financial Institutions
Third-party payment	September 2010	Payment Service Management Practices and Enforcement Rules for Non-financial Institutions
Prepaid card	May 2011	Opinions on Normalizing the Management of Business Prepaid Card
	September 2012	Prepaid Card Business Management Practices for Payment Institutions
	September 2012	Management Practices for Single-purpose Business Prepaid Card
Provisions	June 2013	Interim Procedures for Client Provisions in Payment Institutions
Internet payment	January 2012	Management Practices for Internet Payment Business in Payment Institutions
Ban card acquiring service	January 2013	Bank Card Swiping Service Charge Adjustment Scheme
	July 2013	Management Practices for Bank Card Acquiring Service Business
Mobile payment	December 2012	Chinese Finance Mobile Payment Technical Standards

third-party payment companies. While this is mainly up to the role of third-party payment additional business instead of main business.

Thirdly, for enriching business category, more third-party payment companies begin to transfer from payment settlement business to comprehensive payment business in order to solve platform and vertical industry payment transition, provide diversified and professional third-party payment services and increase consumer viscosity.

Finally, with the prompt rise of mobile payment and the popularity of smart phone, more and more consumers choose to pay via mobile terminal for removing constraints imposed by computer terminal on consumption. New payment means like QR code payment, sound wave payment, near-end payment will definitely bring about the revolution of third-party payment, and even rebuild the third-party payment industry.

Throughout the entire development history of third-party payment industry, we may see that because of the effective relief of information asymmetry, third-party payment assisted by Internet, communication technology and other high-tech means will on the one hand develop main payment business and on the other hand enrich payment scenes, means and patterns. In the future, third-party payment will continually practise normative development and develop new business types.

3 The Development Status of Third-Party Payment

The third-party payment in China remains high rate of growth. On the one hand, the market pattern of third-party payment is relatively stable. On the other hand, with the rise of some emerging payment modes, like mobile payment, near-end payment and QR code, all parties keep making innovation in business pattern to enrich payment means, reinforce consumer experience and sustain consumer viscosity. Under the context of service homogenization, companies can only gain market shares through further promoting service quality, and stepping onto the way of differentiation development. In this regard, third-party payment companies seemingly reach a consensus.

Number of Third-Party Payment Companies

Accompanied by the continuous development and expansion of third-party payment, the number of third-party payment platforms is also on the rise (Table 2).

As proved by payment business license gained by these 269 platforms, each payment platform gains discrepant payment businesses. Some payment companies just gain one payment business license. For instance, Guangdong Xinhui E-commerce Co., Ltd only engages in bank card acquiring service business, Heilongjiang Shengya Science and Technology Development Limited Company can only transact Internet payment business. While some third-party payment companies gain more payment business qualifications. For instance, Alipay gains five business qualifications except fixed phone payment and digital TV payment, 99 Bill gain five business qualifications except prepaid card issue and digital TV payment, and SCEA gains six business qualifications except digital TV payment. It therefore becomes the company which has most business qualifications in third-party payment market (Fig. 3).

Now, third-party payment business still concentrates on prepaid card issue, Internet payment and bank card acquiring service. Especially,

Table 2 Third-party payment license issue condition

Batch	*Time*	*Number of issue*	*Accumulated number of issue*
First batch	May 26, 2011	27	27
Second batch	August 9, 2011	13	40
Third batch	December 12, 2011	61	101
Fourth batch	June 27, 2012	95	196
Fifth batch	July 20, 2012	1	197
Sixth batch	January 6, 2013	26	223
Seventh batch	July 6, 2013	27	250
Eighth batch	July 16, 2014	19	269

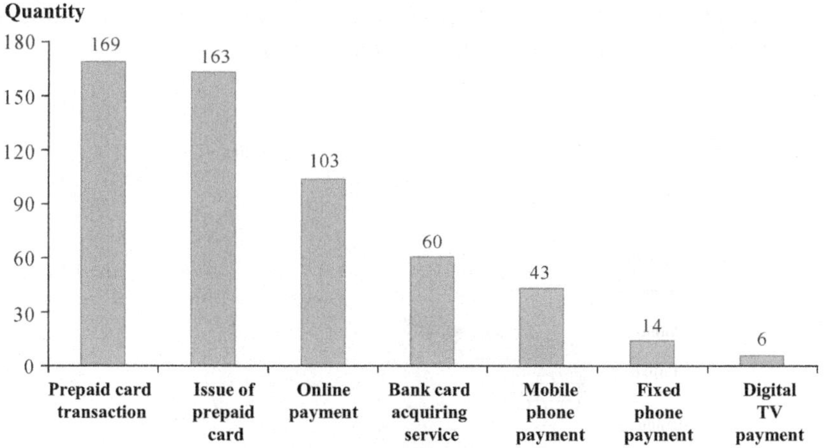

Fig. 3 Distribution of payment business on third-party payment platform

prepaid card issue and acceptance is the topmost business type among third-party payment companies. Internet payment ranks the second place. Though mobile phone payment business does not seize great market shares, it should be noted that mobile payment is the mainstream in the future. It is foreseeable that the number of mobile phone platform will be kept at a high level in the future.

According to the distribution of payment platforms, it is basically related to regional economic growth level. Actually, it is also associated with the properties of third-party payment. The exclusive properties of third-party payment decide that those regions with developed science applications, high-level population and frequent trading behaviors have higher requirements on the use of third-party payment. While these demands also decide that the use of third-party payment is more frequent in economically developed areas. In accordance with the real circumstances, in eastern regions, especially Beijing, Shanghai and Guangzhou, there are more third-party payment platforms. They become the first leading camp of third-party payment. While eastern economically developed provinces represented by Jiangsu, Zhejiang and Shandong become the second camps of third-party payment. But in other areas, the number of payment platforms is still rather limited (Fig. 4).

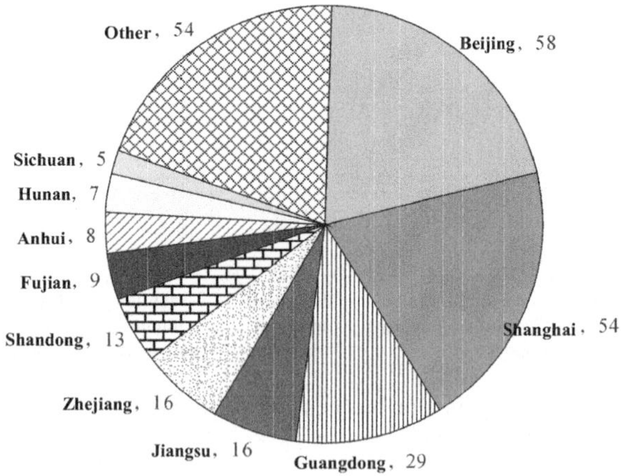

Fig. 4 Quantity of third-party payment platform in provinces and cities

Third-Party Payment Scale

In general, the scale of third-party payment presents the momentum of fast growth. In 2005, the scale of third-party payment only reached 19.6 billion yuan. By 2009, the scale reached 3 trillion yuan. As of 2010, domestic third-party payment business scale has been on high-speed growth, increasing from 6.1 trillion yuan to 17.2 trillion yuan by 2.37 times. At the same time, we must notice the obvious declining trend of growth rate of third-party payment, decreasing from 70% in 2010 to 38.7% in 2013. It is predicted that such high-speed growth is non-foreseeable in the future (Fig. 5).

Pursuant to the structure of third-party payment, bank card acquiring service, Internet payment and mobile payment account for maximum proportion above 99%, and the proportion of other payment types can be basically ignored. Among the three business types, offline bank card acquiring service seizes dominant shares and it reached 80% in 2009. Despite the rise of bank card acquiring service business scale in recent few years from 2.4 trillion yuan in 2009 to 1.7 trillion yuan in 2013, it is undeniable that the growth rate of Internet payment and mobile payment is faster than bank card acquiring service. For this reason, offline acquiring

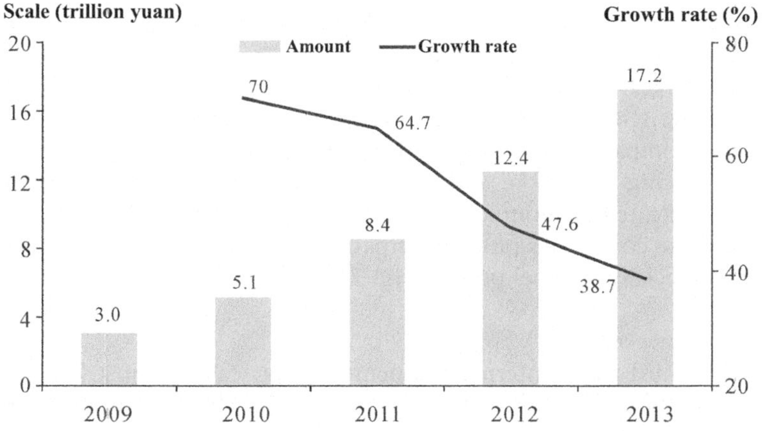

Fig. 5 Third-party payment scale and growth rate from 2009 to 2013 (*Data source* iResearch)

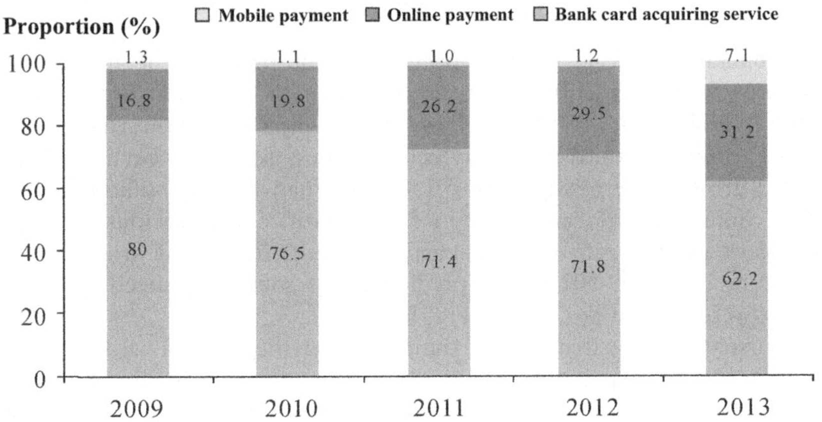

Fig. 6 Third-party payment structure from 2009 to 2013 (*Data source* iResearch)

service proportion is on the decline. By late 2013, it was decreased to 62.2%. But it still dominated third-party payment (Fig. 6).

As proved by the market pattern of third-party payment in 2013, the tripod situation basically takes shape. China UMS seizes maximum market shares as high as 39.8%. China UMS enjoys an advantage over offline payment, and bank card acquiring service far exceeds other competitors in market shares. The two Internet giants of Alipay and TenPay, respectively, seize 28.9% market shares, while independent third-party payment companies just possess 17% market shares. In addition, it is worth noticing that more and more companies now enter the payment industry, like telecommunication operators. Regardless of small market shares, these companies possibly surpass the former by virtue of business power, especially channel power (Fig. 7).

Internet Payment

In 2004, third-party Internet payment trading scale was just 7.2 billion yuan, but the scale of growth was striking. In 2008, it reached 257.8 billion yuan. Before 2012, it grew at the rate of over 100% once a year. After 2011, despite great decline of growth rate. The scale was still approximately 5.37 trillion yuan in 2013, and 5.73 trillion yuan in former three quarters in 2014 (Figs. 8 and 9).

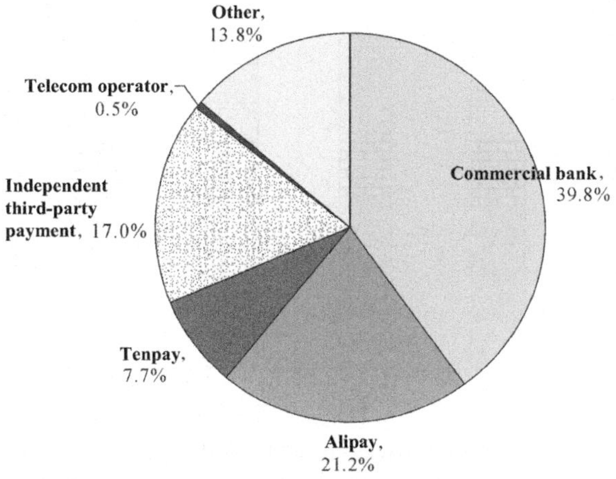

Fig. 7 Layout of Chinese third-party payment market in 2013 (*Data source* iResearch)

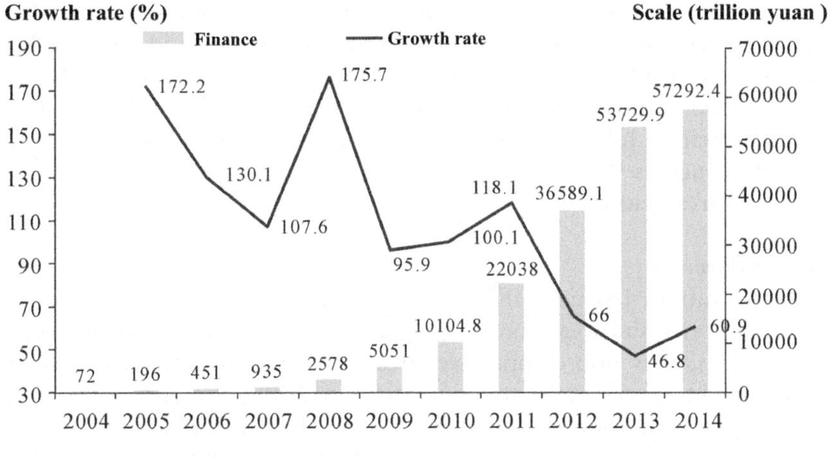

Fig. 8 Third-party internet payment scale and growth rate from 2004 to the third quarter of 2014 (*Data source* iResearch)

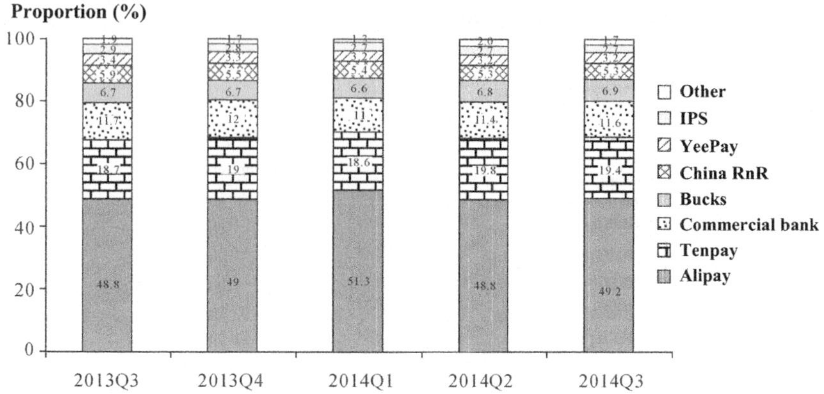

Fig. 9 Third-party internet payment scale and growth rate from the third quarter of 2013 to the third quarter of 2014 (*Data source* iResearch)

Nowadays, the market pattern of Internet payment is relatively stable. Alipay seizes the dominant status with around 50% market shares, TenPay ranks the second place with around 20% market shares and China UMS ranks the third place with around 11% market shares. Obviously, Alipay, TenPay and China UMS take up 80% market shares. The Internet payment market fully demonstrates the Pareto principle. Other payment platforms such as 99 Bill, China PnR, YeePay and IPS only seize limited market shares below 10%.

Mobile Payment

Similarly, mobile payment also undergoes the development stage from a small, minority and weak force to a large, majority and formidable force, and besides, it is non-comparable to any other third-party payment in development speed, scale and potential. In 2009, the scale of mobile payment in China was just 40 trillion yuan. But it doubled in 2011 as around 80 trillion yuan, with a year-on-year growth rate of 89.2%. The growth rate sped up and experienced explosion in 2013. Annual trading volume in 2013 reached 12,197.4 trillion yuan, increasing by 70.7% than 2012. The growth momentum was continued in 2014, in which first-quarter trading volume totaled 14,374.7 trillion yuan, second-quarter totaled 3300.5 trillion yuan with a slight decline and third-quarter trading volume reached by 14,332.7 trillion yuan. The year-on-year growth rate in former three quarters was 835.5%. Such performance is beyond the expectation of everyone.

Together with the fast growth of mobile payment, its business structure is constantly changing. In 2009, short message payment accounted for 97.6% in mobile payment business and seized absolute market shares in this field. The proportion of mobile Internet and near-end payment, respectively, as 2.3 and 0.1% could be basically ignored (Fig. 10).

But after that, the proportion of mobile Internet kept going up in mobile payment business, increasing from 6.2% in 2010 to 51.7% in 2012. It was the first time for mobile payment to surpass short message payment in history. Such trend was followed in 2013 as well, with the proportion rising to 71.7% far beyond short message payment. It therefore became the foremost business form in mobile payment. Simultaneously, the scale of near-end payment was also on the rise, but its growth rate was relatively limited. Its proportion in 2013 was just 3.6% (Fig. 11).

Then why can mobile payment realize ultra-high growth rate? Why can mobile Internet payment surpass short message payment. To sum up, few reasons are worth of noticing.

Firstly, the great popularity of smart phones activates the development of mobile payment and mobile Internet payment. The sales volume of smart phone has been on the rise after 2006. Especially after 2010,

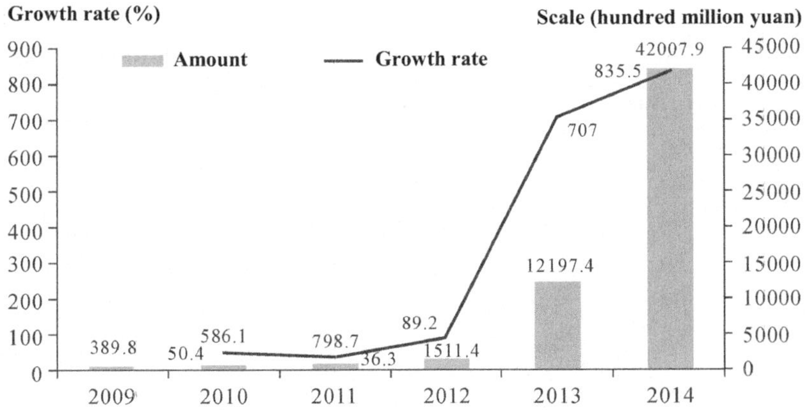

Fig. 10 Mobile payment scale and growth rate from 2009 to the third quarter of 2014 (*Data source* iResearch)

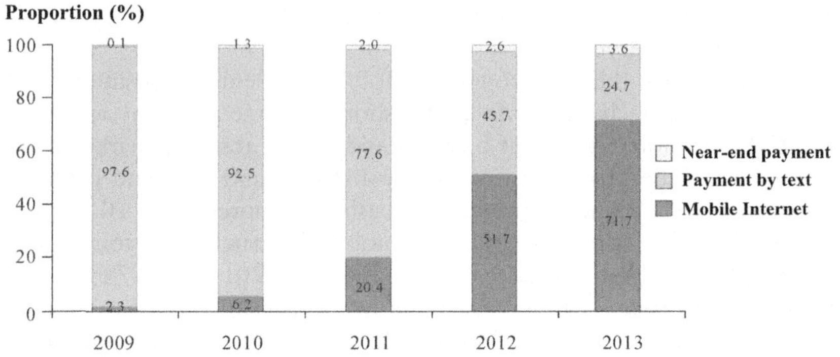

Fig. 11 Mobile payment business composition from 2009 to 2013 (*Data source* iResearch)

the sales volume was maintained above 80% and this greatly promoted the popularity of smart phones. Its role is self-evident in promoting the high-rate growth of mobile payment. Moreover, as smart phones have more functions than ordinary phones, mobile Internet service is of vital importance to the actualization of payment (Fig. 12).

Secondly, the fast advance of technology can support the actualization of mobile payment. Now, QR code payment, NFC payment, sound wave

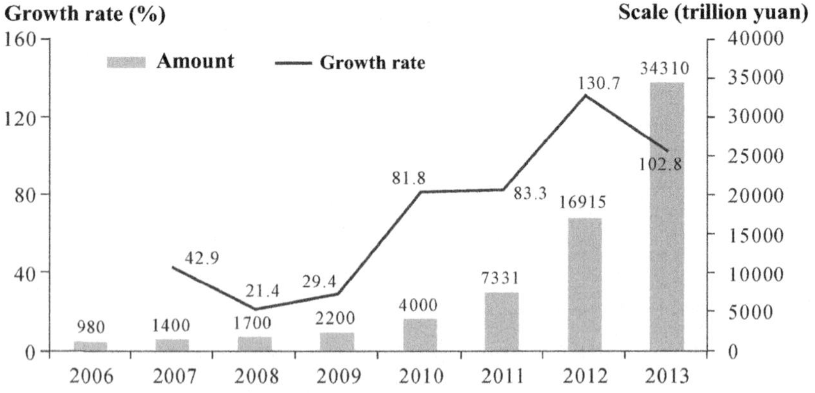

Fig. 12 Sales volume of smart phone in China from 2006 to 2013 (*Data source* In-depth Research Report for Chinese Internet Financial Industry in 2014)

payment and infrared ray payment and other mobile payment patterns are not problems technically, and such emerging payment patterns turn more popular now. It is predicted that technology-driven mobile payment will continually remain at a high-rate growth.

Thirdly, increase of application scenes also supports the fast growth of mobile payment. The application scenes of mobile payment have been greatly enriched, from online shopping to transfer accounts and other traditional payment to recharges, payment of water and electricity fees, offline shopping and other modern payment. As it is, mobile payment possibly overturns the entire payment industry in the future.

Finally, the maturity of O2O pattern is driving the development of mobile payment. As O2O pattern enables consumers to choose online placement of orders and offline payment, it can fully replace other payment patterns, especially Internet payment. The foremost thing is that the scale of mobile payment has been effectively increased by stimulating new payment demands and innovating payment patterns.

As proved by existing mobile payment market layout, Alipay and TenPay still seize large market shares, especially the former. Till the third quarter of 2014, it had seized 82.6% market shares, and its advantages were quite distinct. Besides that, traditional offline payment giant Lacarra also made up 4.4% shares. After all, mobile payment is finished by offline payment patterns in part. Throughout the whole third-party payment industry, bank acquiring service still makes up great market shares. Thus it can be seen that in mobile payment, consumers possibly have greater demands for offline payment such as near-end payment than online payment. If this is true, we must fully excavate the potentials in the payment market. Third-party payment companies shall plan mobile payment and shape consumer habits as soon as possible. Now, backed by their powerful e-commerce platform and social network, Alipay and TenPay have taken an offensive move in this regard. Other third-party payment companies are advised to seek sally ports and avoid market competition from near-end payment and other minor businesses (Fig. 13).

4 The Business Model of Third-Party Payment

Present third-party payment patterns include secured transaction pattern and independent third-party pattern. Though there is some difference in payment patterns, they both satisfy specific payment requirements in respective fields. This implies the necessity of the two patterns.

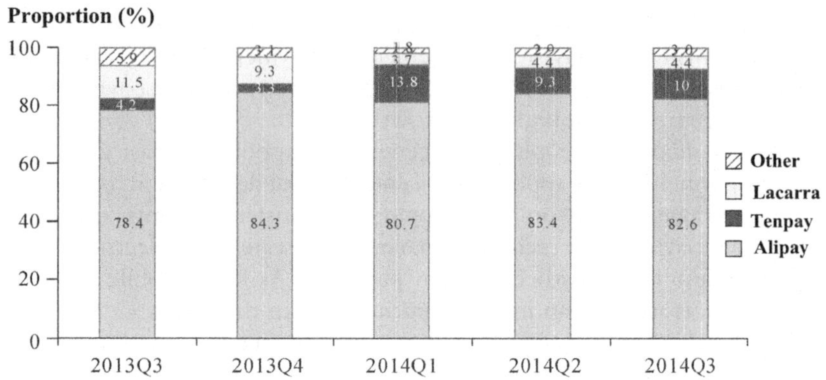

Fig. 13 Third-party payment market pattern from the third quarter of 2013 to the third quarter of 2014 (*Data source* iResearch)

Secured Transaction Pattern

Secured transaction, firstly invented by Alipay, has been widely applied in third-party payment platforms backed by e-commerce platforms, like Alipay and TenPay. Before the rise of Alipay, third-party payment at home and abroad usually serves gateway function. When consumers make payment, third-party payment platforms will be immediately connected to e-bank for payment. But such move has great credit risks. America does not have such worry because it has sound legal system, credit system and risk control system and both the buyer and the seller would provide secured products and loans as per the contract. However, due to the lack of credit system in China, the penalty cost is rather low, and e-commerce accordingly undertakes great credit risks. Third-party platforms can't fully transact such risks. This is also the obstacle hindering the fast development of third-party payment.

Secured transaction is exactly created to solve this problem. Its nature is to solve credit risk—the fundamental problem caused by information asymmetry in trading. The solution is to find an independent third party to entrust capital and promote the success of bilateral trading.

Third-party payment secure transaction pattern is as shown in Fig. 14. First of all, consumers transfer capital from opening bank account A to third-party payment platform account A. secondly, third-party payment platform adds equal amount of money in consumers' virtual account. It

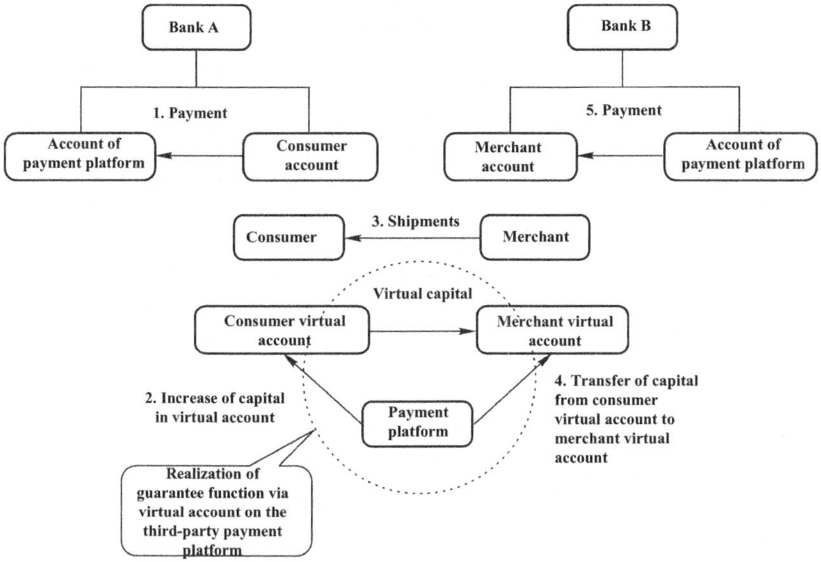

Fig. 14 Third-party payment guarantee trading flow

supposes that consumers now have made payment (but the capital is in custody in third-party payment platform). Thirdly, the seller sends goods and consumers notify third-party payment platform for payment upon acceptance. Fourthly, third-party payment platform transfers the capital from consumers' virtual account to the seller's virtual account. Fifthly, third-party payment platform deducts the capital from the seller's virtual account and transfers the capital from bank account B to the seller's bank account B (Fig. 15).

In this process, we must pay attention to the point that the capital has been placed in third-party payment platform bank account in custody, and the platform does not access the capital directly. The function of the platform is custody by removing information asymmetry between the parties, and lowering credit risks. Third-party payment platform will instantly transfer capital upon the successful completion of transaction.

At first, third-party payment platform realizes the function of capital guarantee by virtual account design. In reality, virtual account indeed fulfills its role. But when third-party payment platforms design virtual accounts, probably they don't know that they may use advanced computer

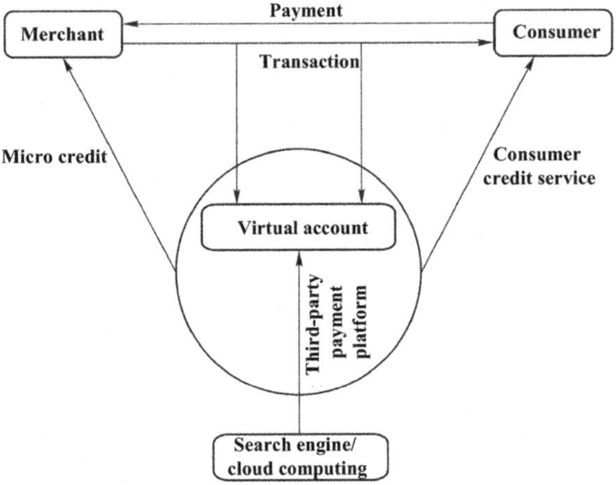

Fig. 15 Logic analysis on the formation of internet finance

technology to analyze transaction data, summarize consumers' consumption characteristics, payment habits, sellers' flow dynamics and operation conditions, and further rationally use the technology according to such interesting discoveries when payment data and transaction data in virtual accounts would add up to such level or say such a giant basis, such as pertinent network marketing and advertising. Furthermore, the platform can also take advantage of data analysis results to gain the accurate portrait of consumers and sellers, assess their credit and provide financial services with higher additional values. Now we can't answer this question. Probably only Alipay itself knows the answer. But fortunately, these thoughts written on paper have been realized and are being realized. For instance, pertinent network marketing has already come true. Careful consumers would find that when they have online shopping, they would often receive similar advertising sent from e-commerce companies. In reality, it is the primary application of big data on initial marketing level. While in face of the great trend of Internet finance now, e-commerce companies have discovered the role of data accumulation. Seemingly careless data accumulation becomes the most important asset of third-party payment platform. The problem now is how to transact such massive trading data and provide consumption credit loan and micro loan services, respectively, to consumers and sellers. Some acute Internet giants have taken steps now.

Independent Third-Party Pattern

What is obviously different from secured transaction pattern is independent third-party pattern. The former is mainly designed according to the e-commerce trading on the platform. Therefore, it is inevitably associated with its own e-commerce platform. But there also exists another sort of payment platform. It does not have any exclusive e-commerce platform, and the rise of such pattern is not to solve credit risk in e-commerce trading, but to offer payment service and payment solutions to companies. So these payment platforms have to be independent from e-commerce platforms.

Comparatively speaking, independent third-party pattern does not have any advantage over consumer base. After all, it does not have giant payment volume like e-commerce platforms. So the market share in third-party payment is rather limited now as 17%. In addition, in market segment, no trace of third-party can be found at all. However, we must admit that the independent third-party platform possesses the same value assets like secured transaction—trading data. As the former has identical virtual accounts, it can not only offer payment settlement service to consumers, but also gather consumer-related information and form information accumulation advantages. Apart from it, the largest problem of independent third-party payment platform is how to survive in the market. Only in this way can it accumulate trading data. During this process, independent third-party payment camps begin differentiation. Some judge that there is no radical difference in industry difference, and the platform may provide a universal and compatible payment solution to meet all industries' payment demands, and some consider that industry properties decide the difference between the payment systems of all industries. The right practice is to take root in a given industry, integrate the industry chain of entire industry and satisfy the payment demands of the given industry. The result is that the former follows the path of integrated payment while the latter follows the path of vertical payment. As proved by facts, both of them satisfy specific payment demands with strong vitality.

Vertical Industry Payment

Vertical industry payment under the category of third-party payment possesses the industry characteristics exclusive to third-party payment, such as virtual account, accumulated payment data, etc. But comparing with other places, vertical industry payment has particular industry service pattern and development path. To put it simply, vertical industry payment serves core companies and related upstream and downstream companies in the industry in payment business, satisfies the payment demands of a given industry. In comparison with platform pattern and integrated payment pattern, vertical industry payment is more flexible and applicable.

Case 1: China PnR

Founded in July 2006, China PnR has accumulated amount of investment totaling 1 billion yuan, and it is mainly engaged in integrated financial service for Chinese small and micro companies, financial institutions, industry clients and investors, like financial payment, account trusteeship, and investment and wealth management. Positioned as a financial e-payment expert, China PnR has established cooperative relations with domestic commercial banks and international bank card organizations. With focus on financial payment and industry chain payment, its core competitiveness is to quickly and accurately customize payment solution for industry consumers, innovate e-payment service products and propel the development of e-commerce in all industries.

China PnR engages in a wide variety of payment businesses. In May 2010, it became the first company that gained the qualification of transacting online fund sales and payment settlement business approved by CSRC. In May 2011, it was among the first batch of companies that gained the payment business license issued by Central Bank. In October 2011, it was among the first batch of companies that gained the license of cross-border payment business pilots approved by SAFE. In December 2014, China PnR Finance gained securities investment funds sales business qualification approved by Shanghai CSRC, and developed wealth management product sales and fund sales businesses. Till then, China PnR has gained fund sales license and fund payment license.

For years, China PnR has been maintaining high-speed development. In 2013, its trading scale exceeded one trillion yuan and it therefore ranked top in the industry, especially in independent third-party payment field. At present, China PnR has served ten thousand industry consumers in fund industry, aviation ticket, business circulation and digital amusement, such as China Assessment Management Company, Air China, Southern Airlines, China Eastern Airlines, Netease, Ping An Insurance, Ctrip, provided financial service for 95% domestic commercial banks and hundreds of leading P2P companies, and built a one-stop wealth management platform for 2 million investors and financial consultants.

Nowadays, on the basis of e-payment, China PnR successively develops small and micro business services, interbank services and financial wealth management services. By way of the integrated service pattern of financial POS acquiring service which combines direct selling and outsourcing, small and micro businesses release "Red POS" which releases service vehicles across the country on trail, promotes POS acquiring service phone client-side, issues POS mini mobile swiping card reader and credit payment 20 product and offers more secure and convenient financial payment service for millions of small and micro business owners. Throughout interbank services, China PnR establishes the first third-party P2P trusteeship account system in China. More than 200 P2P companies at home join China PnR trusteeship account. In 2013, China CNR established the subsidiary China PnR Science and Technology Co., Ltd. to build a "card remittance service platform" and provide prepayment account trusteeship system and value-added service for all industries. Financial wealth management services include its one-stop wealth management platform "Tiantianying" which has been connected with 2 million users, 50 funds and 33 banks. Investors are able to buy the direct-selling products of any fund at any time and place. In terms of professional wealth management, it has released the first one-stop wealth management counseling service platform "Cloud Finance" that specializes in integrated network wealth management services of multiple wealth management products such as trust, insurance and publicly offered fund.

In effect, the real industry advantage of China PnR rests in the payment-side. By customizing special and private payment program according to consumers' industry characteristics, China PnR effectively integrates entire upstream and downstream industry chain of the industry, and realizes industry deepening and vertical reform. This is the supreme characteristic of China PnR in independent third-party payment platform. The "money manager system" developed by China PnR customizes payment operation solutions for core companies and upstream and downstream small- and medium-sized companies in traditional industry, accelerates industry capital turnover efficiency, boosts trading efficiency and management abilities and accelerates industry chain upstream and downstream companies to quickly enter the e-commerce age. Since 2006, it has been successively applied in numerous industries in aviation, hotel, logistics and education. In October 2013, China PnR gained cross-border payment pilot license and marched to cross-border blue ocean market covering aviation, tourism, overseas education and goods trading (Fig. 16)

Money Manager has three prime functions. First of all, it provides high-efficient and low-cost local multi-bank cross-regional business. Secondly, it provides payment, liquidation, sub-account and loaning service. Thirdly, it customizes IT and account management instrument for small- and medium-sized companies. Taking aviation tourism industry, for example, it satisfies the payment requirements in different trading links by multiple payment patterns such as phone payment, credit payment and

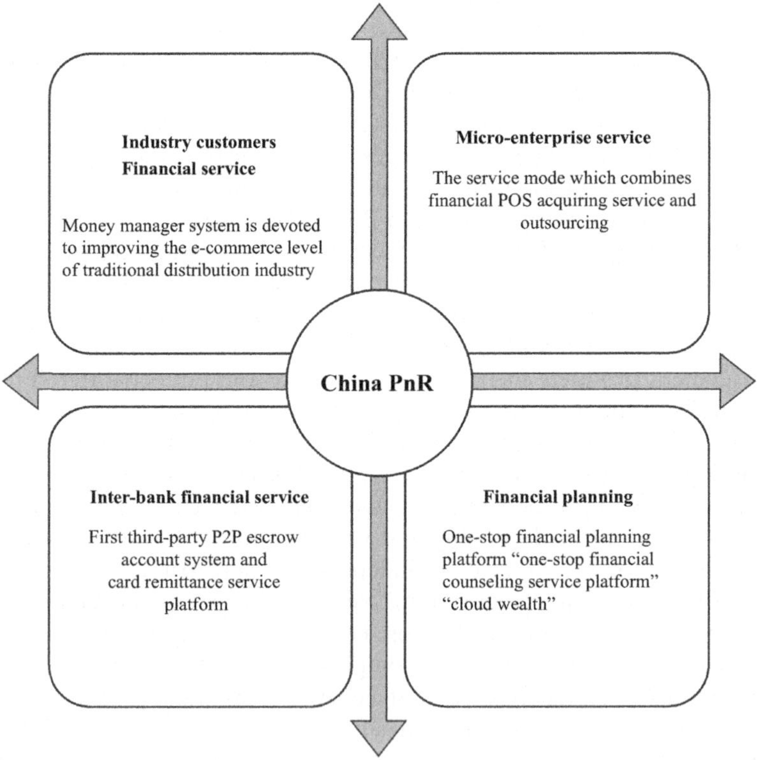

Fig. 16 China PnR business structure (*Data source* http://www.chinapnr.com)

POS payment. More importantly, it provides different forms of payment services at different links of trading. At air ticket agency end, aiming at the large loaning amount of prior ticket, it gives credit granting to analysis of trading data, and provides short-run credit loan to alleviate short-run capital pressures and raise capital turnover rate. For consumers, it can simplify trading flow and realize one-time payment. The payment solution system provided by China PnR improves industry operating efficiency and fully satisfies payment demands.

China PnR succeeds because it caters to the payment requirements and payment characteristics in different industries, and even develop pertinent payment systems to satisfy given demands. This is the foundation of payment in vertical industry.

Furthermore, though China PnR is not the largest third-party payment platform, its development history indicates the "bud" of Internet finance more or less. Obviously, China PnR has gradually diverted the focus from payment to supply chain payment, fund sales and financial services. This is the consistent way for such typical Internet giants to march to Internet finance. It is predicted that China PnR will concentrate on supply chain finance field in the future, as its accumulated payment data are mainly based on the trading data between supply chain companies. This is in particular important to supply chain business finance (Fig. 17).

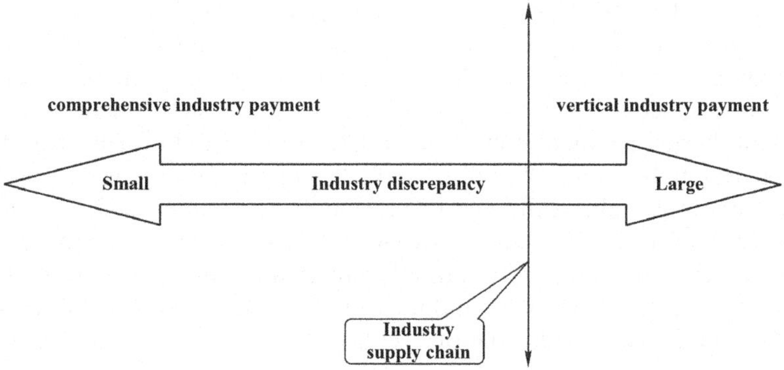

Fig. 17 Difference between two types of independent third-party payment platforms

Integrated Industry Payment
Comparing with vertical industry payment, integrated industry payment insists on totally opposite payment service philosophy. It holds that there is no industry difference during the payment process, and sole difference may be solved by “micro adjustment”. This does not affect the operation of entire payment system, for they primarily provide cross-industry universal payment system and manage to tolerate all involved industry differences.

Case 2: 99 Bill

The business position of 99 Bill is to help companies solve problems in capital inflow and outflow or amount of fund. In the second half of 2017, 99 Bill released offline acquiring service, and expanded pure online payment service to offline service. 99 Bill accordingly grew to be the first company which integrated online and offline payment patterns in national payment industry and began to follow integrated payment pattern. Relying on the strategic cooperation with all major banks, 99 Bill has established an information platform across banks, regions and terminals, and formed full electronic payment and receipt solutions covering all mainstream payment instruments led by computers, POS, mobile phones and phones. Therefore, it can help companies realize efficient capital payment and receipt and integrated management under diverse business scenes. In May 2011 when Central Bank granted the first batch of third-party payment license, 99 Bill had gained permission in 5 businesses, including Internet payment, fixed and mobile phone payment, prepaid card acceptance, bank card acquiring service. 99 Bill and Alipay were sole two full-license payment companies in China then. Additionally, based on the payment business, 99 Bill continually superimposes diverse application scenes throughout the effective match of capital flow and information flow, and solves practical demands faced by companies in operation in a more efficient manner, from high-efficient financial management to pertinent marketing management and inclusive finance service. 99 Bill sustains e-payment effects by information technology.

By far, 99 Bill has over 3 million business partners. Its innovative informatization financial services have been widely applied in more than 20 fields covering retail, business trip, insurance, e-commerce, logistics, manufacturing, medicine and clothing. It has a group of partners including China Eastern Airlines, Southern Airlines, Ping An Group,

China Life Insurance, JD Mall, Dangdang, ZJS Express, Baidu, Sina, Lining, Lenovo, Dell, Digital China and other leading companies in the industry, and expands business in more and more growing small and medium-sized companies.

But it is obvious that the foremost characteristic of 99 Bill should be its integrated payment solutions. Distinct from vertical payment pattern, 99 Bill makes use of diversified payment means, including POS, mobile phone and phone, to make sure of the high-efficient payment of each industry in all application scenes. It can be evidenced by its diverse payment solutions in Table 3. While solving fast payment problem, 99 Bill also assists companies in cash collection and management. With diverse payment means, 99 Bill's integrated payment plans can adapt to the payment demands of different industries. This is the supreme industry characteristic and advantage of 99 Bill.

Vertical industry payment and integrated industry payment are the same in nature, as both of them satisfy the payment requirements of all industries by offering payment services. The difference between the above-mentioned two payment patterns has been fully introduced, and we hereby emphasize two points. First of all, it is consumer industry property that determines corresponding business pattern. Secondly, with the continuous development of payment industry and also the popularity of Internet finance, it is partial to emphasize business patterns anymore. Because both of them belong to the payment industry and can access massive payment data via virtual accounts, data types may vary from pure trading payment data to supply chain trading payment data. It will affect their future network credit loan pattern too. However, these payment data can be all accumulated to lay a foundation for future business expansion. Maybe this is the most important thing. It also explains why third-party payment is the vanguard of Internet finance.

According to third-party payment pattern, it can be fitly judged that there is no radical difference between third-party payment and traditional payment pattern. They both exist as a means of capital transfer. The difference between the two is mainly proved by service characteristics, business composition and profit-making pattern. Comparing with traditional payment, third-party payment more stresses value-added services and integrated payment solutions, and businesses turn more personalized and customized. Likewise, the profit-making pattern increases value-added services (Table 4).

Table 3 99 bill industry payment solution

Industry	*Payment solutions*	*Content*
Aviation	Corporate major client payment solutions	Help airlines expand business from cash settlement business to monthly statement business
	B2C direct sales payment solutions	Satisfy discrepant payment demands of the website and call center business
	Financial management solutions	Create convenience for the uniform financial management of all sales channels in airlines, and improve financial management efficiency
Air ticket agent	Monthly Business trip ssolutions	Help air ticket agents relieve financial pressures
	B2B procurement payment solutions	Help air ticket agents improve the efficiency of issue and relieve financial pressures
	B2C direct sales payment solutions	Satisfy discrepant payment demands of the website and call center business
	Financial management solutions	Create convenience for the uniform financial management of all sales channels of air ticket agents
Retail	Chain store POS card swiping payment solutions	With uniform application and uniform management, it helps companies quickly expand the sales channels
	Online store sales payment solutions	Help merchants access users, raise user conversion rate and retain more users
	Prepaid membership card payment solutions	Cross-store card making, card issue, recharging, consumption and asset management functions to satisfy different consumers' demands
	Capital management solutions	Uniform management of all gathering channels, cross-district capital gathering, batch payment, sound authority management, and improve capital management efficiency

Industry	*Payment solutions*	*Content*
	Financial management solutions	Quick buck financial management backstage can improve merchants' financial management efficiency with its real-time accounting functions and matched orders and capital
Education	On-site course sales solutions	Provide POS payment terminal for convenience of card swiping payment and lower students' tuition fees
	Website course sales solutions	Provide large-sum gateway, credit card and other online payment products to satisfy members' online payment demands and improve website sales payment success rate
	Phone course sales solutions	Provide credit card payment, and e-mail bill products to raise phone sales payment success rate
E-commerce	Website sales payment solutions	Help merchants access users, raise user conversion rate and retain more users
	Phone sales payment solutions	Help call center in phone sales and gathering
	Chain store sales payment solutions	Help merchants collect capital in all branch stores and improve financial management efficiency across districts
	Financial management solutions	Quick buck financial management platform can improve merchants' financial management efficiency with its real-time accounting functions and matched orders and capital
Insurance	Online sales payment solutions	Applicable for the online sales of insurance companies, including account management platforms during the renewal period
	Phone sales payment solutions	Applicable for phone sales, customer center sales, premium phone expending, online sales customer phone tracking and other online marketing channels
	Traditional marketing solutions	Applicable for counter card swiping and door-to-door card swiping and other traditional marketing channels
	Financial processing for capital business payment solutions	Applicable for the financial processing of capital business in the headquarters

(continued)

Table 3 (continued)

Industry	*Payment solutions*	*Content*
	Financial management solutions	Quick buck financial management backstage can improve merchants' financial management efficiency with its real-time accounting functions and matched orders and capital

Data source Chen Xi, Study on Third Party Payment Development Strategies in 99 Bill [D]. Jinan: Shandong University, 2012
Case source https://www.99bill.com/

Table 4 Comparison between traditional payment means and third-party payment means

Type	*Traditional payment means*	*Third-party payment platform*
Service objects	Individuals and merchants	Upstream, downstream and terminal users in core corporate industry chain
Service characteristics	High standardization degree	Individualization, customization, integration
Profit-making pattern	Service charge	Service charge + corporate value-added service charge
Business composition	Basic payment settlement means	Integrated basic payment means and value-added service comprehensive payment solutions
Development direction	Payment settlement platform, new marketing platform, individual consumption credit, individual finance innovation business	Payment settlement platform, supply chain financing, corporate finance innovation business

Data source iResearch

5 The Influence of Third-Party Payment

The rise of third-party payment is not accidental, as it appears to solve credit risks problems during e-commerce trading process caused by information asymmetry. Such means of payment gives rise to huge influences. It not only creates convenience for payment users, but also affects entire payment industry, especially peer business in traditional financial institutions. Moreover, third-party payment which also brings new sales channel is expected to change the traditional sales layout in fund, insurance, securities and other industries. Above all, third-party payment has accumulated massive payment data conducive to the innovation of financing mode. Probably this is subversive to the financial industry.

First of all, third-party payment lowers information asymmetry. Guarantee provided by third-party payment ensures bilateral contract performance ability, and greatly reinforces mutual trust. While this is exactly the key to the development of e-commerce. Information asymmetry reduction widens trading boundary, increases trading possibilities and trading volume. Third-party payment precisely finds the root prohibiting the development of e-commerce, and presents a good fix (Figs. 18 and 19).

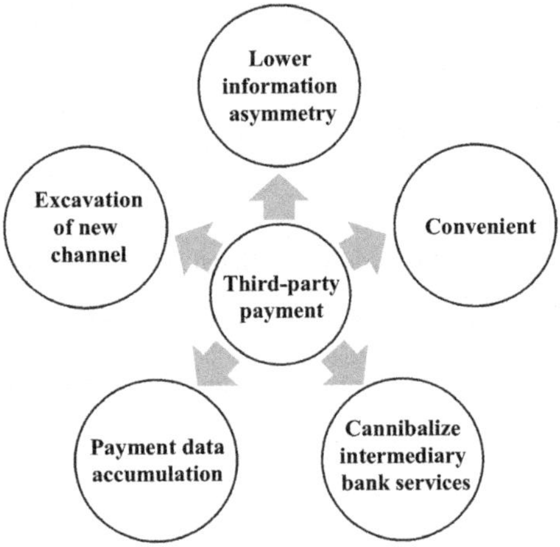

Fig. 18 Role of third-party payment

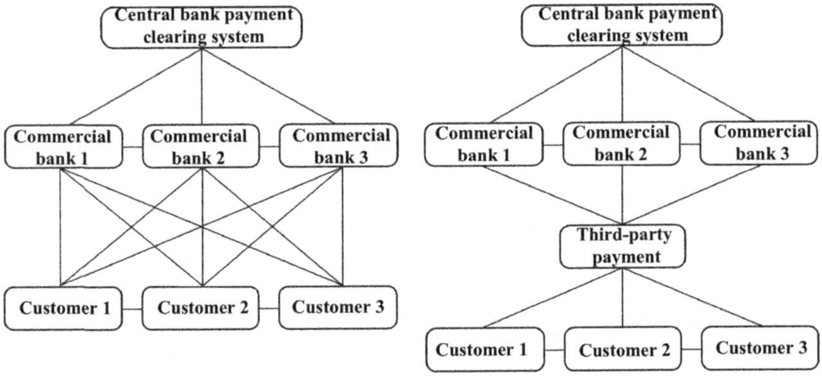

Fig. 19 Comparison of traditional payment mode and third-party payment mode (*Data source* Xie Ping, Zou Chuanwei, Liu Hai'er, *Brochure of Internet Finance*, China Renmin University Press, 2014)

Secondly, third-party payment is relatively convenient and fast. Under traditional payment pattern, consumers make payment settlement via commercial banks and commercial banks close an account via the Central Bank. As consumers shall make payment settlement with each bank, respectively, it requests sophisticated formalities and significantly decreases payment efficiency. Third-party payment platforms make settlement on behalf of both consumers and commercial banks. By offering offset balance via the intermediate account between banks, third-party payment platforms improve payment efficiency to a large extent.

Thirdly, third-party payment business extrudes bank payment business and encroaches median income. Payment settlement and channel are the foremost median business income of commercial banks. Due to its convenience, third-party payment quickly takes over the median business originally exclusive to commercial banks. Especially against the context of interest rate marketization and continuous decrease of interest spreads of deposit and loan, such encroachment aggravates bank income. Original bank payment settlement system does not adapt to market-oriented requirements anymore. It seems that the banking industry has noticed this point already, and positively made itself devoted to the transition to Internet.

The fourth point is about the excavation of new marketing channels. Third-party payment can not only serve as a payment instrument, but also a marketing channel as well. By bridging payment account and fund account, Yu'E Bao allows consumers to buy fund products at any time and place. Some third-party payment platforms also begin to sell fund products online. Supposing what fun it is when users buy these products while logging on the payment instruments. It is definitely more convenient than browse via commercial bank websites, counters, websites of fund companies. Nowadays, third-party payment platforms may cooperate with securities and insurance. The channel role of payment instruments will be more conspicuous in the future.

The last point is data accumulation of third-party payment. This is the most important characteristic of third-party payment platforms. It has been repeatedly emphasized in this chapter. Payment settlement, channel and convenience functions are meaningless before data accumulation. In other words, data accumulation reveals the future of third-party payment platforms. Solving information asymmetry just means solving a tough problem in the payment industry. The solution is short of universality and compatibility. In the future, other financial businesses may also confront information asymmetry dilemma, and such new information asymmetry problems can be only achieved by data accumulation. Therefore, data accumulation is the most important and valuable asset on third-party payment platforms. Data accumulation makes Internet finance possible, and third-party payment platforms deserve the honorable title of "vanguard" of Internet finance.

6 The Risks and Supervision of Third-Party Payment

Third-party payment refers to a means of capital transfer realized with the aid of technologies like Internet. Superficially, it possesses the industry properties of Internet and payment computation. But it should be classified under the category of financial industry in the end. Internet just serves as media. The risk of third-party payment is firstly revealed by the risk of its financial property, including the risk of Internet property.

Risk of Third-Party Payment

There are four kinds of third-party payment risks, namely legal risk, liquidity risk, information risk and operation risk. With the gradual maturity of third-party payment, the Central Bank also gradually improves its management system for third-party payment. All sorts of documents and provisions enacted by the Central Bank, including prepaid card, bank card acquiring service, Internet payment, mobile payment and other mainstream payment, have guiding significance to the normative development of third-party payment. But we should bear in mind that no legal definition for third-party payment has been proposed yet, including setting, operation and regulation of third-party payment. Actually, third-party payment has survived for 18 years in China, and third-party payment has turned rather mature and normative. It is irrational that no definition and specification have been enacted in legal terms by far.

Liquidity risk is one core issue in third-party payment. Capital transfer is the due role of third-party payment. In case of any problem of capital liquidity, third-party payment will lose its meaning of existence. Present regulation policies take the management mode of "two banks + three accounts" for the precipitation capital of third-party payment, rigorously control third-party payment companies' possession, use, guarantee and other illicit behaviors for excess reserves, and fix the role of third-party payment as an intermediary. But for other specific issues, such as interest rate attribution of excess reserves, and withdrawing proportion of loan loss provision, there still lack precise stipulations. All of these will pose severe challenges to the liquidity of third-party payment.

Both operation risks and information risks are Internet property risks. Any operation possibly generates operation risks, even including offline manual operation. After all, the difference is that Internet has faster

Fig. 20 Third-party payment risks

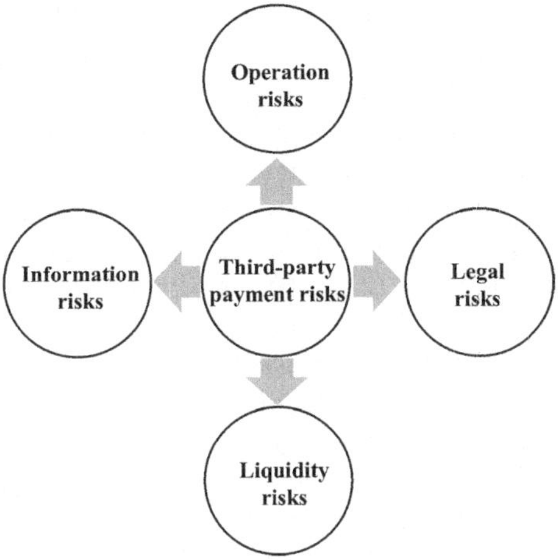

communication speed, stronger influence and larger scope. For this, third-party payment should be more concerned about the prevention of operation risks, and avoid technical and managerial errors such as operation errors, system loopholes and flow chaos. Once these errors occur, a series of severe information risks will be introduced, including information leakage, illicit invasion, and economic crime, which will not only cause risks to the platform but also endanger the personal interests of consumers (Fig. 20).

Supervision for Third-Party Payment

Concerning above-mentioned risks about third-party payment supervision, many studies have raised suggestions and we don't repeat this part here. The chapter hereby stresses that a uniform industry management system should be established. As third-party payment now starts to slowly break up the primitive border of payment, and expands to emerging Internet finance fields represented by online wealth management, network lending and even network search, third-party payment platforms will greatly enrich business contents and business categories, and correspondingly, face more and more severe risks. Then how to manage and control these risks? Given the risky communication of Internet in which one problem on one platform affects other platforms and even platform consumers, Domino effects inevitably exist. Obviously, in this case, supervision for third-party payment does not mean internal risk control or external supervision for a company. It becomes the management affair for entire third-party payment industry. To be sure, we need to supervise third-party payment industry at the industrial level.

Supervision at the industrial level contains three aspects. First of all, industry access threshold must be established. Now, the number of third-party payment platforms increases to 269, and platform number, business scale and business pattern basically satisfy present payment demands. Under such circumstances, it is not sensible to develop more platforms, and attention should be paid to industry quality and business innovation for a rather long time in the future. So rigorous industry access threshold should be formulated, and higher requirements on new and old platforms should be proposed, including registration capital, IT system and license. Only in this way can industry quality be controlled. The second step is to rate third-party payment industry from the perspective of company business type, business scale, business pattern, operation flow, internal risk control and other key behaviors, and determine platform risks. Though it is not proper to allege that companies in entire third-party payment industry are quite a mixed furnace, it is undeniable that these platforms have a large gap in power. Naturally, these platforms have varying credit and risk-resistance abilities. It is necessary to rate the comprehensive level of these third-party payment platforms. The third step is to establish a third-party payment insurance system. Like commercial banks' deposit insurance system, this system aims to establish a risk relief mechanism and company withdrawal mechanism. In this way, it can not only normalize industrial development, improve corporate entry–exit mechanism and reduce internal and external uncertainties, but also protect consumers' interests. Existing platforms such as Alipay has cooperated with Ping An to jointly develop capital security line to ensure the security of users' fast payment. This move fully reflects the spirits of insurance spread risks. But different from third-party payment insurance system, it is just the individual behavior of companies and numerous small- and medium-sized payment platforms can't make it yet. This rests in the difference between powerful platforms and ordinary platforms. But with the continuous development of third-party payment industry, future industry layout will witness sharp differentiation in which industry shuffle, merger and acquisition and restructuring are high probability events. Massive small- and medium-sized platforms ought to give a fast response to such changes, and pay equal attention to research and development and risk control to maintain an advantageous status in the industry.

7 The Development Trend of Third-Party Payment

As to the future development trend of third-party payment, the article judges that new changes will take place in five aspects, payment field, payment means, operational subjects, payment fields and business pattern included.

Diversification and Deepening of Payment Fields

At the moment, the competition in main fields of third-party payment like online shopping, aviation, online games, phone charges is very ferocious and improvement space is rather limited. Future competition possibly transits to other industries. Accompanied by industry diversification, we should also notice industry deepening vertical trend and subdivision trend. Third-party payment platforms will take an active part in industry value chain construction for industry deepening. It marks the mainstream trend in the future. It is predicted that future third-party payment possibly has vertical development in wealth management products' online sales, cross-border payment, education and other industries (Table 5).

For instance, when the government allows cross-border payment and approves the establishment of cross-border e-commerce foreign exchange business pilots, third-party payment platforms begin to develop cross-border payment layout proactively. There are two mainstream patterns at present. The first pattern is to cooperate with overseas third-party payment institutions, share accounts and release cross-border payment. The second pattern is to gather a batch of small cross-border payment transactions, and make bank swap on behalf of consumers. Alipay, TenPay, 99 Bill, UnionPay and other third-party payment giants choose the first pattern, i.e. cooperating with foreign Internet giants like PayPal, VISA and Softbank in cross-border payment.

Diversification of Payment Means

Emerging payment means represented by mobile payment will become the mainstream of future payment industry. Together with the progress of technology, mobile payment, QR payment, sound wave payment,

Table 5 Cross-border payment of third-party payment companies

Companies	*Service/product*	*Covering domain*	*Cooperative/acquisition overseas institutions*	*Covering area*
Alipay	Overseas purchase Foreign card payment	Cross-border online shopping, aviation, travel	SoftBank, PSP, OnCard Payments, VISA, MasterCard	Hong Kong, Macao, Taiwan, China; Japan; South Korea; Europe and America
Tenpay	Cross-border online shopping payment	American express network Merchant cross-border online shopping	American Express	Britain, America
Quick buck	International receipt	Corporate receipt	Western Union	190 countries and regions
Unionpay	Unionpay Internet cross-border shopping payment	Cross-border online shopping	PayPal, Sumitomo Mitsui, BEA	Hong Kong, China; Japan; America

Data source iResearch.

infrared ray payment, WeChat payment and other payment means will break up the limits of Internet and realize instant payment at any time and place. The key is to realize online and offline separation and reconstruction. O2O pattern possibly becomes one of the leading patterns in future payment industry. Now, O2O-based ecosphere construction has achieved initial success. Despite the constraint of trading scale, it maintains promising development momentum. NFC payment now still has low popularity and its product mode remains immature. Though the Central Bank suspended QR code payment out of the consideration for security in March 2014, NFC payment still manifested great development potentials with advanced near-end communication technologies, reinforced industry chain cooperation intention and increasingly popular offline acceptance terminals

Diversification of Third-Party Payment Operation Subjects

In present payment market, China Unionpay has seized most market shares of bank card acquiring service, Alipay has seized half Internet payment market shares, and independent third-party payment markets just account for 17% market shares. Together with the continuous entry of external companies via merger and acquisition and alliance between giants, the layout in third-party payment industry is supposed to change in the future.

The main advantage of China Unionpay rests in its offline market, considerable corporate users, as well as micro users attracted by secure payment platforms and giant e-commerce social contact platforms. Meantime, by virtue of its powerful IT technology and business innovation ability, it wins the favor of numerous consumers. Though independent third-party payment platforms do not have an advantage over consumption end nor offline layout ability, they successfully obtain the approval from numerous corporate consumers because of flexible and customized payment business and capital management ability. In some fields like aviation, retail chain, online games, independent third-party payment platforms have strong user viscosity. Telecommunication operators also enter third-party payment field by virtue of advantages in remote communication, mobile terminal, marketing channel, user quantity, small charging and settlement systems. Taking BestPay release by China Telecom for example, it fully utilizes its advantages in mobile terminals to realize phone payment. The five kinds of payment platforms all possess unique industry advantages in one or few aspects, satisfy consumers' payment demands and gain consumer viscosity, like online shopping, air ticket booking, cash on delivery, card swiping payment. The focus of future competition is on industry segmentation and individualization. The one that has more convenient payment pattern and more wide payment scenes can win more users. While the segmentation and verticality of payment industry determine the limitation of payment pattern and scene application. So future payment layout will be more diverse and sparse. As the saying goes, everyone has his strong and weak points. This is also true of payment platforms (Table 6).

Table 6 Comparison of the advantages of different payment modes

Payment	*Advantages*
Comprehensive payment platform	Payment means featured by strong inclusiveness, compatibility, and adaptability
Vertical payment platform	Flexible payment means with prominent advantages in supply chain payment
Guarantee mode platform	E-commerce platform, social platform, IT technology, business innovation
China UMS	People's Bank of China policy support, offline service network, large corporate user scale
Telecommunications supplier	Remote telecommunication channel, mobile terminal, marketing channel, user, penny billing and settlement system

Decentralization of Payment Fields

In the future, with the saturation of payment businesses in first-tier cities, the payment market will transit to more second-tier and third-tier cities, especially rural areas. Continuous advancement of urbanization will greatly increase the payment demands in second-tier and third-tier cities. Different from first-tier cities, second-tier and third-tier cities have poor adaptability to new technologies, new patterns and new instruments. For this, attention should be paid to increasing payment diversity and trying to satisfy payment demands by mobile payment, TV payment, fixed phone payment and offline payment to exploit the market (Table 7).

Business Pattern Financialization

The business pattern of third-party payment platforms will continually march in the financialization direction. Payment has become the fundamental business of financial services. In addition, owing to the intensification of payment business competition, payment companies will depend on massive payment data accumulated by payment services to engage in financial services with better additional values. In the future, financial businesses led by online wealth management, small and micro company credit loan, supply chain finance, and consumption finance will be the choice preferred by third-party payment companies. All of these are based on payment business. Specifically, they are based on massive payment data resulting from payment business. Future Internet

Table 7 Typical representative modes

Enterprise	*Business mode*	*Profile*
Bestpay	Phone message payment (rural finance)	Phone remittance, withdrawal
China PnR	Bank card acquiring service (red POS, POS mini)	Integrate mobile payment, online payment and offline acquiring business, complete bank outlet functions
Alipay	Convenient payment, rural finance (new rural business division)	Convenient payment: cooperate with all major rural commercial banks, and telecommunications distribution networks to offer payment application guidance and consulting services to rural users, and popularize network payment in the countryside Rural finance: improve rural financial service by innovative technologies

finance field will witness the coexistence of e-commerce, payment platforms, social platforms, search platforms, telecommunication operators and commercial banks.

CHAPTER 4

An Initial Attempt: Roller-Coaster Online Financial Management

Online financial management products represented by Bao series products are the first attempt of Internet finance on the market. Although the model is quite simple, no more than "payment + financial management products", which has realized the seamless connection and online sales of the financial products by taking payment as the flow entrance; the Internet financial thinking and instruments behind it are incomparable. Bao series products are small attempt of Internet finance, but they have gained a complete victory. Behind it is not only the use of a single payment portal, but more importantly, the ability to use big data for liquidity risk control. This is the true reason why Bao series products have amazed the market. Big data accumulated by Alipay can become the raw materials for liquidity management of Yu'E Bao, supporting Yu'E Bao to invest in the agreement deposit of the banks and meanwhile ensuring enough liquidity to cope with the payment demands. This is the so-called practical application of Internet finance. Internet finance does not simply embrace the Internet. More importantly, it uses big data to achieve refined management. From this perspective, online financial management is one of the applications of Internet finance.

Financial management stems from the process of using self-owned assets including cash, stocks, bonds and the like to conduct reasonable investment so as to achieve time transfer, space transfer and credit transfer

Q. Guan and W. Gao, *Internet Finance*,
The Great Transformation of China,
https://doi.org/10.1007/978-981-16-4740-6_4

of the assets. Briefly, financial management is essentially a kind of investment, which realizes maintenance and appreciation of assets through investment. In the past, offline financial management is the majority. People purchased corresponding financial management products through banks, brokers, fund companies, etc. In recent years, with the popularity of the Internet, financial management can be mostly realized through the network without having to conduct offline transactions. From this point of view, whether it is offline financial management or online financial management, it is a normal economic activity, and it has existed for a long time. Why should it be included in the scope of Internet finance? We want to say that the online financial management of Internet finance is essentially different from the past financial management products. The former is to realize the design and risk control of financial management products through the analysis of a large amount of behavioral data. This is profoundly different with the ordinary financial management products both inwardly and practically.

1 The Concept of Online Financial Management

Online financial management in Internet finance refers to the service model of using Internet thinking and network technology to innovate individualized and interactive new financial management products. From this simple definition, we can see that the focus is on Internet thinking and network technology, individualization and interaction. Internet thinking and network technology are the methods to form financial management products, while individualization and interaction are the characteristics of financial management products.

The past financial management products were designed from the perspective of the company, which neglected the features, demands and psychologies of the public consumers. Online financial management is to use the thinking of "pursuit of truth, openness, equality, cooperation and sharing" of Internet to tolerate everything of the public investors, including all of their thoughts, demands, behavioral features, consumer preferences and the like. Only in this way can the online financial management arouse consumers' "sympathy", get their recognition and extensive participation. The past financial management products did not have such consciousness, which only focused on the product design, but neglected the feelings of the public; on the other hand, limited to the support of technology and data, the past financial management products could not obtain the accurate “portrait” of the consumers, thus could not “implant” investors’ information. But now, big data has created necessary conditions for the online financial management products: according to the analysis on big data, the behavioral features of the public investors can be obtained, which can become the key factors of product design, such as customization of personalized products. Meanwhile, big data can be used to conduct risk control and effectively guarantee the safety of online financial management. Such online financial management is the embodiment of the true Internet spirit, and also the sufficient condition to realize individualization and interaction.

2 Development History of Online Financial Management

Online financial management is different from the offline financial management. It mainly relies on the Internet technology, and meanwhile must satisfy the online investment habits of the public investors. The cultivation of such habits mainly relies on the power of e-commerce. Online consumption is a favorable pushing hand for online financial management.

Early in 2009, the rudiment of online financial management had emerged. In June 2009, CUAM initiated the balance financial management model in the way that users could conduct balance financial management, capital appreciation and wealth management through Xianjin Bao. This attempt is a prelude to the fund’s touch, and it is also a landmark event of great significance. However, due to the lack of user base, the subsequent Xianjin Bao did not cause a big market sensation. Objectively speaking, Xianjin Bao at this time was not the true sense of Internet finance, nor was it the true sense of online financial management, because this was just a simple network of financial management, just moving offline financial management to the Internet. But this behavior reflected a problem: public investors could conduct financial management through the Internet. This was a very important point.

June 17, 2013 is bound to be a memorable day. The sudden emergence of Yu’E Bao had started the trend of online financial management of all people. On June 30, 2013, the accumulated users of Yu’E Bao had reached 2.5156 million, and the capital scale reached 6.601 billion yuan. By the end of the 3rd quarter of 2013, the capital scale of Yu’E Bao had reached 55.653 billion yuan, with a year-on-year growth of more than 7 times. Meanwhile, it had made Tian Hong Zengli Bao become the fund with the largest scale, exceeding Hua Xia in the second place by 8.629 billion yuan. Five months later, Yu'E Bao broke through 100 billion yuan for the first time and became the first fund breaking through 100 billion; at the end of February 2014, the users of Yu'E Bao had reached 81 million, with a scale exceeding 500 billion yuan; by the end of the 1st quarter of 2014, the number of users had exceeded 100 million, with a scale of 541.3 billion yuan. In contrast to this, it took A share market 23 years developing only 68 million investors.

When Yu'E Bao spurred a whirlwind of online financial management by all people, other Internet giants, fund companies and banks were not unwilling to remain out of the limelight and had successively launched online financial products. In October 2013, Baidu financial management platform was launched; in December, Baidu Baifa launched Group-buying Finance, NetEase launched Xianjin Bao; in January 2014, WeChat launched Licaitong; in March, Alibaba launched Yule Bao; in October, Guangfa Baifa 100 index fund was put on sale... In no time, "the cities are full of Bao series products", which made people dazzled and not know their whereabouts.

Although the quantity of Bao series products has increased, its yield was on the contrary. The yield on "Bao" in 2013 was up to 6–7%; while it kept decreasing since 2014 and lingered in about 4% until December. As said by Cui Hu in At the Southern Part of the Capital: "Same time last year outside this gate. As red as peach blossom was her dainty face. I've lost where she is when spring breezes again. Only peach flowers are smiling for this one year's date".

In addition to Bao series financial management products, there is also a kind of products in recent years, the development momentum of which is also very fast, that is P2P lending. Strictly speaking, P2P lending is generally classified as a financing method. There must be investment in financing, and investors in P2P are public consumers. From the perspective of public financial management, P2P lending is also a way of financial management. Actually, P2P lending had emerged in China since 2007. Due to various limitations, P2P had not been taken seriously. Until 2012, the scale of P2P lending had started to grow rapidly, and P2P financial management also started to become a part of public financial management. In 2011, the number of P2P platforms was only 50, and the financial management scale was 3.1 billion yuan. In 2012, the transaction scale rose to 21.2 billion yuan, which initially broke through 100 billion yuan in 2013 and reached 252.8 billion yuan in 2014. Compared with online financial management products, P2P has a higher yield, which is basically 20%. Since 2014, the overall yield of the platforms started to decline, which was back to 16%.

3 The Development Status of Online Financial Management

The current online financial management market is the heaven of Bao series products. The market scale of 1.5 trillion yuan formed within a year and a half is unimaginable for anyone. However, no one could ever have imagined that the Bao series products rose to the climax and then uncontrollably declined in the earnings, and the scale also allowed down within the year and a half. Eventually, no one has ever thought of the beginning, seen clearly the scenario, or guessed the ending.

While the "Bao" are slowing down, there is still a force which is accelerating, and that is P2P lending. P2P is also accelerating its development as the same time as the birth of "Bao". The number of platforms has increased, the scale has been enlarged, and the earnings are great; but there are also many problems such as accelerated appearance of problematic platforms, and decline in the yield. Certainly, at least its scale is still expanding. Question: What is the pattern of the financial management market? Answer: both "have their own advantages". It is too early to judge which the winner is.

Bao Series Financial Management Products

Since the birth of Yu'E Bao in June 2013, Bao series products had experienced the rapid growth in quantity and rapid expansion in the scale within a year and a half, meanwhile their yield had experienced the process from high to low. Their great quantity growth, scale expansion and change in the yield all affected people's nerves.

Quantity of Bao Series Products

The number of Bao series products was small in 2013 when they just emerged, which was only 24. Most of them were products of the fund companies, which reached 13, accounting for more than half. There were 5 in the consignment sale system, 2 in the third-party payment system and 4 in the bank system. In 2014, the issuance number of Bao series

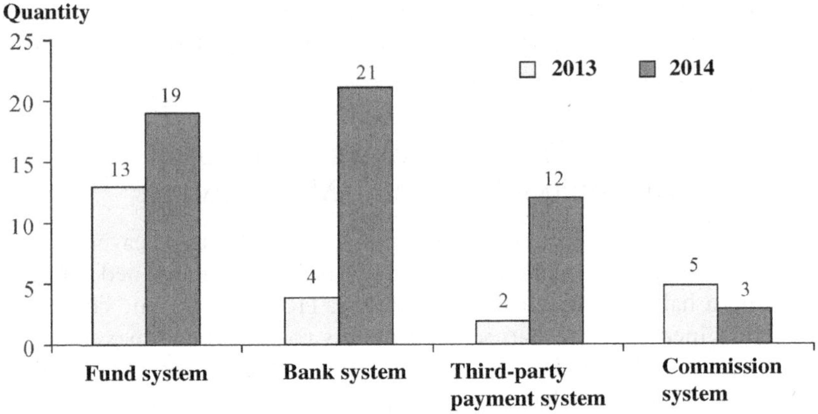

Fig. 1 Quantity of new products of different categories from 2013 to 2014 (*Data source* Annual Report of Internet Finance Financial Management in 2014)

products soared, especially in the bank system, fund system and the third-party payment system, which constituted the main force for the issuance of Bao series products (Fig. 1).

It can be seen that 2014 is the year when the bank system broke out. The most direct influence of Bao series products was to divert the bank's current deposits, then invest them into money fund through the Bao series products. Such deposits flowed into the banking system by means of agreement deposits, thereby raising the bank's debt cost. Therefore, the most seriously damaged and the only damaged by the Bao series products is the bank system. To prevent outflow of the deposits, the bank system started to exert force on Bao series products, which had caught up with the third-party payment system both on the quantity and the yield. 21 had newly increased in the bank system, accounting for 84% of the total in the bank system; followed was the fund system, which was newly increased by 19, accounting for 59.38%; 12 had newly increased in the third-party payment system, accounting for 86%. The increase in the consignment sale system was the least, which had only 3.

Scale of Bao Series Products

The scale of Bao series products in the 4th quarter of 2013 was 523.432 billion yuan, which rose to 1.274032 trillion yuan, with a growth rate of 143.4%. After then, the growth rate had significantly slowed down. The growth rate in the 2nd quarter of 2014 was only 11.8%, with a transaction scale of 1.424654 trillion yuan. The growth rate in the 3rd quarter further declined to 9.8%, with a scale of 1.563893 trillion yuan, which refreshed the maximum value of Bao series products. In the 4th quarter of 2014, Bao series products initially showed a negative growth, and the scale declined to 1.508147 trillion yuan. Although the decreasing amplitude was limited, it had indicated a certain trend.

According to the scale of different kinds of Bao series products, the scale of the third-party payment system was the largest, which reached 788.86 billion yuan. But it declined from the 2nd quarter and the decline amplitude slightly increased. The scale decreased by 7.1819 billion yuan from the 3rd quarter to the 4th quarter. This is the main reason causing to the decline in the scale of the Bao series products. Relatively, among the other three systems, except that the consignment sale system slightly decreased in the 4th quarter and its scale was relatively limited, the scale of the fund system and that of the bank system both increased, even though the growth rate slightly slowed down. It indicates that in the face of the first-mover advantage of the third-party payment system, the fund system and the bank system had been trying to pursue that speed. Although the scale, growth rate and market share of the Bao series products of the third-party payment system slightly decreased, it still could be seen that the market share of the third-party payment system was still more than 45% in a short period, occupying an absolute market share in the Bao series financial management market. The fund system and the bank system had not been able to have a significant impact on it in a short period (Fig. 2).

The market scale of the fund system had been steadily expanded, which rose to 462.009 billion yuan in the 4th quarter from 336.81 billion yuan in the 2nd quarter. The growth rate had slightly slowed down, but still firmly occupying the second largest market share. 2014 is the year when the Bao series products of the bank system caught up pretty fast. The scale had risen to 321.988 billion yuan in the 4th quarter from 144 billion yuan in the 2nd quarter. The growth was great, which was expected to exceed the fund system. However, the scale of the consignment sale system was quite limited, which even declined in the 4th quarter. The consignment system had been shaken off by the other three systems (Fig. 3).

Specific to the products, as of the 4th quarter of 2014, the product with the largest scale of Bao series was Yu'E Bao, reaching 578.936 billion

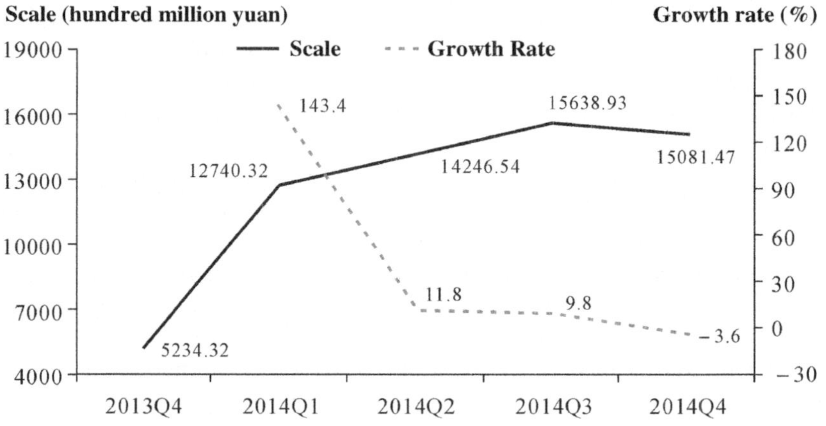

Fig. 2 Bao series products scale and growth rate from the fourth quarter of 2013–2014 (*Data source* Annual Report for Internet Financial Management in 2014, issued by Rong 360)

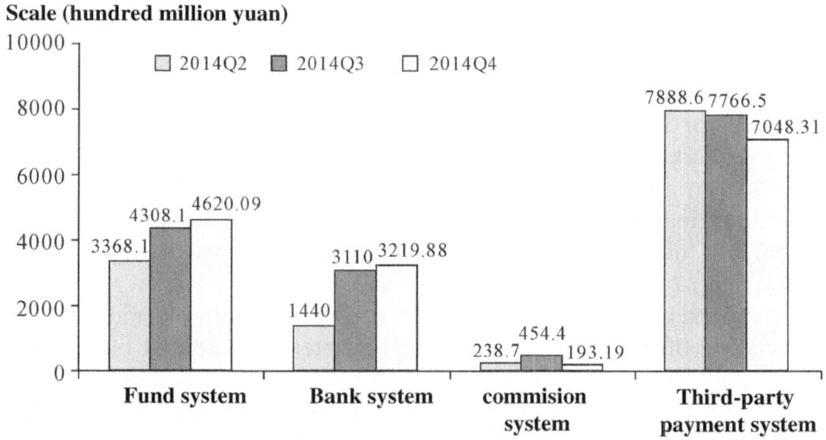

Fig. 3 Scale of different Bao series products from the second quarter of 2014 to the fourth quarter of 2014 (*Data source* Annual Report for Internet Financial Management in 2014, issued by Rong 360)

yuan, far exceeding other products. Among the products ranking top ten, there were only Yu'E Bao and WeChat Licaitong in the third-party payment system, but they accounted for 56.6% of the overall scale; the fund system occupied 5 positions, with the scale ratio of only 29.3%; the bank system occupied 3 positions, which were, respectively, Ping An Ying (Ping An Bank), Shopkeeper Wallet (Industrial Bank) and CBC Suying (China Construction Bank), with the scale ratio of 14.1%. At present, the market pattern differentiation of Bao series products is large. The third-party payment system is dominant in its scale, the fund system is dominant in its quantity, and the bank system has great potential (Table 1).

Yield on Bao Series Products

The yield of Bao series financial management products is in close positive relationship with the scale of Bao series products. Generally, the former is the Granger causality of the latter. The yield of Bao series products also experienced the process that it constantly increased in the 4th quarter of 2013, reached the climax in the 1st quarter of 2014 and then gradually declined since then. By the end of 2014, the average yield of Bao series products had dropped to around 4%, and particular products had even fallen drastically below 4%.

Bao series products are essentially a kind of money funds which use money as an ordinary commodity to conduct transaction in the market and realize pocketing the difference by low purchase and high sale. Therefore, Bao series products and money funds are a kind of investment behaviors. Investments are accompanied by risks, and there is no such financial management product without any risks. Therefore, as an investment behavior, it is quite normal for Bao series products that the yield has any changes or declines. The first thing to do is to allow for the decline, and then consider the factors that cause the decline. This issue will be further elaborated below.

According to the yield of a single product, the product with the highest average daily revenue per 10,000 funds in 2014 is Zhong Lu Xianjin Bao. The product with the highest accumulated revenue per 10,000 funds is Baidu Baizhuan, reaching 514.74 yuan, which is the only exceeding 500 yuan among the Bao series products. The product ranking the second is Yu'E Bao, reaching 469.93 yuan, which is almost the same as Zhong Lu Xianjin Bao and WeChat Licaitong (Hua Xia). The product with the highest on the 7th of the year yield is also Baidu Baizhuan, reaching 5.26%. Relative to the overall performance of "Bao", this yield is high.

Table 1 Top 10 of scale of Bao series products of the fourth quarter of 2014

Ranking	*Product name*	*Product type*	*Asset scale (100 million yuan)*
1	YuE'Bao	Third-party payment system	5789.36
2	ICBC Cash Express	Fund system	1232.48
3	Huaxia Huoqitong	Fund system	890.05
4	Ping An Ying	Banking system	660.46
5	Shopkeeper Wallet	Banking system	551.41
6	CBC Zengzhibao	Fund system	462.27
7	WeChat Licaitong	Third-party payment system	413.25
8	Harvest Huoqile	Fund system	335.26
9	CBC Suying	Banking system	328.89
10	E Fund E Wallet	Fund system	293.35

(*Data source* https://www.rong360.com)

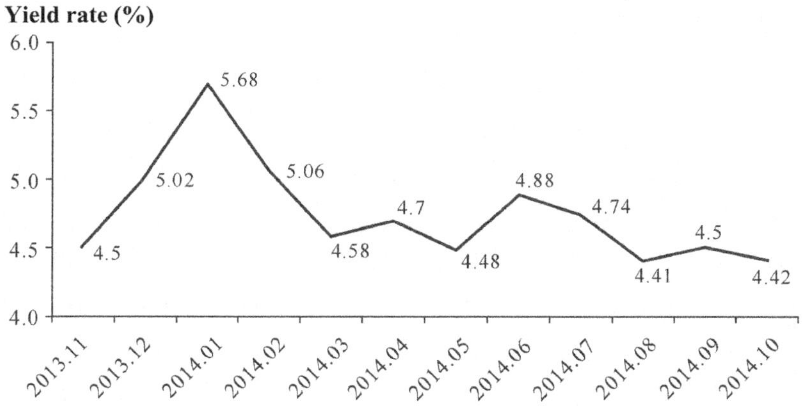

Fig. 4 Monthly average of seven-day annualized yield of Bao series products from November 2013 to October 2014 (*Data source* Annual Report for Internet Financial Management in 2014)

At present, the advantages of Yu'E Bao among the Bao series products are not as obvious as in the past, and the yield is only 4.84%. From the perspective of the stability of revenue, the most stable is WeChat Licaitong (Hui), but actually its yield is very low. It can be seen that the yield and stability of Bao series products cannot be gained at the same time. In both of the two aspects, the better is the CMBC Ruyi Bao, the yield of which is in the middle, but the stability is relatively high (Fig. 4 and Table 2).

Liquidity of Bao Series Products

Profitability and liquidity are two characteristics of Bao series products. Benefited by the good liquidity, Bao series products enable the public investors to gain revenues without affecting their payment. It will neglect neither the consumption nor the financial management. The liquidity of Bao series products can be measured from three indexes, including entry threshold, withdrawal limit and transfer time.

Firstly, from the perspective of entry threshold, the entry threshold of most Bao series products is relatively low, which is more reliable than the financial management products of the banks with an initiate price of 50,000 yuan. The initiate price of 45% of the Bao series products is only 0.01 yuan, and that of 21% of the products is 1 yuan. They are collectively up to 66%. This is truly beneficial to realizing fragmented

Table 2 Overview of some Bao series products' yield rate

Product name	*Revenue per 10,000 funds*			*Seven-day annual yield rate*		*Time*
	Mean (yuan)	*Variance (%)*	*Annual accumulated value (yuan)*	*Mean (%)*	*Variance (‰)*	
Baidu Baizhuan	1.55	66.84	514.75	5.26	0.53	2013.10.31
YuE'Bao	1.29	4.65	469.93	4.84	0.71	2013.6.17
Zhonglu Cash Bao	1.58	73.51	467.91	4.68	0.4	2013.1.28
WeChat Licaitong (Hua Xia)	1.36	48.87	461.71	4.91	0.63	2014.1.16
Yongjin Bao	1.41	47.08	439.31	5.2	1.18	2014.2.23
Shopkeeper Wallet	1.36	3.24	402.94	5.11	0.29	2014.3.10
CMBC Ruyi Bao	1.43	24.78	385.54	4.69	0.10	2014.2.28
JD Xiaojinku	1.55	54.05	354.17	4.76	0.22	2014.3.27
WeChat Licaitong (Hui)	1.24	2.8	346.78	4.63	0.13	2014.3.26
WeChat Licaitong (Yi)	1.3	44.01	320.96	4.64	0.14	2014.4.17
WeChat Licaitong (Guang)	1.25	5.78	308.34	4.68	0.24	2014.4.17
Fuqianbao	1.44	21.24	306.52	5.14	0.41	2014.5.9
Yi Wallet Huoqian Bao	1.57	95.8	303.14	4.88	1.35	2014.5.12
Unicom Call Charge Bao	1.49	90.1	277.68	4.58	0.94	2014.5.20
Zhaozhaoying	1.26	7.59	266.75	4.65	0.18	2014.6.2

Data source https://www.rong360.com

financial management. The products with an initiate price of 100 yuan account for 29%, which rank only second to those with the initiate price of 0.01 yuan; the proportion of products with the initiate price of 500 yuan and 1000 yuan is small, which is collectively 5%.

Secondly, from the perspective of one-day withdrawal limit, different "Bao" products have different regulations. Among the 79 Bao series products, only Rongtong Xianjin Bao does not have the withdrawal limit, and the rest 78 products all have limits in different degrees. From the perspective of ratio, the ratio of withdrawal limit within 50,000 yuan is the highest, reaching to 32%; the second is the withdrawal limit within 500,000 yuan, accounting for 28%; and the ratio of the rest is less than 10%. The smallest one-day withdrawal limit is for the clients of Suning Lingqianbao without real name authentication, which is only 1,000 yuan. Generally, the withdrawal limit of "Bao" of the fund system and the bank system is much larger than that of the third-party payment system (Figs. 5 and 6).

Thirdly, from the receiving speed of redeemed funds, 48% of Bao series products can realize real-time transfer. But the real-time transfer of 41% of the Bao series products is provisory. Particular Bao series products are delayed in transfer and even received on the other day. Similar to the withdrawal limit, the accounting data of "Bao" of the fund system and the bank system is relatively fast. For instance, Harvest Huoqile, CUAM Xianjin Bao and Zhaozhaoying have realized transfer within seconds, and Xinjin Bao of China CITIC Bank can be directly withdrawn without redemption. However, the redemption speed of the third-party payment

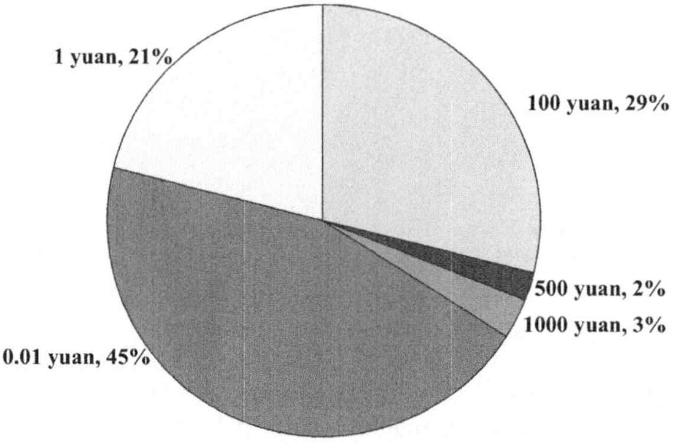

Fig. 5 Distribution of purchase threshold of Bao series products (*Data source* Annual Report for Internet Financial Management in 2014)

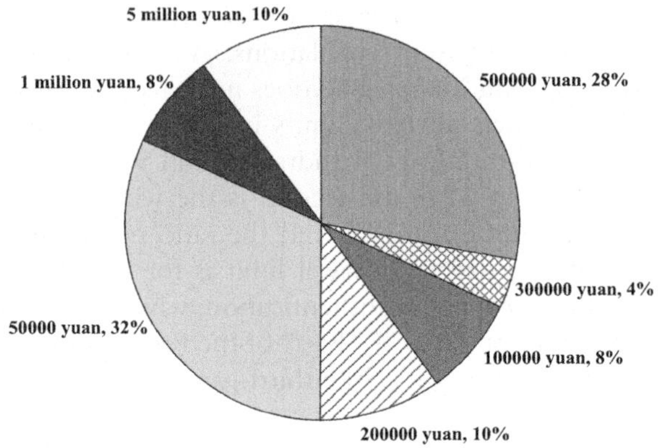

Fig. 6 One-day withdrawal limit of Bao series products (*Data source* Annual Report for Internet Financial Management in 2014)

system is relatively slow, and the transfer time of Yu'E Bao is 1–2 hours at the soonest (Fig. 7).

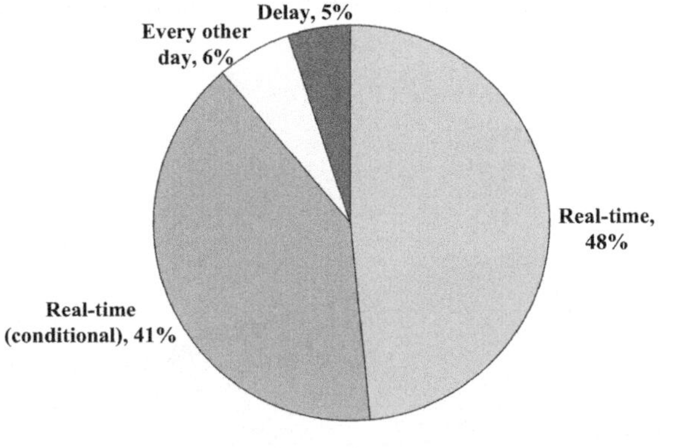

Fig. 7 Withdrawal transfer time of Bao series products (*Data source* Annual Report for Internet Financial Management in 2014)

P2P Lending

The time when P2P lending generated is earlier than "Bao". However, P2P had not drawn too much attention of the public investors for a long time. P2P lending started to enter the fast track of growth since 2012; in 2013 and 2014, the number and scale of the platforms broke out, which constantly stirred the pattern of the financial management market. Although P2P is in the different level of quantity compared with the bank financial management and Bao series products at present, with the constant standardization of P2P industry, the potential of P2P lending is huge.

Scale of P2P Lending

In 2014, the scale of P2P lending was 252.8 billion yuan, which was 2.39 times of that in 2013, and the accumulated transaction scale had reached 382.9 billion yuan. In 2014, except for February when there was a slight decline in the transaction volume, the other months all presented the growth trend. In July, the transaction volume broke through 20 billion yuan, and in November, it again broke through 30 billion yuan. The monthly average growth rate of the transaction volume in 2014 was 10.99%.

Although the growth of the scale of P2P lending is fast, it is still insignificant compared with the scale of 1.5 trillion yuan of Bao series products. It is even negligible compared with the scale of 25 trillion yuan of the bank financial management. The development space left to P2P lending in the future is still large (Fig. 8).

Yield of P2P Lending

In 2014, the yield of P2P lending also presented a trend of slow decline. The yield had declined to 16.08 from 20% at the beginning of 2014. The decline in the yield seemingly did not affect the passion of the investors, and the transaction scale was still growing at a certain rate.

There are three main reasons for the decline in the yield of P2P lending industry: firstly, the capital in the market was relatively sufficient in 2014, therefore the price of funds was not as high as in the last year, and the yield would relatively decline compared to the last year; secondly, with the constant increase in the number of P2P platforms, some platforms established in the earlier stage tend to provide some high yields to attract the investors, and then such yields will gradually return to the normal;

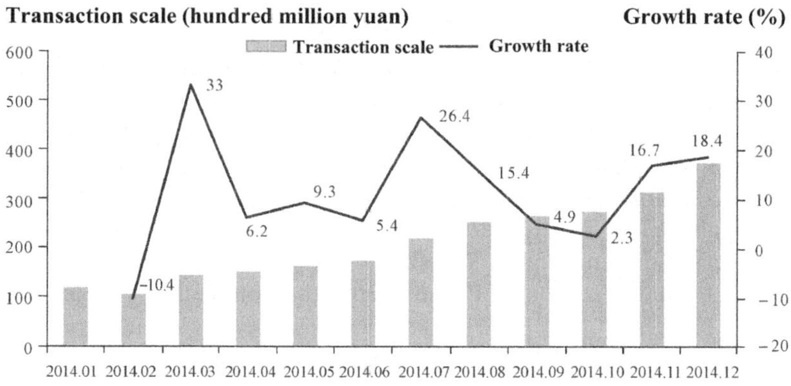

Fig. 8 P2P online lending scale and growth rate from January 2004 to December 2014 (*Data source* Chinese Online Lending Industry Annual Report in 2014)

thirdly, the number of problematic platforms keeps increasing, more and more platforms start to lower their yields to reduce the operation burden. The three reasons have limited further rise of the yield of P2P lending.

Currently, the yields of the P2P platforms in different provinces and cities are different, and some differences are large. The yield in Gansu is the highest, reaching 30.53%, which is also the only one exceeding 30%. Followed by are Anhui and Shandong, which are, respectively, 29.84 and 29.29%. The reasons causing this pattern include: on the one hand, the traditional financial institutions in these areas are usually undeveloped, while the offline demands are large; on the other hand, the newly launched platforms usually attract the investors by improving the yield. In comparison, the yields in Beijing, Shanghai, Chongqing, Liaoning and Hainan are relatively low, which are, respectively, 16.35, 13.52, 12.93, 11.61 and 10%. The financial industry in Beijing and Shanghai is relatively developed, thus the yield is balanced generally; there are many platforms with the background of state-owned assets in Chongqing and other places, while the yield of these platforms is generally low.

According to the circumstances of the investors, high yield will not necessarily attract the investors. The scale of investments with the yield between 15 and 20% is the largest, reaching 61.156 billion yuan and accounting for 52.5%; followed by is the range between 10 and 15%, with a scale of 25.62 billion yuan, accounting for 22.1%; the scale of the investment with the yield above 20% is 18.857 billion yuan, accounting for 16.2%; the platforms with the yield less than 10% have the smallest scale, which is 10.76 billion yuan, accounting for only 9.2%. It can be seen that the investors are not inclined to high revenues. Normally, the investors are inclined to the yield lower than 20%. It can be seen that the investors on the platforms are relatively rational.

P2P Investors and Investment Amount Thereof

In 2013, the number of investors of P2P lending was 250,000, which rose to 1,160,000 in 2014, with a year-on-year growth rate of 364%. As the number of P2P platforms increased and the scale continued to expand, the number of people who conducted investment and financial management through the P2P platforms would continue to increase. As of December 2014, the single-month number of active investors on P2P platforms had reached 882,000. The investor's investment in P2P had sufficiently shown the feature of fragmentation. The investment with amount less than 10,000 yuan accounts for 63.74%, and the investment with amount between 10,000 and 100,000 accounts for 29.1%. The two collectively exceed 90%, and the ratio of the rest investment is relatively small.

4 The Business Model of Online Financial Management

What the Bao series products "really are", and why can have such a huge market impact in a short period, making the banks' current deposits largely lost, the cost of deposits greatly increased, the fund companies expanded rapidly and the public financial management so hot and crazy? All this should start with the essence of Bao series products.

The essence of the Bao series products mentioned above is money fund, because "Bao" is combined with money fund and invested in money fund by raising funds. What is money fund then? It is nothing more than the behavior of investing through the special commodity of money, adjusting the surplus of funds to obtain revenues. Fields in which money fund can invest at present include cash, bank time deposits within one year (including one year), certificates of deposit, bond repurchases, central bank bills and bonds with a residual maturity of less than 397 days (including 397 days) and assets backed securities. It can be seen that the investment field of the money fund is relatively narrow, mainly concentrating on some low-risk deposits and bonds. Based on this, the scale of the money fund has been very limited for a long time, and the yield is also low, most of which are around 3%. So it has not caused extensive concern of people.

How did the money fund develop rapidly? How did it become one of the models of Internet finance? This should start with the third-party payment. The reason why the third-party payment is the advance team of Internet finance is that the models of Internet finance and the core part of Internet finance are essentially derived from the third-party payment. The combination of Bao series products with money funds is also without exception. The growth and development of Alipay, a third-party payment platform, have brought huge resources to Ali: massive payment data, vast precipitation funds and a large number of accounts. But the problem is that the vast precipitation funds deposited in the bank's accounts cannot be properly configured, resulting in a waste of funds invisibly. How to use these precipitation funds to create a reasonable income? There are three problems to be solved here: payment, financial management and risk control. The precipitation funds in Alipay are used by customers to make payment transactions, and meet the daily payment needs of transfer, consumption and so on. Therefore, we must initially ensure that the customer's payment needs are 100% satisfied. Secondly, on the basis of fully satisfying the customer's payment needs, we should know how to preserve and increase the value of the customer's funds. It should be noted that what here mentioned are "value preservation + value appreciation", which put higher requirements on the security of financial management. Once the security is damaged, it is very likely that customers will not be favored; and there must be a good yield in order to gain customer's recognition. The third is how to conduct risk control. This will inevitably involve liquidity risk control and maturity mismatch risk control. It is necessary to satisfy the customer's requirements for redemption at any time, and meanwhile reasonably conduct the maturity mismatch. The requirements in these three aspects seem to be impossible for Alipay. But the truth is, Alipay did it!

The idea of Alibaba is like this: using the funds of customers in Alipay to purchase money funds, and the feature of such funds is stable in revenue. One important thing is that it can invest in bank deposits, which is quite vital. Alipay can propose more favorable conditions to the bank at the time of cooperating with the bank in deposits by means of its powerful fund scale advantage. Such conditions include breaking through the upper limit of deposit interest rate, having access to obtaining higher investment interest, having access to being redeemed at any time, and even withdrawing in advance without default interest. These favorable conditions are unthinkable for normal depositors, and even cannot be obtained by some institutions. Meanwhile, interbank deposits inherently have a special policy dividend, that is, there is no need to pay deposit reserve. In this way, a better yield can be obtained through the money fund; for payment, it is mainly to carry out liquidity risk and maturity mismatch management. This will use big data. It is said in the previous chapter that big data is the most valuable asset of third-party payment companies and the basis for the third-party payment companies to carry out value-added services. Through the analysis of the massive payment data, Alipay can obtain specific information such as the user's payment habits, behavior characteristics, payment time and payment amount, for instance, when the consumer is easy to consume and what the amount of consumption probably is. Through the long-time data analysis, such behavioral information can be fully captured. Then, a large amount of consumer payment conditions are summarized, and then the total amount of payment by the consumers and the payment time corresponding to each total amount can be obtained. In this way, liquidity risk and maturity mismatch risk can be solved. In fact, these two risks can be regarded as one risk. The liquidity risk refers to the amount required for payment, while the maturity mismatch determines the length of time for asset allocation. Combination of the two is the consumption amount at a specific time point. When the data is relatively limited, the maturity mismatch can be used to meet the demand of liquidity. If the data is large enough, the one-to-one matching of the assets can be completely realized. The result is that at the time point when the investment expires, there is a payment demand in the same amount exactly. This is the "seamless joint" under an ideal condition. Therefore, the essence of online financial management is summarized to "payment + financial management + risk control", which are the three pillars of online financial management.

Herein, the importance of big data will be emphasized again, because big data is the source of Internet finance development. Without big data, Internet finance models such as online financial management, P2P, Ali small loans and supply chain finance cannot be discussed at all. Big data is the main line of this book. It is precisely based on the role of big data that various models of Internet finance can come into being. Here, big data is reflected in the massive payment data accumulated by Alipay. The value of such data is huge. Compared with Tencent's social data and Baidu's search data, Alipay's transaction data is more valuable and more widely used. The reason is that the payment data is closer to the funds and it reflects the real transaction behaviors. The real transactions can reflect the characteristics of people's needs, including what commodities they need, when they need them and how many they need. Analysis and summing up of the information are the generalization of the behaviors of all consumers in the network economy, especially the behaviors of Alipay users. In this case, why can't we solve the problem of liquidity and maturity mismatch using Alipay to conduct online financial management, since we have grasped the user's payment characteristics? Just follow the user's behavior to make a reasonable asset allocation. It is nothing but to conduct reasonable asset allocation according to the user's behavioral habits. Therefore, the author thinks that the biggest highlight of Yu'E Bao is the understanding and application of Alipay big data. Understanding is to know what Alipay has and what it can be used for; application is how to process, discard the dross and select the essential and conduct proper use.

Case 1: Yu'E Bao

Many people regard 2013 as the "first year" of Internet finance, because on June 13, 2013, Yu'E Bao was launched. In fact, as early as 2012, Xie Ping first proposed the concept of Internet finance. Many forms of Internet finance, such as P2P lending, big data finance, crowd funding and Internet insurance, have existed for a long time, but they have hardly caused enough attention and concern until the birth of Yu'E Bao.

Current Situation of Yu'E Bao

Yu'E Bao is a financial management product for individual users jointly launched by Alipay and Tian Hong Fund. By transferring the funds in Alipay to the account of Yu'E Bao, the individual users can purchase the product of Tian Hong Fund, Zengli Bao, and then gain the revenues. Moreover, the financial management investment can be redeemed at any time to achieve the "T+0" transfer, without affecting the user's payment transaction. With the low threshold, high liquidity and high profitability, Yu'E Bao has quickly spurred a nationwide financial management fever. As of June 30, 2013, the number of users of Yu'E Bao had reached 2.5156 million, and the scale had reached 4.244 billion yuan; by the end of the 3rd quarter of 2013, the assets had exceeded 50 billion yuan; the scale had exceeded 100 billion yuan in 5 months, and the product became the first fund in China to break through 100 billion yuan; by the end of 2013, the number of users had reached 43.03 million, and the scale had reached 185.342 billion yuan; as of June 2014, the number of users of Yu'E Bao had exceeded 100 million, and the assets had reached 574.16 billion yuan. By the end of 2014, the scale of Yu'E Bao was 578.936 billion yuan.

Model of Yu'E Bao

What kind of product Yu'E Bao is on earth, and how does it work? The operation mode of Yu'E Bao is as shown in Fig. 13. Alipay users first transfer their balance in the Alipay account to Yu'E Bao. The investment in Yu'E Bao is equal to the purchase of Tian Hong Zengli Bao, since Yu'E Bao has been embedded in the Tian Hong Zengli Bao money fund, so the transfer from the Alipay account directly means the completion of the purchase. Meanwhile, the funds will be transferred into the escrow account of Tian Hong Fund from Yu'E Bao. If the users want to redeem the fund, the operation will be contrary to the purchase. Real-time redemption is a creation of Yu'E Bao. On the one hand, Yu'E Bao pays for the redeemed funds through self-owned funds; on the other hand, Tian Hong Fund will reserve some funds in Alipay account for real-time redemption. Through the two methods, users can realize real-time redemption. Although the two methods can satisfy user's requirements for real-time redemption, the real problem is that how much fund does Alipay need to pay in advance, or how much fund does Tian Hong Fund need to reserve? If the prepared fund is less, it will not necessarily satisfy the demand of liquidity. If the prepared fund is more, it will cause idling of the fund. The problem of liquidity reservation decides the problems of maturity mismatch. What kind of maturity configuration should it invest in and how to release a sufficient amount of liquidity at the right time? This is the liquidity problem that Yu'E Bao must deal with while satisfying the needs of financial management. In fact, it is not difficult to manage money. Regardless of the yield and the risk, various products in the financial market can meet the demand. The key issues are: firstly, to choose a financial management product that is suitable for the characteristics of the users' financial management needs; secondly, to ensure liquidity. The first requirement can be satisfied by the money market fund, but what about the second requirement? This requires big data, exactly speaking, the massive accumulation of transaction data. Through the analysis of the transaction data, the user's payment characteristics can be obtained, the payment node is identified, and sufficient liquidity funds are prepared in advance to cope with the payment demand. This is the role of big data, and also the aspect where Yu'E Bao is different from other financial management products, and even the reason why Yu'E Bao can be crowned with the model of the Internet finance. This fully reflects the attempt of Internet finance with big data as the main feature in the financial management market. Because of big data, the traditional financial management model has undergone an essential change, which reflects a new logic and business model (Fig. 9).

Through the way of "Alipay + money fund", Yu'E Bao has provided the users with low-threshold, high-liquidity and high-yield financial management product, enabling the users to satisfy their payment demand and meanwhile conduct efficient financial management. It has gained good user experience, therefore it can get the recognition of the users and the imitation from business competitors in a short time (Table 3).

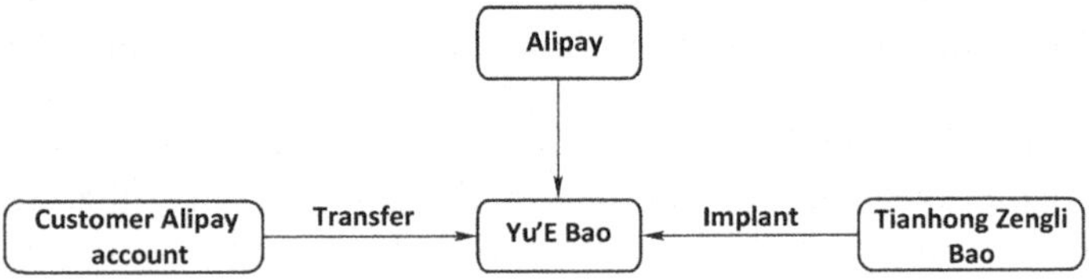

Fig. 9 Operating model of Yu'E Bao

Table 3 Asset portfolio of Tian Hong Zengli Bao (Unit: %)

Type	*2013Q3*	*2013Q4*	*2014Q1*	*2014Q2*	*2014Q3*	*2014Q4*
Fixed-income investment	6.88	6.7	4.01	5.64	7.71	7.97
Bond	6.88	6.7	4.01	5.57	7.57	7.83
Assets support security				0.07	0.14	0.14
Redemptory monetary capital for sale	8.01	0.83	3.5	9.03	2.25	7.11
Bank deposit and deposit reservation for balance sum	84.52	92.21	92.32	85.13	89.81	84.69
Other assets	0.60	0.26	0.18	0.2	0.23	0.23
Sum	100	100	100	100	100	100

Data source Report on Money Market Fund of Tian Hong Zengli Bao from the 3rd Quarter of 2013 to the 4th Quarter of 2014

Investment Structure of Yu'E Bao

Big data has effectively managed the liquidity risk and maturity mismatch risk faced by Yu'E Bao. Then, the remaining problem is the profitability of Yu'E Bao. What does Yu'E Bao profit from? In essence, Yu'E Bao is a kind of money fund, because it is corresponding to Tian Hong Zengli Bao, and the yield of Yu'E Bao depends entirely on the yield of Tian Hong Zengli Bao. Generally, the investment targets of money fund include cash, bank time deposits within one year (including one year), certificates of deposit, bond repurchases, central bank bills and bonds with a residual maturity of less than 397 days (including 397 days) and assets backed securities and the like. The investment target of Tian Hong Zengli Bao is also among them. From its actual operation, more than 80% of the assets of Tian Hong Zengli Bao have been invested in the agreement deposits of banks, and sometimes even more than 90%. Followed by are higher grade bonds, the proportion of which is around 6%. The rest accounts for a relatively small proportion.

Among the bonds, the proportion of policy finance bond is the highest, followed by is the corporate commercial paper underwriting. The proportion of the rest such as national bond and medium-term note can be negligible. It can be seen that the investment targets of Tian Hong Zengli Bao are mainly low-risk and fixed-income assets. Safety and stability are primary, while profitability is secondary (Table 4).

Table 4 Bond investment portfolio classified by varieties of bonds (Unit: %)

Type	*2013Q3*	*2013Q4*	*2014Q1*	*2014Q2*	*2014Q3*	*2014Q4*
National bond	0.71	0.08	0.01			
Central bank bill						
Financial bond	2.99	5.54	2.69	4.54	4.79	4.75
Policy financial bond	2.99	5.54	2.69	4.54	4.79	4.75
Enterprise bond					0.01	
Corporate short-term financing bond	3.18	1.27	1.29	1.18	2.73	3.04
Medium-term note			0.02		0.04	0.05
Others						
Sum	6.89	6.89	4.01	5.72	7.57	7.84

Data source Report on Money Market Fund of Tian Hong Zengli Bao from the 3rd Quarter of 2013 to the 4th Quarter of 2014

From the perspective of investment term of Tian Hong Zengli Bao, the proportion of short-term assets has gradually declined. For instance, the proportion of assets within 30 days has gradually declined to 15.18% from the climax 63.69%, the proportion of 30–60 days has declined to 22.97% from 57.84%; while the proportion of mid- and long-term assets has slightly increased. For instance, the proportion of assets with a term between 60 and 90 days has gradually risen to 42.62% from 14.15%, and that of assets with a term between 90 and 180 days has risen to 17.66% from 2.96%. The change of the trend indicates that the risk control of Zengli Bao has gradually matured, reflected in the configuration of short-term assets to release liquidity and the gradual maturity in the control of liquidity risk, enabling Zengli Bao to realize additional configuration of mid- and long-term assets; on the other hand, the profitability of investment can also be improved (Table 5).

Influence of Yu'E Bao

The influences brought by the development of Yu'E Bao are extensive, which are generally "three prosperities and one loss". Specifically, Yu'E Bao has increased the sales volume of money fund, improved the financial management income of the public users, enhanced the viscosity of Alipay users, meanwhile it has reduced the current deposits of the banks and increased the debt cost of the banks.

Firstly, development of Yu'E Bao has greatly improved the strength of Tian Hong Fund and realized the "counterattack" of medium and small funds. Many people describe the track of Tian Hong as "corner overtaking". Actually, it is not only "corner overtaking", but also "lane

Table 5 Average residual maturity distribution of investment portfolio (Unit: %)

Type	*2013Q3*	*2013Q4*	*2014Q1*	*2014Q2*	*2014Q3*	*2014Q4*
Within 30 days	23.57	63.69	28.19	28.55	15.18	23.89
30 days (included)-60 days	57.84	0.36	23.63	15.14	22.97	37.95
60 days(included)-90 days	14.15	29.71	44.96	24.51	42.62	8.14
90 days (included)-180 days	2.96	8.62	3.18	33.3	17.66	14.58
180 days(included)-397 days	1.06	0.08		0.9	1.38	15.26
Sum	99.58	102.46	99.96	102.4	99.81	99.83

Data source Report on Money Market Fund of Tian Hong Zengli Bao from the 3rd Quarter of 2013 to the 4th Quarter of 2014

changing and overtaking". Tian Hong has realized a great increase in its asset scale by means of Yu'E Bao. Its asset scale of 8.26 billion yuan, ranking the 46th in 2012, rose to 194.36 billion yuan, ranking the 2nd in 2013. It only takes two years. Since 2014, Tian Hong Fund had become the largest fund company. The influence of Yu'E Bao is evident.

Secondly, Yu'E Bao has brought relatively high investment revenues for the investors. The yield of Yu'E Bao was about 4% upon its birth. After then, it kept rising and even reached the climax of 6.5849%. Although it kept declining after the climax, it still maintained at about 4%. It was apparently several times higher than the interest rate of 0.35% of the banks. The reports of Tian Hong Fund showed that the investment revenue of Yu'E Bao in 2013 was 1.79 billion yuan, that of the 1st quarter in 2014 was 5.71billion yuan, rose to 6.838 billion yuan in the 2nd quarter, and declined to 5.7 billion yuan in the 3rd quarter. As of the 3rd quarter of 2014, Yu'E Bao had accumulatively brought the investment revenue of 20.038 billion yuan for the users. Each user had earned 133 yuan on average, which was equal to the money of cinema tickets for a family of three people.[1]

Thirdly, development of Yu'E Bao has brought good user experience for Alipay and enhanced user loyalty. The users transferred the funds to Yu'E Bao through Alipay to conduct financial management. When the funds were needed, they would be redeemed and transferred back to Alipay in time, so that Yu'E Bao had satisfied the double demands of "payment + financial management" of the users, enabling the users to get good use experience. The success of Yu' E Bao had made users more dependent on Alipay, which had enhanced Alipay's user loyalty. In addition, Yu' E Bao can also bring considerable settlement fee to Alipay.

Lastly, Yu'E Bao had moved the cheese of the banks. On the one hand, the fragmented financial management of Yu'E Bao had absorbed a large amount of current deposits, resulting in the rise in loan-to-deposit ratio of the banks, which was not beneficial to the development of the main businesses of the banks; on the other hand, the banks realized contra flow through the method of agreement deposit, invisibly increasing the debt cost of the banks. Calculated on the basis of Yu'E Bao's scale in the 3rd quarter of 2014, which was 534.893 billion yuan, 89.81% of the money had been invested in the banks' agreement deposits. Based on the yield

[1] Data source: http://soft.zol.com.cn/486/4865517.html.

of 4.1%, the banks would pay the interest of 19.696 billion yuan. For current deposits with the same scale, on the basis of the current interest rate of 0.35%, the banks only need to pay 1.681 billion yuan. It thus can be seen that the banks had paid 18.015 billion yuan in addition due to the absorption effect of Zengli Bao, which greatly increased the debt cost of the banks.

5 The Return of Online Financial Management

Compared with 2013, investors' feelings about Bao series products in 2014 were more disappointing and helpless. The declining yield constantly challenged the nerves of investors, which made people unintentionally ask: what happened to "Bao" which was on the altar in the former days? In fact, careful people can easily find that from December 26, 2013, the yield of Yu'E Bao initially fell below 6% to 5.971%. Pandora's box seemed to have opened. Although the overall yield of Bao series products in 2014 was still rising, reaching a maximum of 6.5849% in February, it began to decline since then. As of July 2014, the downward trend could be a linear regression, showing how obvious the "trend" is. Since July 2014, the yield of Bao series products had been relatively stable, and a "small tail" appeared until in November and December (Fig. 10).

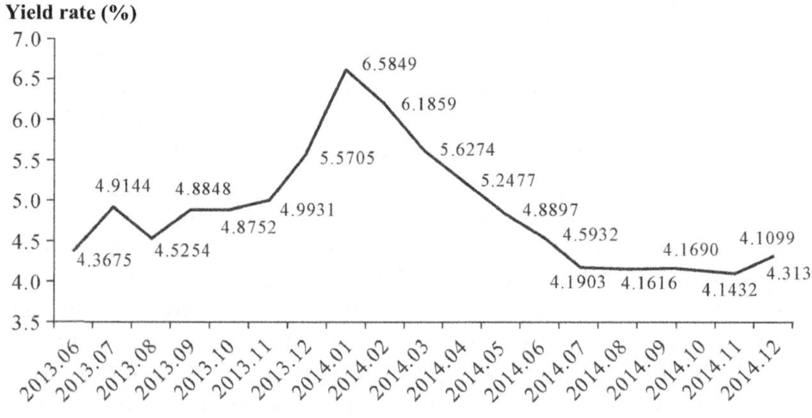

Fig. 10 Average of seven-day annualized yield of Bao series products from June 2013 to December 2014 (*Data source* Wind Database)

Are investments of Yu'E Bao not all bank agreement deposits and high-grade bonds? Is the interest rate not fixed? Is the revenue not very stable? In general, it is true. But it is not entirely true. The original intention of investment of Bao series products in bank deposits and high-grade bonds is to ensure a relatively high yield on the basis of ensuring the investment security. The interest rate of agreement deposit is indeed higher than normal deposit, but the essence of Bao series products is money fund. The commodity for the transaction of money fund is currency, the yield is the price of the currency, and the price of the currency is inevitably decided by both parties. Thus it is not changeless along with the change of the relation between supply and demand. When the supply of currency is less than the demand, the price of the currency will rise, and the yield for the investors will also increase. When the supply is larger than the demand, the yield will decline correspondingly. It thus can be expected that the yield of Bao series products is constantly changing. Even for bank deposits, the demand will also change due to changes in bank liquidity, and the interest rate on agreement deposits will change as well. In general, the yield change of Bao series products in 2014 was influenced by the factors such as monetary policy, interest rate, A share market and bank assessment mechanism.

Firstly, the yield of Bao series products is influenced by the monetary policy of the People's Bank of China. Generally, the monetary policy of the People's Bank of China decides the quantity of the currency on the market, which also decides the price of the currency. In 2014, China's economy had entered into the "new normality", and experienced "overlaid three periods". The pressure of economic downturn had obviously increased. The old economic growth dividends were disappearing, while new economic growth focus had not been formed. Under such circumstances, the monetary policy can't be tightened, because the economy would decline rapidly once the policy is tightened; meanwhile it can't be loosened, because the currency may flow into the industries with excess production capacity again. In general, we should maintain a prudent monetary policy, implement pre-adjustment and slight adjustment, tighten the monetary supply generally and loosen the supply partially, implement oriented adjustment and control and promote development of new industries. According to the operation of monetary policy of 2014, for specific industries such as the fields of "three rural issues", small and micro enterprises and resident housing consumption, they had maintained a relatively loosened status. The deposit reserve ratio had been lowered twice, oriented credit loan placement had been conducted twice, and the housing mortgage interest rate had been guided to decline positively. In November 2014, the benchmark interest rates on deposit and loan had been lowered. According to these measures, the monetary policy of 2014 was relatively loosened as a whole. The actual financing cost is reduced by loose currency, thereby driving the development of the real economy. Therefore, the relatively loose monetary policy implemented by the People's Bank of China based on the consideration of reducing financing costs has greatly increased the supply of currency and lowered the interest rate of the currency. This is good for the bank, but its effect is on the contrary for the Bao series product, which is the fund supplier (Table 6).

Secondly, the yield of Bao series products is closely related to the level of interest rate. Some people said that Yu'E Bao was born in a right time. That's the truth. In June 2013, the banks were encountering "money shortage", when the money was hard to get and the money rate of interest sharply rose, therefore Yu'E Bao had gained popularities from the banks since its birth, and its yield had been constantly rising. Since 2014, the money market rate still kept rising, resulting in the rise in the overall yield of Bao series products. From March 2014, the money market rate started to decline, which once declined to the minimum of 1.75%. Looking back on the money market rate of 2014, except for January, February and December, in the rest months, the rate did not exceed 3.5%. It can be seen that the money market was relatively looser in 2014 than that in 2013. This decided that the yield of Bao series products had declined relatively than in last year (Fig. 11).

Thirdly, the yield of Bao series products is related to the change of bank assessment mechanism. On September 12, China Banking Regulatory Commission, the Ministry of Finance, and the People's Bank of China jointly issued the Notice on Relevant Matters Concerning Strengthening the Management of Deposit Deviation of Commercial Banks (hereinafter referred to as the "Notice"), and newly established the indicator for the deposit deviation at the end of the month to regulate the problem of sprinting the time point of bank deposits. For a long time, the problem of sprinting the time point had commonly occurred. The deposits are high at the end of a month while dropped at the beginning of a month. The deposit deviation is relatively high at the end of the month, which is particularly protruding at the end of a quarter. In June 2014, the bank deposits fluctuated sharply, and the increment of that month accounted

Table 6 A portion of monetary policies of People's Bank of China of 2014

Time	*Content*
January 17, 2014	According to *The Notice on SLF Pilot* issued by People's Bank of China, branches in Beijing, Jiangsu, Shandong, Guangdong, Hebei, Shanxi, Zhejiang, Jilin, Henan and Shenzhen established SLF pilots to solve the liquidity demands in local legal person and financial institution up to macroscopic prudent requirements
March 20, 2014	According to *The Notice on the Establishment of Petty Re-lending and the Expansion of Credit Loan Placement*, People's Bank of China established petty re-lending under the re-lending type supported by credit policy to facilitate financial institutions' credit issue among large, small and micro companies, and grants 50 billion yuan re-lending limit nationwide
April 22, 2014	People's Bank of China decided to lower country-scale rural commercial banks' RMB deposit reserve ratio by 2% point, and lower country-scale rural cooperative banks; lower RMB deposit reserve ratio by 0.5% point since April 25
June 9, 2014	People's Bank of China decided to lower the deposit reserve ratio of commercial banks up to prudent operation requirements and appropriate proportion of agriculture, rural area and rural resident, small and micro business loan (excluding those institutions which had lowered reserve ratio on April 25) and lower the RMB deposit reserve ratio of financial companies, financial release companies and automobile finance companies by 0.5% point since June 16
August 27, 2014	In order to implement national requirements for "aggravating agriculture support, petty re-lending and re-discount efforts", and improve financial services for "agriculture, rural area and rural resident" and other weak links in national economy, People's Bank of China added 20 billion yuan re-lending sum for some branches, guided rural financial institutions to expand agriculture credit, and promoted the reduction of financing cost of "agriculture, rural area and rural resident"
September 2014	People's Bank of China created MLF to provide medium-term basic currency for financial institutions up to macroscopic prudent management practices. MLF helped exert the role of medium-term policy interest rate and lowered social financing cost
September 30, 2014	For further improving the financial services for government-subsidized housing projects, supporting rational resident housing consumption and encouraging the sustainable and healthy development of the real estate market, People's Bank of China and CBRC jointly issued *The Notice on Further Improvement of Housing Finance Services*

(continued)

Table 6 (continued)

Time	*Content*
November 22, 2014	People's Bank of China lowered the RMB lending and deposit benchmark interest rate of financial institutions. One-year loan interest rate was lowered by 0.4% point to 5.6%, and one-year deposit benchmark interest rate was lowered by 0.25% point to 2.75%. The upper limit of deposit interest rate fluctuation range for financial institutions was adjusted from 1.1 times of deposit benchmark interest rate to 1.2 times. Benchmark interest rate term grade was appropriately simplified

Data source People's Bank of China

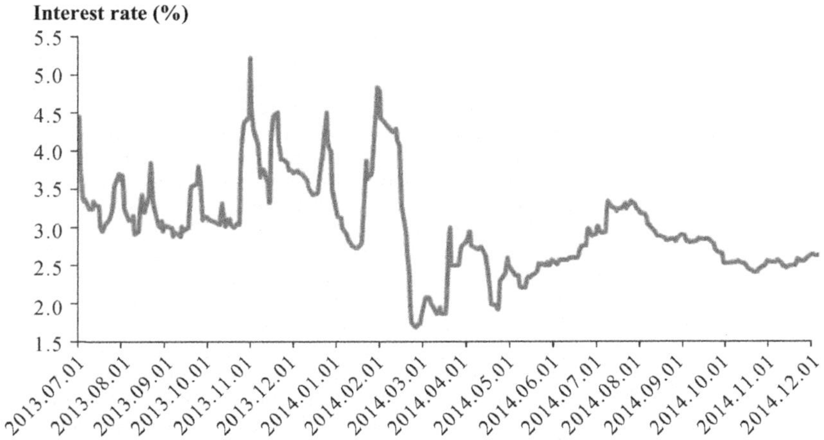

Fig. 11 SHIBOR overnight rate from July 1, 2013 to December 1, 2014 (*Data source* Wind Database)

for 50% of the total increment of the first half of that year. The structured deposit increment of the banks accounted for 30% of the total increment in the first half of the year. This had undoubtedly further raised the costs of bank funds since the cost of structured deposit was much higher than that of the general deposit. This had seriously deviated from the spirit of reducing enterprises' financing costs required by the central government.

The Notice newly set up that: deposit deviation at the end of the month = (various deposits of the last day at the end of the month—daily average deposit of the month)/daily average deposit of the month * 100%. The commercial banks should strengthen the management on deposit stability and reduce the behaviors of sprinting the time point. The deposit deviation at the end of the month shall not exceed 3%. To prevent the commercial banks from sharply increasing the daily average deposit of the month at the end of the quarter, the Notice has restricted the amount which can be calculated into the daily average deposit of the month at the end of the quarter. The calculation of the deposit deviation at the end of the last month of each quarter is that the amount which can be calculated into the daily average deposit of the month should not exceed the daily average deposit of last month * (1 + the average of growth rate of daily average deposit of the last month of the recent 4 quarters). For banks that the deposit deviation at the end of the month exceeds 3%, the access issues should be continuously paused for more than 3 months from the next month; for banks that the deposit deviation at the end of the month exceeds 3% for twice within one year, the annual supervision rating of the banks should be properly lowered.[2]

The yield rise of Bao series products is mostly because of the bank's behavior of sprinting the time point. To complete the deposit task within the regulated time, the banks usually use high yield to absorb short-term deposits without calculating the costs. This is harmful instead of beneficial to the development of commercial banks. The regulator's move is not intended to suppress Bao series products, but to reduce the bank's liability costs by changing the regulatory approach to suppress the behaviors of sprinting the time point, thereby reducing the financing costs of enterprises. As soon as this article is published, the bank's deposit demand will definitely decline, and the yield of Bao series products will also decline (Fig. 12).

Lastly, the decline in the yield of Bao series products is also related to the diversion of the stock market. In the second half of 2014, a bull market occurred in the stock market, and the investors plunged into the stock market one after another to "gain money". At the same time, the decline in the yield of Bao series products had accelerated the withdrawal

[2] Data source: http://kuaixun.stcn.com—0915/11717452.shtml.

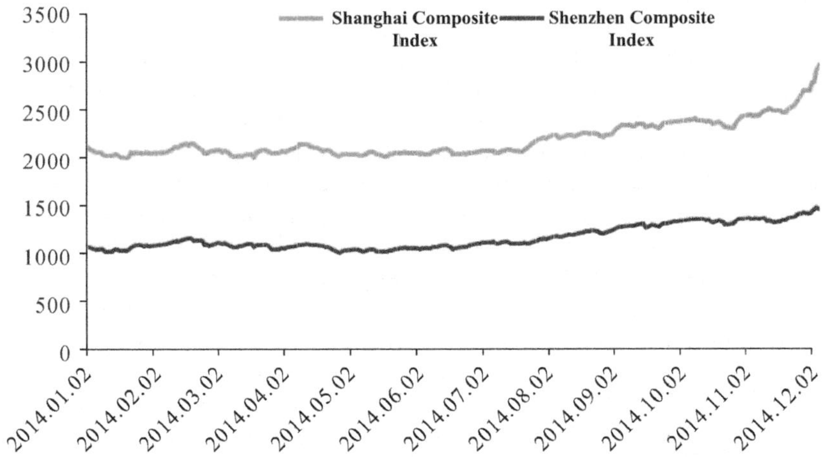

Fig. 12 Trend of Shanghai Composite Index and Shenzhen Composite Index in 2014 (*Data source* Wind Database)

of funds, further speeding up the fund diversion speed of Bao series products.

6 The Essence Re-dialysis of Online Financial Management

Many people said that Bao series product was not a creation in product, but a precise grasp of the policy loophole. This saying may be too absolute. One of the highlights of the above-mentioned Bao series products is that they can reasonably use big data to carry out risk control. After all, risk control is indispensable for the design of a good financial product. Besides, an ideal online financial management product should be interactive and individualized, which will use the precise "portrait" of individual investors created by big data. According to current development status of online financial management, the individualized and interactive customization part is not included. Regardless of the risk control, "payment + financial management" have indeed utilized the policy loophole to some extent, thus the combination is not a perfect financial creation product.

A majority of investment of Bao series products is bank agreement deposit. Both are deposits, what is the difference between the agreement deposit and the general deposit? There are three main points: interest rate, reserve ratio and default interest. For general deposit, its interest rate should not exceed 1.1 times of the benchmark interest rate; besides, the deposit reserve should be normally paid, with large financial institutions paying 20%, medium and small financial institutions paying 16.5%; meanwhile, the interests for advanced withdrawal of fixed deposits should be calculated according to the current interest rate. For agreement deposit of the bank, it is handled with according to inter-bank deposit. The interest rate of inter-bank deposit is determined independently by both parties, which is not limited to 1.1 times of the benchmark interest rate. Besides, inter-bank deposit does not need to pay the deposit reserve, which can effectively reduce the costs for the banks. As a result, the banks are quite inclined to absorb inter-bank deposits. The most important point is that the interest for the advanced withdrawal of the agreement deposit is still calculated at the fixed interest rate, which can effectively guarantee the yield of Bao series products (Table 7).

From the above three perspectives, the financial creation of Bao series products is indeed insufficient. The essence is to use the differential treatment of supervision on general deposits and agreement deposits. Firstly, the bank's current deposits are absorbed into Yu'E Bao through Alipay, and then they are invested in the bank's agreement deposits using the money fund of Zengli Bao. That is, the deposits are transferred out of the bank first and then transferred in as agreement deposits. The nature of the deposits becomes agreement deposit from general deposit after the transfer out and transfer in. The regulatory measures on such deposits also change correspondingly in the way that the interest rate is changed

Table 7 Differences between ordinary deposit and agreement deposit

Differences	*Ordinary deposit*	*Agreement deposit*
Interest rate	Set 1.1 times of benchmark interest rate as the upper limit	Autonomous supply and demand sides
Reserve ratio	Normal payment of deposit reserve fund	Contractual deposit without required reserves
Interest penalty	Prepayment by current interest rate	Withdrawing in advance by original interest rate

from current interest rate to the interest rate for agreement deposits, the deposit reserve is not required from required, and the default interest is canceled for advanced withdrawal. Therefore, Bao series products have only exchanged the concept of deposit, and they cannot be regarded as financial creation. It is no wonder that many people say that Yu'E Bao is a "vampire" lying on the bank. Such attack is not unreasonable.

Under such circumstance, it is an objective fact that Bao series products have moved the cheese of the banks using the policy loophole, and thus it is a matter of course that the supervisor strengthens the supervision on Bao series products.

7 The Supervision of Online Financial Management

For the rapid development of online financial management, the investors, the fund companies and the third-party payment companies all have gained what they want, but the banks have gained nothing and meanwhile are stabbed. Therefore, it is the commercial banks that first proposed to conduct supervision on network financial management. On the one hand, they intend to rapidly develop their own Internet Bao series products and retain the funds in the banks as many as possible; on the other hand, they suggest to strictly standardize the development of Bao series products and incorporate such products into the system of general deposits to conduct effective supervision, so as to restrict the fund-moving "robbery".

On February 25, 2014, China Banking Association convened a seminar for bank deposit self-regulation measures to analyze the agreement deposit management of banks regarding the financial management money funds of the Internet finance. They considered that as an inter-bank deposit, agreement deposit had greatly increased the costs of the banks, and they hoped to incorporate the agreement deposit into general deposit, so that it should strictly execute the upper limit of the interest rate which should not exceed 1.1 times of the benchmark interest rate, pay the deposit reserve and pay the penalty for advanced withdrawal. It can be seen that the banks had fully recognized the essence of the operating mode of Bao series products at that time, which was "trans-boundary interest arbitrage" utilizing the difference between the supervision on policies of the agreement deposit and the general deposit. This measure can be said to hit the "nail" of Bao series products, which gives a dead strike to Bao series products.

In March 2014, the four major banks publicly declared that they did not accept the money market funds of Bao series products. This has a certain impact on the investment of Bao series products. It is said that the main reason why the four major banks reject Bao series products is the consideration of the high costs. After all, the banks must consider their own costs if they accept the agreement deposits from the money market funds. The yield above 6% is almost equal to and even higher than the loan interest rate. Under such circumstance, it is impossible for the banks to accept the price of the agreement deposits.

Soon afterward on March 24, the People's Bank of China made it clear that the creation of Internet finance was supported, but it should also accept proper supervision. Unreasonable clauses such as that the deposits were withdrawn in advance but the interest was still calculated at the original agreed rate are not allowed. This is the first time that the People's Bank of China clearly defined the invisible clause of no penalty for advanced withdrawal within the industry. The abolition of this clause may have a significant impact on the yield of Bao series products. After all, the difference between the contracting interest rate and the current interest rate is still relatively large. For instance, the interest rate of the agreement deposit of money fund is 5%, but the deposit needs to be redeemed in advance during the deposit term, then the interest can only be calculated according to the current interest rate of 0.35%. However, the daily interest of money market funds is calculated according to 5%, the fund company can only get 0.35% but needs to pay 5%, thus there must be a huge loss. In this way, money funds with a high ratio of investment in bank agreement deposits will be greatly influenced. According to the statistics, by the end of 2013, among the 84 funds which published the ratio of agreement deposits, the total scale of agreement deposits was 729.66 billion yuan, and the average ratio of agreement deposits was 47.4%.[3] Among the money funds, there are only 9 of them that the ratio of agreement deposit exceeds 80%, and there are only 3 of them that the ratio of agreement deposit exceeds 90%. The proportion of agreement deposit of E Fund Yilicai currency launched by E Fund is the highest. The proportion of agreement deposit of Tian Hong Zengli Bao corresponding to Yu'E Bao is up to 92.21%. However, Wang Dengfeng, fund manager

[3] Data source: http://www.p5w.netfundfxpl/201403/t20140326_532633.htm.

of Yu'E Bao, expressed that Yu'E Bao had never withdrawn the agreement deposits in advance. The investment horizon of 70% of its assets is within 1 month, which will not have great influence on the liquidity of Yu'E Bao.[4]

On December 29, 2014, the People's Bank of China published the Notice on Matters Related to Deposit Reserve Policy and Interest Rate Management Policy after Adjustment of Deposit Approaches, specifying that the agreement deposit was classified as general deposit, which was required to pay the deposit reserve. The deposit reserve ratio was temporarily determined as zero. This Notice specified the nature of the deposit reserve for the agreement deposit of the money fund. The days when the agreement deposit does not need to pay the deposit reserve had gone for ever. However, the current situation is quite special, the reserve ratio is zero, but the possibility that it will increase at any time is not ruled out. It can be calculated based on Yu'E Bao's scale of 534.893 billion yuan in the 3rd quarter of 2014 that the proportion of its investment in bank agreement deposits is 89.81 – 5% = 84.81%.[5] Considering the 1.62% of statutory deposit reserve rate, if the agreement deposit is required to pay the deposit reserve in accordance with the general deposit, it is approximately 5343.93 × (89.81 – 5%) × 20% × (4.16 – 1.62%) = 2.305 billion yuan. That is to say, the income of Yu'E Bao will be decreased by 2.305 billion yuan if it still invests in the agreement deposit, which is equal to the reduction of yield by 0.43%. In consideration of the yield of 4.4% of Yu'E Bao at present, once the deposit reserve is collected, the yield's drop below 4 will be inevitable. Based on this, it can be foreseen that the yield of Bao series products will further decline, unless some "Bao" products can lower the proportion of the agreement deposits. For instance, the proportion of agreement deposit of HSBC Jinxin currency is only 8.03%. In this way, the influence of deposit reserve will be small (Table 8).

In addition, another regulation of Notice is the interest rate management policy. The limit of 1.1 times of the highest benchmark interest rate is still not executed for the interest rate of agreement deposits as the general deposits at present, which is still determined by both parties based on the principle of marketization. This has constrainedly maintained

[4] Data source: http://www.idcps.comnews20140327/70632.html.

[5] The proportion of deposit reservation for balance is about 5%.

Table 8 Supervision on policies of Internet financial management products

Supervision target	*Time*	*Content*
Interest rate Deposit reserve Penalty interest	February 25, 2014	Banking Association's bank deposit self-discipline regulating measures seminar suggested incorporating "Yu'E Bao" and alike Internet financial money fund into bank ordinary deposit instead of financial institution deposit which subscribes the deposit reserve by rule. Banking Association would enact related self-discipline authority files and normalize related deposit interest allowance, demanding all industries to rigorously conform to related regulatory stipulations. Interest rate ceiling is 1.1 times of the benchmark interest rate of the same grade. The interest rate of withdrawal in advance of money fund follows demand deposit interest rate or gathers default interest
Deposit	March 7, 2014	The four banks explicitly stated the rejection of Internet financial product contractual deposit
Penalty rate	March 24, 2014	Central bank: Offline financial businesses transferred to online counterparts shall observe existing laws and regulations and capital constraints. No irrational contract terms that charged original agreed term interest rate or standard fee for withdrawal in advance or prior termination of services are allowed
Reserve ratio Interest rate	December 29, 2014	*The Notice of People's Bank of China on Related Affairs about Deposit Reserve Policy and Interest Rate Management Policy after the Adjustment of Deposit Caliber* classified contractual deposit under the type of ordinary deposit required reserves as 0 The interest rate policy for aforementioned deposit remained unchanged, and the interest rate was negotiated by the parties as per marketization principle

Data source Sorted according to relevant materials

the foundation of the yield of Bao series products. Otherwise, Bao series products can be directly equal to bank deposits. In that way, rather than placing the money into current deposits through Yu'E Bao, why the users do not directly deposit the money by themselves?

From the current supervision on Internet financial management, it is not difficult to see that for three key points for online financial management, including interest rate, deposit reserve and no penalty: it has been clearly stated that no penalty cannot be maintained; the deposit reserve is already on the line, it's just that the reserve ratio is temporarily zero, leaving the time and space for Bao series products. When the line will be broken depends on the development of Bao series products, the looseness of bank funds and the like. The future trend is that the deposit reserve should be collected as general deposits, and this will further lower the yield of Bao series products; as for the unlimited interest rate, it still exists for the time being, which is the only life-saving straw for the current Bao series products to make agreement deposit investment. The future prospects are bleak, and Bao series products should cherish the present.

8 The Development Trend of Online Financial Management

From the development trend of online financial management, there are two main aspects: one is the constant deepening of the application of big data in online financial management. Its position will continue to move from the back end to the front end; the other is the diversification of investment targets. It is no longer limited to money funds, structured financial management, bill financing, P2P lending and other methods will be sought after by investors.

In-depth Big Data Application

The initial network financial management relied more on the role of the channel which simply connected the money fund and the users, and the most important role was the sales. Product marketing is conducted by enriching the user experience. Compared with traditional financial management, its advantage lies in the low threshold of financial management and high liquidity. The key point is the application of big data. At this time, big data has not yet moved to the front end to participate in the design of financial management products, what's more is to carry out prevention and control of risks, especially liquidity risk and maturity mismatch risk. This model is better reflected in the current Bao series products represented by Yu'E Bao. The risk control application for big data has also been introduced in detail above. From this stage, the application of network financial management based on big data has become one of the models of Internet finance. The application of big data will also be promoted constantly. In the scene consumptions, financial management products will continue to expand the application functions of the traditional "Bao", and investors can obtain value-added services in terms of payment, financial management, revenue and discounts at the time of house purchasing or traveling. It is represented by Tencent's Goufang Licai Bao. After the user uses WeChat payment to pay the earnest money for the house, such money will be automatically transferred to Licaitong for purchasing the money fund to generate revenues. After the house is purchased, the financial management fund can be converted into house payment.[6] In the next stage, Internet companies, such as Alibaba, will be more adept at using the large amount of payment data in their hands to match their users with products, including the type, quantity, price and term of products. Compared with the previous stage, big data is more widely used, not only for risk control. But more importantly, big data has moved to the front end, which can be used to select goods. The ideal state is to achieve the precise one-to-one matching between the users and the products. But this model also tests the operating capability of the platform, whether it can precipitate enough big data and be fully analyzed and applied. Its representative product is Ali's Zhaocai Bao. The final stage is product strategy. Here, big data will be fully utilized, from risk prevention and control, one-to-one matching to product design. At this time, network financial management has truly achieved personalization and interaction. Thanks to the role of big data, the product providers can get what the characteristics of the users are and what kind of financial management products the users need, so that they can provide the products desired by the users specific to the characteristics and needs of the users. The accumulation, digging, analysis and application of big data are the essence and spirit of Internet finance. This is just a masterpiece of the initial attempt of Internet finance (Fig. 13).

[6] Data source: http://www.rong360.com/gl-12/30/62963.html.

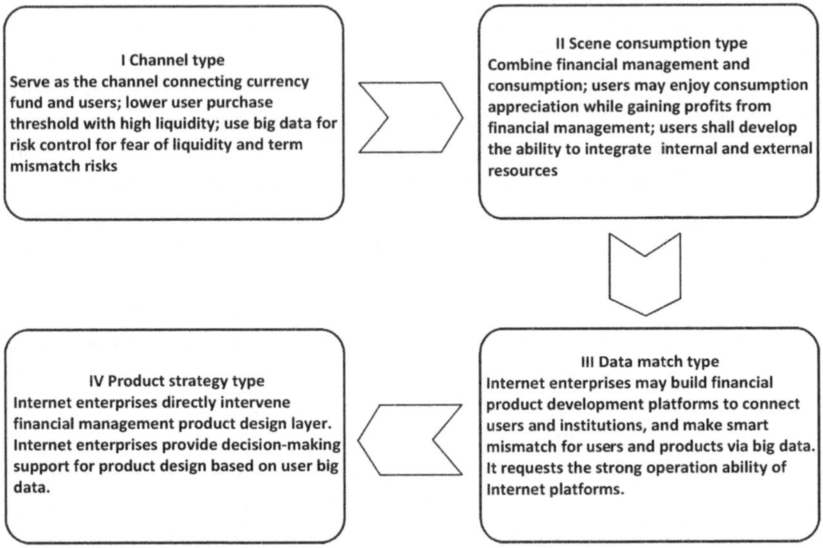

Fig. 13 Network financial management mode development trend (*Data source* The Research Report on Internet Finance in China [2014])

Diversification of Investment Target

With the gradual improvement of the government's supervision of the money fund, it is expected that the future yield of network financial management will continue to decline, and the yield of 5% to 6% in the past will be difficult to trace. It can be expected that in the future, the public will have a more complete understanding of network financial management and their investment will be more rational. In the future, structured financial management, bill financing and P2P lending will become new hot spots.

Although the People's bank of China cut interest rates asymmetrically in November 2014, a large amount of funds flowed into the stock market, and a new wave of bull markets rose. In less than a month and a half, the Shanghai Composite Index rose from 2,500 points to 3,200 points, with an increase of nearly 30%. Specific to the stock market rally, the structured financial management products issued by banks will become the hotspot pursued by the public. In the case of the unchanged monetary policy, the stock market will continue to be strong in 2015, so structured financial management will also rise.

Under the circumstance that the revenues of Bao series products and financial management products of the banks had declined, bill financing, uprising against the trend in 2014, had become the new hot spot of investment. Relying on the advantages of payment by bank acceptance, low entry threshold and high yield, bill financing had gained popularity from massive investors. At present, the term of bill financing is mostly 60–160 days, and the starting point of subscription is 1,000 yuan. The yield of 6% is still advantageous compared with Bao series products and financial management products of the banks.[7]

In 2014, the new entrants and runners on the P2P platforms were "both numerous", which intensified the competition in this industry. Through continuous survival of the fittest, the pattern of brutal growth, disorderly growth and extensive growth in P2P industry are expected to be alleviated. The development of P2P industry will be further rationalized, standardized and healthy. With the upcoming P2P supervision regulations, the development prospects of the P2P industry are bright. Although it may no longer have a platform yield of 20–30% as in the past, the yield of more than 10% has far exceeded that of Bao series products, financial management products of banks and bill financing, which is still very attractive to investors.

From the general trend, the future investment target of network financial management will break through the single kind of money fund. With the increase of investment rationality, the enhancement of anti-risk ability and the deepening of the understanding on revenue and risk, investors will be more inclined to investment diversification and risk diversification, and choose online financial management products that suit their own conditions.

In addition, online financial management may also take the form of an integrated financial service platform. On this platform, various financial management methods such as insurance, bills, bank financing, funds, private placements, trusts and P2P lending can provide users with financial products in different risks, different yields, different liquidities and different investment thresholds through the support of big data. In this case, the types of financial products will be greatly increased to meet the needs of different investors.

[7] Data source: http://www.rong360.com/gl01/08/63344.html.

No matter how the form of online financial management changes and how rich the types are, the essence of online financial management cannot be changed. Its essence is the application of big data in financial products. From the initial risk prevention and control, to the matching of users and products, then to the design of products, they are all the embodiments of big data application. It is with big data that the transformation of online financial management from channel to product designer can be realized, new financial products can be created, and application of Internet finance in the field of financial management products can be realized.

CHAPTER 5

Prominence of "Value" Accumulation: Big Data Finance

Big data finance is one of the effective applications of big data in the field of Internet finance. Internet finance platforms may rely on considerable accumulated user data to offer all sorts of financing services to different users, including platform finance, supply chain finance and consumer finance. While these patterns are based on the credit rating formed with considerable accumulated data. This is the most explicit application of big data, and also the expression of big data value accumulation. By virtue of the data advantages accumulated over a long period of time, Alibaba and JD develop all kinds of big data finance patterns such as Alibaba Micro-lending, Jing Baobei, JD Micro-lending, Ant Check Later and JD Baitiao. While other platforms lack of data accumulation are at a disadvantage in related big data finance businesses. The role of big data in Internet finance is quite self-evident. However, the problem of big data finance rests in its dependence on credit investigation. Though it creates great convenience for financial services to a large extent, it also exposes platforms to risks in credit investigation link.

As stated above, third party is the "vanguard" of Internet finance that help companies accumulate big data. Online Internet wealth management is nothing but an attempt made by big data to help control the risks of wealth management products, prevent liquidity risks and term mismatch risks. If the former two show how big data paves way for Internet finance, this chapter will focus on the prominence of big data value. Following

Q. Guan and W. Gao, *Internet Finance*,
The Great Transformation of China,
https://doi.org/10.1007/978-981-16-4740-6_5

third-party payment and online wealth management, Internet companies begin to make full use of big data in capital financing, namely big data finance, and its business scope is not limited in third-party payment and wealth management anymore. On the contrary, it diverts the focus to financing. This goes further at the business level, the role of bank included.

As is known to all, the nature of finance is financing, i.e. the exchange and match of capital in time and space. Then what is supporting financing? Is it pledge, mortgage, guarantee, joint guarantee or other means? As a matter of fact, either physically or virtually, the backbone of financing is always credit. Whether it is represented by a physical object or someone else or even itself, credit suggests the security of trustworthy capital mismatch. But the problem now is many people or companies lack essential material assets, guarantors or joint guarantors. What is the fix? In another word, how should people prove their credit? We have been beset by this problem for a long time so that many people and companies can't rely on their own credit to do financing. Now, there is one solution to this problem—an accurate "portrait" of individuals or companies can be drawn according to their behavioral characteristics and laws so that involved risks will be fully revealed and risk pricing will be made. Admittedly, different risk coefficients correspond to different interest rate levels. In this way, no credit problem is left. Either individuals or companies can measure their risks as per accumulated data, solve credit problems and realize financing without substantial assets or others' guarantee. This explains the logic of big data finance (Fig. 1).

1 The Definition of Big Data

We've been talking about big data. Then what is big data? It is difficult to figure it out. Does big data mean a large size of data or a sort of computation method? We think that big data means more than that. When it comes to the topic of Internet finance and big data, big data here actually refers to big data in financial application instead of a mathematical or computer technology. Therefore, this concept should be big data in Internet finance.

On the whole, big data of Internet finance should contain four layers of meaning, in which the first one denotes considerable accumulated informatization figures, including credit information, trading information, payment information, social contact information, search information,

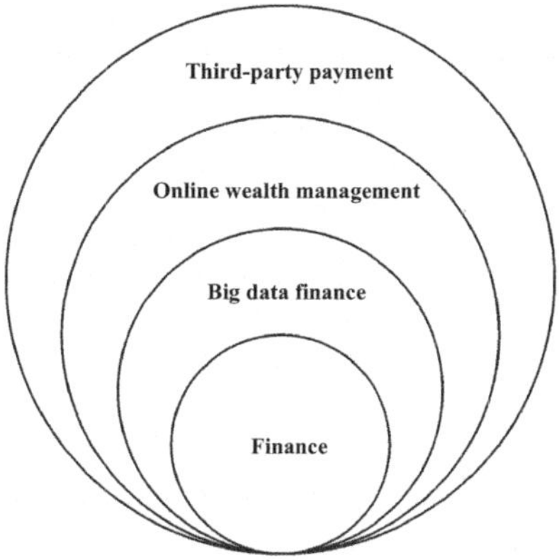

Fig. 1 Progress of the permission of internet finance into finance

mobile operation information. It is a combination of all behavioral information data. The second layer denotes data search and excavation. In face of the discrepancy in data diversity, data non-structural property and data validity, general types of data also have varying validity. The data closer to authentic transaction has higher degree of validity. For instance, trading information and payment information on Taobao seem more valid than social information on Tencent, because the former is closer to actual transaction and more easily reflect traders' business actions. How should we find required data in a timely, convenient and high-efficient manner in the midst of massive digital information, and effectively excavate data to gain user classification, behavioral preference, trading characteristics and other key information? The third layer denotes credit investigation with excavated information. Combining with user classification, behavioral preference, trading characteristics and other key information, it is possible to measure users' credit condition, including occupation, income level, age structure, payment deadline and default rate. Credit condition lies in the foundation of financial activities. Risk pricing is followed by credit investigation. The fourth layer denotes personal and interactive product design made with big data which aims to achieve the quantity match and deadline match of financial products.

What will happen when finance runs into big data? Absolutely, the answer is finance. After all, finance involved here is superior to traditional finance. As it contains data processed by computer technology used to

Fig. 2 Classification of big data finance

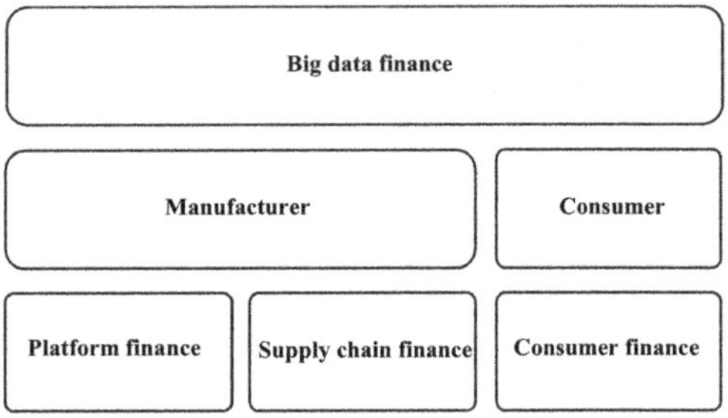

finish user credit investigation and realize match of financial products, it is known as big data finance. Big data finance specializes in the provision of different kinds of financial services tailored for different consumers. To be specific, manufacturers are usually provided with financing service to alleviate liquidity pressures. Big data finance falls into platform finance and supply chain finance in line with the means of operation. Consumers are usually provided with financing service to solve their consumption demands. Consumption finance reduces the constraint of income budget on consumption by consumption finance. Irrespective of the difference between overall financing means in object, pattern and flow, they are the same in nature, which means that they all gain financing objects' credit condition throughout big data analysis and therefore offer risk pricing financing service (Fig. 2).

2 Platform Finance

Platform finance under big data means e-commerce companies analyze considerable accumulated corporate trading data to assess the credit rating and loan payment ability of platform companies, and provide necessary financing support. The main thinking is to utilize considerable data accumulated by small- and medium-sized companies throughout long-term operation on the platform, including trading data, financial data and credit data to estimate corporate operation and cash flow, assess consumer credit and loan repayment ability, and offer lending evidence. In general, the development history of Chinese platform finance reflects the development history of Alibaba Micro-lending. Each development stage, development orientation and development characteristic of platform finance is indicative of the trace of Alibaba Micro-lending. In this sense, the review of platform finance means the review of Alibaba Micro-lending.

Development History of Platform Finance

When it comes to the development history of platform finance, it is inevitable to talk about Alibaba. Alibaba is the first company that begins to accumulate related platform finance elements, try platform finance business and improve platform finance. Platform finance under big data in China has undergone three stages as below.

Element Accumulation Stage in 2002–2006

In the year of 2002, Alibaba released Trust Pass business by building credit files for small- and medium-sized companies engaged in domestic trading. Through employing third-party agency for credit rating, Alibaba presents trading integrity records to buyers and reinforces sellers' credit. This move effectively reinforces sellers' credit and makes for the progress of bilateral trading parties. However, it remains to be seen whether the credit rating measure is proposed for financial lending at first. But it is certain that the credit rating measure not only provides credit data for small- and medium-sized companies in financing, and reinforces the credit of small- and medium-sized companies. More importantly, it affords the thinking of credit rating to small- and medium-sized companies, and points out the way to solve credit loss among small- and medium-sized companies caused by information asymmetry. In a manner of speaking, the establishment of Trust Pass marks the beginning of credit investigation for small- and medium-sized companies.

In 2004, Alibaba further released Trust Pass index to measure member companies' credit, which could more explicitly demonstrate member credit than pure assessment or record. This move lays a solid foundation for Alibaba's subsequent building of credit model for small- and medium-sized companies.

The giant trading scale also brings about a steady flow of data for Alibaba, and gathers considerable value data for its petty loan business.

Initial Attempt Stage in 2007–2009

As indicated by Alibaba's survey for platform companies, only 12% small and micro companies have gained bank loan financing, and remaining 88% small and micro companies even can't raise a loan from banks. The finding inspires Alibaba to open micro-lending business. How could it help small and micro companies gain a loan? What Alibaba has is just accumulated data and credit index of small and micro companies. Alibaba assumes that banks can acquire small and micro companies' operation conditions and capital conditions by means of data analysis and then issue loans with no guarantee or pledge. In May 2007, Alibaba jointly released online guarantee loan services in cooperation with CCB and ICBC, stipulating that any combo composed of three or more companies might apply for a loan with no pledge. Upon receiving the loan application, Alibaba submitted corporate trading data and credit record to banks and then banks decided whether to lend after audit and approval. Moreover, the cooperation also launched multiple loan products represented by "E-lending Pass" and "Easy Financing".

The cooperation between Alibaba and CCB and ICBC manifests the embryo of platform finance under big data, as it fully adheres to the thinking of big data finance which utilizes small and medium companies' trading data and credit data in credit assessment, lowers information asymmetry and controls corporate financing risks. After all, the subject responsible for risk assessment here is the bank.

Unfortunately, Alibaba's cooperation with CCB and ICBC came to an end in April 2011. Concerning the cause of it, many ascribe this to the discrepancy among parties in financial concept, including credit style, risk prevention and control, and business operation. Here is the analysis made by journalist Hu Rongping, Lan Binzhen and Zhang Ke in *The Economic Observer* on August 24, 2012.

In reply to journalists of *The Economic Observer* in the interview, Alibaba Finance expands on changes of Alibaba and banks in thinking and means, and confesses that the varying judging standards for small and micro companies' credit obstruct their cooperation.

As stated by Alibaba Finance, such operation indeed helps some small and micro companies solve their financing demands, but it is essentially based on former credit operation of banks as usual. Consequently, despite the strong lending demands of small and micro companies on e-commerce platform, only a small number of small and micro companies have access to bank credit. Moreover, accumulated credit records of small and micro companies on the network do not gain the full approval from banks yet, and they shall still apply for a loan with guarantee, pledge or joint guarantee. Obviously, such operation puts e-commerce small and micro companies' financing move at a disadvantage. Due to the large quantity and low financing limit of small and micro companies, traditional credit operation means can't achieve financial demands in a high-efficient way, and has low business efficiency.

However, banks in cooperation with Alibaba tell a different story. According to banks, the reason why the cooperation decreases and even calls it quits is that Alibaba later wants to have a finger in the pie over bank loan interest and charges loan-related expenses from companies. Banks refuse the proposal of Alibaba, as they hold such move aggravates consumers' burdens and bank risks. As they say, Alibaba that has developed Alibaba Micro-lending is unsatisfied with being an e-commerce platform and corporate information provider for banks, and it wants to charge 2% loan as a fee.

Alibaba considers that its integrity network has constituted the core competitiveness of all major banks, and it is reasonable for it to gain some earnings as the provider of core competitiveness. It sounds irrational to banks. The banking industry universally views it as irrational charge, and predicts its risks.[1]

Probably the truth doesn't matter at all. What counts is that during this period, Alibaba successfully utilizes its trading data to develop a set of credit assessment indicator system, credit database and loan risk control measures. This means that Alibaba has launched a combat of big data. Even if it loses support from banks, Alibaba can still make it with big data.

Great Leap of Platform Finance Since 2010

In 2010, when Alibaba was still cooperating with CCB and ICBC, it had attained the license of petty loan. In June 2010, Alibaba jointly established Zhejiang Alibaba Petty Loan Co., Ltd with Fosun International Limited, Yintai Group and Wanxiang Group, with registered capital totaling 600 million yuan. Next year, Zhejiang Alibaba altogether issued 2.8 billion yuan to over 40,000 micro companies and 99.9% of the loan was below 500,000 yuan. In June 2011, Alibaba cooperated

[1] Data source: http://www.ccb.com/cn/ccbtoday/20120827_1346054064.html.

with Fosun International Limited, Yintai Group and Wanxiang Group to establish Chongqing Alibaba Petty Loan Co., Ltd, with registered capital totaling 1 billion yuan. Chongqing Alibaba continually utilized accumulated consumer credit data and behavioral data, and combined with advanced micro-lending technology and professional risk control experience to map e-commerce behavioral data to corporate and individual operation conditions and dynamic trends. It is also devoted to providing short-term and convenient pure credit petty loan services with the upper limit of 500,000 yuan for platform merchants.

The successive establishment of Zhejiang Alibaba and Chongqing Alibaba marks the birth of platform finance under big data. This is the platform finance in real sense. Alibaba fully uses all sorts of accumulated data on the platform to finish credit rating on merchants. In September 2012, Alibaba Chongqing Shangcheng Financing Guarantee Company was founded. Its foundation solves the misgivings of Alibaba Micro-lending and signals Alibaba's organic combination of deposit, loan and remittance business.

Suning follows the step of Alibaba. It established Chongqing Suning Petty Loan Co., Ltd in September 2012, with registered capital totaling 300 million yuan. Hong Kong Suning and Suning Commerce Group, respectively, account for 25 and 75%. Chongqing Suning primarily offers petty loan service to micro companies on Suning platform.

Subsequently, Alibaba established the second petty loan company in Chongqing in August 2013—Alibaba Micro-lending Co., Ltd, with registered capital totaling 200 million yuan. Baidu and Tencent were also unwilling to lag behind. In September 2013, Baidu established petty loan company in Shanghai, with registered capital totaling 200 million yuan. Tencent established TenPay Network Finance Petty Loan Co., Ltd in Shenzhen in December 2013, with registered capital totaling 30 million yuan. It is committed to providing petty loan business for Tencent e-commerce operators.

By late 2013, Alibaba Micro-lending had served 642,000 users, and issued 172.2 billion yuan. Average household credit was 130,000 yuan, and loan balance was less than 40,000 yuan. The non-performing loan ratio was below 1%. In particular, it additionally issued 100 billion yuan in 2013.

Business Pattern of Platform Finance

Comparing with supply chain finance, the business pattern of platform finance does not take all companies in the industry chain into consideration, but just analyzes buyers' credit records and trading data accumulated by the platform to assess buyers' credit condition and repayment ability, and then decide whether to issue the loan.

Case 1: Alibaba Petty Loan

Alibaba Petty Loan is the earliest big data-based platform finance company in China, and also the most sound and representative operation mode for the time being. Comparing with commercial banks which prescribe sophisticated formalities and rigorous credit loan conditions and private petty loan companies which hardly access corporate and individual credit investigation data, Alibaba Petty Loan inevitably possesses overwhelming advantages in this field. Alibaba Petty Loan not only cultivates substantial small- and medium-sized company users and commands their core data, but also provides credit support. The perfect combination of the three constitutes online platform finance. By analyzing and excavating online data, Alibaba Petty Loan presents credit reports of small- and medium-sized companies and utilizes Internet to issue loans promptly and timely.

It not only tackles the chronic illness faced by traditional banks in high threshold and sophisticated formalities, but also compensates folk petty loan companies' disadvantages in data inadequacy. As shown by the statistics of Alibaba, annual micro-lending financial business income in 2012–2014, respectively, reached 108 million yuan, 540 million yuan, 174.8 billion yuan. Comparing with other petty loan companies, Alibaba Petty Loan has a rather large mass. In June 2014, Alibaba announced to launch a pure credit loan product "Network Business Loan Advanced Edition" oriented toward small- and medium-sized companies in cooperation with 7 banks. Just one month after the launch, 58 companies passed the audit, and accumulated credit granting balance reached 1.2 billion yuan.

At present, Alibaba Petty Loan mainly comprises Alibaba Loan, Taobao Loan and Factoring Loan. Especially, Alibaba Loan targets at Alibaba's B2B companies, including "Trust Pass" credit loan (oriented toward "Trust Pass" small and micro member companies engaged in domestic trading), Network Business Loan (oriented toward former Alibaba cross-border trading "China Supplier" small and micro member companies), AliSecure (provide security deposit for "China Supplier" members and ensure buyers' prepayment security), AE Fast Loan (an instant credit product designed for Alibaba "AliExpress" members to quickly recoup capital) and order loan. Taobao Loan is mainly aimed at small- and medium-sized buyers on Taobao and Tmall, including order loan and credit loan. Factoring Loan business is aimed at air travel merchants' factoring business, including air travel factoring business, air travel credit loan and payment in advance.

According to specific loan type, Alibaba loan includes circulating loan and fixed loan. Like excess reserves, circulating loan is available at any time with no interest rate. Fixed loan issues one-time loan to applicants. The daily interest rate of circulating loan and fixed loan is 0.06 and 0.05%, respectively. Both of the two types of loans have the longest term of one year and the limit ranging between 50,000 and 1 million. Taobao/Tmall order loan sellers are able to apply for loans via the shipment order, and the longest term of loan lasts for 60 days with 0.05% daily interest rate. By virtue of credit records, Taobao/Tmall credit loan sellers can directly apply for loan with no guarantee and pledge and the longest term of loan lasts for one year. The daily interest rate of 12-month credit loan, six-month credit loan and three-month credit loan is 0.05, 0.06 and 0.05%, respectively (Table 1).

Alibaba Petty Loan application includes the following stages:

Application stage: Consumers who have prepared to apply for a loan may log on Alibaba Petty Loan's homepage to submit the application online. The applicant shall fill in personal information like name of company, name of legal person, phone, e-mail address and application limit. After receiving the application, Alibaba Petty Loan will investigate consumers' accumulated information on the platform, including credit records, trading records, financial information and inventory information. For non-B2B business, the trading is transacted and automatically assessed via the platform with no need of offline investigation. While as to its B2B business, Alibaba Petty Loan empowers third-party professional agencies to directly make field visit to companies, keep track of corporate business conditions and take a picture of it if necessary. Afterward, Alibaba Petty Loan will confirm the survey results of third-party institutions with consumers via phone for ensuring information authenticity.

Table 1 Overview of Alibaba Loan and Taobao Loan

Feature	*Alibaba Loan*	*Taobao/Tmall Order Loan*	*Taobao/Tmall Credit Loan*
Platform type	B2B Provide credit loan for Alibaba corporate consumers	B2C C2C Provide order loan for Taobao and Tmall buyers	B2C C2C Provide credit loan for Taobao and Tmall buyers
Loan limit	50,000 ~ 1 million yuan	Upper limit 1 million yuan	Upper limit 1 million yuan
Longest term	1 year	60 days	1 year
Means of loan	Circulation loan: set an amount of money as the reserve with no interest rate in unused state and consumers can borrow and make payment at any time Fixed loan: issue the loan upon approval	Buyers can apply for a loan with shipment orders	Buyers can also apply for with no guarantee and pledge by virtue of credit records
Loan interest rate	Circulation loan: daily interest rate 0.06% (approximately 21.9% annual interest rate), simple interest Fixed loan: daily interest rate 0.05% (approximately 18.25% annual interest rate)	Daily interest rate 0.05% (approximately 18.25% annual interest rate)	The daily interest rate of credit loan with 12-month credit granting term is 0.05%, and that of 6-month and 3-month credit granting term is respectively 0.06% and 0.05%

Data source China Internet Finance Report 2014

Approval stage: The approval stage of Alibaba Petty Loan is the core of the procedure. First of all, Alibaba Petty Loan analyzes consumers' credit data, trading data and payment data accumulated at Alibaba, Taobao, Tmall and Juhuasuan platforms, and confirms the authenticity of consumer information with network data pattern, online video survey pattern, crosscheck technology (assisted with third-party verification), therefore converting consumer big data to behavioral "portrait" to the uttermost, and further assessing their credit level and repayment ability.

The supervision stage: Upon payment, Alibaba and AliCloud will supervise merchants' trading condition and cash flow in real time and make sure of the proper use of capital. In case of any variation of capital use, the system will emit risk alarm and recollect the loan ahead of time.

The recycle stage: By resorting the Internet platform to supervisor corporate operation dynamics and behaviors, all behaviors possibly affecting normal performance of contract will be warmed. Given that, it is sensible to execute online store/account shut-down mechanism, improve consumer penalty cost and effectively control loan risks.

In terms of its means of repayment, Alibaba Petty Loan chooses installment average capital plus interest repayment means. Consumers are supposed to transfer repayment capital from bank card to Alipay or directly leave enough balance in Alipay for auto-deduction. In condition of prior repayment, Alibaba Petty Loan would also charge 3% of principal as the service charge. In condition of expiry, it would collect 1.5 times of daily interest rate as the penalty cost.

By far, the non-performing loan ratio of Alibaba Petty Loan is just 1.02%. Comparing with the 5.5–6% non-performing loan ratio level among small and micro companies in entire banking industry, Alibaba has done a fairly good job in risk control. Now, the foremost and most valuable asset of Alibaba should be its accumulated big data. How to rationally develop and use data rests in the key to success. The success of Alibaba Petty Loan demonstrates that Alibaba has been on the right track of applying big data in credit rating. Once small and micro companies' credit problem has been solved, and credit pricing has been made as per corresponding credit level, financing will be no more a bother.

Case source http://blog.sina.com.cn/s/blog_8d95b38c0101bkjs.html and http://kuaixun.stcn.com/2014/0207/11146957.shtml.

Furthermore, mainstream big data financial products on the market are basically the same in loan provider, credit granting evidence, loan limit, interest rate, application condition, service scope and loan term. The loan flow is basically designed to cater to the characteristics of small- and medium-sized companies featured by short term, high frequency and fast speed. It signals the core of big data finance. Prime data comprises trading data and business reputation data (credit data). Thus it can be seen that alike companies inspired by Alibaba all afford credit granting service to small- and medium-sized companies based on the two types of data. Concerning source of capital, probably different modes have different sources. Table 2 shows that besides Alibaba Petty Loan, other platforms all cooperate with banks to issue loans (Table 3).

Table 2 Comparison of big data financial products

Characteristics	*Alibaba Petty Loan*	*HC 360.com New E-lending*	*CCB Dunhuang.com E Insurance Pass*	*Wangsheng Gold Trust*	*JD*
Loan prodiver	Alibaba Petty Loan	CMBC	CCB	CEB, CITIC and other banks	JD and BOC
Granting evidence	Trust Pass Trading data	HC 360.com business reputation data	Dunhuang.com trading records and accumulated credit	Toocle data	JD Trading data
	No guarantee and pledge	No guarantee and pledge	No guarantee and pledge	Guarantee pledge	No guarantee and pledge
Loan limit	50,000 ~ 100,000 yuan	30,000 ~ 500,000 yuan	Upper limit 20 million yuan	50,000 ~ 5 million yuan	
Interest rate	18% Fixed loan Annual interest rate 21.9% Circulation loan Annual interest rate	11.52% ~ 16.25% installment loan Annual interest rate 14.04% ~ 16.25% Circulation loan Annual interest rate	BOC six-month coterminous rate rises by 20%, and monthly interest rate is below 1.2%	6.56% ~ 13.3%	10% ~ 30% Benchmark interest rate rises by 10%-30%
Application conditions	Trust Pass "China Supplier" member	HC 360.com "Maimaitong" membe	Dunhuang.com Registered	Member of Wangsheng Toocle	JD Mall supplier
	Company Legal person certification	Company Legal person certification	Legal person certification or individual business qualification	Company Legal person certification	

(continued)

Table 2 (continued)

Characteristics	*Alibaba Petty Loan*	*HC 360.com New E-lending*	*CCB Dunhuang.com E Insurance Pass*	*Wangsheng Gold Trust*	*JD*
	Two-year working or real estate proof	Work or house property certificate		Financial statement in recent three years	
Service area	Shanghai, Zhejiang, Jiangsu	People's livelihood branch location (69 areas)	Nationwide	Zhejiang	Nationwide
Length of maturity	12 months	Valid for 3 years, convenient lending and repayment	For 12 months Circulation loan	Lasting for 3 or 6 months	

Data source http://huaban.com/pins/165806138/

Table 3 Comparison of platform finance and supply chain finance

Comparison	*Platform finance*	*Supply chain finance*
Common points	They all belong to big data finance; assess and issue loan according to trading data and credit accumulated by the platform; face data analysis risks, credit risks and consumer shortage risks	
Differences	They usually do not engage in trading; just provide bilateral trading data; just focus on sellers	Some platforms may intervene in trading and constitute the supply chain; review loan from the holistic perspective of supply chain

We hereby place platform finance and supply chain finance together for comparison. It clearly shows that the two are basically the same in nature. Both of them assess the credit of financing companies on the basis of big data analysis, lower bilateral information asymmetry and reduce loan risks. So they are both in the field of big data finance. Admittedly, the two are also exposed to risks of big data finance, including data analysis risks, credit risks and consumer shortage risks.

On the other hand, there also exist a great many differences between the two. E-commerce platforms in platform finance usually keep away from trading but just present the data of bilateral trading parties. Likewise, they just notice sellers in loans. At times, e-commerce platforms would intervene trading in supply chain finance. For instance, JD is one link of supply chain. While offering loans, such e-commerce platforms tend to review companies from the perspective of entire supply chain.

Bottleneck of Platform Finance

Shortage of Loanable Capital

Liquidity is a universal problem faced by petty loan companies. The reason is that petty loan companies usually have rather low registered capital, ranging between 100 million ~ 1 billion yuan. As consumers increase or loan scale expands, they inevitably feel short of loanable capital. However, as stipulated by *Guidance on the Pilot Projects for Petty Loan Companies* issued by CBRC and PBC, the capital source of petty loan companies is limited to equity and donation, and financing capital from banks shall not exceed 50% of net capital. The net capital of three Alibaba Petty Loan companies totals 1.8 billion yuan. In this way, external loanable capital just makes up 900 million yuan, and loanable capital totals 2.7 billion yuan. Though related encouraging policies in Zhejiang and Chongqing allow petty loan companies to raise the financing proportion to 100% net capital after satisfying specific conditions, general loanable amount just totals 3.6 billion yuan far from satisfying loan demands. Even if Zhejiang Internet Bank has been approved, related problems have not been solved yet, including non-on-site opening of account. Because of this reason, Alibaba Petty Loan can't solve the plight of capital shortage by attracting deposits via Network Business Bank.

The practice taken by Alibaba to solve liquidity inadequacy is asset securitization, i.e. transferring securities to other financial institutions to gain enough liquidity. Corporate asset securitization generally transfers creditor's rights or foreseeable income of the issuing company as core assets to corresponding special project management programs. Special project management programs are internally made up of priority income voucher and secondary income voucher, in which the former is held by investors and the latter by the issuing company. Above-mentioned voucher income is paid by the cash income generated from core assets.

In June 2012, Chongqing Alibaba Petty Loan issued "Alibaba Finance Micro-credit Asset Usufruct Investment Program Collective Trust Plan" to Shandong Trust and raised 240 million yuan from the society. Subsequently, in September, Chongqing Alibaba Petty Loan re-issued "Alibaba No.2 Star Collective Trust Plan" to raise 120 million yuan from the society. The reason why it decides to cooperate with a non-securities company is the term mismatch between Alibaba Petty Loan featured by small amount, short term and convenient lending and repayment and assets backed securities featured by long term.

In March 2013, *Provisions for Asset Securitization Business in Securities Companies* formally issued by CSRC allowed companies to buy new underlying assets generated by underlying assets cash flow in circulation to compose a basic asset pool. This made Alibaba's asset securitization possible.

On July 4 2013, Oriental Securities Asset Management—Alibaba No.1- No.10 Special Asset Management Plan gained the approval from CSRC. It is the first securitization program based on credit asset in the securities industry. The issue takes the creditor's right formed by Alibaba Petty Loan's loan totaling 5 billion yuan as the basic asset and raises capital by 10 non-scheduled special asset management plans within 3 years, with each issue granting 200 million –5 million yuan. The asset securitization is a special asset management plan in which Alibaba Petty Loan sells its loan totaling 5 million yuan to Oriental Securities and altogether issues securities worth of 5 billion yuan by loan portfolio. Based on the portfolio, investors subscribe prior securities worth of 4 billion yuan and Alibaba subscribe secondary securities worth of 1 billion yuan. The securities are to be repaid by the capital and interest totaling 5 billion yuan in the loan portfolio. In particular, prior securities should be repaid before secondary securities. In reality, Alibaba Petty Loan sells the loan totaling 4 billion yuan to securities investors by asset securitization and recollects 4 billion yuan to issue new loans. In another word, small- and medium-sized companies that have gained loans totaling 4 billion yuan successfully acquire financing in the capital market. Before the expiry of securities, if the loan in loan portfolio is paid, the capital gained can be used to buy new loans. It interprets how to compose a basic capital pool with capital flow caused by basic assets and buy new basic assets in circulation. Such circulation lasts until the expiry of securities. By way of this means, the term mismatch between short-term loan and long-term loan could be fixed. At the same time, Alibaba Petty Loan can also gain extra income from asset securitization. The annual loan interest rate of Chongqing Alibaba Petty Loan ranges between 18 and 21%, and the expected income rate of asset securitization products is around 6%. Except expenses in asset securitization operations, Alibaba Petty Loan can also gain income. By October 2013, Alibaba had issued No.1–4 special asset management plans.[2]

In July 2013, Alibaba cooperated with Wanjia Fund-Wanjia Win–win Asset Management to issue Wanjia Win–win-Alibaba Petty Loan Special Multi-consumer Asset Management Plan and invested 200 million yuan. The basic asset of the securitization product is the loan provided by Zhejiang Alibaba Petty Loan and corresponding priority and sub-priority proportion is 9:1.[3]

In July 2013, Alibaba Petty Loan and THAMCO Asset Management under Minsheng Insurance jointly issued Alibaba Petty Loan Program Asset Support Plan. It is the program asset support plan set based on Alibaba Petty Loan's credit asset, and also the first insurance

[2] Data source: http://tech.ifeng.com/internet/detail_2013_04/08/23955154_1.shtml.

[3] Data source: http://www.taoguba.com.cn/Article/852806/1.

asset management asset securitization program. Initial fund-raising sum amounts to 200–300 million yuan, in which insurance capital subscribes priority shares and Alibaba subscribes remaining shares.[4]

In 2014, Alibaba, CMBC and CITIC jointly invested in Alibaba Petty Loan creditor's right bank wealth management products. "Alibaba Star No.4" jointly issued by Alibaba and CMBC was launched in two stages, respectively, on November 17 and 24, and "CITIC Benefit Plan Robust Series No.8" jointly issued by Alibaba and CITIC was launched in three stages. It is the first bank wealth management product invested in petty loan companies. Phase 1 CITIC Benefit Plan Robust Series No.8 (wealth management serial number: A120A0068) was founded on September 26, 2012 and expired till September 26, 2013. Upon expiry, product annual yield of rate was 5.5%. Product capital invested in the receivable creditor's right in Zhejiang Alibaba Petty Loan and Chongqing Balibaba Petty Loan with 100% investment proportion.[5]

By far, capital sources of Alibaba Petty Loan involve trust, securities, fund, insurance and banks. In addition, with the launch of Alibaba self-built network banks, Alibaba Petty Loan solves former technical problems such as non-on-site opening of account, and is able to compensate the inadequacy of loanable capital by direct deposits.

Restriction of Loan Region

According to *Guidance on the Pilot Projects for Petty Loan Companies*, petty loan companies can only develop petty loan pilot projects in counties of the province (prefecture and city) where they are located in. By contrast, Alibaba Petty Loan has a wide range of consumers nationwide. Its loan service oriented toward other consumers outside Zhejiang and Chongqing obviously breaches related provisions about petty loan pilot projects. In 2011, Toabao Order Loan passed the review at the joint conference presided by Zhejiang Province Financial Affairs Office and Trade and Industry Bureau, and was approved to expand the target of network loan to the whole nation. This decision removes barriers in the cross-regional business operation of Alibaba Petty Loan to some degree. But many other problems should not be overlooked as well. As petty loan business in other regions is managed by local Financial Affairs Office,

[4] Data source: http://finance.sina.com.cn/roll/20130719/022616173401.shtml.

[5] Data source: http://finance.21cbh.com–xintuo_1019/863074.html.

Zhejiang Provincial Government's approval concerning the expansion of loan target may not gain the recognition from other peer units at the same level. Therefore, the feasibility of the policy remains pending. Moreover, no specific regulation policy for Internet loan has been formulated yet. Alibaba Petty Loan claims that though its consumers spread across the country, business operation is transacted by the headquarters in Hangzhou. Therefore, it does not engage in cross-regional operation. It remains to be seen if such claim is tenable.

3 Supply Chain Finance

Core companies in traditional finance have been always the focus of banks, and banks usually provide substantial capital support, preferential capital interest rate and flexible loan term. While as upstream and downstream suppliers and distributors of core companies lack scale, power and valid mortgage, and face high business cost, great risks and weak scale effects, they can't obtain the preference of bank credit capital all the time. Since suppliers need to handle with the long term of payment, and distributors need to handle with the slow term of repayment, upstream and downstream companies of core companies are under heavy capital pressures. This severely affects the efficient operation of entire supply chain. Subject to the lack of credit rating, financial companies can't make credit rating or risk pricing for upstream and downstream companies in a traditional way. Under such circumstances, banks can only reduce the scale of credit for security (Fig. 3).

Different from traditional finance which focuses on core companies' financing demands, supply chain finance is more concerned about the adequacy of corporate capital in the supply chain from the perspective of supply chain. In line with the "cask theory", the amount of water is decided by the shortest plank. By the same token, the development of a company is more decided by the cooperation among companies in entire value chain, instead of any single company. For instance, if upstream manufacturers provide inadequate raw materials, downstream manufacturers can't finish the production of large orders. If downstream manufacturers come to a halt in sales, any supply of upstream manufacturers is of no use. Therefore, entirety of whole supply chain is the key to decide the success of products in many cases. Supply chain management is especially necessary for industries with long supply chain such as airplane, vehicle, steel and iron (Table 4).

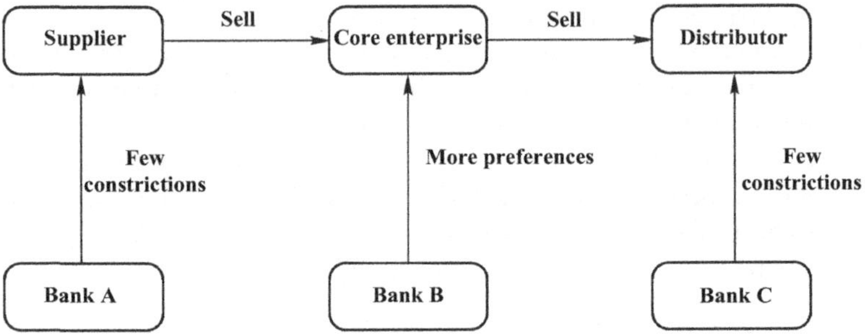

Fig. 3 Relation between banks and supply chain members in traditional finance mode (*Data source* Research Report for Chinese Internet Finance Industry Investment in 2014)

Supply chain finance is produced to solve corporate financing problems in entire supply chain during supply chain management process. Generally, a supply chain is usually composed of the "1 + N pattern", one core company and N cooperation companies included. When ordinary companies cooperate with core companies, they should on the one hand ensure timely supply of products, and on the other hand undertake burdens caused by long term of repayment. In particular, for corporate suppliers who have long term of repayment, their capital pressures are far beyond imagination. Inadequate capital liquidity in turn restricts the supply of suppliers, and further affects the operation of core companies and entire supply chain. It is far from satisfactory to solve the capital liquidity of one or few companies in supply chain. The task of supply chain finance is to ensure the smoothness of corporate capital in entire supply chain.

Case 2: Baorui Hengxin

Beijing Baorui Hengxin Commerce Co., Ltd (Baorui Hengxin) is a medium-sized supplier of JD. It provides four loans totaling 1 million yuan for JD once a month, with 10% interest rate and 30-day term of payment. Plus storage and liquidation procedures, the repayment takes around 45 days. Besides, the company has fortnight security stage reserves totaling 2 million yuan. Annual interest rate totals $100 \times 10\% \times 12 = 1.2$ million yuan, and corresponding capital rate of return is $120/200 = 60\%$. By way of JD supply chain financial service, JD provides guarantee, banks issue loans, and Baorui Hengxin just needs to pay 5.8% annual interest

Table 4 Comparison of traditional credit and supply chain finance

Differences	*Traditional credit*	*Supply chain finance*
Credit granting target	Single company	Single or multiple companies in specific supply chain
Participant	Commercial banks, financing companies	Banks, core companies, logistics, small- and medium-sized companies
Lending time	Short-term, mid-term and long-term lending	Short-term lending
Credit granting condition	Fixed asset pledge or guarantee	Pledge of movables, property pledge
Repayment capital	Corporate working capital	Pledge realization, receivables repayment
Counter-guarantee role	Non	Core company
Loan property	Successively issued credit loans	Self-liquidated, closed and constant
Bank risks	High	Low
Product type	Single species	Diverse species
Rating perspective	Corporate credit rating or pledge condition	Entire strength and trading authenticity of supply chain
Risk control methods	Static focus on corporate	Dynamics track of corporate operation conditions
Consumer development methods	Point-to-point development	Development of upstream and downstream nodes in core companies
Consumer development cost	High	Low
Service target	Capital demands of a single company	Continually decrease the capital cost of supply chain
Service proposal	Homogeneity	Strong pertinence and huge discrepancy

Data source Tian Jiahuan, *Supply Chain Finance and Credit Risk Control*, Zhejiang Industry and Commerce University Press, 2013

rate. In this way, the capital operating efficiency of Baorui Hengxin is greatly promoted. The price of Baorui Hengxin is to pay loan interest rate in exchange for higher capital turnover rate. Weekly delivery amount of Baorui Hengxin is 250,000 yuan. It gets payment at the moment and then makes preparations for storage next week and security storage for the week after next. Weekly security storage here refers to the storage the week after next. It doesn't necessarily refer to security storage. After all, if the company needs to prepare fortnight storage, it does not take any security storage at all. It means that Baorui Hengxin can therefore take 500,000 yuan to transact the business worth of 2 million yuan. The annual profits remain $120 \times (1-5.8\%) = 1{,}130{,}000$ yuan after deducting the interest rate, and capital rate of return increases by 2.77 times to 226%. Throughout supply chain finance, Baorui Hengxin improves its capital rate of return and capital operating efficiency and greatly alleviates its capital pressures.

Case data source Chen Yanyan, Suning and JD's Attempt in "Petty Loan", *Securities Daily*, December 12, 2012.

Supply chain finance based on core companies in supply chain comprehends upstream and downstream companies' production and operation conditions via core companies, provides financing services to satisfy their capital demands. In comparison with traditional finance, supply chain finance is more concerned about the pivotal role of core companies, and meantime, stresses the financial support for upstream and downstream companies. In this way, it ensures capital liquidity in entire supply chain. Supply chain finance, centered around core companies, judges the operation condition and repayment condition of small- and medium-sized companies according to the trading relation between core companies and small- and medium-sized companies, like procurement, sales and storage. Comparing with traditional finance which simply examines small- and medium-sized companies' operation conditions, it proves to be more efficient. At this point, supply chain finance has inherited plain big data thinking, but it fails to walk out of the scope of traditional finance. It is because that it is still a traditional risk control means in need of guarantee and pledge (Figs. 4 and 5).

Admittedly, traditional supply chain finance indeed alleviates the financing dilemma faced by small- and medium-sized companies in supply chain, and increases financing efficiency. But it is far from satisfactory to the financing demands of numerous small- and medium-sized companies, especially those on e-commerce platform. Short of guarantee and pledge, the loan demands of these companies are limited, frequent and fast. The core to this problem is corporate credit investigation. Then how to measure and assess corporate credit? The solution can be found from big data. Backed by big data accumulated on the e-commerce platform,

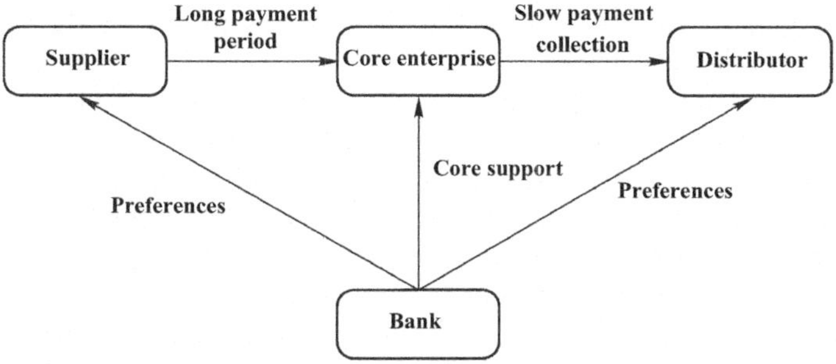

Fig. 4 Relation between banks and supply chain members in supply chain finance mode (*Data source* Research Report for Chinese Internet Finance Industry Investment in 2014)

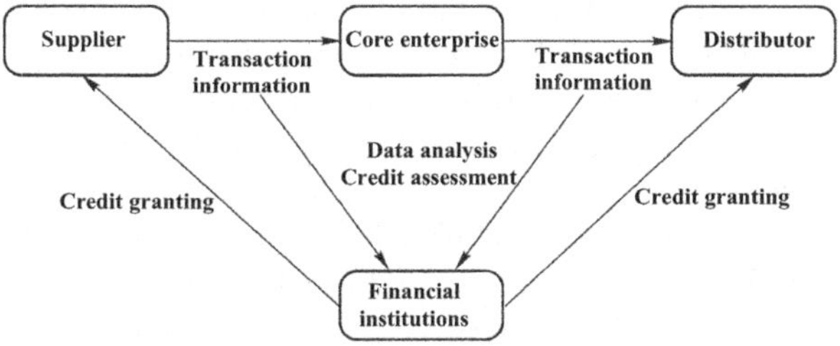

Fig. 5 Relation between financial institutions and supply chain members in supply chain finance mode under big data

it is totally practical to measure the credit rating of small- and medium-sized companies. Therefore, even without pledge assets and guarantee, small- and medium-sized companies can still satisfy financing risk control requirements by credit rating, and successfully obtain loans. This is the expression of big data in supply chain finance.

Development History of Supply Chain Finance

Supply chain finance business in China began in mid and late 1990s. At first, it came into existence because joint-stock commercial banks explored supply chain business to avoid ferocious market competition. Shenzhen

Development is the pioneer of this field which ushers in the trend of supply chain finance.

Shenzhen Development has been always leading supply chain finance. As early as 1999, Shenzhen Development began to exploit loan business for small- and medium-sized companies. Through assessing supply chain and core companies, it broke through the bill business for upstream and downstream industries, and launched pledge business pattern oriented toward small- and medium-sized companies. This is the embryo of earliest supply chain finance. In 2003, Shenzhen Development further launched self-liquidated trading financing business and "1 + N" supply chain financing operation philosophy to reinforce core company-based credit of upstream and downstream companies in the supply chain and issue wholesale loan. In 2005, Shenzhen Development formally launched supply chain finance service, and independently developed debt rating system oriented toward supply chain companies to relieve corporate credit investigation difficulties. Through innovating supply chain financing products in the field of receivables, advance payment, inventory and electronic settlement, Shenzhen Development proposed the concept of "pool financing". Till late June 2010, Shenzhen Development supply chain finance loan scale totaled 145.4 billion yuan, with non-performing loan ratio of 0.35%. Its business scope included more than 20 industries, like iron and steel, vehicle, oil, coal, non-ferrous metals, minerals, rubber, and plastic. In 2011, Shenzhen Development credit balance totaled 224.6 billion yuan and its non-performing loan ratio decreased to 0.26%.[6]

In effect, after Shenzhen Development's launch of supply chain finance business, numerous joint-stock banks represented by CMBC (2002), CGB (2003), CMBC (2005), ICBC (2006), Industrial Bank (2006), SPDB (2007) and Huaxia Bank (2008) successively marched to this industry. For a time, supply chain finance turned to be the hot spot of business innovation in all major industries.

In 2002, by virtue of its advantage on electronic technical platforms, CMBC began to engage in "electronic supply chain finance" business and managed to develop supply chain finance Internet business. It intended to serve the whole supply chain through offering a series of electronic financial derivatives. CMBC electronic supply chain finance pertains to supply

[6] Zheng Xiaowei, Research on Supply Chain Finance Pattern and Risks, Shijiazhuang: Hebei University of Economics and Business, 2014.

chain finance networking conducive to raising financial service efficiency. Its nature is still traditional supply chain finance.

In 2003, CGB released financial service plan covering 18 credit granting innovation patterns. In November 2005, CMBC established Trading Finance Department and positioned the development strategy of "insisting on a professional path and releasing featured trading finance".

In June 2005, ICBC launched Wal-Mart supplier factoring business pilot projects, and took advantage of Wal-Mart's credit to offer full-process financing support for suppliers and solve their financing difficulties. At present, "Wal-Mart Supplier Financing Solution" has become one of the typical cases in commercial bank supply chain finance business practice. In July 2010, ICBC further launched online supply chain financing service and extended the scope of service once again.

In July 2006, Industrial Bank developed "Golden Sesame" to design 18 products for the procurement, sales and production link of small- and medium-sized companies in the operation process. In 2008, Industrial Bank joined the trading facility service developed by SWIFT Organization, and processed centralized matching orders, shipping documents and invoices to cut down information asymmetry between companies and the bank. In September 2010, Industrial Bank prepared to build Trading Finance Center and established supply chain finance basic framework. In 2011, Industrial Bank supply chain finance confirmed the "M + 1 + N" development pattern and widened its scope of business.

In 2007, SPDB launched supply chain financing overall solution and integrated supply chain financing service, electronic service and offshore bank service into supply chain finance service, including purchaser support plan, online account management plan, intra-district corporate trading financing plan, supplier support plan, ship exporting service plan, engineering contract credit support plan etc.[7]

In 2008, Huaxia Bank launched its supply chain financial brand "Financing Win–win Chain", covering future property in goods, pledge of property in goods, goods pledge, receivables, overseas repayment, global certified payment and international voucher. In the meantime, it also integrated the international and domestic business of supply chain finance and resorted international business to expand scope of service.

[7] Chen Cheng, Supply Chain Finance and Risk Management Strategy, Shanghai: East China Normal University, 2011.

Prior to 2008, supply chain finance was still the exclusive feast of banks. As of 2009, with the continuous entry of e-commerce giants, supply chain finance patterns and implications had experienced drastic changes, and supply chain finance pattern featured by big data was shaping up step by step.

Accompanied by the sustained and prompt growth of e-commerce, small- and medium-sized buyers on the platform encounter increasingly prominent financing constraints. In order to solve this problem, e-commerce giants start to consider making credit rating on small- and medium-sized companies with considerable data accumulated by the platform and solve their difficulties in financing because of lack of pledge and guarantee. E-commerce giants connect considerable data to core companies. By associating upstream suppliers, core companies and downstream distributors and logistics companies in the supply chain, they provide supply chain financing via data analysis, and realize financing networking. A series of e-commerce-based supply chain financial modes like JD supply chain and Dunhuang.com successively spring up. These supply chain financial patterns are totally different from past traditional bank supply chain finance patterns. Such difference can be either proved by source of capital, but also severe deviation in credit investigation, rating, credit investigation and risk control behavioral concepts. Big data begins to dominate supply chain financing process.

As proved by the development history of supply chain finance, Chinese supply chain finance has undergone three stages, i.e. traditional supply chain finance stage, online supply chain finance stage and e-commerce supply chain finance stage. In the first stage, commercial banks cooperate with companies in the supply chain offline, and offer capital support based on the assessment of entire supply chain. In the second stage, the core is the online service of supply chain finance. Commercial banks begin to connect with the system of core companies so as to keep pace with online and offline companies' business operation conditions in the supply chain and offer financing services. The third stage is e-commerce supply chain finance stage. E-commerce companies are able to make credit investigation and credit granting for upstream and downstream companies with big data analysis method. The removal of pledge and guarantee marks a big revolution in supply chain finance. In the strict sense, the first stage is not the supply chain finance under big data. The role of big data emerges till the second stage, but it is still the online form of service in the first stage. The third stage witnesses big data supply chain finance in real sense. In the third stage, big data plays a decisive role.

Case 3: Wal-Mart Supplier Financing Solution

The thinking of supplier financing solution provided by ICBC for Wal-Mart suppliers is that "suppliers apply for order financing from ICBC to organize production and preparation upon receiving Wal-Mart's orders and ICBC issues the loan. When suppliers finish production and transport products to Wal-Mart, they shall submit invoice, warehouse warrant and other documents to ICBC. ICBC transacts receivables factoring financing for suppliers. In this way, suppliers can repay order financing loan. Upon the expiry of loan, when Wal-Mart makes payment to suppliers, they may directly transfer the capital to suppliers' receiving account in ICBC and ICBC therefore recollects factoring financing". With this solution, suppliers can complete pre-order financing and post-delivery receivable financing and relieve capital pressures during full production process. Therefore, the business gains widespread praise in the industry.

Case data source Jiang Rong, E-commerce Giants' Successive Access to Supply Chain Finance, *China Business Journal*, December 24, 2012.

Supply Chain Finance Pattern

Receivable Financing

Traditional receivable financing takes place when upstream suppliers deliver products to downstream companies, and downstream companies issue receivable invoices. Following suppliers' submission of invoices to commercial banks as the pledge, commercial banks will issue a loan and downstream companies repay the loan to banks in the end. In this pattern, upstream suppliers actually transfer loan creditor's rights and commercial banks gain the qualification of loan. In nature, such move is pledge for loan behavior. The sole credit risk is whether downstream companies can make timely payment. On the part of supplier financing, it is nothing about credit (Figs. 6, 7, and 8).

While the big data-based receivable financing flow is much more concise. When suppliers sign up the contract with downstream companies and transport the products, financial institutions may perform online credit assessment and risks control on considerable data in order, inventory, finance, and sales, and automatically issue loans to suppliers upon

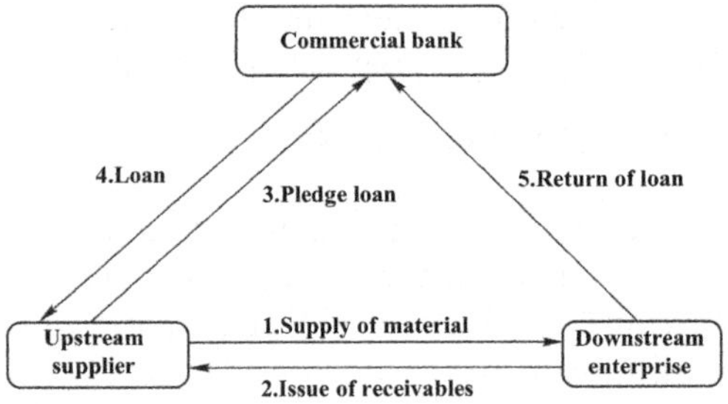

Fig. 6 Account receivable financing flow

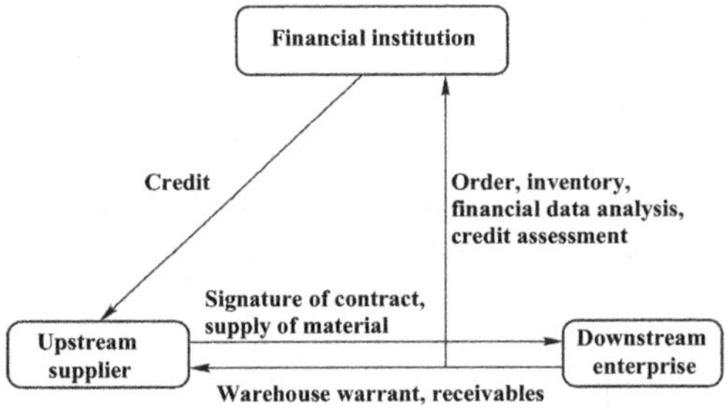

Fig. 7 Receivable financing flow under big data

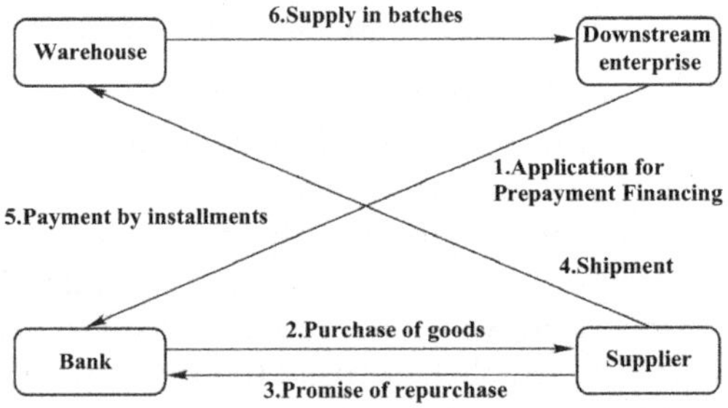

Fig. 8 Prepayment financing flow

approval. The whole process is finished via network. As the risk rating here is made by big data, no asset pledge and guarantee are involved. It means pure credit loan. Credit rating here mainly depends on big data.

Prepayment Financing

Prepayment financing requests the concerted cooperation among downstream companies, suppliers, commercial banks and warehouse. Banks begin to procure products from suppliers once downstream companies submit prepayment financing application. For fear that downstream companies fail to make payment to banks and this aggravates bank risks, suppliers must make promise to do counter purchase if necessary. Then suppliers shall transport products to the designated warehouse of banks. Whenever downstream companies make payment by installment, the warehouse will send pertinent products. Such prepayment financing means alleviates downstream companies' heavy prepayment pressures.

Prepayment financing based on big data is also a similar method. It directly analyzes considerable data, including order, sales, inventory and finance, and directly issues prepayment amount.

Inventory Financing

Inventory financing refers to the action in which financing companies apply for a pledge loan with existing inventory from banks. After submitting the financing application to banks, financing companies shall pledge the inventory in the warehouse designated by banks, and then present proof to banks. Banks offer credit loan to financing companies accordingly (Fig. 9).

Inventory financing under big data may be also completed with related inventory data of financing companies, rather than inventory pledge. To sum up, big data-based credit rating here replaces mortgage and pledge. They are two totally different means of solving credit risks.

As proved by the comparison of above-mentioned three traditional supply chain financing means, it can be fitly judged that all companies in the supply chain should have pledge, either creditor's rights or products, in financing no matter what position they are in the supply chain, what stage they are in and what the purpose of financing is. Whereas, the

Fig. 9 Inventory financing flow

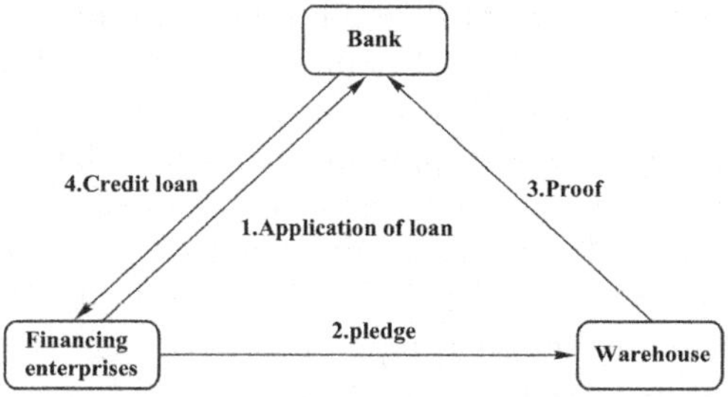

Table 5 Comparison with traditional financing mode

Differences	*Receivable financing*	*Repayment financing*	*Inventory financing*
Pledge	Creditor's right	Procurement of products	Inventory
Third-party	Non	Warehouse	Logistics
Financing purpose	Procurement of raw production materials	Payment by installments delivery in batch	Procurement of raw production materials
Financing company location	Upstream supplier creditor enterprise	Downstream manufacturer and distributor	Any enterprise
Production period of financing enterprise	Waiting for collection before delivery	Production of procured materials	Any period

problem is that considerable small- and medium-sized companies do not have proper pledge, but their financing demands indeed exist. The challenge is how to make credit rating on them. Under such a context, big data analyzes considerable trading data of these small- and medium-sized companies and decides whether to approve of the credit granting. This technology removes the constraint of guarantee and pledge. Therefore, e-commerce platforms enjoy an edge in this regard (Table 5).

Category of Supply Chain Finance

As to main companies of supply chain finance under big data, there are three types of business, namely bank-company cooperation, e-commerce self-built platform cooperation, and e-commerce cooperation. The three types of business have different advantages and disadvantages, and all of them may exert their advantages to some degree. Whereas, none of them is prefect. They all request the test of substantial practices.

Bank-company cooperation type can be viewed as the online form of traditional supply chain finance. Banks acquire core companies and upstream and downstream companies' sales data, inventory data and financial data from the database of core companies, and issue loans according to the credit rating level. "CITIC + Haier" is a typical representative of such type. The advantage of such pattern is that its capital source comes from banks and cooperative companies just undertake limited risks. Besides the low cost of capital, bank financial products are diversified and have strong risk control ability. However, the drawback is that the high corporate financing threshold and long term of approval set by banks affect capital availability efficiency and obstruct corporate production progress. Therefore, such mode possesses more financing advantages to large and powerful entity companies. For instance, as traditional companies like iron and steel and vehicle involve many manufacturers, core companies can only provide adequate data.

E-commerce self-built platform pattern is the most promising branch of supply chain finance, such as JD's self-built supply chain financing products like Jingbaobei and JD Petty Loan. The advantage of such mode is that it can make credit rating via e-commerce big data, and quickly satisfy merchants' financing demands at a low cost. However, the accuracy of risk rating based on big data can be hardly ensured. Comparing with banks, e-commerce platforms naturally have limited risk control abilities. It is challenging for them to effectively use big data. Or otherwise, any careless mistake easily triggers considerable credit risks. Such pattern is very proper for merchants on e-commerce platforms. Such platforms which command merchants' data information can make rational assessment and timely issue a loan.

Case 4: JD Supply Chain Finance

JD supply chain finance is the best performer in this field by far, and also, its experience is very typical. Different from platform pattern, JD's engagement in supply chain finance is to solve e-commerce platform suppliers' payment period problems at first. All suppliers face varying payment period problems. Buyers on e-commerce platforms can gain a loan on time. However, JD supplier take around 38–40 days of payment period. During this period, suppliers should not only make delivery as usual, but also possibly undertake greater capital pressures if greater quantity of demand is ordered. Though the payment period lasting for 38–40 days is not very long, it is very influential on some companies. Accordingly, JD conceives the proposal of supply chain finance. Its original intention is to help relieve capital pressures of upstream suppliers, and improve capital operating efficiency. In 2012, JD business volume exceeded 60 billion yuan. Since its foundation, it maintains 2005 high-rate growth once a year. As a large and trustworthy giant of e-commerce, JD has the confidence to do supply chain finance.

"JD + Bank" Pattern

JD began to involve in supply chain finance since January 2012. On November 27 2012, JD officially launched supply chain finance business. In the cooperation with BOC Beijing Branch, the bank promises to grant hundreds of millions of line of credit and JD vouches for merchants with its credit and scale. JD takes receivable as the pledge for BOC. To be specific, JD is responsible for corporate credit granting and loan approval and BOC is responsible for issuing loans. The interest rate is usually 10 ~ 30% above benchmark interest rate, far below 20% market level. The interest rate is counted by day. The term of loan ranges between 15 days and 90 says. Upon expiry, merchants may apply to extend the term by another 30 days and freely set the term of repayment. By December 2012, supply chain finance loan scale totaled 1 billion yuan. By November 2013, JD had approximately issued loans totaling 8 billion yuan to suppliers via supply chain finance business, and average limit of loan was between 800,000 –1.10 million yuan (Table 6).

Such "JD + Bank" pattern supply chain finance flow consists of the following three parts.

Table 6 Development history of JD supply chain finance

Time	*Progress*
January 2012	Conducted first supply chain finance business and formally entered supply chain finance business
June 2012	Deployed online supply chain finance system, and cooperated with multiple banks
August 2012	Self-developed asset packaging transfer planned products and collaborative investment planned products gained approval from CBRC
October 12, 2012	Held 8 "JD Supply Chain Financial Service Introduction and Marketing Event" for overall suppliers, raised 1.5 billion USD, and gained over 5 billion yuan credit business from financial institutions represented by Bank of China, China Construction Bank, Industrial and Commercial Bank of China, Bank of Communication
January 2013	Set up business insurance company and petty loan company in Shanghai
December 2013	Launched Jingbaobei and updated supply chain financial platform

Data source Liu Shu'e, Solve the Bottleneck in the Retail Industry: JD Supply Chain Finance, *Journal of Beijing Vocational College of Finance and Trade*, 2014 (8)

① Credit granting. JD first assesses suppliers' credit rating according to historical sales data and supply settlement data accumulated on the platform and then determines the limit of credit. Suppliers may apply for a loan within the limit of credit.
② Approval. When suppliers need financing, they shall submit sales contract, freight invoice, warranty and JD confirmation document to JD, and JD informs banks to issue a loan upon approval.
③ Loan. Banks issue a loan to suppliers after receiving JD's notice. The loan is guaranteed by JD, with receivable as the pledge.

JD supply chain finance greatly improves the time and efficiency in issuing loans. Suppliers can basically gain the loan in half a day. There are four types of loan, namely procurement order financing loan, inventory financing loan, receivable loan and expansion financing loan. Among them, in procurement order financing loan, suppliers raise financing requirements while signing supply contract with JD, banks issue a loan to suppliers according to the order and JD directly pay to banks after delivery. In inventory financing loan, suppliers request the loan requirement to banks with warehouse warrant as the pledge. In receivable financing loan, suppliers transfer receivable securities to banks and apply for a loan from banks. Meanwhile, this process is accompanied by asset packet transfer plan and coordinated investment plan. After issuing a loan, banks will sell the loan off to JD and other persons with idle capital. At the end of the term of loan, JD pays the loan back to banks. During the full process, suppliers gain capital, banks gain credit resources and JD gains wealth management income. In expansion financing loan, JD provides capital, and banks issue the loan, supervise the loan and assist it to recollect the loan on behalf of JD. In this process, JD assesses the rating and guarantees for suppliers based on historical trading data.

Jingbaobei

On December 6, 2013, one year after the launch of supply chain finance, JD released a loan product named "Jingbaobei". Different from all past products, Jingbaobei business is transacted by JD itself in the whole course, including supplier rating, credit granting, online audit, and loan issue. The most distinct characteristic of Jingbaobei is that it realizes flexible financing and repayment and consumers may gain the loan within 3 min without guarantee or pledge. The loan interest rate is usually 10%. For a time, Jingbaobei quickly swept the market. In January 2014,

Jingbaobei's financing scale totaled 1 billion yuan. In 2014, Jingbaobei maintained monthly compound growth rate as 30–50%.

Jingbaobei's operation flow is different from the former way:

① Credit granting. Corporate grating and credit granting are indispensable links to any financing means. Jingbaobei would give A-E grating levels pursuant to suppliers' product inventory, sales, term of cooperation and other related indicators, and compute the limit of loan. Jingbaobei just provides financing support with no guarantee and pledge for three levels.
② Approval and risk control. Jingbaobei doesn't request suppliers to provide order, warehouse warrant, receivable and other bills, and it can automatically finish the approval and risk control for loans throughout centralized data processing and analysis on procurement, inventory, sales, settlement and finance via the IT system.
③ JD automatically issues loans to suppliers after approval. The whole process just takes 3 minutes.

Jingbaobei's financing threshold is rather low, as any supplier who has provided products for JD for over 3 months can submit an application. At present, available types of loan include receivable financing loan, order financing loan and prepayment financing loan. These financing products are all operated with considerable data accumulated by JD, including inventory data, financial data, order data, and procurement data, for analysis and risk control. By October 2014, JD Group had accumulated over 40,000 suppliers and related sales data, and it had the capacity to perform full credit investigation and credit analysis on suppliers.

JD's supply chain finance business and Jingbaobei business belong to supply chain finance under big data in the strict sense. It also belongs to big data finance. Many supply chain finance patterns are just the online forms of traditional supply chain finance which just transact past offline approval formalities online via the Internet. Though such practice improves approval efficiency, the spirits and nature of traditional supply chain are not changed. Therefore, it still requests guarantee and pledge. But the two patterns of JD have possessed the characteristic of supply chain under big data, which is most evidently expressed by the application of big data in credit granting. Especially, Jingbaobei has completely demonstrated the characteristic of Internet finance. Concerning the first pattern, many describe JD as a financial intermediary who provides consumers for bank loans. It makes sense a little bit, but it ignores a very important fact—if JD can't do rigorous credit rating and business approval, JD shall undertake the repayment responsibility as a guarantor (Table 7).

"E-commerce + platform" pattern refers to a means in which e-commerce provides related trading data and banks provide capital. Typical representatives include "Dunhuang.com + CMBC". The advantage of such pattern is that the parties can supplement each other's advantages. Banks are responsible for capital supply and e-commerce is responsible for data supply. Both of the two exert comparative advantages. But the disadvantage is that the parties assume different risks and besides, the difficulty in interest partition easily leads to economic disputes.

Case 5: Dunhuang.com

Dunhuang.com engaged in supply chain business since 2011. It mainly chooses to cooperate with banks. During this process, Dunhuang.com does not provide guarantee for small- and medium-sized companies, but just presents corporate business-related information, including consumer trading sum, frequency, risk control, integrity credit, to help banks make the judgement. In terms of lending conditions, approval speed and lending proportion, Dunhuang.com would negotiate with banks in detail.

In 2011, Dunhuang.com and CCB jointly developed the order-based online real-time lending service, and launched three order-based types of loan, including E-lending Pass, E-invoice Pass and E-factoring Pass.

Table 7 Comparison of two supply chain finance modes of JD

Link	"JD+Bank" mode	Jingbaobei
Credit rating	Perform supplier credit investigation and rating and grant the line of credit according to JD big data. This fully indicates the application of big data in supply chain finance	
Material approval	Offline approval	Online systematic and concentrated approval and analysis
Fund source	Bank	Equity fund
Service object	Partial suppliers	Entire suppliers
Source of profit	Service charge	Lending interest and service charge
Lending basis	Final statement	Warehouse warrant

Taking E-insurance Pass, for example, qualified users are supposed to send delivery information back to Dunhuang.com after the formation of orders, Dunhuang.com shall confirm the information and give feedback to the bank, and CCB eventually issue 80% capital to users. The remaining 20% capital will be only issued when buyers receive the products. By August 2013, the number of buyers who applied for E-lending Pass totaled 1000, and accumulated sum of loan totaled 100 million yuan.

In May 2013, Dunhuang.com and CMBC jointly launched the co-branded financial service card "Dunhuang.com Business All-purpose Card" and provided integrated financing, settlement and wealth management financial services for small and micro companies. At present, any user who has half a year of trading records can apply for the debit card on the official website of Dunhuang.com and transact overall settlement businesses free of charge. When users obtain the debit card, Dunhuang.com will transfer corporate operation dynamics to CMBC. In accordance with the match between users and CMBC credit value, users may apply for a loan with the limit of 50,000–1.5 billion yuan. The number of applicants reached over 2000 two months after the launch.

In October 2013, Dunhuang.com cooperated with CMBC to release CMBC-Dunhuang New E-lending Platinum Credit Card. With an advantage over high limit, high efficiency, high withdrawal rate, high age limit and low interest rate, the credit card can provide convenient capital service for platform buyers. The maximum line of credit reaches 500,000 yuan.

Such cooperation means of Dunhuang.com is different from that of JD. On the one hand, comparing with the cooperation between JD and BOC, JD is responsible for approval and credit granting, and the bank is responsible for supply of capital. By contrast, Dunhuang.com just provides user trading information for the bank for reference. To be sure, the role of trading information can't be overlooked as well, or otherwise the bank will not choose to cooperate with Dunhuang.com. What Dunhuang.com can provide is trading data alone. The bank mainly uses available data to make credit rating on users. On the other hand, comparing with JD's Jingbaobei in which JD makes use of its equity capital in supply chain finance, Dunhuang.com uses the capital of bank. In the entire supply chain finance, Dunhuang.com neither performs credit granting nor provides guarantee and capital. It just provides data in exchange for information service charge. But why is such pattern called big data-based supply chain finance? Because the key to business approval is the trading data provided by Dunhuang.com. It is the basis on which the bank makes credit analysis. Therefore, in this sense, "Dunhuang.com + Bank" pattern still belongs to supply chain finance.

Case source Xue Juan, Dunhuang.com's First Move in Supply Chain Financial Service, *China Economic Times*, August 22 2013.

Above-mentioned three types of subjects prove that "bank-company cooperation pattern" is essentially the Internet extension of traditional supply chain finance. Though the bank now gains quality consumers via cooperation and improves efficiency via Internet, it doesn't change its credit analysis method. In the strict sense, it is not under the category of big data finance. If the bank gradually utilizes big data to change its conventional credit analysis method, then a great leap will be created. Maybe e-commerce plays two different roles in e-commerce self-built platforms and "e-commerce + platform" pattern, but both of the two modes begin to adopt big data in risk rating. This is the fundamental property that makes it different from traditional supply chain finance, and highlights the advantages of big data credit investigation. Despite the problems in the short run, e-commerce will have better performance in this aspect as more operating experience is accumulated. Internet finance inspires us that with the accumulation of considerable data, we can control the accurate information of consumers and manufacturers and use available information to make credit investigation and risk rating on companies. In this way, information asymmetry problem that has beset us for a long time can be fully solved theoretically, and this is true of more related problems like financing (Table 8).

4 Consumer Finance

Different from platform finance and supply chain finance which stress seller financing, consumer finance, as its name suggests, more views the financing problem from the perspective of the buyer. In general, consumer finance is actually the action which provides capital financing for the seller. Against the macroscopic context of new normal economy in China in current stage, an important move to boost the transformation and upgrading of Chinese economic structure is to vigorously develop consumer finance, stimulate consumption and invigorate domestic demands.

In line with different criteria of classification, consumer finance falls into different categories. For instance, it can be divided into housing loan,

Table 8 Comparison of the type of supply chain finance companies

Comparison	*Bank-company cooperation network*	*E-commerce self-built platform*	*E-commerce + platform*
Advantages	Low fund cost; Diverse financial products and services; strong risk control ability	Low fund cost	Complementary advantages
Disadvantages	High bank access threshold; Long period of approval; Low fund raising efficiency	Restricted risk control ability; Susceptibility to risks	Risk return game
Nature	Extension of traditional finance Internet; Raising efficiency via network; access of quality clients; non-involvement of financial management terminal; unchanged credit analysis method	Gain wealth management capital via e-commerce, lower financing cost; Effective use of big data credit investigation	

vehicle loan, tourism loan, student loan as per consumption purpose; it can be divided into short-term loan and mid and long-term loan as per term of loan; it can be divided into buyer credit and seller credit as per target of loan; and it can be also divided into pledge, guarantee, mortgage and credit as per guarantee (Table 9).

Table 9 Classification of consumer finance

Means of classification	*Content*
Purpose of consumption	Housing loan, automobile loan, travel loan, student loan
Term	Short-term loan and mid and long-term loan
Lending object	Buyer credit loan and seller credit loan
Guarantee	Mortgage, guarantee, pledge, credit

Data source Report of Chinese Internet Consumer Finance Industry Trend in 2014

Development Conditions of Consumer Finance

Scale of Consumer Finance

Consumer finance in China now has presented high rate of growth. The scale of consumer finance just totaled 3.3 trillion yuan in 2007. The figure continually went up in successive years. By 2009, the growth rate totaled 48.7%, and the scale amounted to 5.5 trillion yuan. The growth rate dropped slowly henceforward and reached the bottom as 17.6% till 2012. It recovered the robust trend then. In 2014, the growth rate of consumer finance was approximately 20%, and corresponding scale was 15.6 trillion yuan.

The robust and prompt development of consumer finance is benefited by three contributors. First of all, the stable growth of Chinese residents' living standards and consumption level expands domestic demands for consumer finance. Secondly, as Chinese economy enters the new normal state, former pattern which depends on investment and export to drive economic growth is non-sustainable, and consumption-cored new economic growth pattern is taking shape now. Thirdly, with the continuous deepening of financial reform, and the rise of diversified, personalized and inclusive finance greatly meet consumers' consumption demands (Fig. 10).

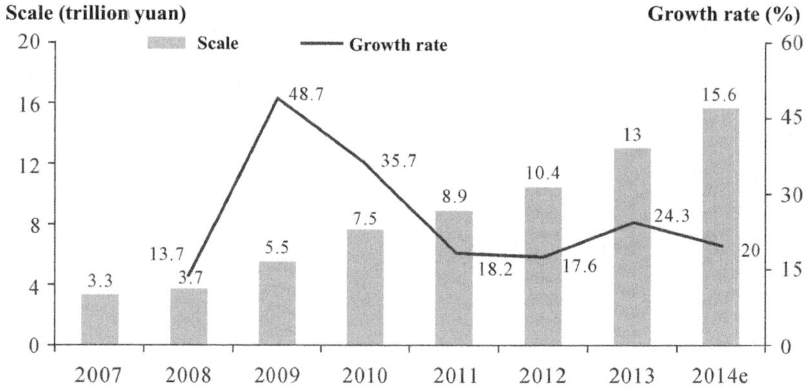

Fig. 10 Chinese consumer finance scale and growth rate from 2007 to 2014 (*Data source* Report for the Trend of Chinese Internet Consumer Financial Industry in 2014)

Consumer Finance Structure

If domestic consumer finance structure is classified by consumption purpose, present residents' individual housing loan still makes up overwhelming market shares. It is because housing loan has larger scale and term of payment than vehicle and some other objects. For this reason, individual housing loan will still maintain high market shares in a rather long period of time. But we must admit that due to the increase of other loans, especially credit card loans, the proportion of housing loan will experience a gradual slowdown. The figure dropped down to 73.8% in 2014. It is predicted to continually decrease step by step in the future (Figs. 11 and 12).

The growing trend of credit card is in particular prominent. In 2007, the loan scale of credit cards was just 2.3%. But the figure increased to over 10% till 2012 and then 15.2% in 2014. It is predicted that the proportion of credit card loans will further increase. This is closely related to the amount of credit card issuance. According to related statistics, there were just 90 million credit cards in China in 2007, and the figure increased to 140 million in 2008, 200 million in 2010, and 300 million in 2012. By late 2013, it went up to as high as 390 million. In recent years, the growth rate of credit card issuance amount is fairly stable, and basically kept at around 20%.

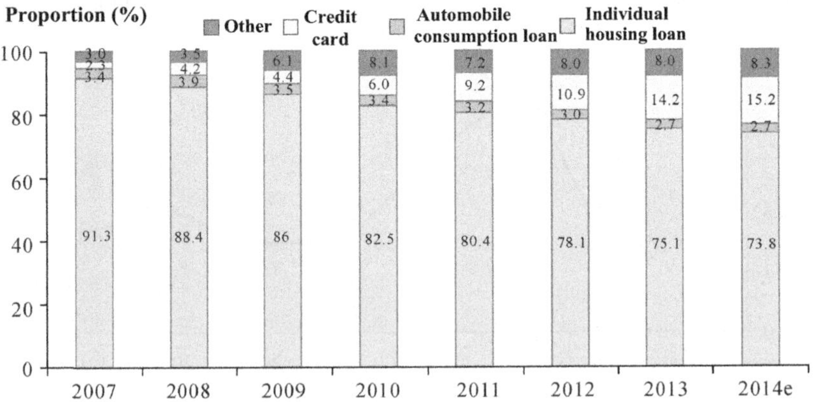

Fig. 11 Chinese consumer finance structure categorized by consumption purpose from 2007 to 2014 (*Data source* Report for the Trend of Chinese Internet Consumer Financial Industry in 2014)

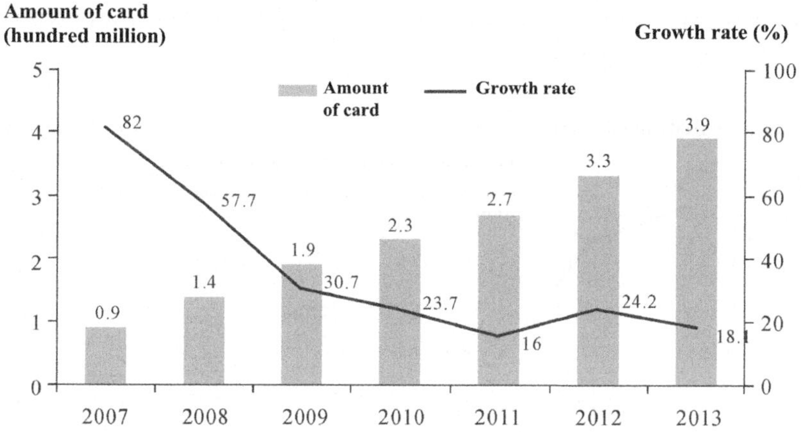

Fig. 12 Issue and growth rate of credit card in China from 2007 to 2013 (*Data source* Report for the Trend of Chinese Internet Consumer Financial Industry in 2014)

In 2007, gross credit granting amount of credit cards in China was 557.71 billion yuan and corresponding term-end receivable was 75.02 billion yuan. While gross credit granting amount and corresponding term-end receivable in 2009 was 1 trillion yuan and 254.76 billion yuan respectively. In 2010, gross credit granting amount reached 2 trillion yuan. In 2012, gross credit granting amount reached 3.49 trillion yuan and corresponding receivable also reached 1 trillion yuan. By late 2013, gross credit granting amount was 4.57 trillion yuan, and receivable was 1.84 trillion yuan. Thus it can be seen that the sustained growth of newly issued credit cards in future few years will activate the stable growth of credit card loans.

From the viewpoint of consumer finance loan term, affected by individual housing loan, mid and long-term consumer loan still occupies a large proportion in present stage. Though it seems to decrease slightly, it is still predicted to maintain 79% growth rate. Correspondingly, it is foreseeable that the growing momentum of short-term consumer loan in recent few years is very prompt, and Internet companies represented by e-commerce and third-party payment gradually march to the field of consumer finance. It is predicted that short-term consumption financial demands will further increase and have unlimited development potentials in the future (Figs. 13 and 14).

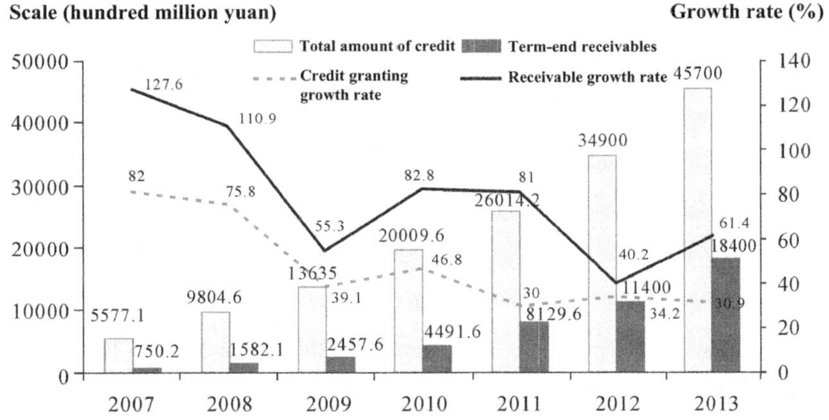

Fig. 13 Overview of Chinese credit card loan from 2007 to 2013 (*Data source* Report for the Trend of Chinese Internet Consumer Financial Industry in 2014)

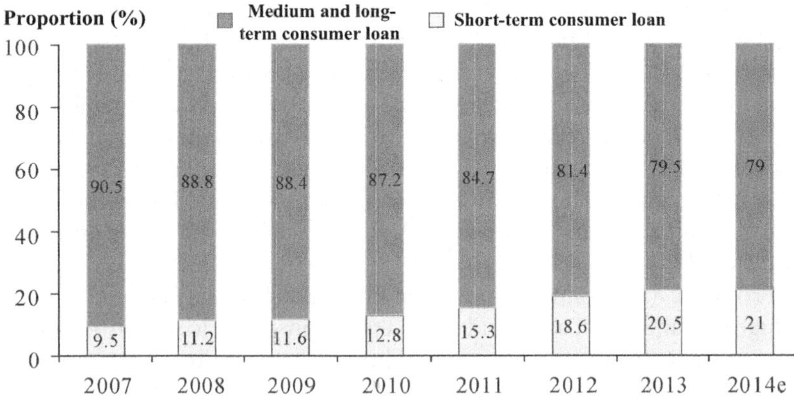

Fig. 14 Chinese consumer loan structure classified by term from 2007 to 2014 (*Data source* Report for the Trend of Chinese Internet Consumer Financial Industry in 2014)

Consumer Finance Industry Chain

The industry chain of Chinese consumer finance is primarily composed of consumers, consumption companies, financial institutions and regulatory agencies. Consumption companies here include retail companies, vehicle companies, real estate companies, air travel companies, education overseas study institutions and other traditional companies in the service of consumer products and services. Financial institutions here include commercial banks, credit card companies, petty loan companies and consumption finance companies. Regulatory agencies include PBC, all industry guilds and ministries and commissions in the field of consumer goods (Fig. 15).

For a long time, the core of consumer finance industry chain has been always commercial bank. At the demand side, commercial banks provide housing loan, credit card loan, vehicle loan and other financial products for consumers. At the supply side, commercial banks provide financial loan for seller credit. To a large degree, all of these facilitate the development of consumer credit in China. But the non-negligible point is that commercial bank-dominated consumer credit also has numerous constraints. First of all, the consumer credit in commercial banks is easily affected by physical network sites, which means that commercial banks can't provide credit loan service in places with no physical network sites. Secondly, products which lack innovation and are severely homogeneous and individualized can't meet diversified credit demands. Thirdly, imbalanced regional and urban–rural development causes great difference in consumer credit.

Accompanied by the rise of e-commerce in China, Internet companies represented by e-commerce platforms and third-party payment begin

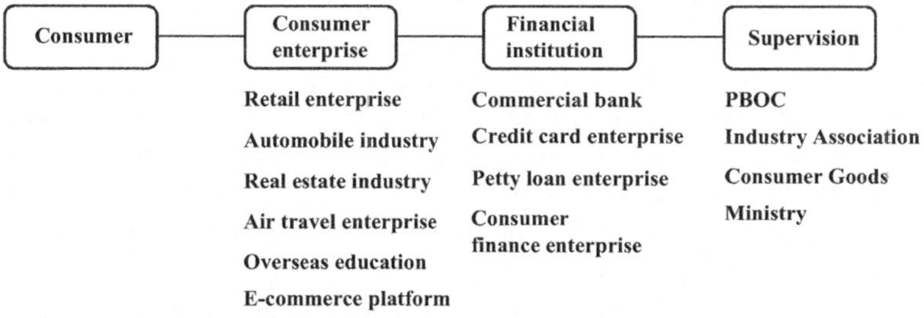

Fig. 15 Consumer finance industry chain (*Data source* Report for the Trend of Chinese Internet Consumer Financial Industry in 2014)

to enter the industry chain of consumer finance, and gradually form Internet consumption financial pattern. The great development of e-commerce makes e-commerce giants an important part of consumer companies, and simultaneously, encourages these companies to successively enter the finance field and provide credit service for consumers. For instance, Alibaba releases Tmall installment and Ant Check Later, and JD Mall releases Jingdong Baitiao to offer consumer credit to consumers. For a time, e-commerce giants' consumer finance products quickly gain the preference of consumers due to the low-threshold, low-cost, high-efficiency and excellent user experience. In the future, Internet companies represented by e-commerce will more embrace consumer finance, and Internet consumption finance will further expand. At the same time, traditional consumer finance represented by commercial banks will be successively released to overturn traditional consumer finance pattern.

Bottleneck in the Development of Consumer Finance

The development of Internet consumer finance shows the bottleneck of traditional consumer finance. In effect, the development of traditional consumer finance is constrained by three aspects as below.

The first one is mismatch between consumer finance and commercial bank credit pattern. Having been engaged in the loan business for large companies in the long term, commercial banks mainly concentrate on corporate asset balance sheet, cash flow statement and profit statement and corporate pledge, mortgage or guarantee. Under the control of interest rate, relying on the loan business for large companies can not only ensure the security of credit, but also gain substantial interest spreads of deposit and loan. As to consumer finance, as small- and medium-sized companies and individuals have poorer credit qualifications than large companies and state-owned companies, they usually lack effective guarantee and pledge. Consequently, in face of stern loan conditions of consumer loan, they usually fail to pass the audit of commercial banks.

Secondly, high consumer credit cost hardly contributes to scale economy. The loan for large companies usually has a long term, large scale and high interest rate. Comparing with short, flat and fast consumer loan, large companies easily form scale advantages. Now that commercial banks have high risk control cost on consumer loan, they can hardly maintain high initiative.

The third problem is the lack of individual credit system. Both commercial banks' constraints in consumer credit and consumer finance's bottleneck in the development process reflect one issue—the lack of individual credit system. By far, there still lacks a complete individual credit investigation system in China. On January 5, 2015, PBC released *Notice about the Preparation Work for Individual Credit Investigation Business* and requested eight institutions to prepare for individual credit investigation business within six months, including Zhima Credit Management Co., Ltd (under Alibaba Ant Finance Service Group), Tencent Credit Investigation Co., Ltd, Shenzhen Qianhai Credit Investigation Center Co., Ltd, Pengyuan Credit Investigation Co., Ltd, Zhongchengxin Credit Investigation Co., Ltd, Zhongzhicheng Credit Investigation Co., Ltd, Lacarra Credit Management Co., Ltd and Beijing Huadao Credit Investigation Co., Ltd. This means that the eight companies probably become the first batch individual credit investigation commercial institutions which gain individual credit investigation business operation qualification. They mainly rely on commercial banks' credit records recorded by Central Bank's credit investigation system. Till late October 2014, Chinese credit investigation system altogether included the credit information of 19.63 million companies and other organizations and 8.5 billion natural persons. Comparing with foreign credit market which has been developed for nearly 200 years, the credit investigation system built in 1992 in China is less sound. The lack of individual credit causes it difficult for banks to comprehensively estimate credit risks. Moreover, owing to the lack of security guarantee, banks' credit risks have been further aggravated. While throughout long-term data accumulation, Internet companies subtly combine individual users' payment information, trading information and other historical data with individual credit rating, and attempt to judge individual users' credit conditions in accordance with users' historical behaviors. In this way, in spite of the lack of pledge guarantee, banks may also issue credit loans to individuals and thus solve consumer credit difficulties in an effective means.

E-commerce companies' Internet consumer finance is a beneficial attempt made to break through the constraint of credit rating. It acutely reflects the importance of individual credit system building. In the age of Internet, credit is the carrier that ensures the fast liquidity of capital flow, information flow and logistics.

Development of Internet Consumer Finance

Benefited by the development of Internet and the rise of people's income level, the past decade witnesses the prompt development of Internet finance. In 2006, Chinese online shopping trading scale was just 26.31 billion yuan, and online permeation rate computed as online shopping trading scale/total retail sales of consumer goods was just 0.3%. In 2008, online shopping trading scale exceeded 1000 billion yuan and corresponding online permeation rate also exceeded 1%. During this period, trading scale increased at a rate of 100% once a year. Though the growth rate decreased to less than 100% as of 2010, it was still maintained above 70%. In 2012, online shopping trading scale broke through 1 trillion yuan, and corresponding online permeation rate exceeded 6.3%. In 2014, online trading scale totaled 2.42 trillion yuan, and corresponding online permeation rate exceeded 9.1%.

The prompt expansion of online shopping trading scale activates the rise of a group of e-commerce platforms represented by Alibaba and JD and also third-party payment platforms represented by Alipay and TenPay. The two use considerable trading data and payment data accumulated over a period of time to exploit in the field of Internet finance. Supply chain finance, Internet insurance, wealth management product sales, big data finance and other innovative financing patterns rise in response to proper occasions. Among them, e-commerce-based consumer finance will be the focus of big data finance in the future.

Actually, consumer finance mainly serves the buyer. The operation mode of e-commerce platform-based consumer finance is as shown in Fig. 18. In the first place, consumer finance shall deal with consumers' credit issue. Therefore, considerable historical data accumulated by e-commerce platforms and third-party payment platforms can be used to assess the credit of consumers. Those consumers who earn high credit level may acquire proper limit of loans via consumer finance service. Such policy not only meets consumers' consumption demands, but also activates the increase of e-commerce sales volume. This is the reason why so many consumer finance products are provided by e-commerce platforms, like JD Baitiao and Tmall installment (Figs. 16, 17, and 18).

Scale of Internet Consumer Finance

Internet consumer finance belongs to an emerging finance pattern. In 2011, the gross scale of Internet consumer finance was just 680 million

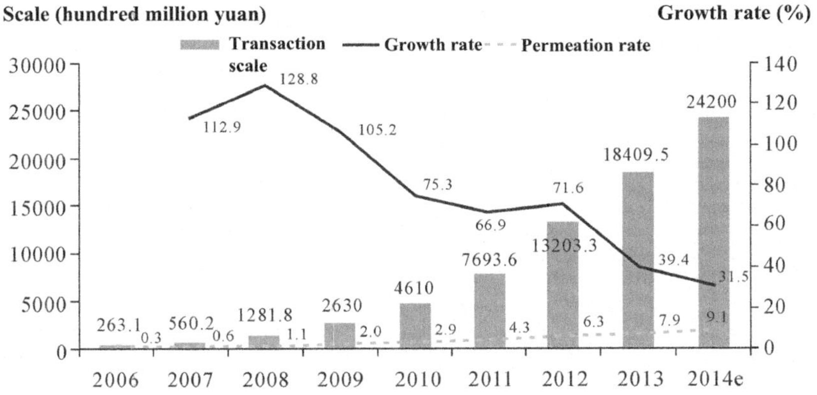

Fig. 16 Online shopping transaction scale, growth rate and permeation rate of China from 2006 to 2014 (*Data source* iResearch)

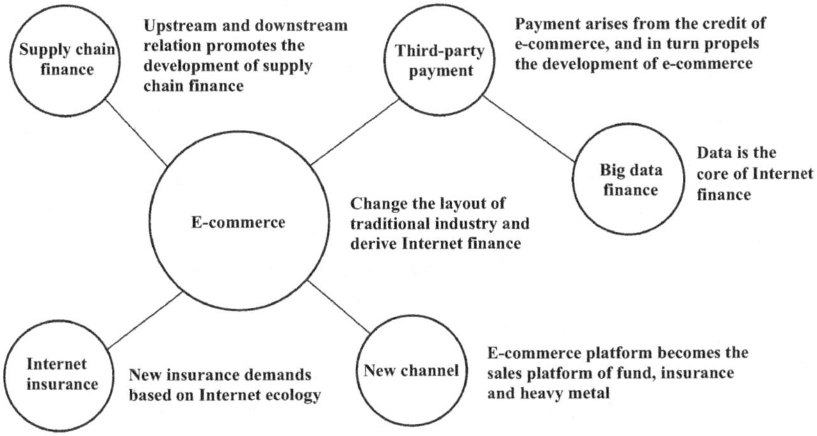

Fig. 17 Diversified finance business types deriving from E-commerce (*Data source* Report for the Trend of Chinese Internet Consumer Financial Industry in 2014)

yuan. It could be even overlooked compared with the 8.9 trillion scale of consumer finance. Afterward, Internet consumer finance increased at a fast speed of nearly 200%. Till the year of 2014, Internet consumer finance

Fig. 18 Operation mode of internet consumer finance

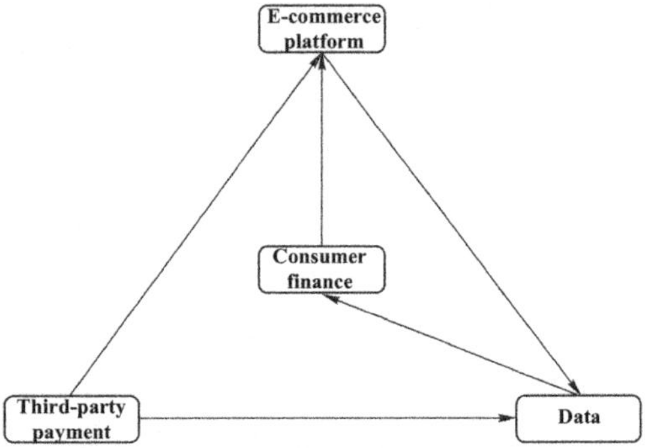

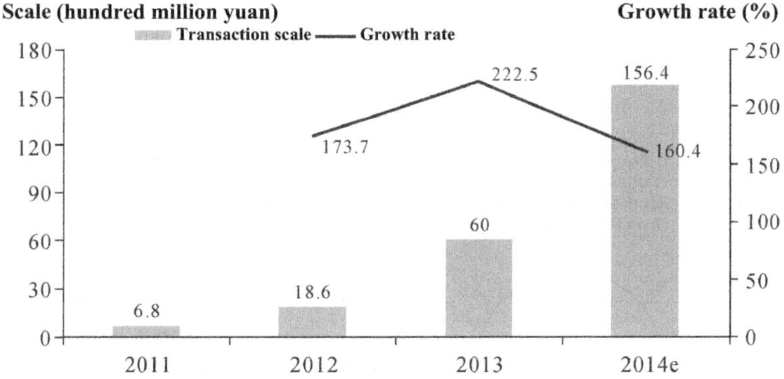

Fig. 19 Chinese internet consumer finance trading scale and growth rate from 2011 to 2014 (*Data source* Report for the trend of Chinese internet consumer financial industry in 2014)

reached 15.64 billion yuan, accounting for 0.1% of entire consumer finance credit (Fig. 19).

Structure of Internet Consumer Finance

Concerning Internet consumer credit, P2P credit makes up overwhelming shares. P2P credit is also a major pattern which promptly rises in the field of Internet finance during the past few years. In 2011, the proportion of P2P credit in Internet consumer credit was simply 99%. Before the rise of e-commerce consumer credit till 2013, P2P consumer credit had always accounted for more than 97.5% shares in entire Internet consumer credit. In 2014, e-commerce credit products officially came into existence and accounted for 32% of Internet consumer credit. Correspondingly, the proportion of P2P credit decreased to 60.5%.

Both P2P consumer credit and e-commerce consumer credit belong to online consumer credit, but there are some differences between the two. In terms of data source, P2P consumer credit's data mainly come from P2P platforms, while e-commerce consumer credit's data come from e-commerce platforms. In terms of risk control, P2P credit gains considerable financial data via the platform, collects and accumulates loaners' information from the perspective of region, capital scale, loan term, payment means and interest level, and analyzes and excavates available data to infer loaners' risk tolerance and investment rate of return, credit level, and other key information. E-commerce platforms assess consumers' credit with accumulated considerable multi-dimensional trading data, payment data, behavioral data and user assessment. On the one hand, it is ascribed to the similarity between P2P credit and e-commerce credit. As to main business, P2P credit focuses on capital source, while e-commerce consumer credit focuses on capital demanders. As to the form of payment, as P2P credit directly offers credit capital to demanders, it can't control the use of capital. E-commerce consumer credit that directly provides goods for consumers is able to effectively control the purpose of capital. As to the use of capital, P2P credit is mainly used in large-amount consumer fields covering vehicle, real estate, decoration and education, while e-commerce consumer credit is used to buy less expensive and frequently used durable consumer goods (Table 10).

In nature, P2P companies belong to capital lending platforms, and the fundamental purpose of such companies is to realize financing. Beginning with e-commerce platforms, e-commerce finance aims to promote the sales of platform products through solving consumers' shortage of capital. In this sense, P2P platforms more stresses capital lending, and e-commerce platforms sell products by lending capital. The former will not control the purpose of capital, and the latter is necessarily used in e-commerce system.

But one point worth of mentioning here is that the earliest P2P platform in China was created in 2007, but P2P doesn't enter the fast lane of development until last two or three years. In another word, present P2P platforms in China have a short life span of duration in no more than 7 years. Moreover, most of them just survive for less than 7 years. This suggests that the short life span determines the limited data accumulation

Table 10 Comparison of P2P credit loan and E-commerce consumer loan

Comparison	P2P credit loan	E-commerce consumer loan
Data source	P2P platform accumulation	E-commerce platform accumulation
Risk control	Accumulate substantial financial data via P2P platform, gather information concerning lenders from the perspective of region, fund scale, loan time limit, means of repayment, interest rate level, and analyze and excavate related information to derive key information such as risk tolerance, return on investment, credit level.	Assess consumer credit according to substantial transaction data, payment data, behavioral data, and user assessment data accumulated on the e-commerce platform
Emphasis	Preference to fund source providers instead of fund demanders	Preference to fund demanders
Form of payment	Provide credit fund, but can't control the use of fund	Direct payment for products, and effective control of the use of fund
Use of capital	Automobile, real estate, decoration, education and other bulk consumption fields	Purchase of petty-sum and high-frequency durable consumer goods

amount on P2P platforms. While full accumulation of data is the sufficient condition for P2P platforms to engage in credit business. Now, P2P platforms usually fail to adopt big data in ordinary meaning in risk and credit assessment to transact credit business. This rests in the most fundamental difference between P2P credit and e-commerce consumer credit in current stage. Therefore, from this perspective, P2P consumer credit is not a part of big data finance. But together with the sustained development of P2P platforms, and accumulation of data, P2P platforms are expected to make full use of accumulated big data to make risk and credit assessment like e-commerce platforms. Then P2P credit will also be part of big data finance. While it is not yet. This point must be clarified.

Scale of E-commerce Consumer Finance

The year of 2014 is the first year of e-commerce consumer finance. On February 13, JD released JD Baitiao business to provide consumer credit business for JD consumers. Next, on July 7, Alibaba released Tmall installment to compete with JD Baitiao and seize the market shares of e-commerce consumer credit. On December 28, Alipay further released Ant Check Later consumer credit business to help consumers buy products in most shops on Taobao and Tmall. In 2014, the trading scale of e-commerce consumer credit totaled 5 billion yuan, accounting for 0.2% of entire online shopping trading scale. It is predicted that in future few years, e-commerce consumer credit trading scale will maintain a high growth rate of over 100% and its proportion in entire online trading scale will also increase. It possibly reaches 1.2% till 2017.

Case 6: JD Baitiao

On February 13, 2014, JD launched the first credit payment product JD Baitiao oriented toward individual users. Consumers are able to buy products via JD Baitiao in JD Mall, either by deferred payment or installment payment. Users may apply for the quota of JD Baitiao online, with maximum line of credit of 15,000 yuan. In addition, the service fee of the product is just half of bank. Consumers can apply for the credit granting of JD Baitiao just within one minute and use it the next day.

JD Baitiao Application Flow
JD users can activate JD Baitiao after logging on the account, inputting name and ID number, and binding the credit card of JD cooperative banks. This step is also known as "claiming Baitiao". When it is time to settle the account, users may pay in installment, i.e. "issuing Baitiao". Upon the arrival of pay day, JD will send a text to remind users to make payment, which is known as "repaying Baitiao".
JD Baitiao Service Terms
JD Mall primarily releases the accounts receivable management business for platform products among consumers, and creates convenience for consumers to buy products in JD Mall, excluding self-support products, gold, accessories, and other hard currency. Consumers are accessible to flexible choices in payment means and payment terms. To be specific, they may either choose to delay the payment for 30 days with no interest rate or make payment by installment. In particular, there are four choices of installment, including 3-month installment, 6-month installment, 12-month installment and 24-month installment. The service fee per month is 0.5%. Gross installment service fee = consumption capital × 0.5% × number of installment. Overall installment service charge is collected in down payment. The service rate of JD Baitiao is just half of bank. Taking CMBC for example, its credit card bill can be paid by installment for 2 months, 3 months, 6 months, 10 months, 12 months, 18 months and 24 months, with corresponding service rate as 1, 0.9, 0.75, 0.70.66, 0.68 and 0.68% respectively. Supposing the 10,000 yuan consumption amount

is to be paid in 3 months by installment, then JD's service rate is 10000 × 0.5% × 3 = 150 yuan, and that of CMBC is 120 yuan more than that as 10,000 × 0.9% × 3 = 270 yuan. Likewise, the service rate of 3-month installment in CCB is 0.75%, 75 yuan more than that of JD. Overdue liquidated damages = current account payable × 0.03% proportion of liquidated damages × number of default days.

JD Baitiao Risk ManagementJD Baitiao Risk Management
JD Baitiao is superficially about receivable management, but it is essentially under the category of big data finance. Across e-commerce, payment, and logistics industry, JD has accumulated considerable basic user data, purchasing behavior and preference data, payment data, offline logistics data and other non-structural data. This is the core asset for JD to engage in consumer credit. By reference to data in different dimensions, JD can completely estimate consumers' income level, payment ability, payment ability, default probability and other core factors. Specifically speaking, JD's risk control falls into three steps. In the first step, JD assesses user credit with its own credit assessment system. It assesses consumers' credit level based on basic user data, trading frequency, purchase amount and other consumption information, as well as additional logistics data including payment data, distribution information, sales return information, shopping comment, and gives credit investigation at varying credit levels. Secondly, JD may test consumers' actual purchase behaviors and control users' capital flow on this basis. Thirdly, users may automatically make repayment via e-bank wallet. In case of payment expiry, JD will urge users to make payment via text or phone to ensure credit capital security. All users shall use the capital on JD platform. This makes for JD's risk control (Table 11).

JD Baitiao not only satisfies JD consumers' consumption demands, and in the meantime, allows JD to complete the closed loop in JD Mall

Table 11 JD financial system

	JD financial system		
Contracting parties	Seller		Buyer
Service objects	JD suppliers	JD cooperative merchants	JD consumers
Credit services	Supply chain finance	Platform finance	Consumption loan
Product name	Jingbaobei	Jingxiaodai	JD Baitiao

credit. On the part of the seller, JD has constructed supply chain finance represented by Jingbaobei to satisfy JD suppliers' credit demands and also platform finance represented by JD Petty Loan to serve JD sellers rather than JD suppliers. On the part of the platform, JD does not intervene the trading of these stores. Therefore, JD Petty Loan is not under the category of supply chain finance. But it has the same principle with Alibaba Petty Loan, for both of them have used big data. This implies that JD Petty Loan should be classified under platform finance in big data finance which has been proposed to satisfy JD partners' credit demands. For buyers, JD provides consumer credit represented by JD Baitiao to satisfy buyers' credit demands too.

Case Source http://www.ithome.comhtmlit/75246.htm and http://epaper.tianjinwe.comtjrbtjrb/2014-02/27/content_7046752.htm.

Case 7: Tmall Installment

In July 2014, Alibaba formally launched Tmall installment which allowed consumers to make payment within 3.6 or 9 months in Tmall. Moreover, down payment was avoided. This decision marked the entry of Alibaba to the field of consumer finance following the step of JD Baitiao.

Different from JD Baitiao, Tmall installment does not request users to submit any application. Any consumer may pay by installment as long as his or her qualification meets system rating. While picking up products, consumers may check if the chosen products allow for installment. Consumers can directly select the term of installment within the limit of consumption. In condition that user consumption limit is out of use, consumers have to freeze capital in Yu'E Bao to prepare for installment payment.

As to service terms, Alibaba users can buy all products available on Tmall, except gold and virtual products. Consumers have access to 3-month, 6-month and 9-month installment. There is no service charge in former three months, but 1.5% service charge is collected per month later. In general, gross service charge for 6-month installment is 4.5% and that of 9-month installment is 6%. This is basically the same with bank installment payment rate. Overdue charge = current amount × 0.05% × number of default days.

Tmall also follows big data risk management pattern. It specifically comprises three steps as below. In the first place, considerable user data come from Alibaba e-commerce platform and Ant Finance. Besides consumer trading data, external payment data and daily finance behaviors are also included. This is of vital importance to consumers' credit rating. In the second place, with data provided by Alibaba e-commerce, Tmall screens high viscosity users via Tmall membership rating system. By the same token, with e-commerce data and financial system data, Tmall refers factoring company's rating model to judge user credit, and grants the line of credit. This is how Tmall determines consumer credit throughout the dimension of member system and factoring company's rating model. At the same time, consumers can also increase the line of credit through Yu'E Bao asset pledge, and satisfy installment requirements by freezing Yu'E Bao capital. Thirdly, Tmall marks consumers' member level and corresponding line of credit, and consumers pay by installment within the line of credit

Case Data source Report for Chinese Internet Consumption Finance Industry Trend in 2014.

Case 8: Ant Check Later

On December 28, 2014, Alipay launched Ant Check Later to provide consumers with consumer credit loan. Users can apply for the service after logging on Alipay and inputting the payment password. Alipay then determines users' line of credit according to their online shopping frequency. The maximum is 30,000 yuan. It is worth noticing here that Ant Check Later, Tmall installment, Tmall Try and Buy and Taobao Try and Pay share the line of credit, which means that the use of any service will lower the general line of credit, and decrease the credit limit for other products.

Most products on Taobao and Tmall support Ant Check Later business. Consumers just need to make payment prior to the 10th day next month after confirming receipt. No interest is involved. In this sense, the longest interest-free term of Ant Check Later extends to 41 days. Ant Check Later approves of automatic payment from affiliated account balance, debit card or Yu'E Bao. The line of credit automatically recovers after payment. In case of overdue expiry, Ant Check Later will charge 0.05% penalty per day with compound interest. This is much similar to the bank.

Akin to commercial banks' credit card, Ant Check Later also offers micro-consumer credit to consumers. Different from the credit card issued by financial institutions which requests rigorous audit on individual property, income, occupation, and work unit, Ant Check Later takes sophisticated big data operation and risk control model to analyze massive data accumulated by Taobao and Alipay and judge consumer credit according to their online shopping and payment habits. This is associated with consumers' consumption behaviors, payment means, credit and account, instead of simple correspondence. Therefore, Ant Check Later is also part of big data finance (Table 12).

5 The Risks of Big Data Finance

Data Risks

Big data finance supported by data lacks considerable data, and therefore, it can't finish the credit rating and risk pricing for loaners. Therefore, it is impossible to realize financing.

Big data information processing includes three links, including data collection, data screening and data analysis. The first link of data collection ensures data size and data dimension. Larger data size and more data dimensions can ensure efficient data application. The second link is data screening. How to find most effective and useful data from considerable non-structural data is the key to decide analysis quality. Despite the possible large size of data, more invalid information may be also included. How to screen information and remove invalid data is a big problem faced by consumer credit companies. The third link is data analysis. Data analysis results directly determine consumer credit limit and risk pricing. If there is a problem in data analysis link, it means that consumer credit hasn't been fully estimated. The reason is probably ascribed to overestimation. So the possible outcome is that companies see a rise of bad debt resulting from loan defaults.

Consequently, Internet companies now compete against each other in data accumulation, data screening and data analysis. Alibaba and JD exactly take a lead in the field of big data finance because of data advantages. E-commerce takes the offensive move in big data field. Afterward, social contact field represented by Tencent, search field represented by Baidu and mobile operators represented by China Telecom all enter the market of Internet finance. They all depend on the data advantage accumulated over time. But how to make data screening and analysis from then on remains the test of market. At present, the bad debt rate of

Table 12 Comparison of bank credit card and E-commerce consumer credit

Project	China Merchants Bank	Ping An Bank	JD Baitiao	Tmall Installment	Ant Check Later
Efficiency	Submit the application seven days in advance, with real-time tracking in following days	Submit the application seven days in advance, with real-time tracking in following days	Submit the application on the first day, with real-time tracking on the next day	Qualifications	Use upon registration
Formality rate	Payment by installments in 2, 3, 6, 10, 12, 18, 24 with corresponding formality rate as 1%, 0.9%, 0.75%, 0.7%, 0.66%, 0.68% and 0.68% respectively	Payment by installments in 2, 3, 4, 5, 6, 7-24 with corresponding formality rate as 0.92%, 0.9%, 0.85%, 0.82%, 0.8% and 0.78% respectively	Payment by installments in 3-24month, with formality rate as 0.5%	0 for former three installments, and 1.5% for subsequent months	No interest during this period
Default interest	5% of remaining part + 0.05% of interest per diem	5% of remaining part + 0.05% of interest per diem	Interest per diem 0.03%	Interest per diem 0.05%	Interest per diem 0.05%
Application material	Credit card, password	Credit card, password	Name, ID card	No need of application	Payment password
Limit	2,000~50,000 yuan	100,000 yuan	150,000 yuan	30,000 yuan	30,000 yuan
Term	Free of interest for 50 days, payment by installments in 3~24 months	Free of interest for 50 days, payment by installments in 2-24 months	Extension of free of interest for 30 days, payment by installments in 3~24 months	Installments in 3,6 and 9 months	Repayment on the 10th day of the next month upon acceptance of goods
Payment convenience	Input of card password	Input of card password	No need of Input of card password	Input of payment password	Input of payment password

(continued)

Table 12 (continued)

Fund source	Bank	Bank	JD equity fund	Alibaba Petty Loan	Ant Micro-lending
Use scope	Online and offline circumstances in support of payment by credit card	Online and offline circumstances in support of payment by credit card	JD Mall, except some products	Tmall, except gold and virtual products	Taobao, Tmall

Data source http://news.mydrivers.com/1/362/362611.htm, http://baike.baidu.com/link?url=mgX8A1upVvyPdiL6XK6MMLpa_hzP0uPWTONePwD5VtvWfLG-G4i0F8ig2pniuKl39bAqpdbD1jIY5uTuhUgMBK-V9h6w1nw0p_AJL0RGRMq, http://baike.baidu.com/link?url=mgX8A1upVvyPdiL6XK6MMLpa_hzP0uPWTONePwD5VtvWfLG-G4i0F8ig2pniuKl39bAqpdbD1jIY5uTuhUgMBK-V9h6w1nw0p_AJL0RGRMq

Alibaba and JD is maintained at around 1%. With the expansion of business scale, more challenges will be proposed to test their data analysis abilities.

Credit Analysis

In reality, all financial credit businesses are developed around consumer credit risks. Due to the inability to comprehensively know about consumer credit, such financial credit businesses have to suppose the past, determine the future and judge consumer credit throughout analysis on big data and consumer behaviors. This is about feasibility. On the other hand, can the past be consistent with the future? It comes down to the difficulty to measure consumer credit. Especially, the default cost of small- and medium consumers can be nearly ignored in contemporary context short of credit. Therefore, even if high credit rating can be presented, it is still possible for consumers break the contract for lower cost considering the low default cost.

Consumer Risk

Another risk in big data finance is consumer risk. Now big data finance mainly serves existing consumers on the platform, and utilizes consumer big data in risk rating. But there are few consumers on the platform. In case of any bottleneck in quantity, big data finance can hardly expand its business scale further. This problem emerges since the start-up stage of e-commerce finance. It is a problem that deserves reflection.

6 The Development Trend of Big Data Finance

Vertical Development

Vertical development is a major trend of big data finance in the future. Nowadays, big data contains a wide variety of types of data, and it is hard to incorporate all industry characteristics into any single mode. Therefore, vertical big data finance will appear sooner or later. Two dimensions are involved here, namely industry vertical dimension and consumer vertical dimension.

Big data finance serves a lot of industries, such as vehicle, tourism, education, digital code, household appliances, real estate, etc. Each industry has different operation patterns and industry chains and naturally requests discrepant financial services. So it is a good idea to design financing services for a specific industry, like air travel, according to the financing demands and payment characteristics. Such services definitely gain the preference of consumers.

Similarly, another tip is to classify consumers, learn about the financing demands of each type of consumers, like students, entrepreneurs and white-collar workers, because different roles have different financial service demands.

Vertical development means professionalism and individualization. In face of ferocious Internet competition, some companies naturally abandon the former service mode which pays equal attention to entirety, and walk on the vertical professional path.

Cooperation Between Banks and E-commerce Companies

Firstly, traditional corporate e-commerce is the main trend of future corporate transition which is realized by launching online operation business, cutting down corporate operation cost and raising productivity. E-commerce platform is one non-negligible link in corporate e-commerce business. After all, flow is the desirable resource of each merchant in online business. E-commerce is the owner of such resources. Banks with enough capital can provide sufficient credit for consumers. Therefore, in the future, we may see the cooperation of "company + e-commerce + bank" in which bank is responsible for supply of capital, e-commerce offers data and the company gains loans. During this process, e-commerce platforms solve their capital and consumer shortage problems, banks gain consumers and companies gain capital. The role of e-commerce is a credit intermediary, instead of a financial intermediary. The efficiency of such financial cooperation is much higher.

Acceleration of Credit System Building

The fundamental contribution of Internet finance is that it provides a new path to solve credit rating. Therefore, future credit system building will accelerate to jump out of the circle of companies and industries, focus on the level of country, and present a general planning for credit system building. *Notice about the Preparation Work for Individual Credit Investigation Business* on January 5, 2015 released by PBC marks the initiation of this trend. Experience proves that America tends to build a pure credit intermediary and Europe advocates the Central Bank-dominated public credit investigation system. In the future, we possibly imitate Europe and enact a Central Bank-dominated uniform credit investigation collection system to break up the barrier across industries and normalize nationwide credit market. The building of such a credit market is imperative for the development of big data finance.

CHAPTER 6

A Bridge Between Capital Supply and Demand: P2P Online Lending Platform

P2P online lending is also one mode of big data application. Therefore, from this perspective, there is no significant difference between P2P online lending and big data finance as both of them are investment and financing actions based on big data credit investigation. However, different from big data financial platforms, P2P online lending platform just plays the role of information intermediary, and does not intervene in trading. It is worth noticing here that the platform uses related big data to conduct credit assessments about borrowers and shows investors the result. Therefore, investors can decide whether to make investment or not. The Internet finance mode based on big data can more effectively achieve the free matching of capital. While all of these take the effective application of big data as the premise.

Though big data finance solves the financing difficulties of small- and medium-sized companies, especially small and micro companies on e-commerce platform, solving e-commerce financing problems is not only an advantage but also a disadvantage at present. After all, the number of e-commerce companies remains limited. As a mature and effective mode, it should focus more on the financing problem of small- and medium-sized companies in a wider scope. In this sense, most data finance platforms can't effectively cover all service scopes, which means that small and micro companies beyond e-commerce platforms can't rely on big data to solve

Q. Guan and W. Gao, *Internet Finance*,
The Great Transformation of China,
https://doi.org/10.1007/978-981-16-4740-6_6

financing problems. Aiming at this problem, how does Internet finance develop?

P2P online lending platform may compensate this shortcoming. As a matter of fact, P2P online lending platforms and big data finance in China nearly rise at the same time. Comparing with big data finance, P2P online lending has its own advantages. In particular, its service target far exceeds the scope of big data finance. This compensates the business financing demands of Internet finance. This chapter analyzes P2P online lending platform.

1 The Definition of P2P Online Lending

At present, there are a great many popular online lending platforms. All sorts of companies, including Internet companies, and entity companies successively enter this industry. Moreover, these companies seek constant changes, which makes customers dazzled and dizzy. In reality, overwhelming P2P online lending platforms in the market are not real and classical P2P online lending platforms, but transformed P2P online lending platforms instead.

Typical P2P online lending refers to the action in which the borrower and the lender directly get contact via online lending platform, and the investor decides whether to make investment through examining the borrower's credit condition and purpose. In this process, P2P online lending platform just plays the role of information intermediary, i.e. the borrower and the lender post information on the platform via free matching, and do not intervene trading but simply retrieve related service charge. Throughout mutual communication, if the borrower and the lender reach investment agreement, capital will be transferred by way of third-party payment, and the borrower will make payment on schedule. Consequently, P2P online lending platform makes non-intermediary direct financing possible. Full communication between the borrower and the lender reduces information asymmetry. Internet is able to reduce trading cost and meantime raise trading efficiency.

However, it is just an ideal state. In real operation, only few modes totally adhere to such means. The main reason is because of information incompleteness about lending. For this, most platforms have made changes more or less in the operation mode of P2P online lending, and some of them even totally get rid of the original intention of P2P online lending and evolve into traditional folk finance. It is nothing but its extension on Internet. These matters will be introduced in detail in subsequent sections (Fig. 1 and Table 1).

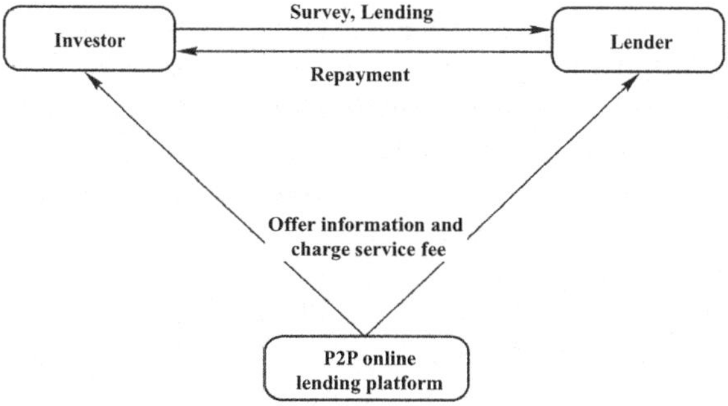

Fig. 1 Classical P2P online lending flow

Table 1 Comparison of bank financing and P2P online lending

Differences	*Bank financing*	*P2P online lending*
Property of financing	Direct financing	Indirect financing
Supply and demand matching	Term mismatch	One-to-one match
Assumption of risk	Credit risk and liquidity risk	Risk free
Property of platform	Information intermediary, fund intermediary, risk intermediary	Information intermediary
Profit model	Interest spreads of deposit and loan	Service charge
Supervision requirements	Capital adequacy ratio, liquidity, reserve fund	Intermediary, no guarantee, no capital pool, no illicit attraction of deposits

P2P Online Lending and Bank Loan

Comparing with traditional bank financing, P2P online lending has experienced some drastic changes. From the perspective of financing property, it can be easily seen that bank financing belongs to indirect financing in which the depositor transfers capital to the bank and the bank makes investment on behalf of the depositor. The borrower raises a loan from the bank so that the borrower and the lender do not directly get contact, but realize capital flow via the intermediary of bank. Banks usually provide long-term capital, but collect short-term capital. This inevitably causes term mismatch. However, capital on P2P online lending platform is in one-to-one relation, in which one borrower matches with one investor. Banks ought to undertake credit risk and liquidity risk for investors, but P2P platforms do not need to undertake related risks. Banks serve as information intermediary, capital intermediary and risk intermediary, but P2P platform just serves as information intermediary alone. Banks earn interest spreads of deposit and loan via financing and investment, but P2P just earns service charge and never intervenes trading. Banks are subject to capital adequacy ratio, liquidity, reserves and related supervision measures, but P2P platform just needs to cooperate with intermediary, and never engages in guarantee, capital pool and illegal sequestration.

P2P Online Lending and Big Data Finance

As proved by the operation mode of P2P online lending, it is a more open, extensive and free financing and investment mode than big data finance. Such openness is mainly reflected by two points.

The first one is platform data access. Big data finance primarily relies on the trading data inside e-commerce companies, but such trading data is just limited within the platform and serves limited customers. Outside of the platform, because of the lack of related trading data, big data finance can't cover all fields. It actually suggests the bottleneck problem of platform customers. This problem has been narrated in last chapter. But it is not a problem in P2P online lending. P2P online lending serves more customers. As there is no restriction on scope and region, the platform possibly takes information in more dimensions to assess the lender's credit and is not confined to e-commerce platform. Consequently, P2P online lending breaks up limitations on e-commerce platforms, and gets rid of the constraint on customer quantity. This is one of the reasons why P2P online lending is more open than big data finance.

Secondly, P2P online lending solves the problem of capital inadequacy. Big data finance e-commerce companies provide loan to small and micro companies with equity capital via the cooperation with banks. But equity capital is limited. So even banks take advantage of asset securitization or other means to transfer capital, the efficiency will be reduced greatly. However, by directly introducing investors to offer capital to the borrower at the liability side, PEP online lending totally solves the inadequacy problem of loanable capital. As long as there are enough investors, they can ensure capital adequacy and solve loan capital source difficulties.

Actually, from the two aspects, P2P online lending is indeed more open and inclusive than big data finance. P2P online lending moves further than big data finance in capital supply and demand. Devoid of capital intermediary, supply and demand parties can directly contact each other, and negotiate about loan scale, interest rate, term and purpose. It has more overt open and dis-intermediation characteristics than bank loan, big data finance and other modes, better propels disintermediation, and more approaches direct financing. But it is worth mentioning here that P2P online lending and big data finance are just two directions of online lending, and their main difference is in data accumulation. In the early stage, the thinking of big data finance advocates data accumulation. When the data accumulates to some degree, big data finance will try to use data in credit approval and involve online lending. However, it can be only launched in a given scope. On the contrary, P2P online lending does not have considerable data accumulation, but tries to use external data, like sound social credit investigation system, to directly assess credit. After all, in the Chinese context, the form of P2P online lending possibly changes.

2 The Development History of P2P Online Lending

The concept of lending has a long history. Either non-official folk finance or official banks, securities, trust and other financial institutions, they are all different forms of lending. P2P online lending is more like one-to-one lending in folk finance. But different from traditional folk lending, it is pure credit loan as it does not need pledge or mortgage. Actually, credit lending in folk finance comes into being in early time than we thought. For instance, typical Rotating Savings and Credit Association (ROSCA) predates currency, and its history in China lasts for more than one hundred years. By ROSCA, we may see through the thinking and bud of P2P online lending in early time.

ROSCA belongs to a credit mutual-assistance association. Usually, the founder requests few relatives and friends to join the conference once a month or once a season, and members shall pay certain amount of capital each time. The capital is used by each member by turn. In most cases, the founder can use the capital in the first round. Then it is the turn of members according to the order. Those members who gain the capital first ought to pay another sum, similar to payment after loan installment. Correspondingly, those who gain the capital later will gain overall capital in the end, similar to fixed deposit by installment and loan after deposit. By way of such means of organization, members can conveniently gain desirable loans to alleviate financing difficulties. But it is clear that such mode is run on the basis of two premises. The first one is the credit between relatives and friends. It rests in the key of ROSCA risk control. Friends and relatives are familiar with one another and aware of respective credit, including assets, default rate, cash flow. In consequence, they may also realize pure credit loan without asset pledge. The second premise is to lower trading cost. As relatives and friends are close to one another, they do not need to investigate respective background. This creates convenience for trading and lowers trading cost. Exactly benefited by the two conditions, ROSCA can ensure its effective operation in a specific scope. But at the same time, the two factors also prohibit the further development of ROSCA. Similar to big data finance, the influence of relatives and friends is limited, and it is hard to expand the scope. It is hard to guarantee the credit of strangers, which means that it is impossible to entrust strangers to use the capital according to their credit. As long as the trading scope is expanded, corresponding trading cost will also increase with distance. Credit risk and trading cost limit the trading scope of ROSCA. Then how to make breakthroughs in the two aspects is the key to operate P2P online lending.

Development History of Abroad P2P Online Lending

P2P online lending appeared in the year of 1976. As there was no Internet at that time, then financial activities were in a small scale in terms of loan scale, number of participant, etc.[1]

In the 1980s, Mohammed Yunus, a Bangladesh economist, founded "micro-loan". In his opinion, capital gap can be compensated as long as the rich lend to the poor. This thinking precedes ROSCA as it breaks up the restriction of scope, and realizes capital loan in a wider range. But limited by technical reasons, micro-loan is restricted in number of participant and region. Thus it can be seen that though Yunus' micro-loan is offline, it basically possesses the spirits of modern P2P online lending.

In May 2005, four young men—Richard Duvel, James Alexander, Sala Matthews, and David Nicholson from Britain founded the world's first P2P online lending platform Zopa, officially announcing the birth of P2P online lending in real sense. P2P online lending therefore sought a leapfrog progress than ROSCA and micro-loan. First of all, it breaks up the constraint on the mutual relation between the borrower and the lender. Even if people non-related to one another may acquire online lending. For this, it greatly increases the number of participant than ROSCA. Secondly, it gets rid of the constraint of lending conditions. Internet makes long-distance lending possible, and removes regional restrictions. Till then, lending free from region and social relation restrictions eventually comes into being.

After that, Prosper and Lending Club were successively founded in America in 2006 and 2007, and they gradually became the benchmark of international P2P industry. But the development of P2P online lending is not easy all the time. Till 2008, both Prosper and Lending Club were banned by SEC. According to SEC, online lending earnings voucher on P2P platforms belonged to securities, but Prosper and Lending Club lacked the qualification of registered broker. This proved that American regulatory authority's supervision on P2P industry was contradictory and divergent to some degree. Though Lending Club and Prosper recovered approval in current and next year, respectively, American regulatory authority still worried about the emerging industry. British P2P industry was also subject to British financial regulatory agency in April 2014.

[1] Data source: Case Research Report for Typical P2P Petty Loan Credit Patterns, 2014.

Accompanied by the development of P2P industry, institutional investors take interest in quality P2P companies. On February 11, 2014, Zopa, the largest P2P online lending platform in Europe, gained new financing sum totaling 15 million pounds (approximately 25 million dollars) from hedge fund company Arrowgrass Capital Partners. Before that, Zopa had gained financing totaling 56.6 million pounds. In America, Prosper and Lending Club were unquestionably the most popular and well-received entities. On January 23, 2013, Prosper announced that it had gained the financing totaling 25 million dollars from Sequoia Capital and Blackstone Group. On May 5, 2014, it gained the new-round financing totaling 70 million dollars led by San Francisco investment company Francisco Partners and followed by another two risk venture companies—Institutional Venture Partners and Phenomen Partners. Similarly, Lending Club also attracted the attention of considerable investors. In late 2007, it finished A-round financing totaling 102.6 million dollars from Norwest Venture Partners and Canaan Partners. In 2009, it gained B-round financing totaling 12 million dollars from Morgenthaler Ventures. In 2010, it gained C-round financing totaling 204.5 million dollars from Foundation Capital. In 2011, it raised D-round financing totaling 25 million from risk venture companies Union Square Venture and Thomson Reuters. In risk investment and financing in 2012, KPCB invested 15 million dollars, and John Mack, former CEO of Morgans invested 2.5 million dollars. In May 2, 2013, it gained another round of finance totaling 125 million dollars from Foundation Capital and Google. Together with the successive entry of institutional investors, P2P industry develops in the orientation of oligarch market.

On December 12, 2014, Lending Club was listed on NYSE as the world's first listed P2P company. This marked that with the development of industry and supervisory norms, P2P industry is predicted to gradually transit from fast development stage to rational development stage. It is very likely to see industry differentiation phenomenon in the future.

Case 1: Zopa

Zopa was founded in Britain in March 2005. As the first P2P online lending platform in real sense, Zopa sets a good example to following P2P platforms in industry criteria, business flow, risk control and a series of aspects.

For realizing lending service on Zopa, the parties must register as members, and provide basic personal information and credit information. The platform will make a comprehensive assessment on personal credit report provided by the borrower and third-party credit rating agency Equifax, rank the borrower's credit level in A, B, C and D. The borrower may apply for a loan totaling 1000–25,000 pounds. Afterward, the borrower should input sum of loan, capital purpose, the affordable capital interest rate, etc. The platform will divide borrowers according to their credit level, and wait for the bid of investors. Upon investors' submission of investment sum and interest rate requirements, the platform can either automatically match the loan or otherwise make investment as per online lending list. Zopa's interest rate is determined by bid. In case that many investors join in one bid, the borrower may reach an agreement with one with lowest offer.

It should be noted there that for controlling risks, Zopa also requests borrowers to make fixed payment per month and investors shall invest in at least 50 borrowers.

During the full trading process, Zopa just plays the role of trading aid, including pre-loan borrower credit authentication, capital transfer, information matching between the borrower and the lender, providing lending trading-related legal documents, retaining third-party agencies to reclaim the loan for investors. Whereas, it never intervenes trading. In another word, it is a pure platform or say a pure intermediary.

Case data source http://www.douban.com/group/topic/6224469/.

Case 2: Kiva

Kiva was a non-profit P2P online lending platform founded in 2005. It is mainly oriented to low-income poor people in developing countries.

In cooperation with global petty loan agencies and volunteers across the world, Kiva learns about local poor groups' capital demands, masters the basic information of borrowers, and posts their pictures on Kiva website via field visit. Kiva lists applicants' basic information, picture, sum of loan, purpose, repayment term and other information on website lending list. The limit of loan ranges between 25–1000 dollars.

When a project raises enough capital, Kiva would lend capital to local petty loan agencies where the borrower lives in without interest, and then these agencies lend the capital to borrowers with low interest. Kiva allows partners to collect low interest for operation.

As to operation means, though Kiva is a non-profit organization, it is more like online "micro-loan" in Bangladesh or say the Internet edition of "micro-loan".

Case source http://baike.baidu.com/link?url=hwPQcZmcYK2p9x3 lOsSZz5GdRQe3Xg3LcRndBAb0gw2qaeIXKXrUj_QCxghJzsfhyGyLn fzYQew NWYQ0-M8Zgq.

Case 3: Prosper

Prosper is the first P2P online lending platform built in America in February 2006 by Criss Larson. Adhering to Zopa's pure intermediary spirits, Prosper aims to provide services and reach trading. But it also makes some changes.

The borrower and the lender shall be the registered members of Prosper at first. Upon successful registration, the platform would rank members' credit according to name, residence, social security number, personal liability, financial balance, and personal credit report provided by third-party credit rating agencies.

Proper consults the assessment made by Experian Company, and requests borrowers must have over 640 credit points. Prosper divides borrowers' credit into AA, A, B, C, D, E and HR (High Risk) levels, with different credit levels corresponding to different loan interest, service charge, loanable sum, and loan term.

Borrowers who pass credit approval must clarify sum, term, purpose and maximum interest of loan so as to generate the lending list. The lending list will demonstrate loan sum, term, purpose, interest, monthly sum of payment, borrowers' credit records, financial state and employment state to investors so that investors can choose proper investment targets for bid.

Prosper is the first platform that applies a full set of auction system called "double blind". The so-called double bind auction system is actually Dutch auction. When borrowers propose the lending application, Prosper will post the requirement on the platform for investors to join the bid, and the one with minimum interest offer wins. But such means makes the whole lending trading process time-consuming and low efficient as the system is hard to operate and investors lack pertinent positioning for bid. In October 2008, Prosper securities business was banned by American Securities and Exchange Commission. In July 2009, Prosper provided two solutions after its re-registration. First, investors can still use former auction system. Secondly, the platform can set interest rate for loan according to credit assessment system.

WebBank issues a loan to borrowers upon the completion of bid, and then transfers the loan to investors. Investors therefore gain earnings voucher.

Case source http://www.yinhang.com/a_2014_0320_194411.html.

Case 4: Lending Club

Lending Club was founded in March 2007 in America. At first, Lending Club just posted lending information on Facebook. It is keen on the social contact properties of Facebook as a social platform, as it thinks that friends familiar with one another have rather low information asymmetry, and lending business is easier between friends out of mutual trust and high communication. Then Lending Club found that Facebook customers were generally young, and this went against its customer requirements in credit record and capital condition. From then on, it embarked on the building of its own website. In March 2008, at the request of American Securities and Exchange Commission, Lending Club was requested to make registration as its bill belonged to securities. In October 2008, Lending Club was re-launched online. The new Lending Club quickly grew to be the world's largest P2P online lending platform. On December 12, 2014, it was listed on NYSE.

Qualification Approval

Lending Club sets up the access threshold for borrowers and investors on the platforms. For borrowers, Lending Club requests that all borrowers shall be American citizens aged above 18 who have social security account, financial agency account, over 660 FICO credit points, less than 35% debt revenues, over three-year credit history and less than 6 times of loan application records during the past 6 months. For investors, Lending Club requests that investors shall reach given requirements in income and wealth, such as less than 10% investment sum in wealth. The main purpose is to protect the interests of investors.

Loan Application

When borrowers apply for a loan from Lending Club, they ought to not only provide information concerning personal credit conditions, but also illustrate capital sum, term and purpose. Lending Club may not verify the authenticity of information. Even so, loan application rate is still rather low. Till late 2012, it was simply 11%. The loan sum of Lending Club ranges between 1000 and 35,000 dollars, and term of payment includes three-year installment and five-year installment. According to loan purpose, re-financing accounts for a large proportion, which is followed by credit card loan. All of these are under the category of consumption credit.

Risk Control

Risk control is the core technology of Lending Club. Lending Club controls borrowers' risk via the link of credit rating and interest pricing. The credit rating of Lending Club is, respectively, A, B, C, D, E, F, G from high to low, and each level is divided into 1–5 level. In another word, there are 7 × 5 = 35 credit levels in Lending Club. It takes two steps to determine credit level. Like Prosper, Lending Club will firstly determine borrower credit pursuant to FICO credit rating and other credit characteristics. In the second place, it makes adjustment of borrowers' loan sum and term on the basis of basic rating. Generally, greater sum and term results is greater decline of credit level.

The loan interest of Lending Club is fixed. It determines loan interest rate as per borrowers' credit rating. Generally speaking, higher credit level means smaller loan sum and shorter loan term and corresponding, lower loan interest. As shown in Table 2, just like credit level, there are also 35 loan interest levels, with a minimum of 6.03% and maximum of 26.06%.

Lending Flow

First of all, investors choose proper borrowers. Investors may also choose proper borrowers for investment in Lending Club, or use investment

Table 2 Lending Club loan pricing

Credit rating	*1 (%)*	*2 (%)*	*3 (%)*	*4 (%)*	*5 (%)*
A	6.03	6.62	7.62	7.9	8.9
B	9.67	10.99	11.99	12.99	13.67
C	14.3	15.1	15.61	16.2	17.1
D	17.76	18.55	19.2	19.52	20.2
E	21	21.7	22.4	23.1	23.4
F	23.7	24.08	24.5	24.99	25.57
G	25.8	25.83	25.89	25.99	26.06

Data source Xie Ping, Zou Chuanwei, Liu Hai'er, *Internet Finance Manual*, Beijing: China Renmin University Press, 2014

portfolio of Lending Club to build instruments, set up indicators such as earnings rate, default rate and service tariffing, and build an investment portfolio with the system automatically. As a general rule, investors who make dispersed investment tend to suffer from less loss. According to the statistics of Lending Club, the loss probability of investors who buy 100 bills is 1%, and that of investors who buy 400 bills decreases to 0.2%. If the number of bill exceeds 800, investors may not suffer from any loss at all. Lending Club stipulates that the minimum investment sum made by investors in single bill should be 25 dollars. The investment only achieves success only when investors' subscription reaches the loan amount.

Secondly, Lending Club issues usufruct voucher. When all investors' investment amount reaches the loan amount, investors will succeed in investment. Lending Club will then issue usufruct voucher to investors. This is the evidence for investors to gain investment and earnings.

Thirdly, WebBank, the cooperative bank of Lending Club, is responsible for issuing a loan to borrowers.

Finally, WebBank transfers the loan to Lending Club and the latter pays to the former.

Such business mode of Lending Club in which WebBank issues a loan and transfers creditor's right to Lending Club could be said as the prototype of CreditEase in China (Fig. 2).

Income Source

Lending Club charges 1% service fee against each payment received by investors. For borrowers, Lending Club collects loan service charge at one time. Service charge rate is related to borrowers' credit rating and

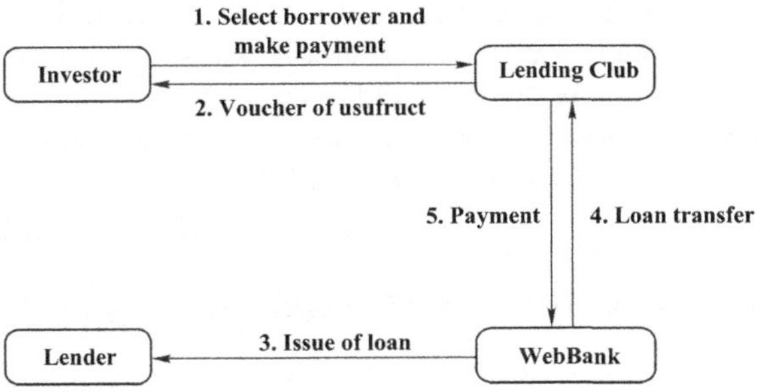

Fig. 2 Lending Club business flow

Table 3 Lending Club loan service charge

Service charge		*Term*	
Credit rating and grade		*3 years (%)*	*5 years (%)*
A	1	1.11	3
	2–3	2	3
	4–5	3	3
B	1–5	4	5
C	1–5	5	5
D	1–5	5	5
E	1–5	5	5
F	1–5	5	5
G	1–5	5	5

Data source Xie Ping, Zou Chuanwei, Liu Hai'er, *Internet Finance Manual*, Beijing: China Renmin University Press, 2014

loan term. Lower credit level means longer loan term and higher loan rate (Table 3).

As proved by the survey of four main P2P online lending platforms in foreign countries, these platforms share many points in common, which could be revealed in four aspects. First of all, concerning, platform positioning, all of them play the role of information intermediary. Foreign P2P platforms show distinct intermediary characteristics. They do not intervene lending trading, but just promote the lending business as much as possible. Secondly, investors are all keen on dispersed petty loan. Thirdly, borrowers are all individuals. Fourthly, the loan is mainly used for consumer loan. Though the four platforms are different from one another in interest formation and risk control, they all make full use of the sound individual credit system and multi-dimensional individual information in the west. Exactly on this basis, credit assessment mode and interest pricing model remain invincible, and pure platform, pure intermediary and guarantee-free mode survives. This is the foremost enlightenment to Chinese P2P online lending industry (Table 4).

Development History of P2P Online Lending in China

The development history of P2P online lending in China is very long. Early in June 2007, the rise of a group of online lending platforms represented by PPDAI marked the birth of P2P online lending in China. As of

Table 4 Comparison of four operation modes

Differences	*Zopa*	*Kiva*	*Prosper*	*Lending Club*
Interest rate formation	Matching formation	Platform formation	Auction formation of corresponding credit rating	Corresponding credit rating
Risk control	Coercive installment repayment, disperse investment	Post-lending management with local institutions	Credit rating Interest rate formation	Credit rating Interest rate formation

2007, P2P online lending in China has taken place drastic changes in the eight years. From past obscurity to present high popularity, P2P industry surmounts the expectation of all. In accordance with the development changes of O2O industry in China, its history falls into three stages as below.

Exploration Stage in 2007–2008

In 2007, adhering to the pure online and pure intermediary P2P online lending spirits, PPDAI began to develop in China. However, P2P platforms failed to attract enough attention as investors, borrowers and financial capital were not confident about such mode. At that time, bubbles in the share market had ruptured, but investors did not timely exit the market and waited for the advent of next-round bull market. In addition, such pure platform and guarantee-free investment mode is non-acceptable to Chinese investors lack of investment awareness. Therefore, P2P platform does not gain high attention in former two years in China, and platform data and trading scale could be nearly overlooked.

High-Speed Growth Stage in 2009–2013

The P2P industry in China takes fundamental changes since Hongling Capital's proposal of principal payment on account concept in the year of 2009. This practice has been successively followed by many platforms. Principal payment on account, guarantee mode, loan loss provision and many other transformed modes successively come into being. For a time, platform quantity and trading volume rapidly increase and P2P industry directly transits from the exploration stage to high-speed growth stage. In

2010, there were just 10 P2P lending platforms in China. But the figure rose to 50 in 2011, 200 in 2012 and 600 in 2013. Till late 2014, there were 1575 platforms and corresponding trading volume also went up. In 2011, online lending trading volume was 3.1 billion yuan. The figure was 21.2 billion yuan in 2012, over 100 billion in 2013 and over 250 billion in 2014. Thus it can be seen that P2P industry is extremely popular in China now.

As proved by its development history, high-speed growth should be fundamentally ascribed to the change of business mode. Out of all kinds of practical reasons, Chinese P2P industry can't satisfy realistic demands by the pure platform mode, and has to experience "sinicization" transformation to develop a unique P2P mode with Chinese characteristics. The foremost expression should be the rise of principal guarantee. Behind principal guarantee, what matters is the change of entire business property. Classical P2P online lending belongs to direct financing in which investors undertake investment risks and gain investment earnings. But in China, such principal guarantee mode reflects the concept of indirect financing in which borrowers lend capital to borrowers and the platform or guarantee company assumes corresponding lending risks. This is basically the same with loan in commercial banks. The sole difference is that the platform is just petty loan company without bank license tag, and this is the online form of petty loan mode. Exactly out of this reason, P2P platform quickly expands in China.

All the time, traditional financial institutions such as commercial banks can't satisfy the credit demands of considerable small- and medium-sized companies and individuals. At the same time, limited by interest non-marketization regulation, these institutions can't set a rational interest for residents so that residents can't raise a loan and banks can't dispose excess amount of money. The gap between high folk lending demands and non-access of small and micro companies and individuals to traditional financial institutions, and lack of individual investors' investment channels is the fundamental motivator of P2P online lending in China. But due to the lack of credit system, banks can't provide corresponding credit loan, and non-mortgage and non-guarantee loan can't gain recognition from investors. Against such circumstances, guarantee mode is created. Thus it can be seen that the root of this problem is in the building of credit system. It is also the most important enlightenment given by western P2P industry.

Normative Development Stage After 2014

In the midst of fast development, there also rise some problems in the P2P industry. To be specific, platform crisis, runaway business, fraud, capital pool and illegal fund-raising problems also emerge in endlessly. In 2013, 76 platforms collapsed. The number rose up to 275 till 2014. Considering this, the regulatory agencies sped up the normalization of P2P industry.

The year of 2014 was called the first year of P2P industry regulation. In April, banks clarified the four red lines in P2P industry, namely intermediary property, non-guarantee, capital pool and illegal sequestration. This is of great significance to the normative development of P2P industry. As some platform self-guarantee modes will be banned, lending risks are expected to drop significantly. Accompanied by the successive enactment of *Internet Finance Instructions* issued by People's Bank of China in July and ten major principles in P2P regulation in September, P2P industry regulatory norms are about to be gradually implemented and P2P industry also goes on the path of normative development.

3 The Development Status of P2P Online Lending

Throughout two-year exploration stage and five-year high-speed growth stage, domestic P2P online lending platforms have become the most dazzling starts in the field of Internet Finance and turn more popular than former Bao series products. It not only causes huge impacts in platform quantity, lending scale and number of participants, but also brings more profound, extensive and intensive influences to the market.

Quantity of P2P Platform

Quantity of Operation Platform

Concerning the quantity of platform operation, there were just 10 P2P platforms in China in 2010. But the scale kept growing as of 2011, and maintained a high growth rate above 300% for consecutive three years. Till 2013, the number rose to 800. Though the growth rate mitigated in 2014, the overwhelming quantity was still 1575, around twice more than that in 2013 (Figs. 3 and 4). From the perspective of platform background, banks, listed companies, state-owned companies and other traditional companies successively enter the industry. At present, these platforms can be divided into four types as per the varying context, namely

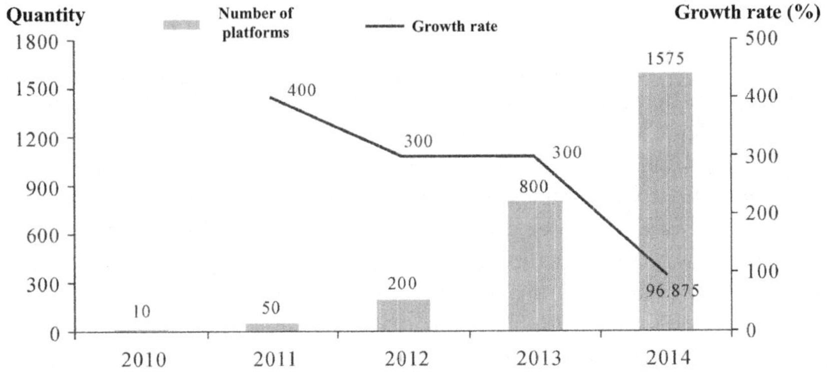

Fig. 3 Number of Chinese P2P operation platforms of China from 2010 to 2014 (*Data source* Annual Report for Chinese Online Lending Industry in 2014)

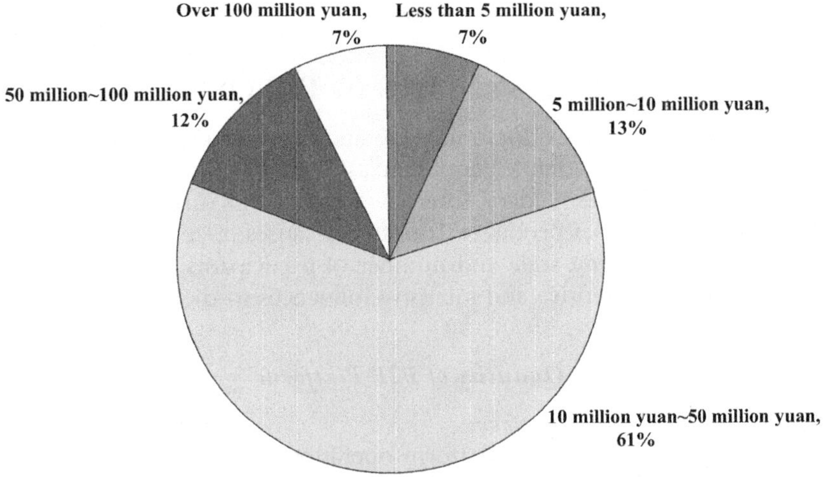

Fig. 4 Scale distribution of new P2P platforms in 2014 (*Data source* Annual Report for Chinese Online Lending Industry in 2014)

risk venture, business, listed company and state-owned assets platform. Among the four platforms, risk venture platform is in largest quantity totaling 29. The quantity of listed companies and state-owned assets platforms is 17. While the quantity of banks is 12.

Table 5 Comparison of different P2P platforms

Type	Advantages	Disadvantages	Representative companies
Banking department	Risk control mode and management with bank's characteristics; Great security; Original clients from banks	Low yield rate	Micro-Company E Home of China Merchants Bank
State-owned asset system	Strong credibility	High investment threshold	Kaixin Loan
Venture capital system	Low investment threshold; High yield rate	Limited brand influence and credibility	Hongling Capital
Listed company system	Substantial capital strength; Normative operations	Insufficient personnel and professionalism	Yinhu.com

Data source Annual Report for Internet Finance Wealth Management in 2014, revised version

Different platforms have different backgrounds. On the whole, bank P2P platform risk control modes and management flow incorporate the characteristics of banks. For this, this mode has relatively high security, and many customers used to be fixed customers of banks. But its drawback should be its relatively low earnings rate. Backed by the brand power of state-owned companies, state-owned assets P2P platforms demonstrate strong credibility, but their investment threshold is relatively high. Though risk venture platform has low investment threshold, and high earnings rate, it has limited brand influence and credibility given the folk assets property. Listed company P2P platforms enjoy an edge in financial power and normative operation, but take a disadvantaged place in manpower and professionalism (Table 5).

Quantity of Problematic Platforms

Concerning the quantity of problematic platforms, it began to drastically increase from 2013. The quantity of problematic platforms was just 10 in 2011, and 6 in 2012. However, it increased to 76 in 2013 and 275 in 2014.

Concerning the appearance time of problematic platforms, problematic platforms usually rise in the end of year. The quantity of problematic platforms significantly increase as of September. This comes down to two reasons. The first one is that platform payment usually takes place in the end of the year. Those platforms found to be in poor operation conditions and liquidity risks will face the great challenge of payment. Some of them even close down for this. Secondly, in the end of the year, banks usually tightened the budget. If some borrowers can't raise a loan, they can't make payment, and this also results in problems in the platforms. In addition, the bull market in the end of the year also replaces investment capital dissociation and investment capital inadequacy in turn accelerates platform payment and collapse.

Concerning the operation time of problematic platforms, most of these platforms run for less than one year, and 77 platforms which have run for 1–3 months run into most problems. It is successively followed by platforms which have run for 7–12 months. Short operation time is one of the remarkable characteristics of problematic platforms. This indicates that many platform founders lack a full understanding about P2P industry at the very beginning, and they even underestimate the risks on P2P platforms. Unsound credit assessment mechanism and risk control mechanism eventually lead to the quick collapse of platforms.

Concerning the type of problematic platforms in 2014, withdrawal difficulty proves to be the foremost reason. Altogether 112 platforms run into this problem, accounting for 41%; 60 platforms run off with money, accounting for 22% and 56 platforms commit fraud, accounting for 20%. The three reasons contribute to 83% business failures. Few platforms close down because of cease of operation, loss of contact, police intervention or document forgery.

Concerning the distribution of problematic platforms, Guangdong, Zhejiang, Shandong, Shanghai and Beijing have most problematic platforms, and the number of problematic platforms there is 58, 41, 39, 25 and 17, respectively. This matches with the quantity of operation platform. Others places also have such problematic platforms, including 12 in Hubei, and 13 in Hunan.

P2P Online Lending Scale

In respect of P2P online lending scale, both trading volume and online lending balance continually go up with the increase of platform quantity. In 2011, online lending trading volume was just 3.1 billion yuan, and online lending balance was 1.2 billion yuan. In 2012, the two, respectively, rose to 21.2 billion yuan and 5.6 billion yuan. In 2013, online lending trading volume broke through the limit of one hundred billion yuan, and online lending balance also surmounted the trading volume in previous year. Till 2014, online lending trading volume doubled than that in 2013, and online lending balance approached that in 2013.

As indicated by monthly statistics in 2014, the scale of trading volume quickly expands. The trading volume is just ten billion yuan at the beginning of the year, but it approximates 40 billion yuan at the end of the year. Regardless of the "collapse" tide at the end of the year, probably the figure rises in trading volume.

Concerning the regional distribution of O2O online lending trading volume in 2014, it shows a clear differentiation trend in national P2P online lending business. It can be divided into four levels according to trading volume. The first level comprises Guangdong, Zhejiang, Beijing, and Shanghai. In particular, Guangdong ranks first with 8463.7 billion yuan and 33.48% trading volume. Other three provinces and cities rank 2-4th place, respectively, with more than 11% proportion. The second level comprises Jiangsu, Shandong, Sichuan, Hubei and Chongqing, with monthly trading volume totaling 500 million-2 billion yuan. The third level comprises Anhui, Guizhou, Shanxi, Fujian, Henan, Hunan, Jiangxi, Shanxi, Yunnan, Tianjin and Hebei, with monthly trading volume ranging between 100 million-500 million yuan. The fourth level comprises Heilongjiang, Guangxi, Ningxia and other regions in which there are less than 10 P2P online lending platforms and corresponding monthly trading volume is below 100 million yuan.

Concerning the regional distribution of P2P online lending balance, Beijing and Guangdong have maximum online lending balance, respectively, as 2718.7 billion and 2676.2 billion yuan. Shanghai ranks the 3rd place with 1896.7 billion yuan. The online lending balance in Zhejiang, Jiangsu and Shandong is 3 billion ~ 8 billion yuan, respectively, and that in other provinces is 1327.9 billion yuan. P2P online lending balance demonstrates conspicuous concentrated characteristics.

P2P Online Lending Interest

The earnings rate of P2P online lending does not increase together with online lending trading volume, but first rises and later decreases. Such decline tendency is in particular prominent in 2014.

As of 2011, P2P online lending interest continually rises from 18.9 to 19.13%. In 2013, it further reached as high as 21.25%. The year of

2013 also witnessed the prompt development of P2P online lending platform. In 2014, annual P2P online lending interest decreased to 17.86%, reaching the bottom line for recent four years.

Concerning monthly interest trend in 2014, the interest maintained high at the beginning of the year. Especially, the interest rose in January–February. But as of March, it continually declined till the end of the year. Such trend determined the general interest level throughout the whole year of 2014. This is probably related to entire macroscopic environment and industry. First of all, in 2014, the whole economy undertook heavy downward pressures, and national currency policy was rather loose. But due to the inadequacy of demands, loose currency gave rise to the decline of lending interest than 2013. Secondly, with the oncoming enactment of supervisory policies for P2P online lending platforms, some irregular P2P platforms expedite to exit, regular platforms which adhere to pure intermediary mode and show strong credit assessment ability and high risk control level become the mainstream and the "virtually high" trend of interest obtains effective containment. Thirdly, as investors reinforce their investment awareness, earnings rate is no more the decisive factor of investors, and the importance of security turns more prominent.

Concerning the interest platform distribution in 2014, most platforms set the interest range between 15% ~ 20% and account for 28.89%. This conforms to general interest level. Secondly, 26.26% platforms set the interest range between 20–30%. It is much similar to above range in quantity, but it has slightly higher earnings rate. 30–40% platforms are in the same quantity with 12% ~ 15% platforms with a similar proportion of around 15%. Besides that, the proportion below 12% and above 40% is less than 10%.

Concerning interest regional distribution, Gansu, Anhui and Shandong have highest interest, respectively, as 30.53, 29.84 and 29.29%. By contrast, Beijing, Shanghai, Chongqing and Liaoning have lowest interest, respectively, as 16.35, 13.52, 12.93, 11.61 and 10%. The interest in Gansu and Hainan even doubles. Thus it can be seen that P2P online lending is divergent across regions in China, and lending capital uneven distribution trend is in particular prominent.

So how about the comparison between P2P online lending interest and other financing modes? Let's do a comparative research for this.

Bank financial products' annual yield is approximately 5.1%, and threshold of single investment amount is 50,000 yuan. Bank loan interest is 7–10%. Plus other implicit cost, general cost of loan ranges between 8–12%. Trust wealth management individual investors often raise fund via third-party wealth management and private banks, and the threshold of single investment amount is around 3 million yuan. Average earnings rate is 8.8%, financing cost is in the range of 13–20%, and average financing limit is 190 million yuan. Individual investment in fund subsidiary is usually made via third-party wealth management party and threshold of single investment amount is 1 million yuan. Average interest is 10%. The financing cost via fund subsidiary ranges between 15–24%, and the threshold of single financing amount is 300 million ~ 0.2 billion yuan. Stock market entrust loan average earnings rate is 8%. But only 20% investors can achieve the goal, 30% investors break even and half investors suffer loss. The financing cost of stock market entrust loan is 15%, and the threshold of single financing amount is 500 million ~ 0.5 billion yuan. The earnings rate of creditor's rights private fund is 12%. Creditor's rights private fund earnings rate is 15% and investment threshold is above 10 million yuan with great risks. Financing cost is 24% and the threshold of single financing amount is 500 million ~ 0.5 billion yuan. The earnings rate of P2P online lending is 12%, and there is no threshold in investment. Corresponding financing cost is around 20% and single amount of financing is rather small (Table 6).

According to the earnings rate, financing cost, access threshold and risk of above financing modes, P2P online lending earnings rate is not the highest nor lowest. But in terms of access threshold and risk, its earnings rate is relatively high and this caters to mass investors. In reality,

Table 6 Comparison of ordinary financing channels in interest rate

Financing mode	*Yield rate (%)*	*Financing cost (%)*
Bank	5.5	8 ~ 12
Trust	8.8 ~ 10	13 ~ 20
Fund subsidiary and bond asset management	13	15 ~ 24
Equity market entrusted loan	8	15
Private equity	12 or 15	24
P2P lending	12 ~ 20	20
Usury		Monthly interest (three points at least) with no ceiling

Data source Sohu Finance

the nature of Internet finance is inclusive finance. Therefore, P2P online lending featured by low financing amount and moderate interest level is especially proper for small and micro companies and individual borrowers.

P2P Online Lending Term

Another characteristic of P2P online lending in 2014 should be the extension of online lending term. The term of P2P online lending in 2011–2013 gradually decreased from 6–9 month to 4–73 month, but it increased up to 6–12 month in 2014. Like interest decline, this also forms a sharp contrast with the past.

According to online lending term in each month in 2014, the trend of term extension is very significant. Rising from 4–23 month in February, it even reached the peak of 6–88 month. Due to the loose monetary policy and decline of lending interest, borrowers are no more keen on short-term capital but apt to choose low-interest and long-term target. This is the main cause of prolonged online lending term.

Concerning online lending term platform distribution in 2014, online lending platforms with 1–3 month term of payment account for the largest proportion as high as 59.17%. It is followed by the platforms with 3–6 month term of payment which account for 22.54%. Thus it can be seen that online lending now is mostly short-term lending, but there will rise long-term lending in the future. It is predicted that lending platforms will increase the proportion of 3–6 month term and even longer term. Lending platforms with over one year term account for the least proportion as 1.27%.

Concerning the lending term in all provinces, regions or cities, Shanghai, Beijing and Liaoning have longest lending term above 10 months. Hainan, Zhejiang and Guangxi have shortest lending term less than 2 months.

Online Lending Participant

In 2014, there were 76,500 average daily participants of P2P online lending, twice more than that in 2013. This proves that with the development of P2P online lending, more and more people begin to trust in and enter this industry. In early 2014, the number of P2P online lending was just 38,600 per day. But till the end of the year, this figure rose by around 100,000 to 136,100 per day. It fully shows the fast development speed of this industry.

Concerning the number of borrowers on online lending platforms, there were 250,000 investors and 150,000 borrowers in 2013. The number reached 1.16 million and 0.63 million, respectively, in 2014, with respective growth rate as 364 and 320%. The growth rate is very prompt. Especially for investors, it belongs to a new investment and wealth management means.

4 The Mode of P2P Online Lending

The main mode of western P2P online lending is pure online intermediary mode, such as Zopa, Prosper and Lending Club. To a large degree, the development of such P2P online lending platforms is benefited by the sound credit investigation system in western countries. As western countries have mature consumption habits, and long history of lending, they have built a complete and systematic individual credit rating system. This is inseparable to P2P online lending. Every individual's credit records could be documented. Therefore, information asymmetry problem can be effectively alleviated at a low cost, which promotes the development of P2P online lending. In consequence, most foreign P2P online lending platforms belong to information intermediary that never intervene trading nor undertake risks. They strictly adhere to the so-called intermediary role of P2P online lending and disintermediation historical mission.

Comparing with foreign P2P online lending in foreign countries, there still lack individual credit assessment system in China. In another word, China now still lacks a complete individual credit investigation system. PBC's credit investigation system covers a limited scope and dimension, and additionally, it is not accessible to P2P platforms. Moreover, as P2P platforms just start in China, it is impossible to accumulate considerable trading data nor make credit assessment like big data finance. This is the plight faced by P2P online lending industry in China. Under such circumstances, Chinese P2P online lending platforms create a new form full of Chinese characteristics and wisdom, such as "online + offline mode", guarantee mode, loan loss provision mode, etc. To put it simply, these P2P online lending platforms want to assess borrowers' credit by all means even at the cost of its original spirits.

Pure Intermediary Mode

Pure intermediary mode means that P2P online platforms just take charge of borrower credit assessment, lending information matching, interest formation work, and investors automatically determine the investment decision. The platform does not intervene the trading. In platform intermediary mode, when the parties register on the platform, the borrower shall provide identity certificate, loan sum, interest, purpose, time of repayment and other information for approval. Upon the approval of P2P platforms, borrowers' loan information will be posted on the platform. Investors can browse each borrower's lending information, make free matching, and determine investment amount and interest. Investment risk is completely undertaken by investors alone. The investment completes once borrowers raise enough fund. The platform charges management fee and service fee

Such pure "information intermediary" mode basically preserves classical P2P online lending spirits and nature, in which the platform does not intervene trading and maintains its own intermediary property. But different from the classical mode, pure intermediary mode forsakes the practice of free information matching. It is the platform that first makes information approval and credit assessment, and raises fund online upon approval and assessment. In this way, the platform can help investors to discern borrowers, and increase lending success rate. On the other hand, as the platform forsakes free information matching principle, it still intervenes trading to some degree. Such mode is a universal practice taken by mainstream pure intermediary modes. From the perspective of Internet finance, this mode makes for data accumulation. It is also vital to the long-term development of the platform. But in the early development stage of platform, lack of enough data aggravates difficulties to the development of platform. Related statistics show that the overdue rate of pure intermediary platforms reaches 10% and bad debt rate reaches 5%. Thus it can be seen that it is very difficult to develop pure intermediary P2P platforms in China.

Case 5: PPDAI

PPDAI is the first P2P online lending platform founded in June 2007 in China. It is one of the few P2P online lending platforms which adhere to pure online and pure intermediary mode at present. PPDAI preserves the advantages of most primitive and classical online lending platforms.

Through completing user development, credit approval, contractual agreement and payment recovery flows online, PPDAI realizes intermediary, platform and network transformation in real sense.

PPDAI's online credit approval continues the practice of Lending Club. By collecting borrowers' related data, PPDAI builds a credit assessment model to rationally estimate borrowers' credit conditions, and consults risk pricing model to determine loan limit and interest. To be specific, credit approval takes two steps. In the first step, PPDAI verifies borrower name and identity information via authoritative data centers, such as the ID information inquiry center in Ministry of Public Security, Trade and Industry Bureau, and Court. In the second step, according to borrowers' online behavioral data, including network social contact data such as MicroBlog, QQ and WeChat and also data uploaded by individuals such as individual bank credit conditions, financial ability and data in other dimensions, PPDAI assesses borrowers' credit with the credit assessment model and therefore acquires the general credit conditions of borrowers. In present stage, besides these data, PPDAI is also busy in seeking external cooperation, like gaining corporate trading data in cooperation with e-commerce platforms, accessing data on other platforms, possibly expanding the database to reinforce credit approval ability.

PPDAI classifies borrowers' credit level into six levels from A to B, C, D, E and HR. Borrowers' lending limit and success rate are also affected by credit level. As to loan interest, PPDAI follows the practice of Prosper that allows investors to determine interest via bid. The platform such formulates the criterion of each credit level and minimum interest for each type of loan, and interest is negotiated by the parties (Table 7).

Apart of credit assessment, PPDAI also establishes the principal guarantee plan to ensure investors' interests. The principal guarantee plan stipulates that investors who have finished identity authentication can make investment for over 50 times, and the minimum amount of each investment is less than 5,000 yuan. The sum of capital should be less than 33% of gross amount of borrowing. In case of bad debt, PPDAI should pay for it completely. But if it is limited to the principal, no interest loss is involved. Therefore, it can be fitly judged that principal guarantee plan lowers investment risks by encouraging investors to make dispersed, petty and combined investment.

The credit assessment mode of PPDAI more conforms to the spirits of Internet Finance. But as a typical representative of P2P online lending, PPDAI has obvious drawbacks. The foremost expression is data absence.

Table 7 PPDAI credit rating and interest rate principle

Credit rating	*Score interval*	*Online scores*	*Offline scores*	*Minimum interest rate (%)*	*Maximum interest rate*
A	126 ~ 150 points	Identity authentication + 10 points	House property certificate; Marriage certificate; Certificate of salary	12	No more than four times of contemporary bank lending rate, with ordinary ceiling as 24%
B	102 ~ 125 points	Phone real-name authentication + 10 points		14	
C	76 ~ 100 points	Video authentication + 10 points		16	
D	51 ~ 75 points	Diploma authentication + 5 points		18	
E	26 ~ 50 points	Due repayment<15 days + 1point		20	
HR	1 ~ 25 points	Due repayment>15 days-2points		22	

Data source Yang Weiwei, Study on P2P Online Lending Behaviors and Risk Assessment, Qingdao: Ocean University of China, 2014

Third-party payment, online wealth management and big data finance all burst out throughout considerable data accumulation in early stage. With a sound social individual credit investigation system, Europe and America support the pure online intermediary development of P2P online lending. But no domestic P2P online lending platform possesses such prerequisite. Devoid of a sound social credit investigation system and considerable data accumulation in early stage, such pure online intermediary P2P platforms are faced with great challenges. As credit assessment models take limited data dimensions, model assessment results are less accurate and reliable and have poor risk control ability. Nearly all P2P platforms in China now confront such a problem. After all, different platforms have different choices before the problem. This is the fundamental cause of platform differentiation.

Case source Shi Yakun, Research on the Innovative Development Mode of P2P Lending Platform, Master's Paper in Henan University, 2014.

"Online + Offline" Mode

Different from traditional online mode, such mode on the one hand preserves online business, and on the other hand transfers some businesses offline. Usually, the online business is wealth management side which attracts mass investors via network, and the platform is responsible for publishing lending information and lending contract. Out of the purpose of risk prevention and control, the platform more transfers borrower seeking and credit assessment flow offline and entrusts offline stores or agents to make field survey so as to determine borrower credit and effectively prevent borrower risks.

This mode is created by the platform to compensate borrower credit information inadequacy online. By way of field survey, the platform can better learn about borrower credit. Its original intention is to increase the credit of borrowers. Comparing with pure online mode, such mode platform still stays away from lending trading. The sole difference is that it makes offline credit survey and assessment. Even if it does not fundamentally smash P2P online lending spirits, it more or less touches offline business (Table 8).

Table 8 Comparison of online mode and offline mode

Mode	*User expansion*	*Risk control*	*Capital transaction*
Online	User scale expansion and pertinent marketing Low operation cost Accumulation of user data Promotion of user education and viscosity in the long run	Convenience for data and risk control accumulation Conservation of cost Rise of risk control efficiency, and reduction of moral risks Subject to the constraint of data scale and dimension	Mastery of transaction data Evasion of policy red line Conservation of cost Rise of efficiency
Offline	Fast growth of trading volume in the short run Efficient persuasion and education for users High cost	Low innovation risks in traditional risk control mode Susceptibility to moral risks High manpower cost Long cycle	Predisposition to cross policy red line Inability to access core data

Data source Case Study Report for Typical P2P Micro-credit Modes, 2014

Concerning credit operation, the "online + offline" mode is somewhat similar to traditional commercial banks. Online business is just to attract deposits and add flow. In respect of capital trading, it also adopts the same mode with banks, namely the so-called offline approval. But this does not demonstrate the superiority of Internet and deviates from the spirits of Interne finance. It can be viewed as a traditional online finance without traditional finance institutional guarantee. Though the "online + offline" mode could well fix credit assessment inadequacy problem, its nature is changing now.

Case 6: Renrendai

Founded in May 2010, Renrendai is a successful representative in which pure online mode transits to "online = offline" mode. At first, Renrendai just focuses on pure online mode. But for better excavating potential consumers and improving platform risk control ability, Renrendai merges with its subsidiary Youxin and Youxin takes charge of seeking quality consumers and making field survey offline. Throughout this means, Renrendai gains a huge success. Till late 2013, Youxin gained financing totaling 1.3 billion dollars, thus hitting the record of Lending Club. Youxin also became the largest financing entity in P2P field in the world.

Renrendai has a similar lending flow to PPDAI. First, the parties should register on the platform to be members. Borrowers must be citizens aged 22–55 with income and repayment ability and investors must be aged above 18. Secondly, borrowers choose type of loan, and submit related documents. Renrendai has three types of loan, including payroll loan, business loan and network business loan, and each type of loan is different. Borrowers shall choose a type of loan and submit required documents. Thirdly, Renrendai should audit borrower material and present corresponding credit level and loan limit. Renrendai classifies borrower credit level into 7 levels, including AA, A, B, C, D, E, HR. Fourthly, when borrowers' loan application is approved, they can post their information on the website for investors to make a choice (Table 9).

Additionally, Renrendai also establishes principal guarantee plan which allows the platform to transfer proportional capital from each sum of loan in risk fund account. In case of severe overdue over 30 days among borrowers, Renrendai will pay due principal or interest with risk fund.

In 2012, in order to better excavate quality borrowers and make risk control, Renrendai and Youxin cooperated to involve offline business.

Table 9 Renrendai lending product

Product type	*Payroll loan*	*Business loan*	*Network businessman loan*
Application conditions	Citizens aged 22–55 At least 3 months working experience in current company; Monthly income over 2,000 yuan	Citizens aged 22–55 The enterprise has been in operation for at least one year	Citizens aged 22–55 At least half a year of operation on Taobao/Tmall; Transaction volume in recent three months exceeds 30,000 yuan, and number of transaction exceeds 50
Borrowing limit	3,000 ~ 500,000 yuan	3,000 ~ 500,000 yuan	3,000 ~ 500,000 yuan
Annual interest rate	10% ~ 24%	10% ~ 24%	10% ~ 24%
Term of loan	3, 6, 9, 12, 18 and 24 months	3, 6, 9, 12, 18 and 24 months	3, 6, 9, 12, 18 and 24 months
Review time	1 ~ 3 workdays	1 ~ 3 workdays	1 ~ 3 workdays
Means of repayment	Average capital plus interest, monthly payment	Average capital plus interest, monthly payment	Average capital plus interest, monthly payment
Application material	ID card, individual credit investigation, certificate of employment, account statement	ID card, individual credit investigation, evidence of business transaction, account statement	ID card, website, QQ video review

Data source Zeng Zhi, Research of P2P Online Lending in China, Chengdu: Southwestern University of Finance and Economics, 2014

The company even specifically built a professional marketing team and risk control team, to expand business in 48 stores across the country. Different from online mode, Renrendai is more concerned about offline marketing team and risk control team. It demands workers to make field visit, approval and post-loan collection. Through this means, it can not only seek more borrowers, but also make better risk control, lower borrower default risk and guarantee investor interests. Practical platform operation experience shows that field authentication target quantity and sum both exceed credit authentication target and institutional guarantee target. Obviously, comparing with pure online mode and guarantee mode,

Table 10 Trading overview of different targets of Renrendai in 2013

Type	Sum of transaction	Sum (yuan)	Proportion
Credit authentication target	2,616	83,967,850	5.35%
Institution guarantee target	3,950	209,076,900	13.33%
Field authentication target	26,223	1,275,990,300	81.32%
Sum	32,789	1,569,035,050	100%

Data source Zeng Zhi, Research of P2P Online Lending in China, Chengdu: Southwestern University of Finance and Economics, 2014

investors more prefer traditional lending and short-term investment habit is not changed yet. While Renrendai's "online + offline" mode satisfies investors' demands, and meantime, expands investors' scope online. As a result, it gains a huge success (Table 10).

Case source Yan Miao, Study on P2P Online Lending Platform Modes, Problems and Countermeasures, Beijing: Chinese Academy of Social Sciences, 2014.

Guarantee Mode

For protecting investors' interests, some platforms launch the guarantee mode, including third-party guarantee and platform guarantee. Third-party guarantee means guarantee companies or petty loan companies provide guarantee for investors. In case that investors run into investment risk and borrowers can't make payment, guarantee companies or petty loan companies shall acquire investors' investment and pay for investors, then the guarantor shall claim recovery from borrowers. Platform guarantee includes equity fund guarantee and loan loss provision mode. The former means that the platform provides guarantee for investor investment with free capital, and the latter means the platform sets up loan loss provision to guarantee investor investment capital.

In third-party guarantee mode, P2P platforms just provide financial information service, and guarantee companies take charge of approving borrower qualification and providing loan guarantee. P2P platforms pay guarantee companies certain guarantee fee and channel fee. Under this mode, P2P platform has evolved to be an intermediary and guarantee company intervenes lending transaction in the capacity of a third party (Figs. 5 and 6).

The concept of platform equity fund guarantee was first raised by Hongling Capital in 2009. Under this mode, once borrowers are founded to have overdue repayment, then the platform shall acquire investors' creditor's right with equity fund, and incorporate overdue creditor's right. Then it will claim recovery from borrowers. At present, the policy stipulates that any platform shall not provide guarantee. So this guarantee mode is transiting to other modes now.

There is some difference between loan loss provision mechanism and third-party guarantee. The platform extracts proportional sum of each loan and interest revenue as loan loss provision and reserves it in specific

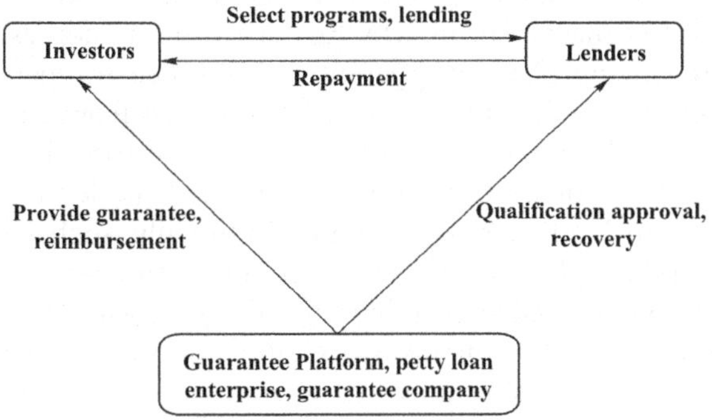

Fig. 5 Third-party guarantee mode lending flow

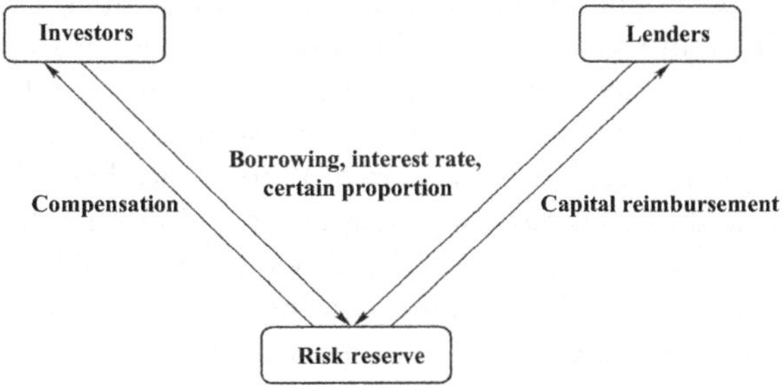

Fig. 6 Risk reserve mode lending flow

loan loss provision account. It is not the revenue of platform, but the compensation made to make up investors' overdue creditor's right. Once borrowers make overdue payment, the platform will compensate investors with loan loss provision, claim compensation from borrowers, and put recovered capital in loan loss provision account. As proved by its flow, loan loss provision still belongs to prior control action which can reduce investors' loss to some degree. However, it doesn't lower lending risk. This is also true of third-party guarantee mode. In consequence, for reducing lending risk, the platform needs to pay more efforts in credit assessment and risk control. Only in this way can the platform gain a virtuous cycle.

Guarantee mode appears under the specific circumstances in China. Due to the absence of social credit system, P2P platforms lack effective credit assessment. Residents' poor investment and wealth management awareness are the main reasons why guarantee mode comes into being. Through introducing platform guarantee, insurance company and guarantee company, it can fully prevent investor interests from being impaired by borrowers, and stimulate the initiative of investors. But under this mode, the platform or third-party has intervened the lending trading as the third party in lending relation, and additionally, such mode doesn't remove risks and simply transfers risks from the platform to the guarantor. Once there are some problems in lending, the platform or guarantor will acquire creditor's right from investors, and continually claim recovery from borrowers. The establishment of guarantee mode means the establishment of a starting procedure. It will be timely initiated in case of default. But in most cases, such mode damages P2P online lending spirits. Under guarantee mode, relation between the investor and the borrower is no more a pure lending relation, as the investor does not undertake investment risks and guarantee institution guarantees investment uncertainties and risk uncertainties. This damages Internet P2P platform's de-intermediary agent and direct financing spirits. It is the third party that provides guarantee. There is no radical difference between this mode and bank. In addition, it also lacks risk control ability in the bank. As a consequence, in strict sense, guarantee mode is variant P2P. Considering the great context of Chinese online lending in China, some platforms adopt this mode to attract more consumers. In the short run, such mode adapts to investors' investment concept. But in the long run, it does not have sustained vigor. It reveals the necessity of de-guarantee. At present,

P2P platform guarantee has been clearly prohibited, and it is predicted that the guarantee mode will be prohibited in the future, too.

Case 7: Hongling Capital

Hongling Capital founded in March 2009 launched the mode of "principal payment on account". It arouses a huge controversy in then period dominated by pure intermediary mode represented by PPDAI. But from then on, principal payment on account nearly becomes the "standard configuration" in P2P industry. Each platform announces that it will implement "principal payment on account" system.

As stipulated by Hongling Capital, investors can become VIP clients after paying 180 yuan annual fee. When borrowers make overdue payment, Hongling Capital will make principal payment on account, or otherwise it just gives 50% principal payment on account. There are three sources of capital in Hongling Capital. The first source is petty cash extracted from profits. The second source is risk guarantee capital extracted from 10% investor interest. The last source is registered members' annual fee.

The proposal of Hongling Capital's "principal payment on account guarantee mode" changes the development course of Chinese P2P industry. Afterward, guarantee availability becomes the first criterion that investors use to measure P2P platforms. Though it corresponds to investors' investment preference for the time being, it shows great "extrusion" effects on orthodox mode such as PPDAI. Concerning industry development, de-guarantee will be the general trend. Especially for platform guarantee mode represented by Hongling Capital, it can't withstand the test of market at all. Hongling Capital is also experiencing changes. In March 2014, it formally launched loan loss provision mode with initial capital of 50 million yuan and each sum of loan withdraws 1.2%. Such transition is positive to its future development.

Case source http://www.nbd.com.cn/articles/2014-08-13/855677.html.

Case 8: Lufax Third-party Guarantee Mode

Lufax is the online investment and financing platform built by Ping An Group in April 2011 with 4.2 billion yuan. The borrower and the lender may realize capital lending via Lufax. Lufax has unique characteristics different from other P2P platforms.

Firstly, it combines online mode and offline mode. Even if Lufax is an online investment and financing platform, and the borrower and the lender finish lending online, borrower qualification approval, risk control and other links are all finished offline.

Secondly, different from direct capital lending on other platforms, Lufax realizes financing by designing wealth management products. Moreover, the borrower and the lender do not finish lending business in person. Lufax first releases wealth management products according to lending demands, and then sells wealth management products to investors. Investors are unaware of specific information and capital purpose of borrowers.

Thirdly, Borrowers' lending is guaranteed by the Financing Guarantee Company Ping An Guarantee (Tianjin) Co., Ltd under Ping An Group. The guarantee company takes advantage of Ping An Group's credit consumption risk management data model to approve borrower qualification offline. When borrowers raise lending application online, Lufax will learn about borrowers' lending purpose, repayment ability and other information via phone, such as work, residence, credit card, house and car. Ping An Guarantee will also approve such information offline. However, in case of overdue payment of borrowers, Ping An Guarantee shall repay due principal, interest and interest penalty (Fig. 7).

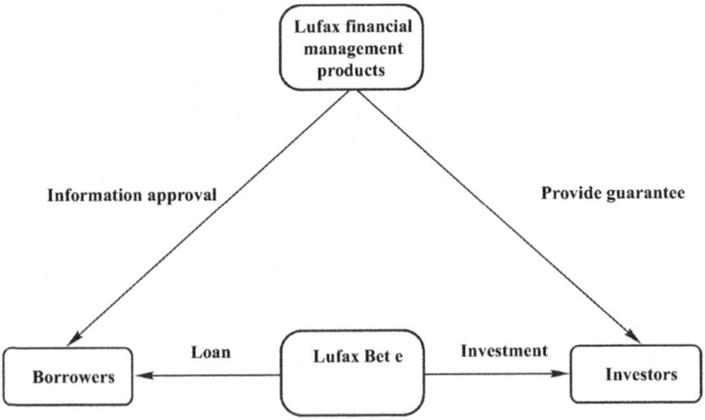

Fig. 7 Lufax guarantee mode

The third-party guarantee mode of Lufax excellently controls risks, which could be evidenced by the 0.9% default rate on the platform. The rate is even below the integral level of the industry. In Lufax's mode, the platform plays the role of a pure online intermediary, and the guarantee company undertakes the responsibility of credit approval and default compensation. This adheres to P2P online lending spirits so that many consider it as the networking of Ping An Guarantee. However, such statement is biased, because it totally ignores the commercial pattern behind this mode. The sole problem is that both Lufax and Ping An Guarantee belong to Ping An Group. Therefore, the third-party guarantee mode of Ping An Guarantee is easily denounced by people. In June 2014, Ma Mingzhe announced at the shareholders' meeting that Lufax would gradually revoke guarantee. Lufax aims to develop in the orientation of pure intermediary, and simultaneously, platform guarantee aims to revoke related-party guarantee mode. In a word, de-guarantee will be the development goal of Lufax and also the development trend of P2P industry in the future.

Case source Zhang Chenjiao, Legal Risks and Supervision of Chinese P2P Online Lending Platform, Shanghai: East China University of Political Science and Law, 2014.

Case 9: Renrendai Loan Loss Provision Mode

Renrendai established loan loss provision mechanism in early 2012, i.e. extracting proportional loan loss provision from loan to guarantee investors' interests. Different credit level and different product category apply different risk withdrawing standards. In credit authentication, the maximum withdrawing ratio is 5% and the minimum is 0. The withdrawing ratio of both smart wealth management target and field authentication target is 1%. No withdrawing is involved in institutional guarantee. As to the use of loan loss provision, credit authentication target just pays for the principal. Payment of smart wealth management target includes unpaid principal, overdue current interest and waiting-period interest. Filed authentication target includes unpaid principal and overdue current interest, but capital source is not necessarily loan loss provision. Institutional guarantee target does not use loan loss provision in payment (Table 11).

Table 11 Renrendai loan provision withdrawal and use

<table>
<tr><th>Product type</th><th colspan="2">Withdrawal proportion</th><th>Scope of compensation</th><th>Fund source</th></tr>
<tr><td rowspan="7">Credit authentication target</td><td>AA</td><td>0</td><td rowspan="7">Unpaid principal</td><td rowspan="7">Risk reserve</td></tr>
<tr><td>A</td><td>1%</td></tr>
<tr><td>B</td><td>1.5%</td></tr>
<tr><td>C</td><td>2%</td></tr>
<tr><td>D</td><td>2.5%</td></tr>
<tr><td>E</td><td>3%</td></tr>
<tr><td>HR</td><td>5%</td></tr>
<tr><td>Smart wealth management target</td><td colspan="2">Over 1%</td><td>Unpaid principal
Overdue current interest
Interest in waiting period</td><td>Risk reserve</td></tr>
<tr><td>Field authentication target</td><td colspan="2">Over 1%</td><td>Unpaid principal
Overdue current interest</td><td>Field certification institutions or risk reserves</td></tr>
<tr><td>Institution guarantee target</td><td colspan="2">0</td><td>Unpaid principal
Overdue current interest</td><td>Cooperative institutions</td></tr>
</table>

Data source Chinese Internet Finance Report, 2014

Debt Assignment Mode

Debt assignment mode means that P2P platform first issues a loan to borrowers to gain corresponding creditor's rights, then splits creditor's right amount and term to creditor's right packages, and transfers these creditor's right packages up to mass investors' investment demands. In this way, the platform matches borrowers' lending demands and investors' investment demands via the transfer of creditor's right (Fig. 8).

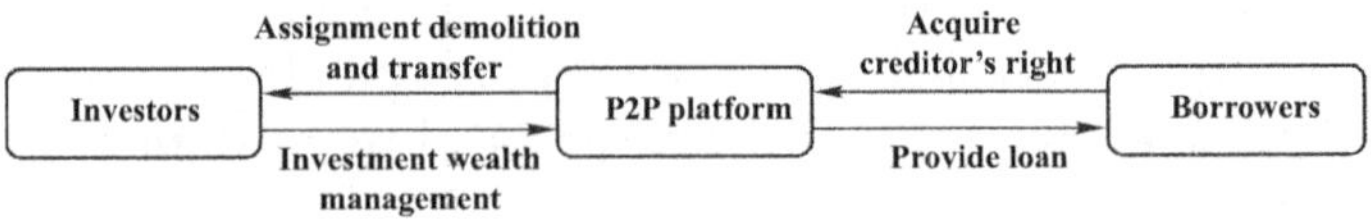

Fig. 8 Credit assignment transfer mode lending flow

However, there exist a great many risks under this mode. The first risk is guarantee risk. Though guarantee is less conspicuous under this mode, it exists implicitly. When P2P platforms transfer creditor's right to investors, the platform undertakes security payment pressures and policy red line alone. The second risk is legal risk. Creditor's right transfer mode can be also viewed as sort of asset securitization action, i.e. the action in which P2P platform sells creditor's right package. This possibly violates the legal red line of *Securities Law*. It is at the risk of issuing illegal securities once there are over 200 issues. The third risk is mismatch risk between capital pool and term. P2P platform splits occurred creditor's right from the perspective of sum and term. Investors eventually gain an asset package. Though they access the borrower list, they have no idea about borrowers. So capital pool risks inevitably exist. Term mismatch risks come into being whenever creditor's right term is messed up.

At present, the mode of creditor's right transfer is highly controversial. Though no related policies have been enacted yet, it is very likely that government policies will tighten the supervision on related risks. More prudent studies should be conducted about the nature, norm and supervision of such mode.

Case 10: CreditEase

CreditEase is the first platform that implements creditor's right transfer mode in China. Its lending flow takes two steps. In the first step, CreditEase senior executives such as Tang Ning lend equity fund to borrowers in their own name and sign the *Lending Agreement*. Lending in the name of individuals can avoid the legal provision that "companies shall not engage in lending". This is how CreditEase takes advantage of policy loophole. In the second step, CreditEase splits considerable creditor's right, including sum and term, divides it into numerous creditor's right with smaller amount and shorter term, and finally sells creditor's right packages to investors. It is worth noticing here that the investors and borrowers do not correspond to one another. Instead, one investor possibly corresponds to multiple borrowers. It is more like a large capital pool.

Even if CreditEase subtly avoids legal sanction, such as engaging in lending in the identity of natural person, and controlling the number of splitting within 200, this mode is still very controversial. As a platform, CreditEase has actually intervened in the trading process. It not only assumes the role of information intermediary and platform intermediary. More importantly, it exists as a credit intermediary. In this regard, it has exceeded the scope of Internet finance, and evolves to a pure online folk lending product. In essence, CreditEase splitting operation is asset securitization process which has great business risk and faces severe red line breach risks. It is foreseeable that this means will be under rigorous supervision in the future.

Case source Shi Yakun, Research on P2P Online Lending Platform Innovation Development Mode, Kaifeng: Henan University, 2014.

"Platform + Petty Loan" Mode

Under "platform + petty loan" mode, P2P platforms cooperate with petty loan companies and the parties complement each other's advantages. Petty loan companies are responsible for seeking borrowers offline, and making credit assessment. Upon approval, borrowers' lending demands will be posted on P2P platforms and platforms seek online investors. During this process, offline petty loan companies take charge of borrower credit approval, guarantee and recourse. While online P2P platforms just serve as the flow entrance that does not take charge of other lending links.

Under this mode, though P2P platform seems to be a pure intermediary platform, its role is confined to intermediary and it has lost P2P online lending spirits. Adhering to this logic, it does not belong to Internet finance, but a completely offline folk lending instead. After all, the difference is that raised capital has been released on Internet. At this moment, P2P platform is just a website, devoid of any property of finance (Fig. 9).

Case 11: Yooli

In cooperation with petty loan companies, Yooli is just responsible for recruiting investors to match petty loan companies' offline lending consumers. When petty loan companies discover proper borrowers, they first approve borrowers, and recommend them to Fuscent. Following credit assessment, Fuscent will post lending information on Yooli for fund-raising. During this process, petty loan companies provide principal-interest guarantee. In case of overdue debt, petty loan companies shall pay for borrowers. Yooli just raises capital online in this process, with no need

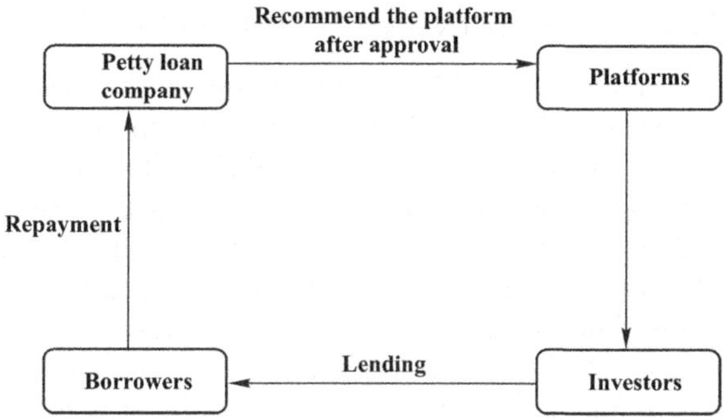

Fig. 9 "Platform + Petty Loan" mode lending flow

of assuming risks. Most risks and responsibilities come down to petty loan companies.

Case source Zhang Chenjiao, Legal Risks and Supervision for Chinese P2P Online Lending Platform, Shanghai: East China University of Political Science and Law, 2014 (Table 12).

Table 12 Comparison of the advantages and disadvantages of five P2P online lending platforms

Mode	Advantages	Disadvantages
Pure intermediary mode	Pure intermediary, pure online platform; Improvement of data accumulation and risk control ability; Low cost	Inadequate prior data accumulation; Poor credit approval ability; High default rate and bad debt rate
Online+offline mode	Absorb capital via Internet constellation effects and long-tail efficiency, and improve risk control level via offline credit review	High cost; Lack big data-based Internet credit review and risk control technologies, and lack Internet finance spirits
Guarantee mode	Guarantee investors' interests	Transfer risks rather than eliminate or decrease risks; Generate moral risks; Lack Internet finance spirits similar to traditional credit loan Internet
Creditor's Right Assignment Mode	Splitting of creditor's right makes for the growth of inclusive finance	High risks, violation of possible red lines and under the pressure of austerity policies
Platform+petty loan mode	Professional labor division	Loss of the spirit of P2P online lending

5 The Rethinking of P2P Online Lending

The development history of P2P online lending in China is just around seven or eight years, and it gains popular in recent four or five years. However, during the few years, Chinese P2P industry has undergone drastic changes in entire scale, platform quantity and number of participants. Even America, the country where P2P online lending is most mature and Britain, the country where P2P online lending is created have been left behind. This proves the vigor of P2P online lending in China. Such new lending mode can provide financial services proper for Chinese economic growth and satisfy the financial demands of whole society. This is noteworthy. But at the same time, in the midst of drastic changes in the industry, P2P platform business mode is also experiencing drastic changes. From pure online mode to "online + offline" mode, from guarantee mode to creditor's right transfer mode, and "platform + petty loan" mode, P2P online lending mode is still in constant changes. Such innovative spirits even outshine future innovation-driven trend. We have to admit that China is fully motivated in this aspect. Unfortunately, innovation in this regard is mostly the infringement against P2P online lending. Such innovation also goes against the sustained and healthy development of P2P industry in China. Foreign P2P industry development is based on two points.

First, foreign P2P online lending platforms mostly exist as a kind of consumer credit. Borrowers compensate the shortcomings of consumer capital through short-term and petty loan. As a consequence, to some degree, western P2P online lending can be viewed as Internet consumer finance.

Secondly, P2P industry development is supported by enough data. As is known, data constitute the basis of credit assessment, and the data have been accumulated by western countries for a long time. Data accessibility directly determines the feasibility of P2P industry lending. Whereas, this is impossible in China. On the one hand, Chinese P2P online lending mostly does not serve consumption. Borrowers are mostly small, medium-sized and micro companies. Only few platforms offer individual consumption finance. On the other hand, there is nearly no big data supporting the development of P2P industry in China. The two points determine that pure intermediary P2P online lending has no market in China. But in reality, considerable traditional finance platforms can't satisfy lending demands. Therefore, classical P2P online lending platforms must be transformed from online approval to offline approval mode, from no-guarantee to guarantee mode and from online lending to offline development. In a word, this "form" must be used to satisfy investment and financing demands. But the change of many platforms leads to the changes of P2P platform nature more or less, and some of them even lose the meaning of P2P platform (Table 13).

What is Internet finance? What is P2P online lending? This goes back to the first question. P2P online lending exactly uses big data to fully reveal the credit of borrowers and lower information asymmetry. Simultaneously, it can be considered as a new direct financing means which uses Internet low cost and convenience characteristics to expand trading possibilities and trading scope. Similar to the core of Internet finance, P2P online lending also consults big data in credit assessment and risk control. In consequence, the foundation of such mode is big data. The first concern is big data. Why can big data finance gain better development and P2P online lending need mode transformation? The reason is very simple, as the former experiences big data accumulation process and the latter lacks data accumulation. However, credit is not valued in China. As people do not care about credit, no data accumulation has been made. At this point, P2P online lending has no prospect in China.

Table 13 Comparison of the characteristics of five P2P online lending modes

Comparison	Pure online mode	Online+offline mode	Guarantee mode	Credit assignment	Platform + petty loan
Operation mode	Pure online mode	O2O	O2O	Offline mode	O2O
Risk control	Online review	Offline review	Offline review	Offline review	Offline review
Guarantee mode	Principal guarantee plan	Risk reserve	Third-party guarantee Risk reserve	Platform guarantee	Petty loan company guarantee
Degree of intervention in transaction	Non-intervention of transaction	Non-intervention of transaction	Intervention of transaction	In-depth participation of transaction	Non-intervention of transaction
Role of platform	Pure information intermediary	Information intermediary	Information intermediary	Information intermediary	Online channel
P2P online lending integrating degree	Typical representatives	Basic retention	Violation of principle	Suspected violation	Loss of P2P online lending spirit

For gaining sustainable development, P2P online lending should also experience long-term data accumulation about consumer and trading. Similar to PPDAI, though PPDAI develops at a low speed, it is the most classical P2P online lending mode. Moreover, it is also the most secure mode with greatest development potentials. Once it accumulates enough data, the platform will turn to be another Alibaba Petty Loan. But this process is very lengthy. Now that the platform does not have data accumulation nor seek data accumulation, what can it do to develop P2P online lending? The sole solution is transformation, such as transiting from online to offline, providing guarantee, and pursuing external cooperation. Even if these modes satisfy the demands of investment and financing consumers, and have gained remarkable achievements in the short run, it lacks vigor. Together with the constant efforts made in supervision in P2P industry, the intermediary property of such platform has been clarified. If self-guarantee mode is not approved, it is foreseeable that with the implementation of policies, creditor's right transfer, "platform + petty loan" mode and guarantee mode all are very likely to be abolished. Therefore, it is necessary to transform these platforms. Why does Lufax suggest gradually canceling guarantee? In the future, the development of P2P platform needs to rely on big data in credit assessment and risk control instead of external guarantee. It is the core competitiveness of future finance competition. For this, it is imperative to transform and foster platforms.

6 The Risks of P2P Online Lending

As a general rule, P2P online lending risks are mainly borrowers' operation risk, credit risk and also risk control risk, legal risk and liquidity risk from the platform. As these risks have varying causes, origins and determinants, they affect the development of P2P online lending to varying degrees. The outburst of any single risk possibly leads to the collapse of P2P platforms.

Operation Risk

At present, operation risk is one of the foremost risks faced by P2P platforms. Operation experience from CreditEase even proves that operation risk rests in the largest risk faced by platforms.

Operation risk mainly refers to the risk caused by borrower information forgery and wrong information submitted by borrowers. Out of different reasons, P2P platforms now do not have data accumulation or lack the support of issue data. To a large degree, it requests borrowers to submit data, including income level, pledge, credit condition, so that borrowers offer some false data and wrong data to improve individual credit level. Whereas, the platform is unable to test the authenticity of data. Under such circumstances, borrowers' credit level will be overestimated, and those borrowers who are used to be excluded by loan can gain a loan now. Corresponding lending default rate is expected to rise.

With the continuous accumulation of platform data, and the mutual communication with external data, it is foreseeable to realize data diversification and cross validation in the future. In this way, the platform can test the information submitted by borrowers and lower artificial operation risks.

Credit Risk

Borrowers' credit risk is another threat faced by P2P platforms. Nowadays, domestic credit environment is very disadvantageous. As borrowers just need to pay low default cost, and information sharing hasn't been reached between platforms, borrowers who have been put on the black list on one lending platform can still raise a loan on other platforms. The existence of credit risk further intensifies borrowers' moral risks. In this way, when borrowers gradually increase in the lending market, corresponding lending interest will witness a rise, and real borrowers will be gradually expelled from the market. This is the so-called "lemon phenomenon". It is also a reverse choice. This goes against the development of entire P2P industry.

In order to handle with this risk, the government must aggravate the punishment for borrower default through building industry union and realizing information sharing. Such practice greatly raises borrowers' default risk and necessarily lowers credit risk in an effective way.

Risk Control Risk

The prime risk of platform is risk control risk. The big data-centered risk control system is founded to be defective in five aspects, including inadequate credit data, limited user network behavioral data, biased network user characteristics, risk control model invalidity, and limited model applicability scope. On the one hand, as mentioned above, without enough accumulated data, P2P platforms can hardly assess borrowers' credit. On the other hand, the accuracy of risk control models in P2P industry remains to be seen. Causes in these two aspects prevent P2P platforms from making accurate credit assessment about borrowers, and effectively controlling lending risks. This is the key factor that determines the development of P2P platform.

All questions are concluded with data. It is not only the core question faced by P2P platforms, but also the reason why P2P platform is a mode of Internet finance. In current stage, Chinese P2P platforms still lack their own core advantages. Nothing is possible without data. In the age of Internet finance, big data means competitiveness and productivity!

Legal Risk

Illegal fund-raising and illegal deposit are legal risks possibly faced by P2P platforms. The positioning of P2P platform is intermediary. The role of intermediary determines that P2P platforms can't access capital nor engage in illegal fund-raising and deposit. However, a great many platforms now still raise fund. For instance, creditor's right transfer mode is a typical illegal fund-raising behavior. Therefore, with the enactment of supervisory policies, such illegal fund-raising mode and alike-fund-raising mode are possibly the first to be supervised. As a consequence, in order to avoid legal risk, P2P platforms ought to regress to the role of a pure intermediary and become a real investment and financing platform.

Liquidity Risk

When P2P platforms intervene trading, many of them split the target to react to borrowers' long-term and low-interest lending requirements and investors' short-term and high-earnings rate investment requirements. They split large-amount and long-term lending target into small-amount and short-term investment products to satisfy bilateral requirements. During this process, the platform must satisfy liquidity demands through building the capital pool via term mismatch. Liquidity risk management contains high technical content. Nearly all platforms have to face this problem. But for P2P platforms, if they are trapped by large-scale term mismatch, liquidity risk is inevitable on the condition of reduced traffic inflow. Capital pool, term mismatch and liquidity are mutually causal. It is exactly the sophisticated relation among the three affects the survival and development of the platform.

7 The Supervision of P2P Online Lending

Policy of Supervisory Department

P2P online lending has developed for eight years in China. Up to this day, things are totally different. But we must admit that though P2P online lending has developed to a large scale in China, present P2P online lending is still in a vacant state without access threshold, without industry standard and institutional supervision. Does it mean that P2P online lending does not request supervision, or the government wants to supervise P2P online lending but never takes measures.

As a matter of fact, government supervision on P2P online lending is still on the way. Out of various reasons, different people hold different opinions about the positioning, functions and modes of P2P online lending. Against the great context of separated supervision, no consensus has been reached about the supervision on P2P online lending. But it does not mean that the government overlooks its supervision on P2P online lending. As indicated by available supervisory policies, the year of 2014 is a boundary that differentiates the attitudes of supervisory department.

Before 2014, supervisory department rarely stated its attitudes toward P2P online lending. It primarily depended on industry union and self-discipline of P2P online lending industry.

On August 23, 2011, CBRC issued *Notice on the Risk Warning of Renrendai*, suggesting that P2P online lending platform possibly had 7 types of potential risks and the banking industry must establish a firewall with P2P platforms. It was the first time for the supervisory authority to issue pertinent supervisory policies for P2P online lending. It suggested that the supervisory department had realized risks in P2P online lending.

After that, together with the great development of P2P online lending, self-discipline regulation dominated by industry union started to take the leading status. This proactively normalizes the development of P2P online lending and compensates the shortcomings of supervisory policies.

On November 4, 2012, China Micro-credit Association P2P Industry Committee was founded. This was the first national membership industry association organization in China.

On August 26, 2013, the committee officially issued *Self-discipline Convention on Individual-to-Individual Micro-credit Information Counseling Service Agency Industry* to propose related self-discipline requirements for P2P institution service sponsors, borrowers, industry management requirements, industry business exit mechanism, industry practitioners and other aspects. For fear of breaking the legal red line, the concept of P2P settlement and separation was raised for the first time.

On December 20, 2012, the first network credit service industry business union in China was founded in Shanghai. On December 19, 2013, the union issued the first online lending industry self-discipline criterion in China—*Online Lending Industry Access Standards* to determine online lending industry operation red line. It stipulated that companies in the union shall not appropriate borrower capital in any means, and equity capital and lending capital isolation mechanism must be established. Term mismatch shall not be used to set up the capital pool.

Throughout exploration for one year, the supervisory department began to deploy P2P online lending supervisory system. On November 25, 2013, PBC Department of Treaty and Law presented three risk warning tips for P2P business, and clarified the business operation red line for P2P online lending platforms. To be specific, the platform shall not provide guarantee, raise fund to build capital pool, illegally incorporate mass deposit, or fund-raising fraud. PBC advised to build a platform capital third-party trusteeship mechanism so that P2P online lending platforms recede to its intermediary nature.

The day before 2014 was the exploration stage of P2P online lending supervision. Industry union, CBRC and PBC all enacted some policy measures to supervise P2P online lending. Regardless of the shortcomings in systematicness, it accumulated rich experience in P2P industry supervision and helped continually improve the supervisory system.

As of 2014, P2P industry supervision began to transit from industry union self-discipline supervision to supervision department red line. CBRC, PBC and other supervisory departments successively expounded the industry principle and policy red line for P2P online lending, which laid a foundation for further statement of industry supervisory policies.

On April 21, 2014, Liu Zhangjun of CBRC clearly presented four red lines in P2P online lending: clarifying the intermediary property of platforms; platforms shall not provide guarantee; platforms shall not raise fund to build capital pool; platforms shall not illegally incorporate public capital. This was the first time for the government to clearly define P2P online lending supervision. This was greatly conducive to the development of entire industry.

In April 2014, PBC issued *Chinese Finance Stability Report*, in which it presented six modes of Internet finance and clarified the five major principles of Internet finance supervision.

In July 2014, Wang Yanxiu, Director of the Innovation Department of CBRC, announced that the focus in P2P supervision was that the platform should submit to the constraint of industry threshold and principal, possess risk control ability, entrust capital, prohibit capital collection, clarify charge mechanism, protect investor information and develop external audit.

On August 2, 2014, Yang Xiaojun, Vice Director of the Innovation Department of CBRC, presented five principles at 2014 Chinese Internet Finance Development Round Table Conference for P2P supervision, including clarifying information intermediary positioning, implementing third-party trusteeship, fostering specific industry threshold, making full information disclosure and risk revelation, and encouraging industry self-discipline. In general, these principles could be summarized by "clear positioning, non-breach of red line, threshold, focus on transparency and strong self-discipline".

On August 22, 2014, Li Zhilei, Vice Director of the Innovation Department of CBRC, presented six principles to develop P2P business at 2014 China Asset Management Annual Conference. First, P2P institution should be an online information intermediary platform instead of a credit intermediary platform. Secondly, the building of P2P companies must adhere to certain threshold and pay contributed capital. Thirdly, P2P companies shall not access the capital of borrowers and lenders. They must be pure and independent intermediaries. The capital may be trusted by banks. Fourthly, borrowers and lenders should submit to the limit of amount. Fifthly, the focus was on professional talents. Finally, counterfeit P2P must be cracked down.

On September 27, 2014, Wang Yanxiu, Director of the Innovation Department of CBRC, presented ten principles for P2P supervision at Chinese Internet Finance Innovation and Development Forum. (1) P2P platforms shall not hold investors' capital nor build the capital pool. (2) Platforms must implement the real-name registration system. (3) P2P was classified as an information intermediary. (4) There must be an industry threshold in P2P. (5) Capital must be introduced into third-party trusteeship system and audit mechanism should be also introduced to avoid illegal fund-raising. (6) Platforms shall not provide guarantee. (7) Platforms must clarify the charge mechanism and never blindly go after high-interest financing projects. (8) Full information disclosure must be ensured. (9) It was imperative to reinforce industry self-discipline. (10) Platforms should stick to micro-credit business. The proposal of ten principles further refined and improved the four red lines and they were of great importance to the development of P2P online lending.

On November 12, 2014, CBRC revealed ten principles for P2P supervision, including clarifying the nature of information intermediary, never building capital pool; transferring capital to third-party commercial banks for trusteeship; cultivating specific technical expertise; clarifying capital constraint mechanism; reinforcing information disclosure; preparing talent reserves; executing black list system; preaching industry self-discipline; exerting the coordinated supervision role of industry association.

On November 26, 2014, Pan Gongsheng, Vice President of PBC, presented five tips for Internet finance supervision at 2014 Payment Settlement and Internet Finance Forum. The first tip was to stick to openness and tolerance principle in supervisory rule and framework design. The second one is to stick to the justice of supervisory rules, reinforce coordinated supervision and prevent supervision arbitrage. The third one is to make market subjects correctly understand the relation between supervision and industry self-discipline. The fourth one is to maintain good communication between supervisory department and employment institutions. The last one is to stick to business baseline, normalize operation and hold prudent attitudes in operation. Internet finance business shows overt diversity and discrepancy characteristics, but each business should adhere to specific business boundary. Taking online lending field, for example, the platform can't provide guarantee, raise fund to build capital pool, illegally raise fund or illegally incorporate mass deposit.

On January 14, 2015, Wang Yanxiu from CBRC presented eight principles at 2015 Chinese New Economy Annual Conference for Internet finance supervision, namely innovative supervision, moderate supervision, classified supervision, coordinated supervision, adherence to financial laws and regulations, innovation around entity economy, full information disclosure, and focus on protection for financial consumer interests.

On January 20, 2015, CBRC built Inclusive Finance Department was responsible for promoting bank inclusive finance, financing guarantee institution, petty loan and online lending, and managing P2P. The establishment of Inclusive Finance Department helped further clarify P2P supervisory department and launch P2P supervisory work.

The successive rise of policy red line, ten principles and supervisory subjects implies that supervisory authority begins to develop supervision on P2P online lending with steps and plans. From the perspective of policy, the general principles should cover platform intermediary, capital trusteeship, building of industry threshold, information disclosure, de-guarantee, and capital pool.

Local Policies

Comparing with authority supervision on P2P online lending, all provinces and cities place emphasis on the execution of various policies to facilitate the healthy development of Internet finance. According to incomplete statistics, by February 2015, Beijing, Shenzhen, Tianjin, Guangzhou, Nanjing, Guiyang, Shanghai, Wuhan, Zhejiang and other provinces and cities had enacted professional measures in Internet Finance. Through optimizing the development environment of Internet Finance in different aspects, such as Internet finance companies, industry parks, incubators, incubation compounds, investment amount, registration reward, office occupancy subsidy, finance contribution subsidy, micro-credit service reward, these measures support the development of Internet finance in an all-round way (Table 14).

8 The Development Trend of P2P Online Lending

Regression to Pure Intermediary Mode

Either from the perspective of worldwide P2P industry or supervisory department's thinking, future Chinese P2P will still transit to the pure online platform mode. P2P platform in itself is an information intermediary, in which the borrower and the lender make free information match and the platform promotes the agreement as much as possible. The intermediary property of the platform is rather self-evident. But in China, out of various reasons, the pure platform mode lacks soil of survival and development, and some platforms are forced to transform to guarantee mode and creditor's right transfer mode. Though these platforms have made some contribution, it still deviates from the development trend of direct financing and goes against the development of P2P industry. The risk

Table 14 Local internet finance policies

Area	*Time*	*Document*
Beijing	August 2013	Internet Financial Industry Development Practice in Shijingshan District
	October 11, 2013	Opinions on Promoting the Innovative Development of Internet Finance in Haidian District
	December 2013	Few Measures Supporting Zhonguangcun Internet Finance Industry Development
Shenzhen	February 13, 2014	Instructions for the Innovative Development of Internet Finance
Tianjin	February 27, 2014	Promotion of Internet Finance Development Action Plan
Guangzhou	June 2014	Measures about the Innovative Development of Internet Finance
Nanjing	July 2014	Measures about Internet Finance Industry Development
Guiyang	July 2014	Few Policy Measures Supporting Guiyang Internet Finance Industry Development
Shanghai	August 7, 2014	Few Opinions on Promoting the Healthy Development of Internet Finance Industry in Shanghai
Wuhan	August 2014	Opinions on Supporting Internet Finance Industry Development
Zhejiang	February 2015	Instructions Supporting the Sustained and Healthy Development of Internet Finance in Zhejiang

brought about by these modes should not be overlooked as well. Thus it can be seen that with the implementation of supervisory policies, the pure platform mode will survive and gradually become mainstream of the industry. Some large P2P platforms represented by Lufax have begun to transit to de-guarantee platform mode. By way of platform mode, it is possible to accumulate user data, and accumulate experience in consumer credit assessment and risk control ability. This is also the core factor affecting future P2P industry competition.

In the transition process to platform mode, the foremost matter is de-guarantee. Nowadays, platform guarantee nearly disappears after four red lines, but third-party guarantee still prevails. Guarantee affects direct financing spirits. In this sense, this trend remains non-complaint. The most direct outcome of de-guarantee is to break up rigid payment so that P2P becomes investors' investment action instead of deposit action. In this regard, education and guidance for investors are still on the way.

Loan Loss Provision Mode Will Be the Transitional Choice

When British P2P platform RateSetter creates loan loss provision to ensure investor interests, this mode has been applied in many platforms. Especially, following de-guarantee trend in China, it is still the choice of many platforms before investors' full acceptance of risk. Thus it can be seen that platform guarantee will not be totally abolished in the short run, while loan loss provision mode possibly becomes a transitional choice to de-guarantee mode.

The difficulty of loan loss provision mode is in the withdrawing of loan loss provision. At this point, P2P platforms may consult the practice of commercial banks. As stipulated by *Bank Loan Loss Withdrawing Guide*, banks should make withdrawing on a quarterly basis, and year-end balance shall not be less than 1% of year-end balance. According to the *Preparatory Management Measures for Commercial Bank Loan Loss*, the loan provision rate (loan loss preparation/ loan sum) in commercial banks is not less than 2.5%, and provision coverage (loan loss/ NPL) is not less than 150%. Loan loss provision should be determined in accordance with the high level of the two. The platform may also extract proper loan loss provision to ensure investors' interests on the grounds of real operation conditions. But it may not be entire interests.

In addition, the platform may also consider introducing the insurance company to cover investors. This measure may also ensure investors' interests to some degree.

Build Third-Party Capital Trusteeship System

For preventing the platform from appropriating investment capital, it is very necessary to implement third-party capital trusteeship system. As the intermediary, the platform shall not contact and use the capital. Though many platforms agreed to cooperate with the third party in the past and form "capital trusteeship" either in pure channel mode or sub-account mode, many third-party payment companies are simply responsible for capital transfer, but they can't differentiate the authenticity of transfer. Therefore, the platform may transfer the capital to its own account via false trading. With the view of completely prohibiting such phenomenon, capital trusteeship must be executed where third-party payment or the bank transfers capital from investor account to borrower account and the platform does not contact capital. Only in this way can the system guarantees capital security.

Improvement and Development of Full Industry Chain

The development of full industry chain is very likely to be the development trend of future P2P industry. In reality, the "platform + petty loan" mode is very heuristic. By improving cooperation in the link of borrower search to credit assessment, platform approval, investor consumer introduction and capital reclamation, industry chain development can be well guaranteed.

In reality, most links are completed by P2P platforms. However, the development of P2P platform is always beset by limited consumers, inadequate traffic or insufficient credit assessment. In view of these problems, it is imperative to integrate the whole industry. On the basis of information intermediary, P2P is able to more effectively complete entire investment and financing operation in cooperation with credit rating institutions, portal websites, and petty loan companies.

The key is that all links need to develop synchronously to exert the synergy of whole industry chain. Taking credit investigation, for example, China must build a full set of credit investigation system.

More Evident Verticality Trend

Due to the aggravation of P2P industry competition, some platforms inevitably abandon all-round development mode, turn to focus on a specific industry or subdivision field, and develop industry subdivision, business subdivision and consumer subdivision. Some platforms will form unique advantages in certain fields, such as car loan, house loan and consumer loan in business field; white-collar worker, small and micro-company, online shopkeeper, college student and other groups in consumer field; tourism, chemical, household appliance in industry field. In the future, there will rise more professional P2P platforms in these fields, and the verticality trend will turn more overt.

Establishment of Industry Standards

The enactment of supervisory policies will normalize P2P industry standards, including platform building, access threshold, and minimum registration capital for fear that some platforms without operation qualifications enter the market. In the past, any entity can engage in P2P online lending once it establishes a website. This phenomenon indirectly reveals the chaos in P2P platform. For solving this problem radically, the government should rigorously normalize the establishment of P2P platforms. Especially, in respect of platform qualification, the platform can only enter the market once meeting the standards in key links such as registered capital, risk control, etc. Only in this way can it lower P2P industry risks from the source.

Information Transparency

The trend of information transparency will be reinforced. At present, only few platforms can achieve information transparency. These platforms rarely disclose information concerning borrower information, and capital flow, and on the other hand, investors can't acquire related information at all. This prevents investors from learning about the investment subjects. Meantime, it is also detrimental to supervise platforms and borrowers' capital use conditions. For this reason, the government must make more efforts in information disclosure and elaborately disclose borrowers' financial conditions, credit conditions, capital purpose and operation conditions so that investors fully understand borrowers and make investment decisions. Or otherwise, these platforms easily build capital pool. More importantly, it also adds difficulty to risk prevention and control.

Acceleration of Credit System Building

Credit system building is the key factor related to the development of P2P industry. But there still lacks a systematic credit system in China. The credit investigation system in the central bank is just accessible to banks, and P2P platforms are excluded from the system. More seriously, this credit investigation system just covers 800 million people, of which only 300 million people have credit records. In addition, as borrowers who raise a loan via P2P platforms usually lack credit records or have poor credit records, the credit investigation system in central bank is less valid.

For speeding up the building of credit system platform, the foremost thing is to gain borrower data. One feasible way is to gradually transit from platform data to external Internet data, financial institution data, government supervision data and eventually social credit investigation system. For this, P2P platforms must reinforce external cooperation, including both cooperation with P2P platforms and cooperation with external institutions. In particular, these platforms shall positively work with the credit investigation system in central bank, thus lowering P2P platform cost and compensating shortcomings in central bank's credit investigation system (Table 15).

In August 2013, NFCS Co., Ltd built the first Internet-based credit investigation system in China—Internet finance credit investigation system to incorporate numerous online lending corporate credit investigation data and realize credit investigation sharing between online lending companies. NFCS is the sole company that integrates individual credit investigation system with corporate credit investigation system, and provides individual and corporate credit investigation and credit rating service in China. As the central bank credit investigation central holding company, NFCS introduces central bank credit investigation experience and standards, including business rules, collection of data format, etc. In this way, there is no technical obstacle in the connection with central bank credit investigation center's individual information basic database. By late

Table 15 Trend of P2P platform data source

Stage I	*Stage II*	*Stage III*	*Stage IV*	*Stage V*
Platform data	External Internet data	Financial institution data	Government monitoring data	Social credit investigation system
Website behavioral data Personal data	E-commerce transaction data Third-party payment data Social network data Logistic data	Bank Security Insurance Fund	Water and electricity payment Taxation Traffic violation	Building of social data system Data sharing

Data source P2P Petty Loan Mode Case Research Report, 2014, revised edition

December 2014, there were altogether 370 online lending institutions, 524,000 consumers and approximately 5000 average daily inquiry.

In current stage, the platform can't access central bank credit investigation system like banks, but it can share credit information with online finance credit investigation system. Once the government clarifies supervisory policy, it will orderly propel the access of qualified P2P online lending.

CHAPTER 7

More Open Financing: Crowdfunding

In a strict sense, the prototype of crowdfunding already occurs. The AA system in dining is a typical representative. Crowdfunding starts with commodity crowdfunding, aimming at achieving a thought or creative idea. Therefore, compared with other Internet finance modes, crowdfunding seems to be independent from the system. Even so, we can't deny the fact that crowdfunding is a new type of financing and investment mode different from direct financing and indirect financing in the past. It can optimize capital allocation to some degree. In addition, as part of Internet finance, crowdfunding also means the effective use of big data. We may learn about investors' behavioral preference, and investors' credit according to big data. All of these make for the success of crowdfunding. On the contrary, without the support of big data, we can't differentiate investors and financiers, and crowdfunding then turns aimless.

As a typical mode of Internet finance, crowdfunding has been always in a moderate state. But as of 2014, both the supervisory department and the industry endow the industry with invincible motive force. Number of platforms, number of participants, projects, financing sum in the industry all witness a huge leap. The enactment of *Management Practices for Private Equity Crowdfunding Financing and Investment* in late 2014 creates an unlimited imaginary space for this industry. But limited by the constraints in crowdfunding industry, it is still rather difficult to develop crowdfunding. Such situation never occurs in other modes of Internet

Q. Guan and W. Gao, *Internet Finance*,
The Great Transformation of China,
https://doi.org/10.1007/978-981-16-4740-6_7

finance before. For the moment, there is still a long way to go in the development process of crowdfunding.

1 The Concept of Crowdfunding

In short, the concept of crowdfunding comprises "crowd" and "funding" in which the former means large number of participants. At this point, it fairly conforms to the spirits of Internet finance inclusive finance. "Funding" means public aggregation of fund. Therefore, the concept of crowdfunding indicates the aggregation of fund under the efforts of a great many people.

Usually, crowdfunding is divided into commodity crowdfunding, equity crowdfunding, lending-based crowdfunding and donation crowdfunding. Commodity crowdfunding refers to the reward to be gained by investors through investment in commodity or service. At present, most platforms in China follow the mode of crowdfunding, such as JD crowdfunding, Taobao crowdfunding, zhongchou.com, etc. According to investment target, commodity crowdfunding can be further divided into comprehensive crowdfunding and vertical crowdfunding. The former covers multiple platform investment targets, such as music, film, art and game and typical representatives include Kickstarter, IndieGoGo and DemoHour; while the latter just focuses on one type. For instance, Tmeng just focuses on film and Musikid just focuses on music. Equity crowdfunding means investors gain corresponding equity from project investment. This is the foremost point different from commodity crowdfunding and P2P investment mode. According to investment mode, equity crowdfunding can be further divided into "leader investment + follower investment mode" and general mode. The former means the platform chooses a professional investor to lead common investors to make investment so as to reduce general investors' investment risks. Typical representatives include AngleCruch and Dajiatou. The latter means ordinary investors choose their own investment projects. Typical representatives include American Fundersclub and British Crowdcube. Lending-based crowdfunding means investors gain corresponding creditor's rights from the investment. It actually indicates P2P platform in common sense. Donation crowdfunding means investors make contribution of capital but they do not gain economic benefits. In another word, it is an act of collection. At present, the focus of domestic crowdfunding industry is primarily on commodity crowdfunding and equity crowdfunding. Especially, commodity crowdfunding remains to be the mainstream of crowdfunding business. In this chapter, we will place emphasis on the two modes in discussion (Table 1).

Though both of them belong to crowdfunding, there is a great difference between commodity crowdfunding and equity crowdfunding. In commodity crowdfunding, issuers promise to provide commodity or service as the reward and users join in investment as ordinary investors. The investment amount is rather low. Moreover, investors may present their suggestions for products to help issuers make design and production. This investment mode is much similar to "pre-order + group buying". Project operation usually takes a short period. It often takes around one year from launch to product acquisition. In case of project failure,

Table 1 Classification of crowdfunding

Type	Characteristics	Subdivision	Characteristics	Typical representatives
Commodity crowdfunding	Raise fund via the platform and give reward by either physical objects or services	Integrated crowdfunding	Crowdfunding projects include music, film, art, game	Kickstarter IndieGoGo JD Equity Crowdfunding
		Vertical crowdfunding	Real estate, PE sports, music or film	Tmeng
Equity crowdfunding	Raise fund via the platform and investors can gain corresponding equity, thus rewarded by realization or dividend	Leader investment + follower investment mode	The platform shall assign a professional leader of investment to guide ordinary investors in investment	AngelCrunch Dajiatou
		General mode	Investor Direct Investment Project	Fundersclub Crowdcube
Lending-based crowdfunding	Investors invest in projects in exchange of creditor's right			Renrendai
Donation crowdfunding	Investors contribute to the projects free of charge			Micro Charity Crowdtilt

Data source Research on the Current Situation and Future Development Trend of Equity Crowdfunding in China, revised edition

issuers may request to refund the capital in part. While equity crowdfunding promises to provide corporate share, and investors may either cash out share or gain dividend. Correspondingly, equity financing has high requirements on investor qualification and investors can only make investment after accumulating enough assets. Investors can also enjoy the rights of ordinary shareholders. However, they can only gain earnings when the company makes profits. This usually lasts for a long period. In case of project failure, investors will not gain any compensation. Though commodity crowdfunding is still the foremost crowdfunding mode in China now, its "pre-order + group buying" mode shows that it primarily collects capital to do some minority products. Despite the large sales volume, investors simply subscribe a new product in advance. After all, project angel round investment or VC has nothing to do with crowdfunding. As a result, for building a multi-layer capital market, commodity crowdfunding is not the prime mode in the future, and it will be the age of crowdfunding represented by equity crowdfunding in the future. Equity crowdfunding is an investment act which targets at equity. Further than P2P, it pertains to corporate financing act and more effectively solves the financing problem of small- and medium-sized companies than P2P online lending (Table 2).

Crowdfunding is greatly different from P2P. In terms of financing means, P2P belongs to lending-based financing in which the borrower raises a loan from the investor for production and operation. While crowdfunding belongs to equity financing in which the investor is the shareholder of the borrower. Even in commodity crowdfunding, investor is also the shareholder of the borrower. Therefore, crowdfunding is completely different from P2P. Creditor's rights can be claimed, but this is not the case for equity. Comparing with crowdfunding, P2P has fewer participants and some P2P platforms even practise 1–1 (Peer to Peer) lending business. By contrast, crowdfunding usually raises fund in 1–N mode. Most P2P platforms engage in individual consumer loan and corporate operation loan, but the target of crowdfunding is often the company. In addition, in the initial stage, it takes a forward lead than P2P companies (Table 3).

Table 2 Comparison of commodity crowdfunding and equity crowdfunding

Differences	Commodity crowdfunding	Equity crowdfunding
Financing mode	Reward by entity	Reward by share
Reward mode	Reward by entity or service	Cash in profits or gain bonus by share
Investor qualification	With loose requirements, registered users usually do not have any restriction on income	With rigorous requirements, it is only accessible to qualified investors
Fundraising amount	Low fundraising amount	High fundraising amount
Investor authority	Investors' right to make suggestions for product design	Investors may enjoy the dividend like ordinary shareholders
Investment purpose	Product preorder + group purchase	Gain investment reward based on rational analysis and prediction, and focus on future development prospects
Reward period	Short term usually lasting for few months or one year	Gain reward only when the company makes profits with a long period of reward
Project failure handling means	The platform shall demand the initiator to return partial fund in condition that the initiator can't provide commodity on time	Investors can't gain profits and initiators do not promise to refund the principal in case of project failure

Data source Study on the Current Situations and Future Development Prospects of Equity Crowdfunding in China, revised edition

Table 3 Comparison of P2P and crowdfunding

Differences	P2P	Crowdfunding
Financing property	Creditor's right	Equity
Number of participant	Limited number of participants	More participants
Financing objective	Consumption loan, corporate operation loan	Project financing, corporate financing
Development stage of the company	Operation period	Initial period
Reward	Interest rate	Equity and commodity
Risk	Guarantee	Great risk

2 The Development of Crowdfunding

Either at home or abroad, the development of crowdfunding is not always smooth, but goes through a circuitous and tardy process until being recognized by the supervisory authority and the market.

Development Process of Crowdfunding

Development Process of Crowdfunding at Abroad

The first crowdfunding company ArtistShare in the world was founded in the year of 2001. Known as "Pioneer of Crowdfunding Finance", it is mainly oriented toward artists and fans in the music circle. Fans are able to sponsor the production of records via the website, and gain records sold online. Artists can also sign more agreeable contractual clauses. Through raising capital from fans via the website, artists allow fans to watch how they produce the records and even some special contents throughout the whole process.

After 2005, crowdfunding platforms appeared like mushrooms after rain, such as Sellaband (2006), SliceThePie (2007), IndieGoGo (2008), Spot.Us (2008), Pledge Music (2009) and Kickstarter (2009). Among them, ArtistShare sets a good example. As the first Internet crowdfunding platform, ArtistShare not only leaves profound influences on American music circle, but also initiates the age of Internet crowdfunding and creates lots of crowdfunding giants.

Data source: Xie Ping, Internet Finance Report 2014.

IndieGoGo founded in January 2008 first focused on fundraising for films and drama, and it then diverted the focus to smart hardware. In April 2009, Kickstarter came into being in America and it raised enough capital for some projects in a quite short time. For a time, this emerging fundraising mode received high attention in the industry. In 2010, Kickstarter finished 3910 crowdfunding projects, and corresponding capital scale reached 37.63 million USD with 43% success rate. In 2011, launchers from 177 countries initiated fundraising projects on Kickstarter, covering 90% countries and regions. Altogether 18,109 projects successfully raised capital and corresponding success rate totaled 85.7%. In 2013, altogether 3 million people became participants of crowdfunding activities, and gross amount totaled 4.8 billion USD. By now, Kickstarter has become the world's most famous and largest crowdfunding platform.

In October 2010, the world's first equity crowdfunding platform Crowdcube was founded in Britain, marking the inception of another new mode in the crowdfunding industry—equity crowdfunding.

America enacted JOBS Bill in April 2012, which provided more convenient financing channels for small companies and allowed small companies to sell more corporate shares to investors via crowdfunding. As stipulated by the bill, small companies do not necessarily make registration in SEC, and they may raise capital less than 1 million USD via crowdfunding within one year. All crowdfunding transactions shall be transacted by registered middlemen, and these middlemen associate the launcher with potential investors on the website. If investors' annual income or net asset is less than 100,000 USD, they shall not spend more than 2,000 USD or 5% income in investment. If their annual income or net asset is more than 100,000 USD, their amount of investment shall not exceed 10% of annual income or net asset (Fig. 1).

According to the statistics, there were just 192 crowdfunding platforms in the world in 2009, and corresponding scale totaled 32.1 billion yuan. After that, the number of platform increased by 40%–50% once a year, and meantime, fundraising scale also increased exponentially. It reached 16.9 billion yuan in 2012, 315.7 billion yuan in 2013 and approximately 614.5 billion yuan in 2014. At the same time, the number of platform also grew up to 1196. In the future, fundraising scale will still maintain a high growth rate as usual.

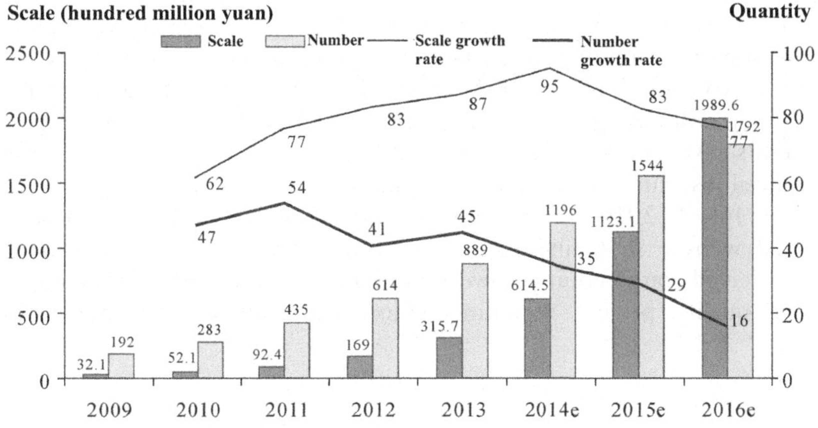

Fig. 1 Global crowdfunding scale, platform number and growth rate from 2009 to 2016 (*Data source* Chinese Internet Finance Report [2014])

Development Course of Crowdfunding at Home
In July 2011, the first crowdfunding website DemoHour was officially launched in China. It signaled the start of network crowdfunding in China. In September 2011, the first crowdfunding platform of public welfare property—Dreamore was established. In November 2011, equity crowdfunding platform AngelCrunch came into existence. After that, Dajiatou, zhongchou.com, China Dream.com and a series of crowdfunding websites was successively launched. But till late 2013, crowdfunding industry was still unknown among people, and the number of platform, financing scale and number of participants were very limited.

Till late 2013, the crowdfunding industry witnessed a great opportunity. Beginning with the "Integral Dream -Micro-welfare" plan issued by CCB in October 2013, the banking industry also entered the field of crowdfunding. At the same time, Tao Dream, later renamed Taobao Crowdfunding, launched in December 2013 later entered the field of science, design, agriculture, craft and recreation. Future emphasis will be placed on science and design innovation projects. It later gave rise to a general trend of crowdfunding led by Internet finance giants. In April 2013, Baidu Crowdfunding was launched. In July 2014, JD equity crowdfunding "Whip-round" was launched.[1] It highlighted the field of smart hardware and pop culture. In the meantime, traditional industry giant Suning Corporation also announced to march to the field of crowdfunding. The newly established Crowdfunding Project Department incorporates members of Suning Crowdsourcing Team. It concentrated on hardware in the early stage, and planned to grow to be full-category crowdfunding platform covering material crowdfunding, donation crowdfunding, real estate crowdfunding, film crowdfunding and equity crowdfunding. In addition, in November 2014, Pinganfang real estate crowdfunding rose in the market. In December of the same year, SPDB's "Xiaopu Recreation" was also launched and more and more financial institution entered crowdfunding field from then on.

On July 1, 2014, Zhongchouzhijia was founded as the first industry portal website in Chinese equity crowdfunding industry. It primarily provided all-round equity crowdfunding news, authoritative data comparison, quality project recommendation and industry communication

[1] Data source: China Network Crowdfunding Analysis Report in 2014.

community service. In the future, it will offer all sorts of special services for equity crowdfunding.

On October 31, 2014, nine equity crowdfunding platforms including Renrentou, Aihetou, Dajiatou, Daibang, Yunchou, Zhongtoubang, Aichuangye, Tianshijie and Yinxingguo, jointly convened the first-session equity crowdfunding conference, built the first equity crowdfunding industry alliance and signed *Crowdfunding Industry Convention*.

There took place drastic changes in the crowdfunding industry in 2014, characterized by the entry of Internet giants, establishment of industry portal websites, and formation of industry alliance. In a manner of speaking, the year of 2014 witnesses the outburst of crowdfunding industry in China, and both platform number and amount of fundraising realized leap-type development. Pursuant to related statistics, there were less than 20 crowdfunding platforms in China in late 2013, and most of them were commodity crowdfunding platforms. But till late 2014, there were 129 crowdfunding platforms in China, including 92 commodity crowdfunding platforms. Gross financing scale totaled 900 million yuan, and especially, equity crowdfunding exceeded 700 million yuan.

In existing crowdfunding projects, smart hardware and cultural creativity products are the foremost two types of products. JD, Suning and Alibaba all concentrate their focus on smart hardware. On September 22, 2014, "Three Dads" smart air conditioner raised capital totaling 11.226 million yuan on the first day of launch, and it therefore became the first project worth of millions of yuan in JD. Throughout development for half a year, JD now ranks the first place in equity crowdfunding project.

It is worth noticing here that accompanied by the prompt expansion of crowdfunding industry, the supervisory layer also changes their attitudes drastically. On March 28, 2014, Zhang Xiaojun Spokesman of CSRC stated that CSRC now was surveying the new business forms of Internet finance including equity crowdfunding, and it would present instructions in response to the times. The general thinking of supervision was still "encouraging innovation, preventing and controlling risks, avoiding disadvantages and pursuing advantages, and realizing sustainability". On March 30, 2014, the Central Bank authorized CSRC to supervise crowdfunding industry. On May 15, 2014, CSRC discussed crowdfunding access threshold, financing amount and positioning based on the survey in first-tier cities. On November 19 2014, Li Keqiang, Premier of the State Council pointed at the executive meeting that "the government shall build capital market petty re-financing mechanism and develop equity crowdfunding financing pilots". It was the first time for the government to officially support, affirm and promote the development of equity crowdfunding. Before that, CSRC had affirmed the positive significance of equity crowdfunding for many times. On December 18, 2014, China Securities Industry Association published the Private Equity Crowdfunding Management Measures (Trial) (Draft for Comment), which preliminarily defined the nature of non-public development of equity crowdfunding, the positioning of equity crowdfunding platform, the definition and protection of investors, and the obligations of financiers. Although the Measures set a relatively high threshold for private equity QFIs, it is the first regulation for the crowdfunding industry, and its positive significance should not be underestimated. On March 11, 2015, the State Council issued the Guiding Opinions on Developing Crowd-maker Space and Promoting Mass Innovation and Entrepreneurship, indicating the need to carry out the pilot financing of Internet equity-based crowdfunding and enhance the service ability of crowdfunding for mass innovation and entrepreneurship. The 2015 Government Work Report focused on serving the real economy and promoting financial reform, and also explicitly proposed to carry out equity-based crowdfunding pilot projects.

Crowdfunding is always controversial since its inception. This is in particular true of equity crowdfunding. After realizing the importance of building a multi-layer fund market in solving the financing and investment plight of small and micro companies, the supervisory layer also changes its attitudes toward equity crowdfunding. Equity crowdfunding will definitely be the leader of crowdfunding.

On March 20 2015, JD began to test equity crowdfunding and planned to adopt "leader + follower" mode where the leader must have certain investment experience, familiarize with the industry of investment project and provide industry resources for entrepreneurs. In current stage, as the supervisory layer hasn't enacted detailed rules and regulations concerning private equity crowdfunding, the mainstream is still private equity crowdfunding. JD stipulates that participants are limited to corporate senior executives and financial institution practitioners whose income is more than 300,000 yuan and financial assets total over 1 million yuan.

As proved by the development thinking of JD, Suning and Alibaba, they all solve entrepreneurs' initial product production and sales promotion via equity crowdfunding in the initial stage, and then turn the project through equity crowdfunding. Thus it can be seen that from primary fundraising to excavation of potential users, product sales and promotion, equity subscription, crowdfunding platforms will help entrepreneurs complete a series of links. Such progressive incubation service is possibly the mainstream choice of future crowdfunding industry.

On the whole, crowdfunding is still in the budding stage in China, and some basic problems are not effectively solved yet, such as legal constraints. Out of this reason, it is unlikely to burst out in the short run like P2P. Together with the continuous release and improvement of policies, equity crowdfunding will definitely welcome its day in the near future.

Current Development Situation of Crowdfunding

As indicated by the statistics of Rong 360, by late 2014, there were 116 crowdfunding platforms in China. Crowdfunding platforms here just consist of commodity crowdfunding and equity crowdfunding. In 2014, the number of new platforms reached 78 and monthly average growth rate reached 10.7%. Especially, equity crowdfunding platform has the largest growth rate. There were only 5 platforms in January 2014, but it reached 27 in the end of the year. Commodity crowdfunding increased from 28 to 69. Consequently, commodity crowdfunding platforms still outnumber equity crowdfunding platforms now, but the gap narrows much.

Annual Brief for Chinese Crowdfunding Industry in 2014 issued by Yiling Finance shows that the proportion of Chinese commodity crowdfunding platforms was 61% in 2014, around 2.44 times more than that of equity crowdfunding platforms. Mixed crowdfunding here refers to both commodity fundraising platform and equity fundraising platform which makes up 11%. While welfare platforms account for the least proportion as 3%.

In 2014, the gross scale of crowdfunding in China reached 915 million yuan, including 705 million yuan from equity crowdfunding and 210 million yuan from commodity crowdfunding. Though the number of equity crowdfunding is less than that of commodity crowdfunding, the financing limit of the latter is 3 or 4 times more than that of the former. In the first quarter of 2014, the financing scale of crowdfunding platforms was 52.45 million yuan, including 5.2 million yuan from commodity crowdfunding and 47.25 million yuan from equity crowdfunding. In the second quarter, the gross scale reached 135.46 million yuan, and corresponding growth rate was 158.3%. In particular, equity crowdfunding financing amount exceeded 100 million, and commodity crowdfunding also reached 27.08 million yuan. In the third quarter, the financing scale was 275.86 million yuan, with corresponding growth rate as 103.6%. Equity crowdfunding exceeded 200 million yuan and commodity crowdfunding exceeded 73.02 million yuan. In the fourth quarter, financing scale was 451.17 million yuan, equity crowdfunding financing scale was 346.82 million yuan and commodity crowdfunding exceeded 100 million yuan (Figs 2, 3 and 4).

As proved by the number of participants on crowdfunding platforms in 2014, the rise of participants before October was not significant, and the maximum reached around 41,100. However, by November, it abruptly rose up to 367,500. The main reason was possibly the Real Estate Crowdfunding launched by JD Crowdfunding in the same month, which directly witnessed the outburst of participants. By December, the number of participants decreased by 50% on the original basis (Fig. 5).

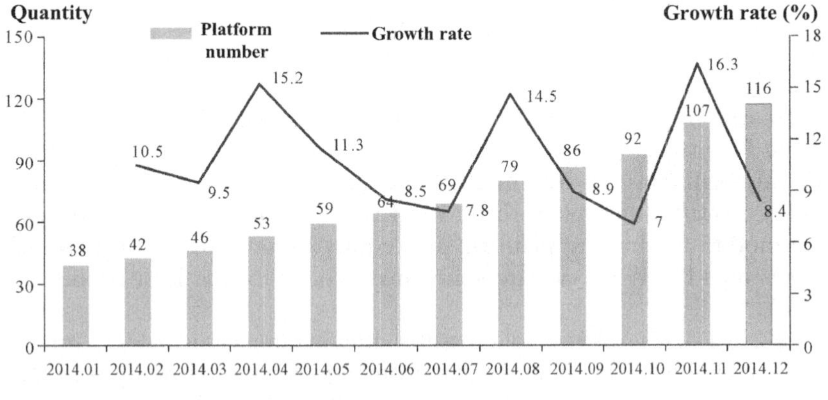

Fig. 2 Chinese crowfunding platform quantity and growth rate in 2014 (*Data source* Internet Crowdfunding Report of China in 2014)

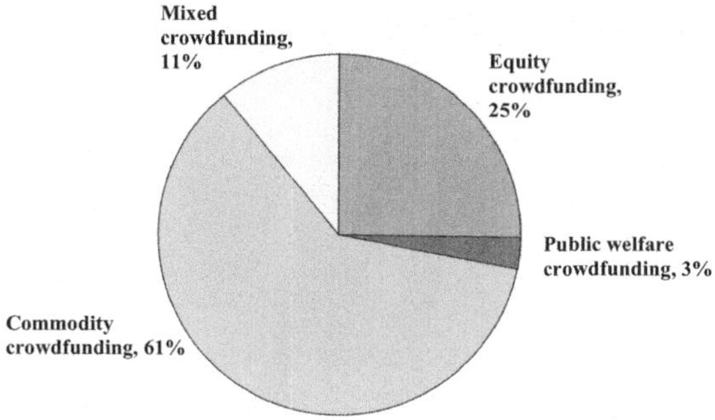

Fig. 3 Distribution of Chinese crowdfunding platforms in 2014 (*Data source* Annual Brief Report for Chinese Crowdfunding Industry in 2014)

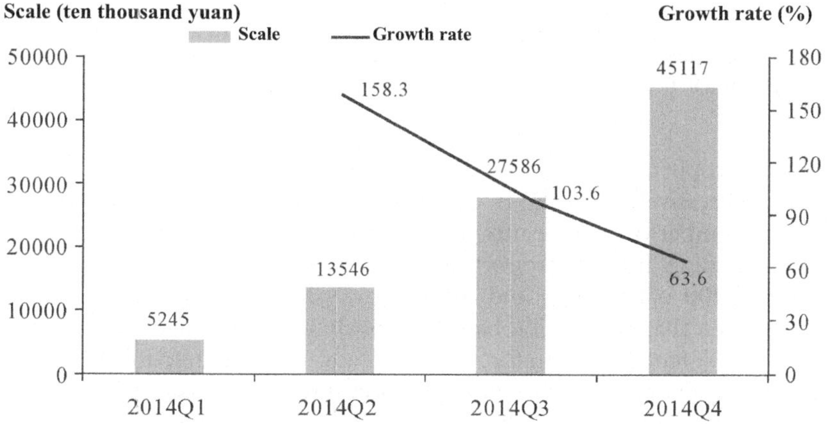

Fig. 4 Crowdfunding scale and growth rate of China in 2014 (*Data source* Internet Crowdfunding Report of China in 2014)

As proved by the market occupancy of each platform, the market occupancy of crowdfunding platforms demonstrates the concentration trend, especially e-commerce platform concentration trend. Among all successful projects, Zhongchou.com makes up the largest proportion as high as 1386, 1000 more than that of Taobao Crowdfunding. The achievement is unmatched by other platforms. But Zhongchou.com does not enjoy an edge in respect of scale and number of participants. Though JD Crowdfunding was only launched in July 2014, it gained the largest fundraising scale in simply half a year as 122 million yuan, and its corresponding

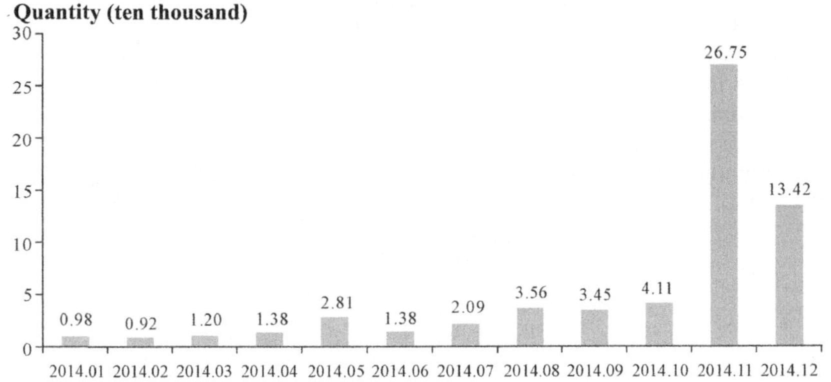

Fig. 5 Quantity of participants on crowdfunding platforms in 2014 (*Data source* Annual Brief Report for Chinese Crowdfunding Industry in 2014)

market proportion totaled 42.23%. Zhongchou.com ranked the second place, successively followed by Taobao Crowdfunding. From the perspective of number of participants. JD still ranks the first as 290,900, and its corresponding market proportion totals 42.6%. Taobao Crowdfunding has 200,000 participants and makes up 29.29% market shares. Thus it can be seen that JD and Taobao can quickly gather participants by virtue of their influential user traffic, and such advantage is unmatched by any other independent crowdfunding platform. From the perspective of single investment project, Zhongchou.com has a small financing scale inferior to that of JD and Taobao, but it enjoys an edge in individual contribution (Table 4).

3 Commodity-Based Crowdfunding

Commodity crowdfunding means a financing mode in which project sponsors launch project financing for a specific project, commodity, or creative idea, and investors who invest in the project may gain commodity or service as reward in the future. The target of commodity crowdfunding projects covers a wide scope, including film, music, game, animation, cultural creativity and electronic products, etc. Existing development trend shows high proportion of smart hardware and cultural creative products, especially the former. E-commerce platforms represented by

Table 4 Comparison of market occupancy of all crowdfunding platforms

Platform	Successful projects		Fund-raising amount		Number of active participants	
	Number	Proportion (%)	Scale (ten thousand yuan)	Proportion (%)	Scale (ten thousand yuan)	Proportion (%)
JD crowdfunding	244	8.1	12235	45.23	29.09	42.6
Taobao crowdfunding	386	12.81	3916	14.48	20	29.29
Zhongchou.com	1386	45.99	4917	18.18	6	8.78
Demohour	282	9.36	3279	12.12	4.37	6.39
Green Orange crowdfunding	83	2.75	603	2.23	4	5.86
Musikid	238	7.9	359	1.33	1.95	2.85
Dreamore	226	7.5	970	3.59	1.77	2.59
MoDian	12	0.4	212	0.79	0.55	0.81
Coinvest	49	1.63	214	0.79	0.26	0.38
The Cube	26	0.86			0.17	0.25
Youjiyouli	17	0.56	25			
Tmeng	16	0.53	149	0.55		
Dajiazhong	16	0.53	59			
Yichou.com	4	0.13	70			
JUE.SO	29	0.96				
Others					0.12	0.18

Data source Annual Brief Report for Chinese Crowdfunding Industry in 2014

JD Crowdfunding unanimously place emphasis on the support for smart hardware.

Generally, commodity crowdfunding project sponsors often have a good product or creative idea and expect to gain the cognition from the public. However, they can't launch the project without enough fund, nor raise a loan from the crowdfunding platform. Comparing with P2P financing, as the project has not been launched, it can't raise a loan from the platform. At this moment, financing can be made via the crowdfunding platform. In the earlier stage, project investors become project shareholders and join project operation, including product design and production. The reward gained is product or some value-added service. For instance, in film crowdfunding, investors can gain film tickets upon the release of films, and additionally, they may contact actors or access souvenirs in the film process. In commodity crowdfunding, investors can also gain products. Under the mode of commodity crowdfunding, investors make investment to gain produced commodity instead of more investment earnings. Therefore, many people generalize the mode as "pre-sale + group buying". Pre-sale mode means investors buy the product via investment prior to production, and sponsors also sell products out. Group buying means many people sell products in batch via investment.

At present, there are two types of product crowdfunding platform, i.e. comprehensive platform and vertical platform. The former releases many types of fundraising projects on the platform, while the latter focuses on the crowdfunding business in a specific field. During the development process of crowdfunding platform, differentiation marks an inevitable trend. Even if comprehensive crowdfunding platforms remain the mainstream, probably more and more platforms would choose vertical paths in the face of ferocious competition in the future. In addition, the competitiveness of vertical platforms is not inferior to that of comprehensive counterparts.

Development Conditions of Commodity Crowdfunding

The fundraising scale of commodity crowdfunding maintains a high growth rate in recent few years. In 2012, the scale of commodity crowdfunding was just 700 million yuan. But it later rose to 200 million yuan with a growth rate of 187.1% in 2013. Till 2014, the scale was around 440 million yuan. At present, there still lack authoritative statistics for crowdfunding in China. Though many statistical reports are authoritative, varying data and statistical indicators can't satisfy research requirements. So the author cites different indicators of many reports to reflect changes of crowdfunding. There inevitably appear similar indicators but different values. The author does not want to verify the authenticity and reliability of data, but want to analyze current conditions of crowdfunding. Therefore, if readers see disunity of data, it is related to different data sources instead of mistakes or assumptions. After that, the scale of commodity crowdfunding still grew annually at the rate of 150% on average. It is predicted that the gross scale will reach 7000 million yuan, and 10 billion yuan in 2017 and 2018, respectively. Obviously, it shows that commodity crowdfunding in the primary stage of industry development will have a great space of improvement in the future.

Current commodity crowdfunding scale has exceeded planned fundraising scale of 68.5642 million yuan, with the extra-fundraising rate above 24.41%. It proves that investors hold high passion for commodity crowdfunding. This is also the outcome of commodity crowdfunding market for years (Figs. 6 and 7).

Development conditions in 2014 illustrate that the fundraising amount on comprehensive crowdfunding platform was 370 million yuan, and it made up 84.1%. By contrast, the scale of vertical platform was just 60 million yuan and it made u0 13.9%. Comprehensive platforms still account for a large proportion in commodity crowdfunding. Comprehensive platforms can launch a great variety of platforms, while external e-commerce platforms create great user traffic, such as JD Crowdfunding and Taobao Crowdfunding. However, the difference is that vertical crowdfunding projects have single variety, and limited number of platforms. Typical representatives are Pinganfang, Tianxiadai, Musikid and Tmeng. Because of this, comprehensive platforms have higher fundraising amount than vertical platforms. In terms of project number, there are altogether 4494 projects and 3787 of them belong to comprehensive platforms throughout the

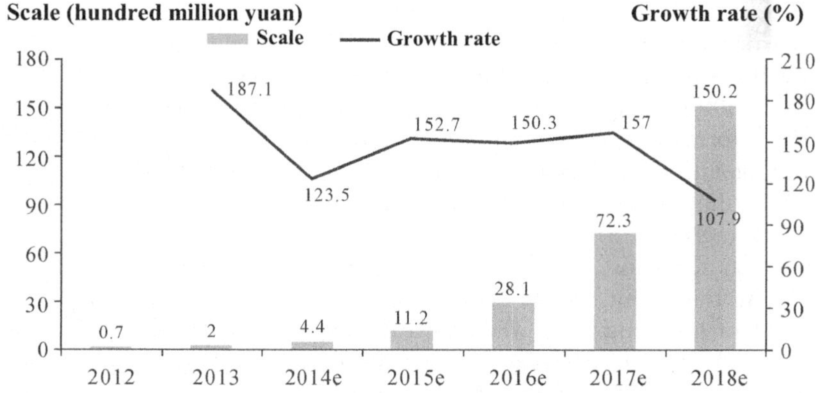

Fig. 6 Commodity crowdfunding scale and growth rate in China from 2012 to 2018 (*Data source* Report for Chinese Equity Crowdfunding Market Research in 2015)

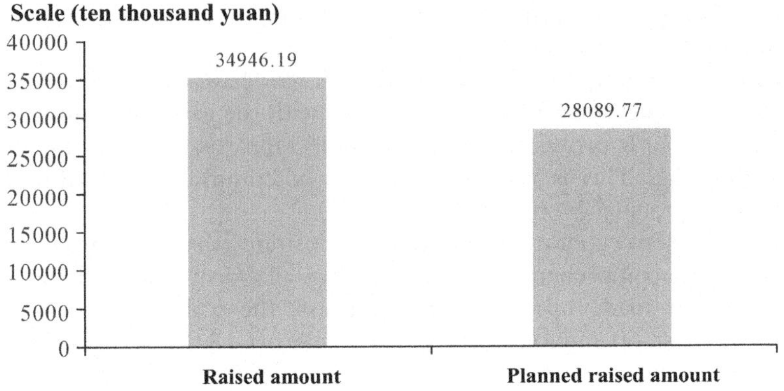

Fig. 7 Commodity crowdfunding raised amount and planned raised amount in 2014 (*Data source* Crowdfunding Industry Report)

year. Comprehensive platforms make up 84.3% in the market. The remaining includes 482 vertical platforms in the market which account for 10.7%. Concerning fundraising success rate, gross project fundraising success rate is 77.2%, comprehensive platform success rate is 78.5 % and vertical platform success rate is simply 67%. Therefore, either in project launch number or fundraising success rate, comprehensive platforms gain an advantage over vertical platforms. Concerning number of participants, approximately over 790,000 participants join commodity crowdfunding, including 69,600 participants on comprehensive platforms and 79,000 participants on vertical platforms. The fact that comprehensive platforms still constitute the main force of commodity crowdfunding development will not be changed in the short run (Table 5).

According to the market distribution law of commodity crowdfunding, market aggregation characteristics are in particular distinct. Large platforms launch most projects and raise most fund with high success rate. At this point, small platforms do not enjoy any advantage. In respect of financing scale, JD Crowdfunding, Zhongchou.com, Taobao Crowdfunding, DemoHour and Dreamore rank the top five place, and altogether raise 270 million yuan with 60.8% market shares. Among them, JD Crowdfunding takes the lead, and raises 140 million yuan, about the sum of remaining platforms ranking the second-the fifth place. Among

Table 5 Overview of the development of Chinese commodity crowdfunding platforms in 2014

Scale		*Totality*	*Comprehensive type*	*Vertical type*	*Others*
Fundraising scale	Sum (hundred million yuan)	4.4	3.7	0.6	0.1
	Proportion (%)	100	84.1	13.9	2
Number of project	Number	4494	3787	482	225
	Proportion (%)	100	84.3	10.7	5
Number of participants	Scale	790,825	695,926	79,082	15,817
	Proportion (%)	100	88	10	2
Fundraising success rate	Number	3468	2972	323	173
	Success rate (%)	77.2	78.5	67	76.9

Data Source Report for Chinese Equity Crowdfunding Market Research in 2015

top 10 product crowdfunding projects in China in 2014, JD Crowdfunding accounts for 70%. This proves the forceful fundraising ability of JD Crowdfunding. Benefited by the great platform flow and sound crowdfunding services, JD provides a series of services such as fundraising, production, promotion, sales and audit. This is the reason why JD can gather so many investors and projects on the platform. Though it is just launched in the market for half a year, it already exceeds other platforms. This point should be learned by many other platforms, especially Taobao Crowdfunding. Zhongchou.com depends on its comprehensive crowdfunding services, Taobao crowdfunding depends on the huge user traffic of Taobao.com, and DemoHour builds specific industry advantages and scale to varying degrees as the first crowdfunding platform in China. But it is worth noticing here that crowdfunding industry in itself is not rather mature. Apart from drastic industry changes, it is very likely to transform the industry. As a result, these platforms shall reinforce platform building and enhance platform competitiveness (Tables 6 and 7).

Concerning the number of launched projects in 2014, Zhongchou.com launches most projects as many as 1444, above the sum the four platforms. But concerning the success of projects, DemoHour ranks the first place as high as 99.3%. It is successively followed by Taobao Crowdfunding with 96.5% success rate. Zhongchou.com ranks the third place with 94.9% success rate. JD Crowdfunding ranks the least place with 83.1% success rate. In respect of financing scale, launched project,

Table 6 Top 10 commodity crowdfunding projects in 2014

Project source	Project name	Project type	Project sum (ten thousand yuan)
JD Crowdfunding	Wukong i8 smart temperature controller	Smart hardware	1,246
JD Crowdfunding	Club together to gain housing 11 yuan at an 89% discount	Other	1,221
JD Crowdfunding	Haier Air Rubik's cube	Smart hardware	1,195
JD Crowdfunding	Three Dads - Air Conditioner for Pregnant Women and Children	Smart hardware	1,123
Demohour	Smart Plug: K2 Universal Socket	Smart hardware	540
JD Crowdfunding	Fluorite Internet Movement Camera S1	Smart hardware	511
JD Crowdfunding	Kisslink: quick access	Smart hardware	430
Zhongchou.com	takee1homogram mobile phone	Smart hardware	376
JD Crowdfunding	IQEGG Smart Air Cleaner	Smart hardware	351
Demohour	Smart massage paste	Smart hardware	333

Data source Report for Chinese Equity Crowdfunding Market Research in 2015

Table 7 Comparison of performance among all platforms in 2014

Scale		JD Crowdfunding	Zhongchou.com	Taobao Crowdfunding	Demohour	Dreamore
Financing scale	Sum (hundred million yuan)	14031.4	4903.9	3950.7	3182.6	965.1
	Proportion (%)	31.6	11	8.9	7.2	2.2
Launched project	Number	445	1444	397	276	253
	Proportion(%)	9.9	32.1	8.8	6.1	5.6
Success rate	Number	370	1371	384	274	223
	Success rate (%)	83.1	94.9	96.5	99.3	88.1
Number of participant	Scale	627297	75271	458374	74326	25957

Data source Report for Chinese Equity Crowdfunding Market Research in 2015

and success rate, no platform is sound in all aspects as they have respective shortcomings.

Concerning project type, different platforms also behave in different manners. It can be easily seen from the top ten crowdfunding projects in China in 2014 that the most popular product in the market now is smart hardware. By virtue of JD's advantage in 3C field, JD Crowdfunding makes up 55.9% market shares. DemoHour and Taobao Crowdfunding make up 19.6% and 15.9%, respectively. In the field of cultural entertainment and publication, Zhongchou.com seizes overwhelming market shares as 85.1% and 66%, respectively. Correspondingly, the proportion of JD Crowdfunding is just 13.3% and 29.6%, respectively. In the field of public welfare, Taobao Crowdfunding and Zhongchou.com basically make up 50% market shares, respectively. While the field of agriculture is divided by Zhongchou.com and Taobao Crowdfunding. In the field of film and TV music, Taobao Crowdfunding seizes 67.8% market shares, and the proportion of JD Crowdfunding and Dreamore is 16.7% and 15.5%, respectively. In the field of animation game, JD Crowdfunding seizes 88.6% market shares, and Dreamore seizes remaining 11.4% shares. Thus it can be seen that these platforms have different focuses of business, and no platform stresses all-round development. In another word, it is rare to see a platform to take up large market shares in any field. As later entrants hardly seek development, these platforms seize specific market shares in some aspects. In reality, the pattern makes for the equilibrium development of all industries and prevents the occurrence of monopoly. But in subdivision field, monopoly seems inevitable (Table 8).

Commodity Crowdfunding Financing Mode

Commodity crowdfunding has a rather simple financing mode, as it does not involve security issue-related problems. Considering its low financing limit, it will not touch the bottom line of law. To put it simply, Chinese investors facilitate commodity production and sales via fundraising. Here are the few steps of commodity crowdfunding investment mode.

The first step is investor registration and approval. For commodity crowdfunding investors, the procedure of identity approval is very simple. By contrast, investors are subject to strict qualification approval, which can be evidenced by investment ability, asset, income and anti-risk ability.

The second step is sponsor qualification and project approval. Sponsors shall submit their identity information and project introduction to

Table 8 Market shares of all platforms in subdivision area

Type	JD Crowdfunding	Demohour	Taobao Crowdfunding	Zhongchou.com	Dreamore
Smart Device	55.9%	19.6%	15.9%	7.2%	1.4%
Cultural entertainment	13.3%		1.6%	85.1%	
Publication	29.6%		1%	66%	3.4%
Public welfare	4%		49.9%	46.1%	
Agriculture			29.9%	70.1%	
Movie and TV Soundtrack	16.7%		67.8%		15.5%
Animation and game	71.9%		28.1%		
Humanistic art				88.6%	11.4%
Others	66.6%		3.5%	15.6%	14.3%

Data source Report for Chinese Equity Crowdfunding Market Research in 2015

the platform by text, image and video. Additionally, sponsors must label fundraising target amount and deadline. The platform then audits both sponsors and projects. These projects can be only posted on the website for investors upon approval.

In the last step, investors choose projects for investment. After browsing the investment project list on the platform, investors may invest in projects that they are interested in. The amount of investment is decided by them at their own will. As to fund management means during the raising period, investors may choose either target entry or immediate entry. The former means when fundraising amount doesn't reach the target, the platform will manage the fund. The platform only transfers fund to sponsors in condition that fund amount reaches fundraising target. The latter means the platform does not manage fund, and investors' fund will be directly transferred to the account of sponsors. In general sense, target entry is out of the purpose of defending investors' interests, because fundraising amount can reflect market acceptance to commodity to a large extent. Once fundraising amount falls short of the target, it means that the market does not accept commodity. Under such circumstances, the project can't be completed as planned if the fund is transferred to sponsors. As a result, the fund can be only refunded to investors. Investors prefer target entry. If project sponsors request fund in emergency, they are inclined to adopt immediate entry in timely project launch.

Nowadays, most commodity crowdfunding platforms apply target entry mode, and divide fundraising amount into two parts. 50% of the fund is prepaid for project launch. Upon the completion of project, sponsors shall obtain the remaining.

Case 1: DemoHour

DemoHour, the founder of commodity crowdfunding in China, was established in May 2011. It sets a good example throughout the development of domestic commodity crowdfunding industry.

Here is DemoHour's project launch flow. The team first makes real name certification on the platform, and then submits detailed production plan, amount and term of fundraising. After registering and releasing products on the platform, the next step is to fill in product information, and upload product image-text material for approval. Products may be displayed on the platform upon approval.

While raising fund via DemoHour, investors can not only gain latest product on time, but also join in product design and creation, propose their own thoughts and ideas, and form virtuous bilateral interaction. On the part of sponsors, they not only gain start-up fund, but also promote products via this platform, and harvest feedback from potential users.

Concerning investment risk control, DemoHour charges 5% of gross fundraising amount as the cash deposit in the end of the activity, and transfers 70% fund to sponsors within 7 workdays. The remaining 30% will be transferred together with whole or partial cash deposit by the platform to sponsors when the project is completed and investors receive commodity.

Representative project: Smart Plug2
Project type: home life
Fundraising amount: 5.397636 million yuan
Deadline: September 18, 2014

Project introduction: Smart Plug2 makes overall improvement for Smart Plug 1. Apart of a series of new functions like time switch, security energy conservation protection, remote control of household appliances, WIFI signal augment and monitoring, it adds five plugs including body reaction, infrared remote control, radio frequency, environmental detection and doorkeeper security. Its core function is still remote control of household appliances via phone which aims to build up a smart house life (Table 9).

Table 9 Project fundraising overview

Sum (yuan)	*Number of participants*	*Reward*
1	5473	Any product under Xiao K Generation II can be bought. Any consumer who has bought the wisdom key may join in the lottery (iPhone6 Plus)
19	1509	1 remote control plug-in
29	2256	1 environmental plug-in, radio-frequency plug-in, or induction plug-in
39	200	1 wireless smart plug-in Xiao K Generation II
49	499	1 wireless smart plug-in Xiao K Generation II
69	1000	1 wireless smart plug-in Xiao K Generation II
79	880	1 wireless smart plug-in Xiao K Generation II
99	1256	Xiao K Generation II super suit: 1 Xiao K Generation II plug-in + 1 remote plug-in + 1 induction plug-in
139	200	Two wireless smart plug-in Xiao K Generation II
199	1000	1 Xiao K Generation II super suit: 2 sockets + 4 plug-ins
219	200	1 Xiao K Generation II super suit: 2 sockets + 4 plug-ins
229	200	1 Xiao K Generation II super suit: 2 sockets + 5 plug-ins
279	100	4 Xiao K Generation II smart sockets
459	100	2 Xiao K Generation II super suits: 4 sockets + 4 plug-ins
2999	30	50 Xiao K Generation II super suits
3999	20	20 Xiao K Generation II super suits (2 + 4)
5799	99	30 Xiao K Generation II super suits (2 + 4)
18,999	78	100 Xiao K Generation II super suits (2 + 4)
55,499	13	300 Xiao K Generation II super suits (2 + 4)

Data source Report for Chinese Equity Crowdfunding Market Research in 2015

Case 2: Zhongchou.com

Founded in February 2013, Zhongchou.com is a comprehensive commodity crowdfunding platform which integrates fundraising, investment, marketing, incubation, and operation services as a whole. The platform primarily concentrates on six business divisions, including science and technology, public welfare, publication, entertainment, art and agriculture.

Service Mode

Zhongchou.com provides a series of comprehensive services such as fundraising, marketing, incubation and operation for sponsors. This is the difference between Zhongchou.com and many other platforms. Before the launch of crowdfunding projects, Zhongchou.com will analyze project demands. After all, the size of market demands directly decides the success of projects. In order to satisfy investors' style and requirements as much as possible, Zhongchou.com is also responsible for project packaging. In the process of fundraising, Zhongchou.com will also formulate project plans to attract more investors. When fundraising activity comes to an end, the platform also offers entrepreneurial tutorship to sponsors, and helps them draw up and improve their business proposals. In entrepreneurial incubation stage, the platform helps entrepreneurs accumulate resources, expand business development paths, manage financial risks and propose suggestions in respect of talent introduction and training. By way of such one-stop comprehensive crowdfunding services, it can help sponsors raise fund, launch projects and facilitate business operation as soon as possible (Fig. 8).

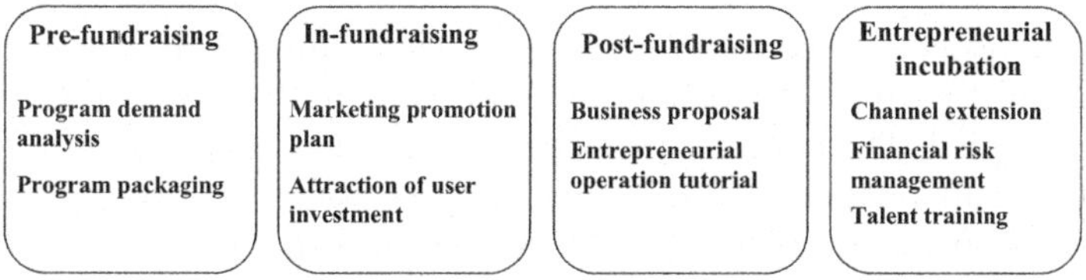

Fig. 8 Crowdfunding service mode

Rick Control Mode

In the period of fundraising, investors entrust fund in third-party payment accounts. On Zhongchou.com, fundraising succeeds if the amount lives up to the target within the deadline. If the project fails to raise enough fund within the deadline, investors' fund will be returned. After successful fundraising, Zhongchou.com will pay 70% of raised fund to sponsors, and pay the remaining 30% when sponsors perform the retribution obligations. If sponsors' commitment is not finalized, Zhongchou.com will spend 30% raised fund to cash in the return.

Data source: Research Report for Chinese Equity Crowdfunding Market in 2015.

Case 3: Taobao Crowdfunding

Launched in November 2013, Taobao Crowdfunding is the first Internet giant that enters the field of crowdfunding in China. Devoted to building up a commodity preorder platform, Taobao Crowdfunding allows everyone to launch fundraising projects on the platform. The platform involves a great many fields, such as science and technology, animation, design, public welfare, film and television, music, book and game.

Launch Flow

Apart from general flows, sponsors who want to launch fundraising projects on Taobao Crowdfunding must register an account of Taobao to be a seller, and make real name authentication on Alipay. Likewise, investors must be Taobao buyers in the first place.

Risk Control Mode

When sponsors succeed in fundraising, collected fund shall be guaranteed by the third party and sponsors themselves gain 1%-50% of the fund as start-up capital. The concrete proportion is decided by sponsors. Sponsors can only gain remaining fund when they perform the promise to give reward to investors. In addition, Taobao Crowdfunding also introduces business insurance to cover sponsors' fundraising behavior, thus further lowering project risks and defending investors' interests.[2]

[2] Data source: http://hi.taobao.com/market/hi/hi-question.php?spm=a215p.7204153.0.0.rcYTq8.

Data source: Report for Chinese Equity Crowdfunding Market Research in 2015.

Case 4: JD Crowdfunding

JD Crowdfunding was launched on JulWhile building up a fundraising platform, JD Crowdfunding platform also places emphasis on the establishment of industry incubation platform. Except fundraising services, JD Crowdfunding also offers a series of services, including production, marketing, sales and audit, to help promote project implementation quickly.

Project Scope

JD Crowdfunding platform demands projects to be innovation and executable. Another concern here is all projects should have a precise target, including smart hardware, pop culture, life aesthetics and public welfare. In current stage, smart hardware remains the focus of JD Crowdfunding.

Launch Flow

Sponsors shall go through identity authentication and qualification authentication online via third-party payment Internetbank first, including ID card, passport, academic degree, etc. Sponsors can only post projects on crowdfunding platforms upon the completion of real name authentication. Additionally, sponsors must be original creators of projects, and the reward must be products or derivative products instead of creditor's rights, equity, interest and dividend.

Service Pattern

JD Crowdfunding platform provides design instruction and crowdfunding proposal instruction for sponsors, and uses JD's former channels to promote projects so as to help sponsors quickly expand the market. JD enjoys rich experience in 3C field. Deeply aware of consumers' consumption characteristics and product demands, JD is able to assist sponsors to finish product design and adjust crowdfunding proposals according to investors' requirements. At the same time, JD can also help sponsors raise product sales volume and brand reputation by virtue of its channel role and facilitating role. Apart from fundraising, these additional services can be hardly provided by any other third-party platform. This is also the reason why JD Crowdfunding can grow up at a fast speed. Moreover, JD Crowdfunding's accurate positioning also plays a vital role. JD has no match in its understanding about smart hardware. Full understanding about the market is of great importance to the expansion of projects.

Risk Control Mode

y 1, 2014. Though it starts late than Taobao, JD Crowdfunding takes advantage of its platform advantage, channel advantage and profession advantage to march to the field of smart hardware and it then becomes the leader of commodity crowdfunding platforms simply within half a year. Its success is worth of pondering.

With the aim of defending investors' interests, all fund shall submit to the online supervision of third-party payment Interbank in fundraising period. Following successful fundraising operation, JD platform deducts 3% service charge and refunds remaining 70% to sponsors within 3 work-days, and allots 30% as cash deposit. When sponsors finish the reward obligation, the platform pays the remaining amount to sponsors.

Data source: Report for Chinese Equity Crowdfunding Market Research in 2015.

4 Equity-Based Crowdfunding

In June 2011, Ctquan, the first equity crowdfunding platform in China, was launched in the market. After that, a group of equity crowdfunding platforms represented by AngelCrunch and Dajiatou were successively established.

The first case of equity crowdfunding in China is Makev. On October 5 2012, Makev began to sell membership cards at the unit price of 100 yuan in its online direct-sale store on Taobao, and the membership cards corresponded to 100 initial offerings. From October 5, 2012 to 12:00 on February 3, 2013, Makev completed two rounds of fundraising, and altogether 1191 members subscribed 68,000 shares. Gross amount of fund totaled 1.2037 million yuan. However, CSRC judged it as initial public offering and called it off. Irrespective of the failed offering, it does not mean that the supervisory layer totally rejected the means. Afterward, equity crowdfunding was known by the public, and some equity crowdfunding platforms, such as Yuanshihui, were founded one by one.

On November 1, 2013, CCTV News affirmed Internet finance's role in changing traditional industry and supporting the development of small- and medium-sized companies in the coverage for equity crowdfunding platform AngelCrunch. This proved that the supervisory layer has affirmed the role of equity crowdfunding platform throughout a period of time. After that, the action of equity crowdfunding platform also begins to expedite.

Comparing with commodity crowdfunding, the sort of investment which aims to gain commodity, equity investment aims at corporate equity, dividend, interest and other earnings. In addition, comparing with commodity crowdfunding, investors show more prominent investment inclination, and more conform to the goal of building a multi-layer capital market of the country. Unfortunately, equity crowdfunding hadn't gained promising prospects for a time in the past, which could be proved by its limited industry scale. Till the year of 2014, the supervisory layer began to notice the industry, proactively made industry survey, designed top planning and released the signal of reform. By the end of the year, the issue of *Measures for Private Equity Crowdfunding Financing* (trial) (exposure draft) even brought a warm spring to people in the chilly winter. For a time, many people predict that the year of 2015 will see the heyday of "equity crowdfunding".

The operation means of equity crowdfunding bears much similarity to that of commodity crowdfunding. Under the two modes, it is always project sponsors that launch a good project in case of capital shortage, and sponsors gain earnings from production with fundraised by crowdfunding platforms. Whereas, equity crowdfunding financing takes equity as the reward. Totally different from commodity crowdfunding, investors gain equity, dividend, interest and cash earnings. It is more of investment property than commodity crowdfunding mode, but not limited to any specific commodity or service. Investment earnings resulting from these platforms is possibly huge. But it also gives rise to some other problems. The first one is investor qualification problem, the second one is investment amount problem and the third one is investment risk problem. Now that there are more than one products, investors can invest more in fundraising process. But this is also accompanied by growing investment risks. In condition of loss, the blow to investors is non-imaginable. Then it means that not all investors possess investment capacity or anti-risk capacity. Generally speaking, only investors who have certain economic power, investment experience, and anti-risk capacity can join the activity. This inevitably bounds the move of a great many investors.

Affected by objective factors like industry property and legal constraints, equity crowdfunding platform has not held enough attention all the time. But together with the continuous expansion of industry, equity crowdfunding not only receives more and more attention from the industry, but also gains great support from the supervisory layer. For instance, JD engaged in equity crowdfunding test as of March 2015. In accordance with *Guidelines on the Development of Mass Innovation Space and the Promotion of Mass Innovation Entrepreneurship* enacted by the State Council in March 2015, the government shall vigorously develop Internet equity crowdfunding financing pilots. Due to the sustained improvement of internal and external environment, equity crowdfunding will also approach the public in the industry.

Current Development Situations of Equity Crowdfunding

The number of equity crowdfunding platforms has been always very small. In 2011, Ctquan and AngelCrunch were successively established. There were 7 equity crowdfunding platforms by 2013. The year of 2014 witnessed the sharp rise of platforms from 7 to 29, with over 300% growth rate. It is not hard to see that owing to the continuous rise of good news in the industry, the number of platforms is expected to greatly increase up.

Chinese equity fundraising financing scale was simply 710 million yuan in 2014, making up 77.6% of entire fundraising financing scale. Though the number of platforms is just one third of that of commodity crowdfunding, its financing scale is three times of the latter. This indirectly proves the formidable financing capacity of equity crowdfunding platform (Figs. 9 and 10).

Despite the forceful financing capacity of equity crowdfunding platforms, raised amount is still less than planned amount from the perspective of financing rate. Moreover, the fund gap is very large. It forms a sharp contrast with commodity crowdfunding fundraising rate above 1. This implies that equity crowdfunding surmounts commodity crowdfunding in fund demands, and the two are not on the same level. In the future, together with the constant liberalization of equity crowdfunding, its financing scale will be further expanded, and its leading role in the crowdfunding industry will be reinforced (Fig. 11).

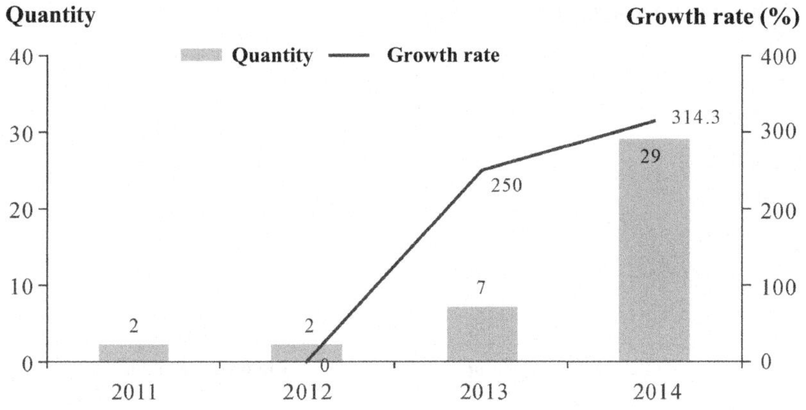

Fig. 9 Quantity and growth rate of Chinese equity crowdfunding platforms from 2011 to 2014 (*Data source* Internet Equity Crowdfunding Inventory Report; Internet Crowdfunding Report of China in 2014)

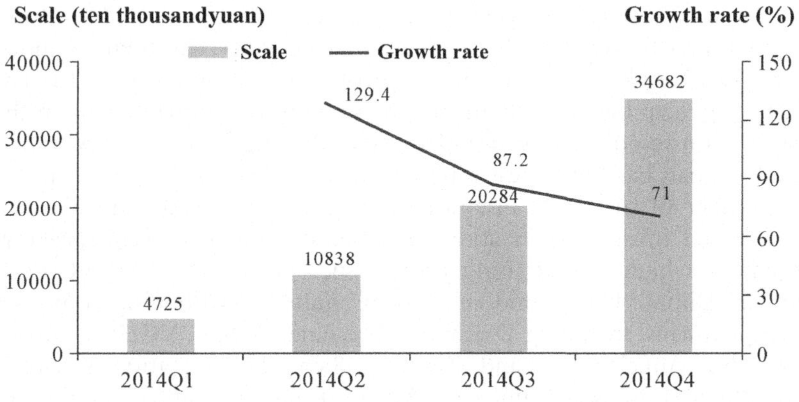

Fig. 10 Chinese equity fund-raising scale and growth rate from the first quarter of 2014 to the fourth quarter of 2014 (*Data source* Internet Crowdfunding Report of China in 2014)

According to incomplete statistics, there were 49,381 projects released on equity crowdfunding platforms from 2011 to 2014, but only 333 of them succeeded. Therefore, the success rate was just 0.68%. Gross

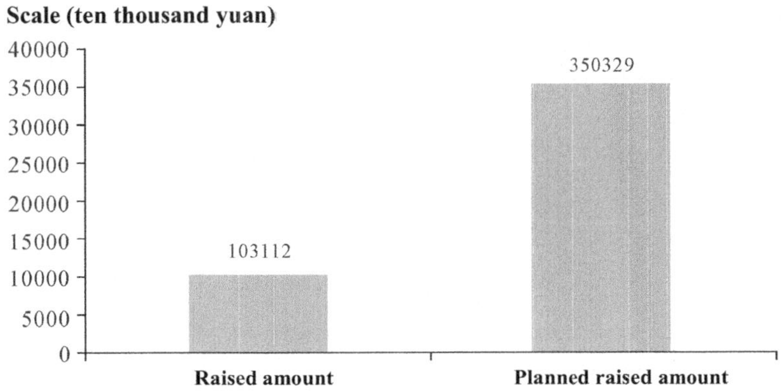

Fig. 11 Equity crowdfunding amount and planned raised amount in 2014 (*Data source* Crowdfunding Industry Report)

amount of raised fund reached 1550 million yuan. The fundraising amount was 710 million yuan in 2014, accounting for 45.8%. Moreover, Ctquan founded in 2011, AngelCrunch and Yuanshihui founded in late 2013 rank top three places in gross fundraising amount. In view of the huge gap between platforms, the three unquestionably rank in the first echelon in equity crowdfunding field. Among them, the first established Ctquan has the largest fundraising scale above 1 billion yuan, and the number of successful fundraising projects totals 230. AngelCrunch has released most projects above 30,000. But comparatively speaking, Ctquan has higher fundraising project success rate than AngelCrunch and Yuanshihui. The second echelon of equity crowdfunding comprises seven platforms, including Dajiatou, Chinae.net, V2ipo, VCHello, Roadshow Bar, Angel Street and Zhongtou8.cn. These platforms usually have specific fundraising amount (above 20 million yuan) or number of projects. In particular, the fundraising amount of Roadshow Bar built in 2014 totals 90.24 million yuan, approximate to the level of the first echelon. While that of the remaining ranges between 20 million and 30 million yuan. Among them, Chinae.net has launched most projects as many as 300, and it is followed by V2ipo as many as 155. The remaining is in the third echelon, and all of these platforms have low financing amount and limited quantity of projects and exert weak influences on the entire industry. Among them, Yunchou.com and Angel Guest have raised a large amount of fund over 10 million yuan (Tables 10 and 11).

Throughout the comparison of three echelons, it can be easily found that commodity crowdfunding platforms share many points in common, and there also exists industry aggregation phenomenon on equity crowdfunding platforms. The number of launched projects in the first echelon exceeds 48,000, accounting for 98% of the industry. The proportion of launched projects in the second and third echelon is 1.68% and 0.31%, respectively. In respect of financing projects, there are 274 projects in the first echelon, more than the sum of those in the second and third echelon,

Table 10 Development conditions of main equity crowdfunding platforms in China from 2011 to 2014

Platform	Time of establishment	Site	Number of project	Number of successful project	Financing amount (ten thousand yuan)
Ctquan	2011.6	Beijing	16090	230	100300
AngelCrunch	2011.11	Beijing	30304	35	20000
Dajiatou	2013.1	Guangdong	47	26	2601
Qidian Venture Capital	2013.8	Beijing	24	0	0
Aihetou	2013.9	Guangdong	20	3	733
Yuanshihui	2013.12	Beijing	2000	9	12000
Chuanyeyi	2013.12	Guangdong	300		2730
V2ipo	2014.1	Beijing	155	0	0
Aichuangye	2014.1	Shanghai	22	0	0
FashionVC Hualiji	2014.3	Beijing	18	0	0
Angel Guest	2014.4	Guangdong	11	4	1099
Drupal China	2014.4	Sichuan	11	5	86
VCHello.com	2014.4	Guangdong	64	7	1950
Yunchou.com	2014.5	Guangdong	15	7	1200
Luyanba	2014.5	Jiangsu	125	5	9024
Angel Street	2014.6	Beijing	77	0	0
Zhongtoubang	2014.7	Guangdong	64	2	3200
Zhongtoutiandi	2014.7	Beijing	20	0	0
Bafangtou	2014.8	Jiangsu	4	0	0
Equity Yi	2014.9	Beijing	10	0	0
Tiantian Capital Transfer	2014.9	Zhejiang	0	0	0
Sum			49381	333	154923

Data source Internet Equity Crowdfunding Inventory Report

Table 11 Overview of different types of equity crowdfunding platforms

Scale		*First ladder*	*Second ladder*	*Third ladder*
Number of launched projects	Number	48,394	832	155
	Proportion (%)	98	1.68	0.31
Number of fundraising projects	Number	274	40	19
	Proportion (%)	82.28	12.01	5.71
Fundraising amount	Amount (ten thousand yuan)	132,000	19,505	3118
	Proportion (%)	85.37%	12.61	2.02

Data source Internet Equity Crowdfunding Inventory Report

and they make up 82.28% of the industry. In respect of fundraising amount, the amount in the echelon totals 1.32 billion yuan, and makes up 85.37%. The achievement is too far beyond to catch up with for the second and third echelon.

Equity-Based Crowdfunding Financing Mode

On the whole, equity crowdfunding financing mode is basically the same with commodity crowdfunding. But concerning equity crowdfunding, there are still some limitations in existing laws and regulations. At the same time, out of the consideration about risk control, present equity crowdfunding financing mode is more sophisticated than commodity crowdfunding in flow.

The first flow is investor approval. Investors are supposed to register an account, submit user name, mailbox, phone number and phone verification code, and fill in personal information, including ID card, passport, etc. Then investors need to bound bank card and make online risk appraisal. The platform shall approve investors' identity. Those investors who pass the approval become formal investors of the platform, while those who fail to pass the approval shall not engage in project investment and can only check project profile.

The second flow is sponsor approval. Like investors, sponsors also need to finish online registration and identity authentication. Sponsors can only launch project financing upon completion of approval.

In the third flow, sponsors need to fill in project information, including basic project information, project team information, project proposal, project demonstration, project flow and business plan. The platform approves projects from three aspects, including basic introduction, project team information and business plan. In most cases, the approval is completed by formal approval instead of immaterial approval. Projects are demonstrated to investors for selection upon approval.

In the fourth flow, investors invest in projects. At present, investors make investment either by direct investment mode or "leader + follower" mode.

Under direct investment mode, investors directly make investment in projects. It is much similar to commodity crowdfunding. Under "leader + follower" mode, professional investors act as leaders and ordinary investors act as investors followers in the investment. This mode is mainly proposed to solve ordinary investors' experience shortage and great investment risks. In this way, if senior investors who have rich experience or thorough understanding about the industry can lead and guide ordinary investors to make investment, ordinary investors' investment risks can be fully lowered.

Equity crowdfunding platforms usually set rigorous requirements on the qualification of leaders. For instance, a leader is expected to satisfy at least one of the following conditions: two-year working experience in Angel Fund or as a VC Fund manager, two-year entrepreneurial experience (limited to first founder), three-year working experience as a corporate director, five-year working experience as a corporate manager, two-year Angel investment experience. AngelCrunch requests leaders to satisfy at least one of the following conditions: leaders must be active investors (who have invested in projects in half a year, and reached new projects in recent one month); leaders must have rich experience, independent judgment ability, rich industry resources and influence, strong risk tolerance ability in specific field; leaders must invest in no less than projects in a year and spend enough time in project expansion; leaders must have retreated from at least one project; leaders must have the competence to improve project BP, appraisal, investment clauses and financing amount, assist in project roadshow and finish financing and investment; leaders must have strong sharing spirits and would like to share projects with other investors. Consequently, it can be fitly judged that equity crowdfunding platforms set very strict requirements on leaders' qualifications. Leaders should fully exert their prominent advantages in projects, and help sponsors and investors finish project financing and investment. In general, the responsibility of leaders is to cut down the cost of sponsors, and simultaneously decrease the risks of investors. Specifically speaking, leaders should be responsible for the following obligations. The first one is project analysis, investigation, appraisal, post-investment management. The second one is to offer project analysis and due diligence conclusion to investors, and help sponsors finish project financing. The third one is to coordinate the relation between sponsors and investors. The last point is to build limited companies.

It is worth noticing here that all investors do not make investment in the capacity of shareholder. Instead, it is the leader that first takes the lead to establish limited companies. Investors' shareholding proportion corresponds to the proportion of subscription. Sponsors become shareholders of launched projects and maintain corresponding shares. The reason why the practice is implemented is to reduce the number of shareholders, conform to the regulations of Corporation Law and more importantly, simplify start-up business equity structure.

Case 5: AngelCrunch

Since its foundation in November 2011, AngelCrunch had launched over 16,090 projects, attracted 2109 investors, and successfully completed over 230 financing projects totaling 10 billion yuan till September 2014. Representatives included Didi Dache, Toohappy Huang, and Breadtrip. Among them, there were 6,456 new projects launched in 2013, and 1,097 of them passed approval and 65 projects successfully raised fund, with a success rate of 5.9%. During January–September 2014, there were 8,410 new projects. Among them, 2,607 projects passed approval, and 77 of them successfully raised fund. The two figures slightly increased up than 2013, but fundraising success rate dropped down.

According to the classification of AngelCrunch successful fundraising projects, most projects are under the category of local life service (12), mobile/SNS social contact (9), media entertainment (5) and financial service (5). They altogether make up 62%. In terms of fundraising amount, the five types of projects also have the largest scale with a gross amount of 68.77 million yuan, and a proportion of 63.17%. As to the fundraising amount of single project, all projects have basically the same amount around 2 million yuan except a few special ones (Tables 12 and 13).

Table 12 AngelCrunch development overview

Scale	*2013*	*January–September 2014*
Number of project	6,456	8,410
Number of approved project	1,097	2,607
Number of financed project	65	77
Fundraising success rate	5.9%	3%

Data source Internet Equity Crowdfunding Inventory Report

5 The Rethinking of Crowdfunding

It seems that people have a better understanding about the implication of crowdfunding when they first get acquaintance with the concept. But as time passes by, there rise more and more misgivings and misunderstanding. Are commodity crowdfunding and equity crowdfunding are Internet finance? Why do they belong to Internet finance? Crowdfunding can be considered as the online form of private offering pursuant to its implication, mode and flow. The sole difference is that the offline mode has been launched online now. Therefore, it is nothing to with innovation. Internet here plays the role of channel. Is this Internet finance? Does Internet finance means finance on the network?

Actually, many people, including some experts and scholars, have overlooked this issue. Most available articles and comments about crowdfunding concentrate on crowdfunding mode, risk and risk control links. Despite the importance of these links, they lack the core, i.e. how crowdfunding exists as a mode of Internet finance. After all, it is definitely more than online private offering.

As the core of Internet finance, crowdfunding can take advantage of big data to analyze financing and investment characteristics and promote financing and investment business. It rests in the radical mission of crowdfunding, and also the most distinctive feature of crowdfunding different from online offering. In our opinion, big data application of crowdfunding is at least shown in four aspects, namely sponsor credit appraisal, project appraisal, investor appraisal and operation appraisal.

First of all, in sponsor credit appraisal, the platform confirms sponsors' identity and appraises their credit in combination with related statistics

Table 13 Statistics of AngelCrunch successful fundraising projects from January to September 2014

Type	Number of successful project	Fundraising amount (ten thousand yuan)	Fundraising amount of a single project (ten thousand yuan)
Local life services	12	2140	178.33
Mobile/SNS social contact project	9	2137	237.44
E-commerce project	2	370	185
Education training project	4	1100	275
Mobile Internet project	2	400	200
Advertising marketing project	1	60	60
Instrument software project	2	550	275
Media entertainment project	5	1450	290
Smart hardware project	3	450	150
Financial service project	5	1150	230
Outdoor tourism project	3	680	226.67
Corporate service project	1	100	100
Traffic project	1	300	300

Data source Internet Equity Crowdfunding Inventory Report

such as identity, income, ability and experience. Credit appraisal constitutes the basis of investment and financing activities, and also an effective means to prevent and lower sponsors' credit risks and moral risks.

Secondly, in project appraisal, the platform shall assess project innovation, feasibility, applicability, market potentials and financing difficulty. The feasible practice is to compare present with former successful or failed cases, and reveal project potentials. This is in particular important to project launch and operation (Fig. 12).

Fig. 12 Application of big data in crowdfunding

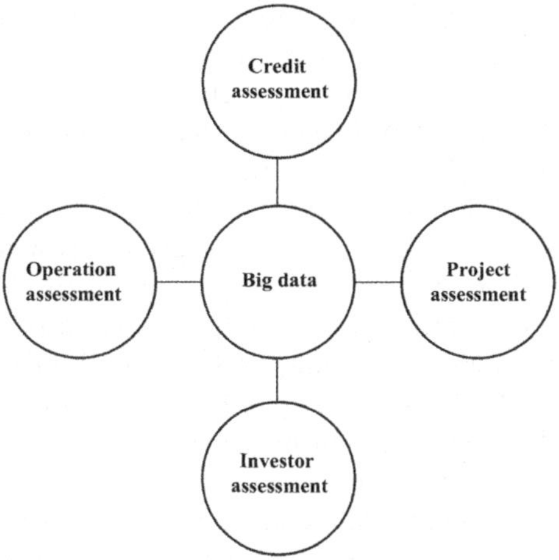

The third link is about the analysis on investor investment property. How about the investor group? What is the preference of investors to projects? What is the amount of investment? It is especially critical to learn about the features of fundraising target. Or otherwise, the project possibly fails if fundraising projects do not conform to or match with investors.

The last link is about project operation appraisal. In the process of project launch and operation, the project may operate and appraise corporate production, marketing and promotion links, present accurate suggestions and help companies better produce and operate projects.

What is crowdfunding? Crowdfunding appraises sponsors, investors, launched projects and production operation based on big data so that it more lives up to expectation and reaches ideal operation effects. Among all influential factors, the core is big data application. But at present, neither commodity crowdfunding, such as JD Crowdfunding and Taobao Crowdfunding, nor equity crowdfunding, such as AngelCrunch, exerts the advantage of big data. Commodity crowdfunding now depends on investors' "interests" in commodity rather than the use of big data. Equity crowdfunding is also the mix of "interest" and "earnings". Therefore, focus of commodity crowdfunding should be placed on the use of big data in the future.

Then where does big data come from? As to this problem, just like P2P, it just means the accumulation of platform data. For instance, both failed cases and successful cases accumulate big data for the platform. In this sense, the platform can only quantify accumulated cases and analyze respective characteristics to sum up a law. This is crucial to the launch of follow-up projects. From this perspective, domestic crowdfunding industry is still in the start-up stage, and its project number and fundraising scale far fall short of those of P2P industry. In other words, there is still a long way to go for crowdfunding.

The reason why crowdfunding is defined as a more open financing mode is that it is not limited to creditors' rights but enters more fields and diversifies financing modes than other modes led by big data finance and P2P. This creates benefits to commodity crowdfunding with commodity demands, donation crowdfunding devoted to public welfare and also equity financing engaged in entrepreneurship. Due to its more flexible investment and financing modes, and more opening characteristics, it gives parties of investment and financing more choices. Consequently, crowdfunding possibly has better prospects than other modes in the future.

Case 6: DemoHour Application of Big Data

As the crowdfunding industry began to differentiate in 2014, the differences in platforms' ability to accumulate, control and apply internal data began to become prominent. Based on three years of data, DemoHour provides very precise guidance for platform projects. For example, DemoHour will tailor production and promotion plans for companies based on the experience of previous successful projects, grasp the resources of online and offline sales channels based on the platform, and guide companies to adjust the delivery quantity at any time. These have played a very important role in the initiation and development of the project (Table 14).

Data source: http://report.iresearch.cn/html/20140529/231939.shtml.

6 The Problems of Crowdfunding

Severe Legal Risks

The reason why crowdfunding fails to realize prompt development is because it suffers from great legal risks in part. Limited by its properties, commodity crowdfunding is subject to fewer limitations in current

Table 14 Instruction of DemoHour to projects in different periods based on platform data

Stage	Characteristics	Product output	Platform service content
Stage I	Project initiator's design thinking	0	Keep thoughts and product design drawing confidential, and establish intellectual property awareness
Stage II	Product prototype and improvement	1~10	Utilize platform fans and former project experience to improve new project proposals and increase user viscosity
Stage III	Give feedback to prior users, improve products and complete trial production	100~500	Launch the product on the platform and contact all mainstream media for secondary product exposure
Stage IV	Further clear out market conditions and prepare for mass production	1,000~3,000	Instruct corporate inventory and formulate production and channel strategy according to the market feedback
Stage V	Product launching	>10,000	Comprehensive application of platform channel resources and market resources

Data source iResearch

context. Because of excessive legal constraints, equity crowdfunding easily breaches related laws and regulations and leads to project failure. Specifically speaking, equity crowdfunding has three main legal risks as below.

The first legal risk arises from illegal fundraising. According to the first clause in *Interpretation of the Supreme People's Court for Specific Application of Illegal Fundraising Criminal Cases*, illegal fundraising should satisfy the following four conditions concurrently: 1. absorb fund without approval from related departments in legal terms or borrow the form of legal operation; 2. make public publicity via media, introduction and marketing event, leaflet, phone messages and other means; 3. promise to repay capital with interest or reward in the form of currency, substance or equity in given term; 4. absorb fund from social public and the society from non-specified objects. Equity crowdfunding satisfies the four conditions mentioned above. The reward of equity crowdfunding is equity. Public fundraising does not target at specific objects, as it also attracts participants via massive promotion and publicity. For this, equity crowdfunding is very likely to be thought as illegal fundraising.

As stipulated by *Measures for Private Equity Crowdfunding Financing* (trial) (exposure draft), both platforms and financiers shall not make publicity, promotion or persuasion to avoid the second clause. Moreover, investors must be registered real-name users who conform to at least one of the following conditions: minimum amount of investment shall not be less than 1 million yuan in single financing project; financing assets shall not be less than 3 million yuan or individual annual average income shall not be less than 500,000 yuan in recent three years. Except related property and income proof, investors must possess the ability to discern, judge and assume related investment risks to avoid the fourth clause.

On the whole, considering the risk of equity crowdfunding, present limitation on equity crowdfunding has not been lifted. Therefore, the development of private equity crowdfunding requests investors who have certain income, anti-risk ability and risk identification ability to cut down equity crowdfunding risks.

The second risk is illegal issue securities. The first clause in Article 10 of *Securities Law* in China stipulates that public issue securities shall meet legal and administrative regulations, and report to the State Council Securities Supervisory Agency or other authorized departments for approval. Any undertaking or individual shall not issue securities without legal approval. Public offering at least meets one of the following conditions. Issue securities to non-specific targets; issue securities to more than 200 specific targets; commit other issue actions stipulated by laws and administrative regulations. Aiming at non-specific objects, the platform usually tests investors' qualification via real-name authentication, and converts non-specific targets to specific targets. The number of specific targets shall not exceed 200. The platform may either predetermine investors' investment proportion or avoid the regulation. For instance, Dajitou stipulates that leaders' minimum investment proportion should be 5%, and that of followers should be 2.5%. In this way, it is far less than the restriction of 200 quota.

The third risk is breach of *Corporation Law*. According to the *Corporation Law*, a limited liability company shall include 200 at most. In order to effectively reduce the number of shareholders in newly established companies, investors may first build up a limited company and then become shareholders of the start-up company in the name of the company.

Unsound Supervisory System

Measures for Private Equity Crowdfunding Financing (trial) (exposure draft) enacted in December 2012 normalizes equity crowdfunding, and clarifies equity crowdfunding private offering property, equity crowdfunding platform positioning, investor definition and protection and financier obligation, etc. In particular, it requests to execute special fund projects to manage fund on equity crowdfunding platform, and clearly list affairs proper for equity crowdfunding platforms. All of these are highlights of the Measures. But undeniably, there still exist lots of problems in the Measures.

First, it sets high requirements on investors. Individual investors are requested to have no less than 3 million yuan financial assets or have no less than 500,000 yuan annual average income in recent three years. This is greatly different from the large number of participants and small amount of fund on crowdfunding platforms.

Secondly, related laws haven't been revised and they still contradict with *Securities Law* and *Corporation Law*.

Thirdly, the regulation that prohibits platform equity transfer service goes against the exit of investors.

Comparing with domestic policies, European and American supervisory policies for equity crowdfunding platforms deserve reference in three aspects: first of all, foreign equity crowdfunding platforms set a relatively low threshold for investors and financiers; secondly, foreign equity crowdfunding platforms practise rigorous supervisory policies; thirdly, foreign equity crowdfunding platforms are subject to high information disclosure requirements (Table 15).

Fuzzy Platform Profit-making Mode

It is estimated that each project crowdfunding platform would charge 5%-10% service fee, including trading fee, value-added fee, traffic import and marketing fee. But the 5%-10% service fee can hardly sustain the normal operation of the platform. Some platforms, such as DemoHour, even canceled service fee in July 2013 to attract investors. But before the formation of a clear profit-making mode, the platform undertakes heavy operation pressures. In April 2014, DemoHour, the giant of Chinese crowdfunding industry, announced to transit to a smart hardware platform and totally lost its crowdfunding label from then on. The main

Table 15 Comparison of crowdfunding regulation in China, America and Britain

Project	*China*	*America*	*Britain*
Regulatory laws	Private equity Crowdfunding financing management practices	Jumpstart our business Startups acts	Regulatory rules on online Crowdfunding and issue of illiquid securities in other means
Investors' requirements	Real-name registered users, including units or individuals whose minimum amount of investment in single financing project shall not be less than 1 million yuan, units whose net assets shall not be less than 10 million yuan, individuals whose financial assets shall not be less than 3 million yuan or individuals whose annual income shall not be less than 500,000 yuan	Investors whose net assets or annual income shall be less than $100,000, and amount of investment shall not exceed $2,000 or 5% of their annual income; investors whose income exceeds $10,000, their annual amount of investment is less than 10% of their annual salary; the amount of investors with more assets shall be limited within $100,000	High asset investors whose annual income exceeds 10,000 pounds or whose net assets exceed 250,000 pounds; mature investors who have gained FCA authorization; immature investors whose amount of investment shall not exceed 10% net assets (excluding mature investors)
Fundraisers' requirements	Real-name registered users of the platform; financiers shall not publicly or implicitly issue bonds to unspecific targets; upon the completion of fundraising, the number of shareholders in the companies set up by financiers or fundraisers shall not exceed 200	The ceiling of fundraisers' annual crowdfunding amount is $1million. Upon the completion of putting on records on SEC in America, fundraisers shall disclose necessary information to investors and intermediaries	
Platform establishment means	Equity crowdfunding platforms shall apply to secruity association for the records within five workdays after establishment	Intermediaries which help fundraisers make public financing shall get registered in SEC in America	Platforms shall gain authorized operation from FCA

Project	*China*	*America*	*Britain*
Crowdfunding platform requirements	Professionals whose net assets are no less than 5 million yuan and have developed private equity crowdfunding financing; no less than 2 senior managers with over three years of financial or information technology working experience	Remove the obligation of crowdfunding platforms as stock brokers or security traders; allow securities issuing office to issue, sell or negotiate securities via the platform; intermediaries that help fundraisers engaged in public financing shall get registered in SEC	Intermediary platforms shall gain the authorized operation from FCA to improve the security of crowdfunding financing
Platform banned behaviors	Raise fund from institutional Internet platform or affiliated parties; provide external guarantee or share-holding entrustment for crowdfunding projects; provide transfer service for negotiable securities in equity or other forms; promote or recommend financing projects for non-real-name registered users; engage in securities underwriting, investment consultant, asset management and other securities institution businesses, excluding securities operation institutions with related business qualifications; have sideline in individual online lending or online petty loan business	Offer investment opinions or suggestions; attract users to buy securities issued on the website by persuasive purchase, sales or means of issue; pay for staff, agencies or other individuals with persuasive behaviors based on website securities; join in other restricted behaviors prescribed by SEC	

(continued)

Table 15 (continued)

Project	*China*	*America*	*Britain*
Information disclosure	Keep investor and financier information, financing record and investor appropriateness management information and other related materials confidential. The term of retention shall not be less than 10 years	Disclose information according to the scale of issue; for the issue amount less than $100,000 or below, income tax returns and unaudited financial statement in past fiscal years shall be confirmed by administrative staff; for the issue of securities worth $100,000–$500,000, financial statement shall be audited by an independent accountant; for the issue of securities worth $500,000–$1 million, financial statement shall be audited	Online lending platforms shall inform consumers about the business in plain languages. Comparative study on deposit interest rate must be fair and clear. Any investment suggestion on the platform may be considered as financial sales behavior. Financial sales-related regulations shall be obeyed

Data source Research on the Current Situations and Future Development Trend of Equity Crowdfunding in China

Table 16 Crowdfunding platform profit-making mode

Source of profit	*Means of income*	*AngelCrunch*
Transaction fee	Raise fund as per specific proportion, usually 5%	5% of financing amount
Value-added service charge	Outsource affairs related to contract, document, law and finance, excluding financing to crowdfunding platform	Provide informatization software service, such as corporate governance software, and charge low fee
Flow introduction and marketing fee	Cooperative marketing and advertising separation	Provide value-added and senior services, provide more services for companies with third-party institutions, such as legal services and financial services

Data source Shenwan Hongyuan Securities

reason is that throughout development for over three years, the platform still fails to find a proper profit-making mode, and it inevitably has to make transition. Thus it is clear that a clear profit-making mode is of great importance to the development of the platform (Table 16).

Great Investment Risks

Comparing with P2P and other mature companies and projects, crowdfunding financing is apparently in the start-up stage. Therefore, it faces more difficulties in the implementation stage than P2P financing projects, and the final outcome is more uncertain. Poor investment experience prevents many investors from engaging in the field of crowdfunding.

Unsound Exit Mechanism

Different from equity crowdfunding, commodity crowdfunding can give reward to investors upon the production of commodity. However, investors can only gain reward from equity crowdfunding when invested projects make profits. Therefore, corresponding investment return period usually lasts for a long time.

As there is no site for public trading, investors' shares can't be arbitrarily transferred. Now that investors are not allowed to transfer shares

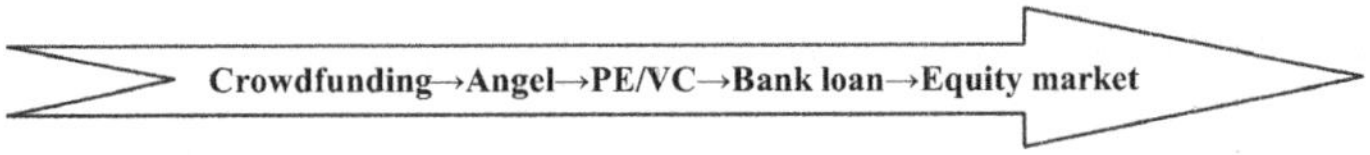

Fig. 13 The position of crowdfunding in the corporate financing stage

upon investment or exit trading, investors' passion is greatly prohibited (Fig. 13).

Platform Fund Management

Whether platform has the qualification to manage investor fund in the capacity of intermediary has always been the focus of discussion. Theoretically, the platform which plays the role of intermediary can't entrust investment fund. Therefore, it is the third party that should be responsible for platform fund management.

Kickstarter exactly entrusts fund in Amazon Payment. Investors transfer all fund to Amazon Payment, and sponsors also transfer the fund to their own accounts via Amazon Payment. "Toufubao" released by Dajiatou in September 2013 also follows the thinking of third-party custody. Toufubao is a sort of investment custody service released by Industrial Bank Shenzhen Branch entrusted by Dajiatou in which sponsors transfer investment fund to the custody account, and then transfer fund to newly established companies upon the agreement of contract. In this way, it avoids fund risks caused by platforms and sponsors.

7 The Future Development Trend of Crowdfunding

Development of the whole industry chain of the platform

More and more crowdfunding platforms are no more pure financing platforms. At the same time, crowdfunding platforms also take charge of integrating upstream and downstream channels, providing management experience and helping entrepreneurs finish projects. This trend is in particular prominent on vertical crowdfunding platforms, such as music, field and other fields. For instance, lianchou.com launched in

October 2014 as the first cultural creativity platform in China affords one-stop comprehensive crowdfunding services for project sponsors, including fundraising, investment, incubation and operation.

Entire crowdfunding comprehensive services include the following three points. The first one is project productization before project financing, which means that platform financing plan demonstrated to investors must be professional enough. Secondly, in the process of financing, sponsors and investors must have full communication. The last point is sustained progress after successful financing, including production planning, market promotion and sales docking (Table 17).

Comprehensive full-industry chain development of the platform should be ascribed to a great many reasons. First of all, ferocious competition forces the platform to provide value-added services. Secondly, value-added services increase platform income. Thirdly, it helps sponsors better develop business. As proved by facts, the guiding role of the platform in project operation is especially prominent. Past successful project experience can be well consulted to guide the production planning, market promotion and marketing of newly established companies.

Table 17 Crowdfunding platform follow-up services

Service project	*Specific content*	*Advantages*
Fundraising	Launch the project and gain user funding	Advantage of traditional crowdfunding platform
Production plan	Provide inventory, manufacturing and logistics instructions for project managers according to past successful experience	Advantage of e-commerce crowdfunding platform
Marketing	Provide fans marketing, online marketing and offline recommendation conferences for projects based on a giant user group	Advantage of traditional crowdfunding platform
Sales docking	Provide sales market for products by personal platform or strategic cooperative partner	Advantage of e-commerce crowdfunding platform

Data source iResearch

Verticality

Vertical platforms come into being because of two reasons. First of all, vertical platforms expand business scope, occupy subdivision market at a low cost, satisfy individual demands and form distinctive industry culture. Secondly, vertical platforms demonstrate platform professionalism, authority and precision, and attract specific investors to make investment.

Due to the continuous differentiation of crowdfunding industry, vertical trend will be continually deepened in the future, and comprehensive platforms will coexist with vertical platforms.

Diversification of Platform Profit-making Mode

The platform shall not only make profits from service fee alone, but should also expand more profit-making points, thus forming a diversified profit-making mode. First of all, it needs to enrich value-added services, greatly support project packing and promotion, and expand services to upstream and downstream parties around fundraising. Secondly, it needs to widen website threshold, introduce traffic and increase advertising income. Thirdly, it seeks external cooperation, and introduces VC to increase intermediary income. Finally, it ought to make strategic investment, choose better projects to buy into shares and add investment income.

CHAPTER 8

Rising Entrance of Flow: Vertical Financial Search

In the Age of Internet, information is explosive. Therein lies the significance of finding proper information to match in massive information. Vertical financial search realizes financing and investment by information match. To realize the rational match of information by way of financial information search, collection, gathering and analysis is a key step in Internet finance. Therefore, the future vertical financial search will become the portal to the Internet finance world. In addition, a great many platforms now are engaged in professional vertical search, mainly responsible for finding financial information that matches searchers, and helping users find the most proper information in the shortest time. Together with the continuous rise of financial products in the future, more and more users will choose vertical search portals outside mainstream platforms to find personalized and suitable financial products. Accurate information search is the future development direction of search platforms.

In this Age of Information, the concept of search has already penetrated deep into the mind of people. Baidu, Google and other search giants are almost known to everyone now. In the field of Internet Finance, together with the continuous innovation of business modes, all sorts of products are also in sharp rise, ranging from Bao series products to P2P money management and crowdfunding. For a time, all sorts of products spring up like mushrooms after rain. But amazingly, investors' strangeness to products forms a sharp contrast with it. As to Bao series

Q. Guan and W. Gao, *Internet Finance*,
The Great Transformation of China,
https://doi.org/10.1007/978-981-16-4740-6_8

products, overwhelming people just know Yu'E Bao but have no idea about other money management products with ultra-high rate of return. Such phenomenon indirectly shows severe information asymmetry in the Age of Internet Finance. Though Internet Finance may solve the information asymmetry problem between fund suppliers, what is function of single financing mode in condition of fund supply–demand information asymmetry? Targeting at this problem, there already appears a mode in the industry, i.e. vertical financial search. Vertical search customized for Internet financing products plays a vital role in alleviating information asymmetry, reducing transaction cost, and raising success rate. Accompanied by the continuous deepening of Internet finance, the business state of vertical financial search will begin to come under the "spot light" and turn to be the flow entrance of Internet ecosphere.

1 The Definition of Vertical Financial Search

Internet vertical financial search refers to a mode which realizes the interaction between fund supply and requisitioning sides via financial search intermediary. Typical mode of vertical financial search is "search + price parity". Product requisitioning party seeks all sorts of financial products suitable for demands by search, compares these products in terms of price, term and rate of return by parity, and finally chooses one product and leaves the contact information. Customer manager will complete the final trade after getting into contact with the customer.

The positioning of financial search is information intermediary who provides information support and information mixture for trading parties, and solves information asymmetry problem of the parties. Financial search in itself does not intervene product design and product trade process, nor competes with money management, P2P, big data finance and crowd funding. It is just like the relation between manufacturer and shopping mall. Therefore, it can more efficiently avoid the regulation of policies.

By financial search intermediary, customers can find proper financial products for themselves, and on the other hand, financial products may be sold out. In this way, the two sides can exchange financial products and fund. At the same time, throughout vertical financial search, it is also possible to discover the characteristics of product requisitioning party and further help product suppliers make improvement.

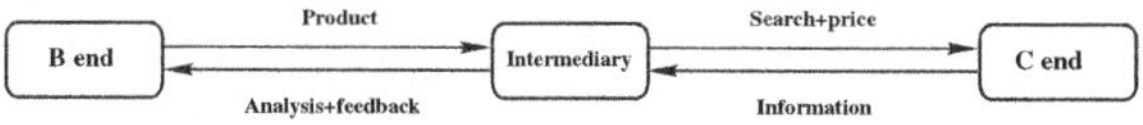

Fig. 1 Two layers of vertical financial search

Layer of Vertical Financial Search

There exist two layers in vertical financial search, namely B2C process and C2B process. The two layers demonstrate the interactive experience characteristics of Internet finance. As a matter of fact, B2C process is a process of "search + price parity" in which consumers find most proper financial products in the market via vertical financial search. During the full process, vertical financial search is more like a product intermediary responsible for pushing products from B-end to C-end, and helping B-end mix and sell products. While C2B process is a process of "analysis + feedback". Combining with analysis on C-end behavior, vertical search platform can excavate consumers' behavioral characteristics and purchase demands, and give feedback to B-end to help finish product re-design and adjustment so that products more cater to consumers' demands (Fig. 1).

Vertical Financial Search and Big Data

The nature of vertical financial search is big data application. At the first layer, vertical search realizes "search + price parity + recommendation" functions by credit rating, search engine, intelligent recommendation, risk pricing model based on consumers' personal qualification data, such as occupation, income, assets, etc. In this sense, big data is the foundation of this function. With consumer qualification data, it is possible to finish the credit rating of consumers, and rationally price consumer risks. With consumer demand data, it is possible to fulfill "search + price parity" functions, and combine quantity with term and risk pricing. In a manner of speaking, vertical financial data realizes online fund quantity match, term match and risk pricing functions by virtue of big data.

At the second layer, when vertical search platform accumulates considerable consumer data, including consumer shopping habits, risk preference and behavioral characteristics, it can take advantage of accumulated big data to perform data analysis and data excavation and therefore gain accurate portrait of consumers, and give feedback about consumer characteristics to financial institutions. This creates convenience for the design and reformation of financial products. In this process, consumer behavior and other related big data are key factors (Figs. 2 and 3).

In reality, finance itself is to solve fund circulation problem. It is faced with two obstacles in general, i.e. credit problem and information match problem. The former corresponds to credit investigation and the latter corresponds to search. In conclusion, the two problems come down to information asymmetry. Credit investigation is nearly the foundation of all economic activities including finance, while search is the flow entrance of Internet finance. Big data not only helps achieve credit investigation, but

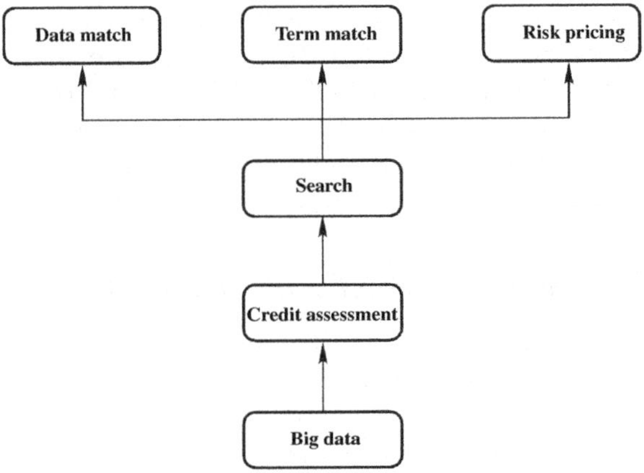

Fig. 2 Application of big data in search

Fig. 3 Application of big data in information feedback

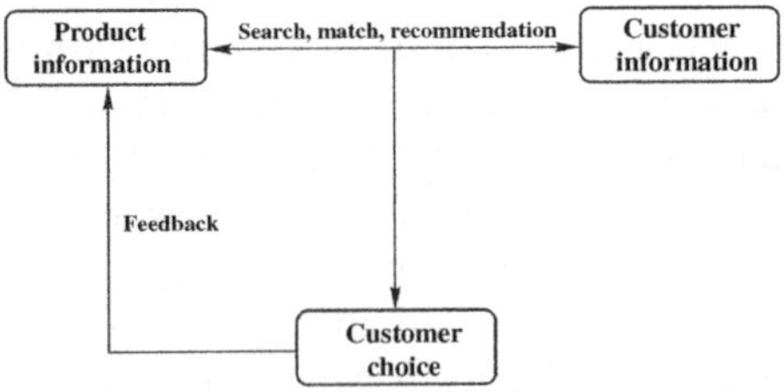

also paves way for information search and match. From this perspective, vertical financial search is the form of big data application.

Industry Chain of Vertical Financial Search

Vertical financial search industry chain is composed of three parts, namely upstream financial product provider, midstream information intermediary and downstream financial product demand side. Upstream financial product providers mainly include traditional financial institutions such as banks, fund, insurance and small loan companies. Product variety is also rather diversified, including trust finance, security trading, money fund, commercial insurance, P2P money management products. For upstream providers, vertical financial search platforms may provide technical service, flow entrance and marketing channel services. Above all, the foremost thing is that online marketing channel enables the demand side to more easily find products. Middle stream vertical financial search platform, as the platform connecting the supply and demand side, is connected to product supplier data upward and output data downward, and offers loan, money management counseling and financial services. Downstream financial product demand side gains related information about products and services via vertical financial search platform, and then buys products online or offline.

Income Source of Vertical Financial Search

In general, there are five income sources of vertical financial search platforms. The first one is consumer recommendation fee. Search platforms help financial institutions screen proper target consumers from massive candidates and recommend them to financial institutions to finish product trade. The fee charged by search platform from financial institutions ranges 50 ~ 100 yuan per capita. The second one is trade commission. Search platforms help users finish entire loan flow, and charge part of loan as the commission ranging between 0.5% and 3%. The third one is advertising income. Search platforms attract advertising release and charge advertising fee based on the huge flow. The fourth one is risk control service fee. Search platforms assess consumer credit with consumer data, help institutions make risk pricing and charge risk control service fee. The last one is information service fee. Search platforms may analyze consumer behavioral characteristics according to accumulated data, and send analysis results to financial institutions for product redesign and information service fee.

2 Source of Vertical Financial Search

With the fast development of Internet, the number of network information witnesses exponential growth. Faced with so much information, how to choose proper information becomes a tough problem. The building of a group of local search websites represented by Baidu (January 2000), Sougou (August 2004), Qihu360 (September 2005) indicates the birth of Chinese search industry. The rise of search engine has significant meaning for information demanders to gain information, lower information asymmetry cost and promote economic benefits in the first time. Since its inception, search engine industry gains prompt development. Till 2006, the scale of Chinese search engine industry totaled 13.9 billion yuan. Afterward, market scale had been continually expanded, and even reached over ten billion yuan in 2010. By late 2014, search engine market scale approximated 60 billion yuan, with a growth rate of 51.9%. In particular, Baidu took the lead with 81.8% market shares, Google ranked the second place with 10.4% market shares, and Sougou and Qihu, respectively, occupied 4% and 2.8% market shares.

But with the continuous growth of search engine, more problems come into being. For those information demand side who has specific demands, ordinary search engines can't find necessary information suitable for individual interests and hobbies. This means that universal search engine technologies do not adapt to specific information search demands. The market now still has huge demands for search engines enjoying great search advantages in a specific professional field (Fig. 4).

The earliest vertical search website in China should be Hexun website (1996) in finance and economics industry. Afterward, vertical search platforms successively rise in real estate industry, automobile industry and finance industry, like Soufang website (1999), Sina Home (2008). The rise of vertical search platform offers great help for specific information demand side to search related professional information. Comparing with ordinary research platforms, the foremost changes in vertical search platforms rest in the profession, accuracy and profundity of search results. Professional search engine platforms usually serve a specific group, and

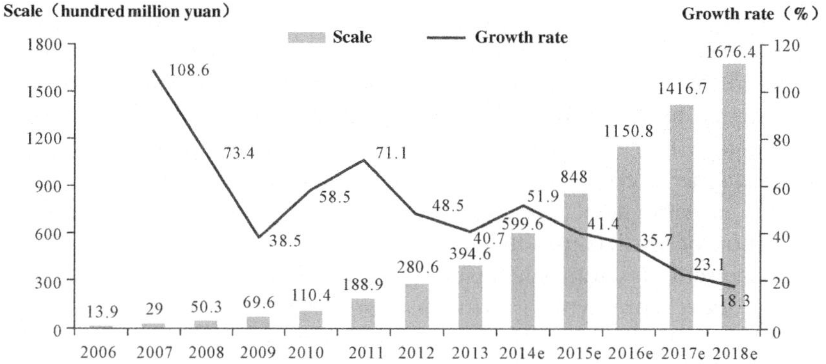

Fig. 4 Chinese search engine market scale and growth rate from 2006 to 2018 (*Data source* iResearch)

satisfy the specific search demands of a specific group. This can't be fulfilled by ordinary search platforms.

In 2005, the first tourism search platform Qunar was established in China which allowed consumers to compare domestic and overseas flight and hotel prices and services. Besides that, navigation websites like Hao 123, entrepreneurial news website Chuangyezone and Rong 360, photography art websites Fengniao appeared one after another.

Search engines in China experience a development history from ordinary search to vertical search. Vertical search has appeared and is gradually accepted by consumers. Accompanied by the advent of Internet finance in 2013, Internet finance products also quickly increase, which provides a fertile soil for vertical financial search. The rise of vertical financial search in China should be attributable to five reasons. First of all, Internet finance initiates the age of national fragmented wealth management, and consumers greatly increase demands for investment and financing products. Secondly, as the category of financial products and service types significantly increases, consumers can't search and compare products nor make decisions. This greatly aggravates information asymmetry. Thirdly, because of the lack of information disclosure in financial products, it is difficult to gain more details about product profile. Fourthly, consumers lack professional investment instruments. Fifthly, online marketing gradually becomes one of the marketing channels of financial institutions. Limited by high marketing cost, traditional marketing channels can't develop consumers in groups. By contrast, online marketing is able to realize scale economy, gain market shares and cut down marketing cost.

As of 2011, a group of Internet vertical financial search platforms represented by Rong 360, 91 Finance, Haodai, Jinfuzi have been successively established and expanded. The emergence of vertical financial search platforms helps consumers find financial products, helps financial institutions develop new consumers, and in the meantime, makes for the recreation of financial products.

At present, in domestic field of vertical financial search, there also appear more sub-division markets. For instance, in loan field, there are Rong 360, Haodai, 91 Finance, and Daixiaomi; in insurance field, there is Dajiabao; in fund field, there are Shumi Fund, and Tiantian Fund; in credit card field, there are Aicredit, and Rong 360; in bank money management field, there is Mr Qian. Additionally, there are also more comprehensive vertical financial search platforms including Cjdao, Bankrate.com, Yitou.com, Cunzhe.com, and Jiyuan Investment.[1]

Comparatively speaking, domestic vertical financial search is just in the start-up stage. As indicated by related reports, online search financial products remain the mainstream in foreign countries. Google's survey indicates that 88% netizens in European and American market would do online search and survey while choosing financial products. Among them, 66% users would directly submit online application after submitting the application, and remaining users usually submit application via phone or face-to-face interview.[2] In current stage, the proportion in China is just around 20%. The proportion of auto loan and housing loan is just 11%. It suggests that overwhelming financial products are still acquired via banks, intermediaries and offline institutions. It is predicted that the proportion will reach 50% in future years accompanied by a giant market scale totaling tens of trillion yuan.

3 The Business Mode of Vertical Financial Search

The vertical financial search mode in China is still in the budding stage featured by small industry scale and single business mode. In general, vertical financial search industry remains in the first layer of industry development, i.e. screening and recommending applicable financial

[1] Data source: http://it.sohu.com/20140620/n401102780.shtml.

[2] Data source: http://www.rong360.com/about/business_model.html.

products for consumers according to their qualification and demands based on search, match, recommendation and other alike data analysis and data excavation technologies. Due to the continuous progress of vertical financial search industry, the industry tùrns polarized crosswise and lengthwise, and forms respective business modes. Now, representative vertical search business modes include comprehensive financial product vertical search platforms, financial service intermediaries and vertical financial search platforms on behalf of three different development thoughts, respectively.

Integrated Financial Product Vertical Search Platform

Integrated financial product vertical search platform means that in financial product vertical search field, searched product category should not be confined to specific product category, but should cover more categories as much as possible. When financial search platforms come into being at the very beginning, many platforms including Rong 360, 91 Finance and Haodai develop business from loan search to vertical search, and gradually evolve polarization in subsequent stages of development. For instance, Rong 360 progressively enriches product category on the basis of loan search and successively releases products like credit card and money management products. In the future, it plans to march into the market of integrated financial product vertical search, and further develop more financial products such as insurance and fund.

Case 1: Rong 360

Company Profile

Rong 360, founded in Beijing in October 2011, was released online in January 2012. It is a platform which provides domestic consumers, micro companies and individual business entities with Internet finance search, recommendation and application services. Combined with data offered by consumers, it is devoted to providing accurate and personalized recommendation service for consumers.

By far, Rong 360 has established cooperative relations with more than 10,000 financial institutions, and provided nearly 50,000 loan, credit card and money management products. It develops business in more than 100 cities across the country, and conducts credit card and money management business in more than 200 countries covering 80% users. Until December 2014, it helps consumers submit 1.2 trillion yuan loan applications. Generally, loan approval proportion recommended by Rong 360 amounts to 10%–20%, including 15%–16% operational loans.[3] The success rate of micro company loan is just 3%.

The fast growth of Rong 360 also gains preference of capital. By now, it has gained three rounds of financing. In March 2012, Rong 360 completed A-round financing totaling 7 million USD sponsored by Light Speed Venture, Kleiner Perkins, Zero 2IPO. In July 2013, it finished B-round financing totaling 30 million USD led by Sequoia Capital and Light Speed Venture, Kleiner Perkins, Zero 2IPO followed the investment. In July 2014, it finished C-round financing led by Lanting Investment totaling 70 million, and Light Speed Venture, Kleiner Perkins, Zero 2IPO followed the investment.

Business Mode

On the one hand, it faces 43 million small- and medium-sized companies, over 30 million self-employed entities and over 100 million individual users. On the other hand, it is oriented toward more than 10,000 financial institutions. The former is faced with sophisticated financial products short of effective means of comparison, and intermediaries have too high cost and low efficiency. The latter develops consumers in batch. Traditional marketing mode is too costly, but intermediaries have rather low credit. As a result, Rong 360 serves as the information intermediary between the two, offers search, match and recommendation service for consumers, helps consumers effectively and conveniently find financial services, and helps financial institutions develop consumers in batch in a high-efficient and low-cost manner. Rong 360 earns information service fee from it.

Nowadays, the income source of Rong 360 comes from five aspects. The first one is recommendation fee charged from customer recommendation service against financial institutions, with each user being charged for 50 ~ 100 yuan. Secondly, when users apply for loan, Rong 360 helps users finish entire loan application flow, and then charges proportional sum of loan as commission at the rate of 0.5%–3%. The third source is

[3] Data source: http://www.financialnews.com.cn/jj/hg/201402/t20140222_50072.html.

advertising income. The fourth source is risk control service fee. Rong 360 helps institutions make risk pricing according to consumer credit investigation and charges fees for the service. The last source is information service fee. In the future, Rong 360 will excavate and analyze user behavior data, and send analysis results to financial institutions in exchange for information service fee. Currently, recommendation fee and commission make up around 95% of entire income.[4]

Business Flow

Rong 360 takes advantage of data collection technology and information provided by cooperation channels to build the database, and gather all available product information. Consumers can gain qualified product list once inputting loan sum, payment term, purpose of loan, occupation, mortgage, income and other necessary information. Through comparing the limit, interest rate, monthly installment payment, time of loan, successful application rate and other indicators of overall products, consumers can choose the optimal plan and submit the application. It is no need for them to go to offline sites for transaction. Such seemingly simple flow at least includes search engine technology, data analysis ability, risk control system, intelligent recommendation technology, financial modeling ability, bank product development and innovation ability, and bank product dynamic operation ability.[5]

At the first level, Rong 360 screens products by reference to loan purpose, loan sum and term. At the second level, it makes credit appraisal on user occupation, mortgage and income for risk pricing. Intelligent personalized recommendation technologies on this basis match products and gain available product list. Therefore, such seemingly simple flow is still decided by big data application. The key to is risk control ability.

Development Thought

The development orientation of Rong 360 is to build an integrated financial product vertical search platform, gradually add credit card and money management service on the basis of loan, and launch insurance and fund service in the future.

[4] Data source: http://kuaixun.stcn.com/2013/1108/10894604.shtml.

[5] Data source: http://www.niwodai.com/view-rong360/article-74433.html.

Rong 360 launched loan business in January 2012, including personal consumption loan, operation loan, housing loan and auto loan. Users are able to compare ten thousand loan products via the unique intelligent match system of Rong 360, screen these products and directly submit application. In July 2013, it later released credit card business. Users can browse the credit card information of all banks on its official website, and directly apply for credit card and credit card loan. Following "recommendation and screening match" mode, users would finally choose the most proper cards. In April 2014, Rong 360 money management service came into existence, including online loan money management, Internet money management and bank money management. On the way to become certain one-stop comparison platform and community which gathers money management products and money management information as a whole, its money management service mainly offers news, assessment and product search services, and helps users make sensible and secure money management decisions.

Except such an integrated financial product vertical search platform, Rong 360 began to open offline loan counseling service ever since November 2014, and tried to organically combine online financial search recommendation service with offline loan counseling service, and build O2O mode. As Rong 360 transits from online "search + recommendation" mode to more professional "decision + service" risk management mode, it more deeply intervenes the loan flow to facilitate loan product innovation and risk management innovation. This is supported by Rong 360's consumer base, big data, risk modeling and professional approval ability.

Under "search + recommendation" mode, Rong 360 does not intervene trade. When users input product demands, the backstage system intelligently recommends proper products. Such practice has proven its effects in alleviating information asymmetry and raising loan success rate. However, 85% consumer demands are still not satisfied yet. Under "decision + service" mode, Rong 360 has to undertake responsibilities for loan due diligence, data collection, pre-approval interview, preliminary loan approval and even post-loan consumer management and collection.[6] This means that Financing 360 collects consumer data offline and more accurately realizes consumer credit assessment and risk pricing online for more

[6] Data source: http://www.bj.xinhuanet.comhbpdjrpdjrpd2014-11/14/c_1113248677.htm.

accurate search match and higher success rate. Offline business matched with risk pricing and product design can more raise the successful match between users and financial products. It is predicted that loan success rate will raise from 15 to 30%–40% on average.

Throughout the development history of Rong 360, it can be fitly judged that integrated financial product vertical search platform has two development orientations. The first one is product line. It is essential to enrich search platform product variety, including loan, money management, insurance, fund and other products, and build the search platform into another "Baidu" in the field of financial product. The second task is to raise match rate and enhance consumers' risk pricing ability. This is up to risk pricing mode and data, especially data access. The original intention for Rong 360 to develop offline counseling service is to gain more reliable consumer data, so as to reinforce consumer credit assessment and risk pricing ability. Only in this way can it increase product match accuracy and success rate.

Financial Service Intermediary

Likewise, though it also begins with financial product search, it gradually transits from investment and financing business with accumulated data, and transits from pure information intermediary to financial service intermediary. The development mode of "product sales + investment and financing + asset management service" initiates another path of vertical financial search in China. A typical representative in this regard is 91 Finance.

Case 2: 91 Finance

Company Profile

Founded in September 1, 2011, 91 Finance belongs to an online financial shopping guide and sales platform. It has established operation center in Beijing, Shanghai and Shenzhen, and conducts business across 87 key cities across country. By June 2014, the number of consumers who applied to buy various financial products per day was over 10,000, daily trading volume was over 2,000 and involved sum of trading exceeded 300 million yuan. It is predicted that in future few years, 91 Finance's annual financial service consumers will exceed 2 million, and involved sum of trading will exceed 300 billion yuan.

By October 2011, it gained 5 million A-round investment sponsored by Matrix Partners. In September 2013, it gained 60 million B-round investment led by Broadband Capital under Tian Suning, and Matrix Partners followed the investment. In July 2014, it gained C-round investment led by Haitong Securities subsidiary Haitong Kaiyuan, and Broadband Capital and Matrix Partners followed the investment totaling 200 million yuan in early stage.

Ecosystem

On the basis of 91 Finance Cloud and 91 Finance Open Platform, 91 Finance releases 91 Finance Supermarket, an online financial product and service-oriented platform, 91 Money King oriented toward small- and medium-sized company money management service, 91 Wealth, Internet direct money management platform devoted to asset security market, 91 Financial Circle, an exclusive information platform for financial practitioners, and establishes a financial ecosystem for thousands of financial institutions, small- and medium-sized companies and hundred million consumers backed by the four basic businesses.

Business Module

The business module of 91 Finance is mainly composed of 91 Finance Supermarket, 91 Money King, 91 Wealth and 91 Financial Circle. To be specific, 91 Finance Supermarket mainly sells financial products, 91 Money King and 91 Wealth provides investment and financing service and 91 Financial Circle targets at asset management services.

91 Finance Supermarket released by 91 Finance in November 2011 pertains to an online guide and sales platform for financial products. At present, 91 Finance Supermarket has grown to be the largest financial product sales platform in China. Designed with a floor classification structure, the platform guides different consumers to pertinent special zone of financial products. Till now, 91 Finance Supermarket offers product categories including loan, credit card, money management, insurance as well as bank service. Different zones fulfill different functions. 91 Financial Supermarket possesses four leading core advantages, including the registration of more than 300 financial institutions, one-stop shopping experience, accurate floor classification product guide and professional and free high-end financial service.

91 Value-added Bao is a financial platform jointly launched by multiple institutions such as Minsheng Royal Fund, Taikang Asset Management, Rongtong Capital and Haitong Securities. Called Yu'E Bao for companies, 91 Money King is mainly oriented toward small- and medium-sized companies. It marks the transitions of 91 Finance from information intermediary to trading intermediary. 91 Value-added Bao enjoys 6 superior advantages, including low threshold—1 million yuan, easy operation—online one-click operation, high earnings—6% expected annual earnings, flexible allocation—monthly subscription and redemption, security and stability—bank money management and bulk inventory, free donation—private banking service by senior managers. Up to now, 91 Value-added Bao has altogether released three products (Table 1).

91 Wangcai, released on March 19, 2014, was designed to provide direct Internet money management service for financing and investment providers. By offering low-cost financing mode for small- and medium-sized companies via house property mortgage, 91 Wangcai offers secure and quality investment assets to consumers. The threshold is 100 yuan, annual interest rate is 8%–12%, and pertinent term is 1–6 month(s). House property should satisfy sufficient value mortgage conditions. Till late 2014, there were more than 200,000 91 Wangcai investors and related online trading volume amounted to 1 billion yuan.

On August 31, 2014, 91 Finance officially launched 91 Financial Circle. Rooted in the trading circle, social contact circle, news circle in the financial market, 91 Financial Circle covers all sorts of financial institutions including banks, trust, insurance, brokers, funds and fund subsidiaries. In the future, it will gather companies and personal investors. At the level of institution, 91 Financial Circle transacts inter-financial institution business via online services. At the level of company, it chooses most suitable institutions and products for companies in accordance with company characteristics, financing and investment demands. At the level

Table 1 91 Value-added products

Product features	Product 1	Product 2	Product 3
Annual yield rate	6%	6%	7%
Subscription amount	1 million yuan	500,000~1 million yuan	50,000 ~100,000 yuan
Yield type	Fixed income	Fixed income	Fixed income
Subscription and redemption	Tuesday or Wednesday	2 months, 1 year	32 days

Data source 91 Finance official website

of individual, 91 Financial Circle combines with platform project data analysis to do professional asset management product rating and select most suitable investment products for individuals. In the future, 91 Financial Circle will be devoted to online professional asset management counseling service for sake of institutions, companies and individuals.

Risk Control System

Adhering to a risk management system which combines online mode with offline mode, 91 Finance includes online big data credit investigation and risk control mode, traditional offline due diligence and post-loan management.

Backed by 91 Finance Cloud and 91 Finance open platforms, 91 Finance now has accumulated massive user data, including basic user information, Internet information, historical loan records, and consulted traditional commercial banks' credit rating system and internationally universal FICO credit rating model to do credit assessment on users and companies, and establish exclusive data credit investigation system.

By virtue of linear and non-linear regression, decision-making tree analysis, neural network modeling methods, 91 Finance performs quantitative and qualitative analysis on users. At the same time, through independently developing the search engine, 91 Finance tracks users' online behaviors, encourages users to associate the account with MicroBlog and other social contact accounts, monitors users' log-in habits, continually accumulates and supplements user behavioral factors, expand and improve big data risk control models.

Given this, 91 Finance comprehensively controls users' individual characteristics and credit investigation conditions, and introduces it to the decision-making engine and business flow of risk approval to better conduct business.

Thus it can be seen that 91 Finance also begins with finance search, but it now gradually deviates from the track of finance search. Through 91 Money King and 91 Wealth, the platform now starts to transit from a financial product search and sales platform to a trading intermediary, but abandons the label of pure information intermediary and matchmaking trading, and begin to engage in product design, product trading and product investment and financing services. While the launch of 91 Financial Circle indicates the starting point of 91 Finance in asset management service. 91 Finance's development path of "product sales + investment and financing + asset management service" suggests its transition from a search information intermediary to a financial service intermediary.

Vertical Financial Search Platform

Vertical Financial Search Platform means that the platform does not make crosswise expansion, but just focuses on a specific field for deep exploitation and manages to take a place in this field. Such development thought forms a sharp contrast with the formation of integrated vertical financial search platform. The latter endeavors to enrich platform product line, and comprehensively satisfy consumers' financial demands, while the former primarily provides profound services for a given subdivision field. A typical representative in this aspect is Haodai.

Case 3: Haodai

Company Profile

Haodai was officially launched online as of March 2013. In July 2013, Haidai gained the risk venture totaling ten million yuan from Cowin Capital. By March 23, 2014, Haodai had opened local online free loan search and consulting services across 108 cities in China, established cooperation relations with more than 5800 banks, 4000 small-sized credit companies, pawnshops and various formal financial institutions, and offered more than 20,000 credit products. The number of credit managers in cooperation with Haodai increased from 500 to 28,000.

Product Category

Haodai has been engaged in loan product search business as of its inception. In terms of product category, Haodai has released consumption loan, company loan, auto loan, housing loan, mortgage loan and other loan products.

Consumption loan primarily includes personal loan for the purpose of overseas study, house decoration, purchase of durable goods and purchase of car. In terms of category, consumption loan includes housing mortgage loan, non-housing loan and credit card loan, and it is characterized by wide consumption purposes, high loan limit and long loan term.

Company loan is mainly used for bulk and long-term investment such as procurement of fixed assets, and technical reform. Company loan falls into working capital loan, fixed asset loan, credit loan, guarantee loan, stock pledge loan, foreign exchange pledge loan, unit fixed deposit receipt pledge loan, gold pledge loan, consortium loan, bank acceptance bill, bill acceptance bill discount, trade acceptance discount, buyer or protocol payment bill discount, with right of recourse for domestic factoring and export rebates and account trusteeship loan.

Auto loan is the credit auto loan approved by banks for car buyers in need of capital. Those who apply for the loan should satisfy the application conditions, such as holding signed car purchasing contract or agreement, having stable occupation and income.

Loan for purchasing house is the credit auto loan approved by banks for homebuyers in need of capital. Those who apply for the loan should satisfy the application conditions, such as holding signed housing contract or agreement, having stable occupation and income, or otherwise proof of income.[7]

Development Thought

Haodai possesses massive user data processing, information matching ability and related technologies and experiences. Therefore, it can bridge borrowers and credit loan officers. This is the advantage and mission of Haodai as a vertical financial search platform. Concerning the development thought, Haodai does not engage in crosswise expansion, but just concentrates on lengthwise expansion of loan business by continually enriching loan product category, tries to be the largest loan search and service platform in China and strives to be the first leading brand in Chinese credit loan search. Such development thought bears similarity with that of Rong 360, but there exists drastic difference between the two. Both of them probe into the field of vertical search, and manage to increase vertical search efficiency and enrich product category. Rong 360 meets consumers' various demands for financial products by enriching search product categories. In this way, it can attract more consumers. By contrast, with focus on loan product search, Haodai is trying to increase loan product category and meet consumers' loan demands. According to Li Mingshun, founder of Haodai, the company can only expand business after taking a place in a subdivision market and growing strong enough

[7] Data source: http://baike.baidu.com/link?url=sHfZngYDTxvTjBbwI4m131WFTqFh6 QGuamUkY0ciwgGgvQgRNxIoQz11z93ompSJJV46UrSlpNUT6eWWqgNzVq.

Table 2 Comparison of three vertical search modes

Characteristics	Comprehensive vertical financial search platform	Financial service intermediary	Vertical financial search platform
Business mode	Comprehensive search	Sales + investment and financing + asset management	Vertical search
Product type	Gradual increase	Multiple types	Single type
Intervention in transaction	Non-intervention	Weakening of intermediary functions in transaction	Non-intervention
Development priority	Risk control, match success rate	Credit assessment	Product matching

with irreplaceability.[8] In the future, the main challenge confronted by Haodai is whether it can accurately match loan demands with all financial institutions. This tests Haodai data analysis ability and data excavation ability. It also decides the success and failure of Haodai.

Moreover, Haodai now is busy in C2B loan product reverse customization exploration with big data application, with the aim of creating greater values to financial institutions and finding more suitable loan products for loaners.

Throughout the comparison of three vertical search modes, the distinct difference between the two may be found out. It can be obviously seen that financial service intermediary mode has gradually weakened the function as an information intermediary. Besides, in the trading process, information intermediaries are trying to enrich product category. The prime difference between integrated vertical search and vertical financial search rests in the number of product category, in which the former gradually increases its product category and the latter just has single product category. Both of the two do not intervene trading process. The three modes share common points in big data rick control. Whether it can favorably assess user credit and make risk pricing determine the final match success rate. The three modes point out the emphasis of future prospects (Table 2).

[8] Data source: http://it.sohu.com/20140620/n401102780.shtml.

4 The Development Trend of Vertical Financial Search

The future of vertical financial search is decided by data. Those who have data can better analyze and excavate data and those who better use data can gain success first. In consequence, data use systematization, customization of financial products and vertical search platform e-commerce will be the three leading trends of vertical financial search.

Data Collection, Analysis and Excavation Systematization

Though search platform is search service, it is still based on big data application. Big data application is employed in consumer credit assessment and risk pricing. The two aspects determine the product match success rate of search platforms. Then why does Rong 360 deploy offline business? It is because that search platforms should more accurately collect consumer data offline for credit assessment and risk pricing. The bottleneck of the three modes rests in data collection and excavation. So whether the platform engages in search or investment and financing and asset management, it should face match rate problem and consumer credit assessment problem. This depends on data. Therefore, data collection, analysis and excavation systematization will be a trend in future search industry.

Financial Product Customization

Now the search industry remains at the first stage, i.e. B2C stage. But as more industry data has been accumulated, it will enter C2B stage sooner or later. The search platform may use its accumulated consumer data to analyze consumer behaviors. This is of vital importance to financial institutions' product design.

Search Platform E-commerce

The cooperation between search platforms and financial institutions will be deepened in the future, especially in initial product design. At that time, search platform is probably not just a data provider, but intervenes product design. Maybe search platforms will grow to be a financial shopping mall, and develop both self-support and external products. In particular, self-support product refers to the product exclusively customized for consumers with platform data.

CHAPTER 9

The Forefront End that is Ignored: Network Credit Investigation

Finance is the operation and management of risks, while credit is the measurement of risks. Innovation of credit assessment is the most important achievement of Internet finance. Internet finance can gather information scattered in every corner and obtain individual credit beyond reach through analysis and arrangement to effectively make up for individual credit. From this angle, credit investigation should be the forefront end of Internet finance. However, this book places it before the conclusion, so it is ignored. The basis of credit investigation is big data. As multi-type mass data help to realize individual credit assessment, this book constantly highlights the importance of big data for Internet finance, which is also the basis of credit investigation, risk management and information matching. Without big data, Internet finance is like water without a source, where no matter how good a model is, it cannot achieve the accommodation of funds due to the failure of credit assessment and risk control.

Though various models of Internet finance look nice, all of them will be out of practical significance if one necessary and sufficient condition, namely the forefront network credit investigation, is not met. Credit is the necessary and sufficient condition of mispairing of capital, time and space, namely the precondition of current financial operation. If network credit investigation is poor, all of these financial models realizing fund transfer, such as big data finance, P2P lending and crowdfunding, cannot work,

Q. Guan and W. Gao, *Internet Finance*,
The Great Transformation of China,
https://doi.org/10.1007/978-981-16-4740-6_9

indicating the action of credit investigation. However, unfortunately, we have never attached importance to the action of credit investigation and ignored the existence of credit investigation. As a result, when we enter in Internet finance, we suddenly realize that the premise of success, namely network credit investigation, is missing. Consequently, various local variants of Internet finance, such as assignment of debt, guarantee and loan loss provision, have no choice but emerge as the times require. We are forced to remedy these inborn defects in a dilemma. We carry out offline credit checking, while accumulating data online. As the saying goes, more preparation may quicken the speed in doing work. Only when the credit investigation becomes perfect, will Internet finance will be successful.

1 Network Credit Investigation and Big Data

The Meaning of Credit Investigation

Credit investigation refers to activity to collect, organize, store and process credit information of natural person, legal person and other organizations, provide credit reports, credit evaluation and services, such as credit information consultation, and help clients judge and control credit risks and conduct credit management.[1]

Credit investigation mainly have four effects. The first effect is to reduce information asymmetry. Information asymmetry is the primary obstacle to restrict financial transactions. If people demanding capital and people supplying capital cannot know each other's conditions, including personal credit status and state of enterprise operation, etc., they cannot come to an agreement. Therefore, the appearance of credit investigation allows both sides to know each other by credit assessment, reducing information asymmetry. The second one is to reduce transaction cost. Both sides of a transaction can easily seek out each other without excessive cost. The third one is to expand the transaction boundary. Credit investigation allows strangers to know each other and breaks fixed circles among relatives and friends, expanding both the transaction range outside the circle of friends and the transaction boundary effectively. The fourth one is to increase the transaction possibility. Reduction of both information asymmetry and transaction cost and expansion of the transaction boundary

[1] Data source: Development Report of China's Credit Investigation Industry (2003—2013).

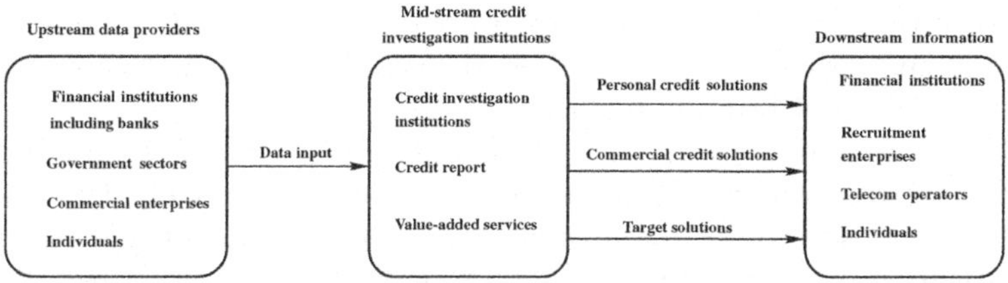

Fig. 1 Credit investigation industry chain (*Data source* Internet Finance Basis: Research Report for the In-depth Development of Individual Credit Investigation Industry, modified)

finally leads to increase of transaction possibility, promotion of transaction and accommodation of funds.

The industry chain of credit investigation consists of three parts, namely upstream data providers, midstream credit agencies and downstream information users. Upstream data providers are in charge of providing enterprises and individuals, including banks, government sectors, business enterprises and individuals, etc., with various data relating to identity, occupation, income, loans, assets, taxes and crimes, etc. According to data provided upstream, midstream credit agencies develop credit reports and value-added services, including personal credit solutions, business credit solutions and target solutions. Personal solutions include credit reports, credit rating, dispute credit reports, victim information of fraud, etc.; business solutions include credit reports, solutions in accordance with industry division (credit, credit cooperation, commercial fraud, finance, insurance and investment etc.); and target solutions include data acquisition, data management, talent identification, ID card verification and fraud detection, risk management, check authentication service, etc. Credit reports developed by credit agencies are applied to financial institutions, recruiters, telecom operators and individuals, etc. (Fig. 1).

New-Type Big Data

Credit investigation has the closest relationship with big data. All financial activity must depend on credit investigation based on big data. Big data is the essential condition of credit investigation. Through analysis of big data, we can evaluate loan repayment ability and repayment willingness of borrowers, understand their credit condition and decide interest rate, amount and term of loan. Hence, big data credit investigation constitutes the foundation of Internet finance.

The connotation of big data also undergoes changes. In traditional credit investigation, credit data of banks is the most valuable data source that is the closest to the credit of borrowers. However, this type of credit investigation has many limitations: 1. as credit data of banks is not shared with the outside world, it cannot realize whole-society credit investigation; 2. due to the high threshold of risk control set by banks, most individuals, small and micro businesses fail to obtain loan because of lack of credit data; and 3. due to the single dimension of this type of credit investigation, it cannot fully reveal the credit condition of borrowers. In this condition, the circumscribed credit investigation cannot meet needs of the whole society, especially needs of the lower classes. Consequently, Internet finance was born to deal with the fragmented large-scale financing constraints, accompanied by network credit investigation based on new-type big data.

In the times of the Internet, there's data outburst and various types of data are full of our interface. New-type big data has characteristics in respect of volume, value, variety and velocity. First, the order of magnitude of big data is much higher than that in the past. Its daily data size is of exponential growth. Second, its data is of multiple dimensions, extensive sources and numerous types. As social contact, communication, e-commerce, search and payment, etc. accumulate massive data, they become new data providers. In addition, data types also change and unstructured data existing in forms of picture, text, sound and symbol, etc. appear, which greatly enriches types of data.

Given the current situation, types of big data include payment data, transaction data, behavior data, social data, search data and communication data besides credit data. These seven types of data almost cover all data characteristics of current individuals and enterprises. That is to say, through analysis of seven types of data, we can obtain the credit condition of borrowers. At present, these seven types of data are held by different enterprises. With a wave of Internet finance, various industries and enterprises want to get involved this emerging industry and develop a credit system belonging to enterprises. For example, Alibaba created Zhima Credit with its payment and transaction data, while Tencent attempted to develop Tencent Credit through social data. Therefore, now it's not easy to exchange and share data among various industries and enterprises and most of them carry out independent development (Fig. 2).

Big data is also characterized by massive redundant information. As a result, big data not only brings about massive data, but also results in reduction of data value density. Therefore, how to conduct data storage, screening and analysis becomes a new problem in the times of big data. Thanks to great development of information technology, such as search engines and cloud computing, processing problems of big data have been solved. The search engine can help us find out valuable data from multi-dimension massive data and conduct data screening. Through cloud

Fig. 2 Composition of big data

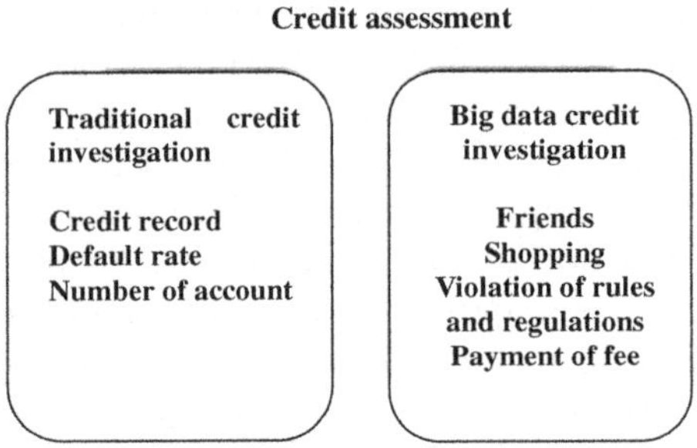

Fig. 3 Comparison of traditional credit investigation and big data credit investigation

computing, various data can be analyzed and combined. According to overall consideration of personal credit conditions, data analysis can be completed. Big data-based network credit investigation is a process to reintegrate fragmented massive information with IT technology. Big data is the basis, IT is a tool and credit investigation is the purpose.

In traditional credit investigation, loan repayment ability and repayment willingness of borrowers are evaluated in accordance with information that is strongly related to them, such as credit records, default rates and numbers of accounts. However, in addition to credit data, big data credit investigation also involves multi-dimension data weakly related to credit, such as social contact, shopping, violation, fine and fee payment. Though these data are less related to credit investigation than credit data, description capacity of data can be strengthened by increasing data dimensions. Hence, big data credit investigation as such cannot only enhance effectiveness of credit investigation, but also reduce dependence on credit data, realizing credit evaluation of people who are not covered by credit data (Fig. 3).

2 The Rise of Western Credit Investigation

The development of the Western credit investigation industry centers on individual credit investigation. Thanks to driving of individual consumption economy, Western credit investigation has made efforts in personal credit evaluation. After development for more than 60 years, Western credit investigation has undergone a process from unscientific to scientific; subjective to objective; and qualitative to quantitative.

Development History of Western Individual Credit Investigation

The Stage of Qualitative Credit Analysis before 1950

Before 1950, Western credit was neither electronized nor modeled and bank lenders usually decided to lend or not according to their experience and understanding on borrowers. This purely artificial lending process included no credit investigation or highly weakened the effect of borrowers' credit, but relied on lenders' experience. Therefore, it was of low efficiency and had no unified and objective standard, and its lending process varied from person to person, which was not scientific.

The Stage of Locally Quantitative Analysis from 1950 to 1979

In 1956, Fair Issac, an individual credit investigation company in the USA, was founded and developed FICO score, a credit score mode. With FICO scores, banks could carry out automated mass credit checking. As it expanded credit and reduced the default rate, it became a revolution in the field of credit assessment. However, as this mode was only adopted in banks with their internal data, its effect remained to be limited.

The Stage of Fully Quantitative Analysis after 1980

After 1980, credit institutions started to share data, which allowed them to fully understand the credit condition of borrowers and reduce information asymmetry. Experian of the USA gathered personal credit information of consumers from different credit institutions and carried out comprehensive quantitative analysis on credit conditions of individual consumers, which was more effective than application of pure credit information of banks.

The Stage of Big data Credit Investigation

As the times of big data comes, we can conduct in-depth mining of multi-dimension and multi-level consumer data through advanced IT technology. Therefore, we can carry out more effective, clear and precise analysis on credit conditions of borrowers than comprehensive analysis and also analyze people who have few credit records, which fully reflects the supplementary role of Internet finance.

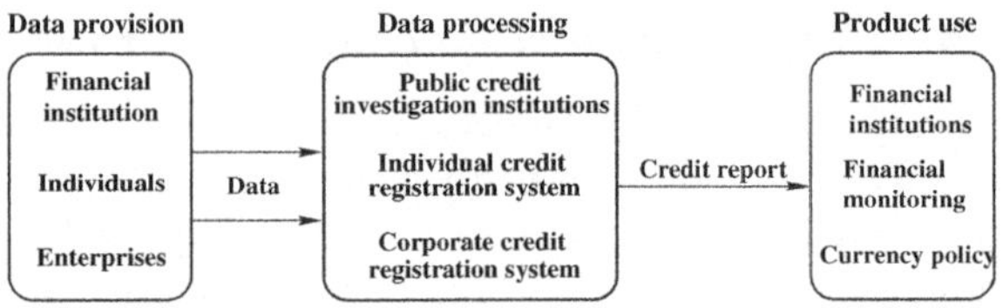

Fig. 4 Public credit investigation mode (*Data source* Cinda Securities)

Western Credit Investigation Models

After development and accumulation for years, the current Western individual credit investigation mainly includes models of public credit investigation, market-oriented credit investigation and industry association credit investigation. Each model has different operation mechanisms and characteristics and applies to different economic environments.

The Public Credit Investigation Model

In the public credit investigation model, the government directly sets up credit institutions and forces financial institutions to submit credit information of enterprises and individuals to the credit department by administrative means. Then the credit department sets up an authoritative database of credit information and sells credit information to financial institutions. This model is mainly adopted by European countries, such as France, Italy and Germany (Fig. 4).

The public credit investigation model has four characteristics: 1. The data authenticity is high. By forcing financial institutions to submit credit information, the credit department can ensure authenticity and reliability of submitted data. 2. Credit institutions are monopolistic. These credit institutions set up by the government are monopolistic in the market and master all credit resources. 3. It lacks competition with low data coverage. Due to lack of competition, the impetus to enrich credit data is insufficient, so it cannot cover multiple types of data. 4. It is non-profit. Credit institutions pay to financial institutions to maintain its normal operation.

The Market-Oriented Credit Investigation Model

In the market-oriented credit investigation model, through legislation, the government permits credit companies to gather, organize and analyze data and provide comprehensive, authentic and precise credit report to

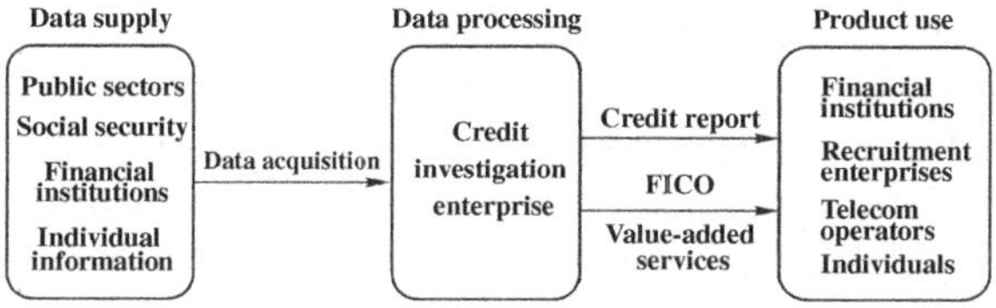

Fig. 5 Marketization credit investigation mode (*Data source* Cinda Securities)

the society. Through adequate market competition, it realizes profits of credit companies and healthy development of the credit investigation industry. This model is mainly employed by the USA and the UK.

Mainstream credit companies analyze users' credit by combining the FICO model with gathered data. In the FICO score model, there are five major factors to consider, namely payment history (35%), debt burden (30%), length of credit history (15%), types of credit used (10%) and recent searches for credit (10%), with different weights. So far, Trans Union, Experian and Equifax have dominated the individual credit investigation industry in the USA through free competition.

Main characteristics of the market-oriented credit investigation model: 1. All data of a company are collected from the market by no compulsory means. Though these data are of multiple types, their authenticity is lower than those in the public credit investigation model. 2. The credit investigation industry is of free competition, instead of monopoly, which is the main characteristic of marketization. 3. Due to competition, the credit investigation industry constantly perfects its mode, optimizes data and improves quality of credit investigation service. 4. Credit companies are profitable and they obtain profits by improving quality of credit investigation service (Fig. 5).

The Industry Association Credit Investigation Model

Japan adopts the industry association credit investigation model. In Japan, credit information institutions include the bank system, the consumption credit system and the selling credit system, corresponding to the banking industry association, the credit loan industry association and the credit industry association, respectively. Members join these associations voluntarily and mainly include banks, credit card companies, guarantee companies, other financial institutions, business companies and retail stores. Members are obliged to submit various types of credit data to associations, while associations are in charge of gathering and processing data and send credit reports to members. These associations are non-profit.

At present, the three major credit investigation institutions, namely KSC, JICC and CIC, start to share individual credit information and data with each other.

Characteristics of the industry association credit investigation model: 1. Data of credit investigation is of high authenticity. The data is gathered by neither compulsory means nor marketization, but voluntary submission of members. Therefore, it avoids both compulsory means and marketization and obtain data of high authenticity. 2. It is of anti-monopoly. As the original intention of these associations was for the common interests of the industry, they are voluntary non-monopoly associations. 3. The industry is non-profit. These industry associations aim at serving members, instead of obtaining profits (Table 1).

All of these three models have both advantages and disadvantages. In general, advantages of the public credit investigation model and the industry association credit investigation model are accurate and low-cost data gathering and good privacy protection, while advantages of

Table 1 Comparison of the advantages and disadvantages of three credit investigation modes

Mode	*Advantages*	*Disadvantages*
Public credit investigation	1. High entirety and accuracy of data information 2. Low charge and user cost	1. Incomplete credit investigation data, low applicability 2. Inadequate marketization of services 3. Service only available to financial institutions
Market credit investigation	1. Wide scope and type of data collection 2. Diverse product and service	1. Poor protection of credit investigation objects' privacy 2. Poor data accuracy
Industry association credit investigation	1. Accurate credit investigation data 2. Low cost	1. Access to members only 2. Professional report with limited applicability

Data source Cinda Securities, revised edition

the market-oriented credit investigation model include wide-channel and multiple-type data gathering and a large variety of products.

3 Samples of USA Credit Investigation

From another angle, we can find that the development of Western credit investigation chooses between marketization and non-marketization. Public credit investigation is typically non-marketization, while the USA model is typically market oriented. As for Japan's model, it is a mixed model of marketization and non-marketization. What model on earth can adapt to the development of China's credit investigation? In our opinion, we should be market-oriented and collect various types of data, instead of single-type data. Only in this way can we meet diversified, multi-layer and personalized demands of China's credit investigation. Through the power of the market, we can strengthen the development of the credit investigation industry, select the superior and eliminate the inferior in the industry, and realize transformation and innovation of the industry. Hence, the development of USA credit investigation is of high referential value for China.

The Development History of USA Credit Investigation

The greatest motivation of USA credit investigation is demands for consumption. With the increase of demands for consumption, the USA credit investigation has undergone steady development and growth.

The Rapid Development Period from 1920 to 1960

The great demand of individual consumption in the USA led to the great demand of credit loan, but the individual credit default rate increasingly increased because of the Great Depression. In order to reduce the default rate, the USA started to establish a credit investigation system. Meanwhile, the appearance of credit cards accelerated the establishment of the credit investigation system.

The Period of Legal Perfection from 1961 to 1980

In order to further perfect the credit investigation system, the USA issued 17 laws of credit investigation, which played a crucial role in ensuring the development of the credit investigation system. In addition, due to the appearance of card organizations, such as VISA and MasterCard, the application of credit cards entered a period of rapid development.

The M&A Integration Period from 1981 to 2000

The banking industry started to carry out trans-regional business and large-scale M&A integration, where the demand of national credit investigation started to appear. Meanwhile, the development of information technology made national operation of credit investigation institutions possible. Hence, credit investigation institutions entered the M&A integration period.

The Mature Period of Stability from 2001 to Now

The domestic market of American credit investigation became saturated. The industry started to expand overseas markets and develop more applications of credit investigation. Professionalization of credit investigation markets and the global trend started to speed up.[2]

Meaning and Boundary of the USA Credit

The USA credit system has been highly mature and formed unified understanding on the meaning of credit. Generally speaking, individual credit is constituted by 5C1S, including Character, Capability, Capital, Condition, Collateral and Stability. In the USA, the credit condition of an individual is investigated from these five aspects (Table 2).

The USA also has unified understanding on the credit boundary. In the United States, the credit boundary includes two major parts, namely information that can be gathered without authorization and cannot be gathered without authorization. The former includes insensitive individual information, such as length of service, credit cards, duty, housing, while the latter includes sensitive information that can indicate individual credit condition, such as check, driving records and crime records.

In general, the USA credit investigation mainly collects information from the following four aspects: 1. basic information, including occupation, income, work stability, block, house and living stability; 2. credit information, including car loan, house loan, credit cards and student loan, etc.; 3. consumption information, including frequency of mall and

[2] Data source: The General Trend of the Credit Investigation Market.

Table 2 The USA credit boundary

Credit boundary	Collection without authorization	Working age Credit card Debt revenue proportion Bank account Credit file age limit Denigration record	Post Housing Address Duration of residence Public undertaking record
	Collection with authorization	Check Driving record Medical record Income	Savings and security account information Criminal record Insurance policy Race, belief, political propensity

Data source The general trend of the credit investigation market

network consumption and limit, etc.; and 4. public information, including court judgement, tax default, ride stealing, traffic violation and debts of friends and relatives, etc.

The USA Credit System

According to objects of credit investigation, the USA credit system can be divided into two parts, namely credit investigation of institutions and credit investigation of individuals. Furthermore, the credit investigation of institutions can be divided into two parts, credit of capital markets and credit of ordinary enterprises. Credit investigation institutions for credit of capital markets include Standard & Poor's, Moody's Investors Service and Fitch Ratings, while that for credit of ordinary enterprises mainly refers to Dun & Bradstreet. In individual credit investigation, the USA has formed three major credit investigation institutions, namely Trans Union, Experian and Equifax. In addition, the United States has more than 400 regional or professional credit investigation institutions attached to those seven companies above or providing data for them. All of these constitute the USA credit system.

The USA credit system has formed a mature industry chain from data sources, data standardization, data processing and product formation to product usage, where various links are of interaction and effective cooperation. The three major credit investigation institutions are the core of the whole industry chain.

Data sources of American individual credit investigation are extensive. By marketization means, credit investigation companies obtain necessary data for credit investigation from financial institutions, credit extension institutions, third-party data processing companies, local credit investigation companies and public records, etc. Metro1 and Metro2 are the unified standard data report format and standard data gathering format, designated by ACR for individual credit investigation business, respectively. After standardization of source data, the data are analyzed and processed by Trans Union, Experian and Equifax to form credit rating products, credit investigation reports and original credit investigation data used by financial institutions, credit extension institutions, recruitment enterprises, data analysis companies, federal government, public service agencies and individuals. These products are applied to various scenes, such as job haunting, loan and renting.

Among the three major credit investigation institutions in the United States, Experian is the largest individual credit investigation institution in the world and offer credit investigation products and value-added services to various industries globally. Its businesses involve credit services (provides individual credit service for consumers in 19 countries and enterprise credit service in 13 countries), decision-making analysis (employs 400 data analysts and statisticians and provides enterprise solutions), marketing service (provides marketing service in more 30 countries, including the USA, the UK, Germany and China) and consumer protection service (including identity theft detection, identity protection and fraud identification).

Experian's credit service products include credit reports, credit rating, identity theft detection, credit checking and their combinations to meet needs of different clients.

Equifax's businesses include credit services (including online consumption information, house loan and consumer financial services), international business (consumers in Latin America, Europe and Canada), labor solution (including authentication and employment service), North American individual solution (avoid theft of personal identity) and North American business service (value-added service of commercial data). Its credit service products mainly include credit detection and ID protection products (Equifax's complete priority plan and complete family plan), credit reports and credit rating service (Complete report, Equifax credit reports and rating) and FICO score products.

The businesses of Trans Union include credit monitoring, credit management and protection, credit reports, credit rating and solution, etc. (Table 3).

4 Development of China's Credit Investigation

Development History of Domestic Credit Investigation

China's credit investigation can be traced back to the first credit investigation institution, Chinese Credit Investigation Institution born in 1932. However, the development and growth of the credit investigation industry occurred after the reform and openness. With the rise of domestic credit transactions, the progress of financial institutional reform and the increasing openness to the outside world, China's credit investigation industry has undergone rapid development. To sum up, the development of China's credit investigation industry can be divided into three stages.

The Exploration Stage from 1978 to 1995

Since the reform and openness, in order to adapt to issue and management of enterprise bonds, People's Bank of China (PBOC) set up the first credit rating company, Shanghai Yuandong Credit Rating Limited Company. Meanwhile, to meet needs of enterprise credit investigation in foreign trade, Foreign Economy and Trade Calculation Center and Dun & Bradstreet provided domestic and foreign credit reports for each other through cooperation.

In 1993, SINOTRUST, a company specializing in enterprise credit investigation, was founded to offer credit investigation services. Afterward a group of professional credit investigation companies were set up one by one. Those companies led to the early exploration of China's enterprise credit investigation, but there was no company specializing in individual credit investigation yet.

The Start-up Stage from 1996 to 2002

In 1996, PBOC started to carry out the enterprise loan system nationally. In 1997, enterprises in Shanghai received credit rating and, permitted by PBOC, Shanghai launched a pilot project of individual credit investigation. In 1999, Shanghai Credit Information Services Co., Ltd was

Table 3 Overview of three individual credit investigation companies in America

Comparison	Experian	Equix	Transunion
Overview	Founded in 1996, the company has 17,000 employees in 44 countries, covering 400 million consumers and 50 million companies across the globe. Business revenues in 2014 totaled $4.772 billion.	Founded in 1899, the company has 7,000 employees in 19 countries, covering 600 million consumers and 80 million companies across the globe. Business revenues in first half year of 2014 totaled $1.198 billion.	Founded in 1968, the company has branches in 35 countries, covering 500 million consumers across the globe. Business revenues in 2013 totaled $1,180 billion.
Business content	Credit service, decision-making analysis, marketing service, consumer protection service	Credit service, international business, labor solution, North American personal solution, North American business service	Credit monitoring, credit management and protection, credit report, credit rating, solution
Operation characteristics	Good at credit investigation, the company analyzes potential customers by data analysis, and runs business in China by subsidiary Xinhuaxin	Rich variety of products, including over 40 individual credit investigation products Make credit risk assessment for consumers without credit records, such as immigrants and college students	Good at estimating potential risks of different industries Run business in Shanghai
Industry distribution	30% finance, 21% consumers, 10% retailers, 6% telecommunication/ electricity, 5% automobile, 4% insurance, 3% media and technology, 21% other	26% finance, 16% mortgage loan, 10% consumers, 10% employees, 6% telecommunication institutions, 6% companies, 6% resale companies, 5% business, 4% retailers, 11% other	
Regional distribution	48% North America, 21% Latin America, 19% Britain and 12% Asia-Pacific Region	77% America, 7% Canada, 6% Britain and 10% other	74.7% North America, 25.3% other

Data source The General Trend of the Credit Investigation Market, revised edition

founded and started to conduct enterprise and individual credit investigation. At the end of 1999, the bank credit registration consultation system was formally launched. In 2002, the system set up a local-provincial-general-level database and realized national-network query.

It can be seen that, in this stage, construction of the credit investigation system accelerated, and companies, pilot projects, systems and database of credit investigation developed continuously. On the whole, in this stage, the credit investigation industry kept trying.

The Development Stage from 2003 to 2014

In 2003, the State Council endowed PBOC with responsibilities of credit investigation management and establishment of a social credit system and approved the establishment of the Credit Information System Bureau. Meanwhile, Shanghai, Beijing and Guangdong, etc. launched pilot projects of development of regional social credit investigation industries and set up a few regional credit investigation institutions. In 2004, PBOC established a nationally unified database of individual credit information. In 2005, the bank credit registration consultation system was upgraded into a nationally unified database of enterprise credit information. In 2008, the State Council adjusted PBOC's responsibility of credit investigation management of as "management of the credit investigation industry" and took the lead in the inter-ministerial joint meeting on the social credit system construction. In March 2013, Control Regulations on the Credit Investigation Industry was formally launched to clearly point out that PBOC was the supervision and regulation department of the credit investigation industry, making the industry have laws to abide by.[3] In September 2013, Regulations for Credit Investigation Institutions was launched, in favor of standardized management of credit investigation institutions. In June 2014, the Social Credit System Construction Program Outline (2014–2020) was published to plan the construction of China's credit system in detail. Since June 18, 2014, PBOC had issued 30 enterprise credit investigation licenses in four batches.

With the continuous development of the credit investigation industry, the supervision of credit investigation was also strengthened. By establishment of supervision institutions and management regulations for the industry and enterprises, the plan for industry development became clear.

[3] Data source: The Development Report of China's Credit Investigation Industry (2003—2013).

By formulation of the industry planning outline, the development path of the industry also became clear. It was greatly beneficial to the long-term development of the industry. Issuing of enterprise credit investigation licenses indicated a new development stage of the industry.

The Polishing Stage from 2015 to Now

On January 5, 2015, PBOC published the Notification on the Preparation for Individual Credit Investigation Business and approved eight institutions, including Zhima Credit Management Co., Ltd, Tencent Credit Co., Ltd, Shenzhen Qianhai Credit Center Limited Company, Pengyuan Credit Service Co., Ltd, CCX, Intellcredit Co., Ltd, Lakala Credit Management Co., Ltd and Beijing Sinoway Credit Co., Ltd, to prepare for individual credit investigation. The market of individual credit investigation was finally opened.

The openness of individual credit investigation business indicated that the credit investigation system of PBOC started to involve big data, which could enrich the credit investigation system and popularize credit investigation (Table 4).

Three Pillars of the Credit Investigation Industry

After developing for more than 30 years, China's credit investigation industry has made great progress. At present, the three pillars of the credit investigation industry are the legal system of credit investigation, the basic database of financial credit information and the credit investigation market. Through harmonious development of the three pillars, the credit investigation industry has sound system guarantee, development basis and space to improve.

The Legal System of Credit Investigation

The legal system of credit investigation includes four aspects, namely industry rules and regulations, the system of the basic database of financial credit information, the system of credit rating management and credit investigation standardization.

In terms of industry rules and regulations, in 2013, PBOC issued Management Regulations of the Credit Investigation Industry to make the industry have laws to abide by and Management Methods of Credit Investigation Institutions to further describe setup and supervision of credit investigation institutions. The publication of these two acts played

Table 4 Credit investigation industry development stage in China

Development stage	*Symbolic events*	*Characteristics*
Exploratory stage in 1978–1996	1. Established the first credit rating company—Shanghai Far East Credit Rating Co., Ltd 2. Cooperated with Dun & Bradstreet for foreign trade 3. Founded Xinhuaxin International Consulting Co., Ltd engaged in corporate credit investigation	No professional individual credit investigation institution engaged in corporate credit investigation
Start-up stage in 1996–2002	1. Implemented corporate lending system in nationwide banks in 1996 2. Launched personal credit investigation pilots in Shanghai in 1997 3. Founded NFCS in Shanghai in 1999 engaged in personal and corporate credit investigation 4. Systematically established tertiary database system in local places, provinces and headquarters by bank credit registration consulting system in 2002 and built nationwide consulting network	Individual credit investigation pilots

(continued)

Table 4 (continued)

Development stage	*Symbolic events*	*Characteristics*
Development stage in 2003–2014	1. Established Credit Information System Bureau in 2003 2. Established uniform individual credit information basic database among banks in January 2006 3. Implemented *Management Practices for Credit Investigation Industry* in March 2013 4. Enacted *Management Practices for Credit Investigation Institutions* in March 2013 5. Enacted *Social Credit System Building Planning Outline* in June 2014 (2014–2020) 6. The Central Bank began to issue corporate credit investigation license since June 18, 2014	Government instructed credit investigation, mainly public credit investigation service
Improvement stage in 2015–present	Informed eight companies including Zhima Credit to prepare for individual credit investigation work since January 1, 2015	Credit investigation industry oriented toward big data credit investigation

Data source Internet finance basis: personal credit industry development in-depth research report

an important role in promoting standard operation of credit investigation institutions.

As to the database system, PBOC published Interim Procedures of the Basic Database Management of Individual Credit Information and Management Methods of Bank Credit Registration Consultation (Trial) to regulate management systems of individual and enterprise credit information databases respectively. Meanwhile, it stipulated the access of new credit extension institutions, especially small-loan companies and financing guarantee companies, to databases.

In respect of credit rating management, in 2006, PBOC issued PBOC's Instructions on Credit Rating Management to manage credit rating of financial products, borrowing enterprises and guarantee institutions conducted by rating institutions. In 2008, it published PBOC's Notification on Management Strengthening of Credit Rating Operations in the Interbank Bond Market to stipulate on-site interview and work time in interbank bond market rating conducted by rating institutions. These two documents normalized business of rating institutions and promoted healthy development of the credit rating industry.

As for credit investigation standardization, PBOC published the Basic Standard Specification of Credit Information System Development, including five financial-industry standards, such as Design and Management of Credit Data Elements. It also formulated standard specifications relating to credit rating, including five financial-industry standards, such as Data Elements of Credit Investigation and Rating and Data Collection Formats of Credit Investigation Data Exchange, promoting standard business of rating institutions.

The Basic Database of Financial Credit Information

The establishment of the PBOC basic database of financial credit information was also carried out for more than 20 years. In terms of enterprise database, in 1992, PBOC started to conduct pilot projects of a loan note system in Shenzhen. In 1996, loan notes started to be popularized nationally and converted into electronic loan cards. In 1997, PBOC started to build a bank credit registration consultation system and formally launched it in 1999. In 2002, it set up a national-provincial-local-level bank credit registration consultation system. In 2004, PBOC started to organize commercial banks to set up the basic database of financial credit information. In 2005, it formally upgraded the system into a nationally unified basic database of enterprise credit information. In June 2006, the national network of the basic database of enterprise credit information was formed (Fig. 6).

In terms of individual database, in the early 1999, PBOC approved Shanghai to carry out pilot projects of individual credit investigation. In July of the same year, Shanghai Credit Information Services Co., Ltd was

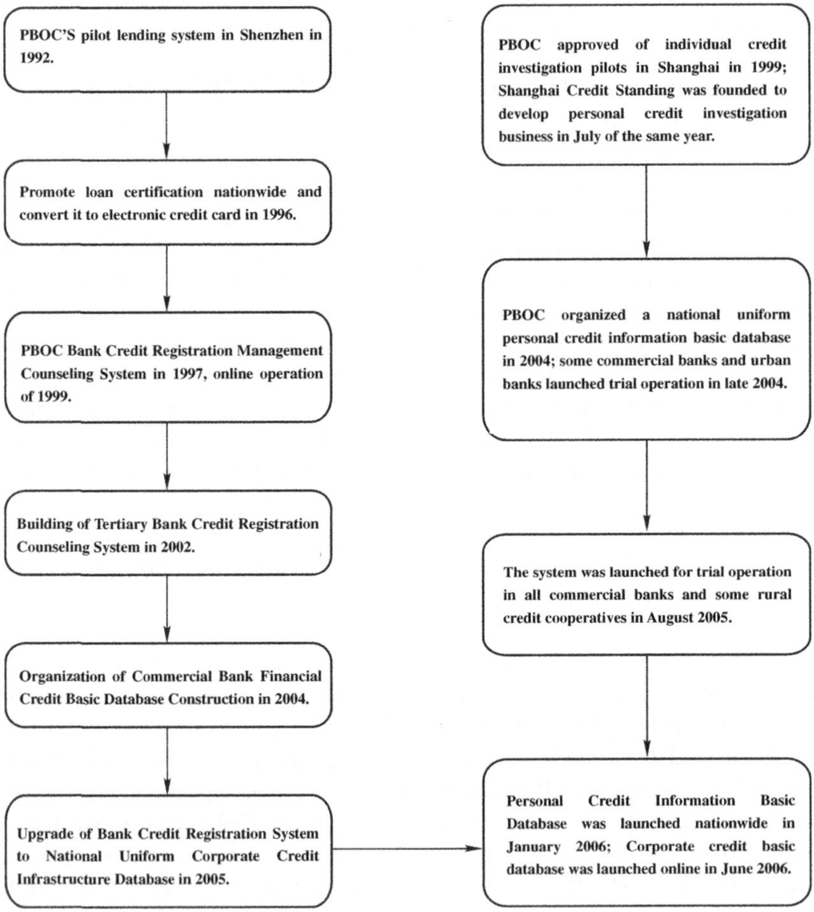

Fig. 6 Construction history of basic database of financial credit information (*Data source* Development Report for Chinese Credit Investigation Industry [2003–2013])

founded and started to conduct individual credit investigation. In 2004, PBOC organized commercial banks to establish nationally unified basic database of individual credit information and at the end of the same year, carried out pilot runs in some commercial banks and urban banks. In August 2015, it was expanded to cover all commercial banks and some rural credit cooperatives. In January 2006, basic database of individual credit information started to run formally in China.

Currently, basic database of financial credit information has been accessed to various credit extension institutions. Its information gathered increases rapidly with stably improved quality. By the end of 2012, basic database of enterprise credit information had accessed to 622 institutions, including 144 city-commercial banks, 108 foreign banks and more than 70 small-loan companies, cooperative financial institutions and finance companies. Basic database of individual credit information had accessed to 629 institutions, including 310 housing provident fund centers, 145 city-commercial banks and a few other institutions.

From the perspective of service scope, the individual database served 830 million people in 2013, including 320 million people who had credit records. By 2012, there were 154 thousand query user accounts, 270 million queries in a year and 749 thousand queries per day on average. In 2013, the enterprise database included 19.2 million enterprises with 133 thousand query user accounts, 100 million queries in a year and 274 thousand queries per day on average (Tables 5 and 6).

Case 1: Credit Reference Center of PBOC

The existing data of the Credit Reference Center of PBOC mainly comes from commercial banks, including loan credit transaction information of clients gathered by commercial banks and non-credit-transaction information that have direct and clear influences on credit subjects. In addition, the data mainly consists of credit data of the financial industry with non-credit-transaction information for auxiliary. It includes five types of information:

① Credit information produced by credit extension institutions approved by CBRC: this is the main data source of the Credit Reference Center, where the compulsory collection right of the Credit Reference Center has been guaranteed through administrative laws and regulations.

Table 5 Types and numbers of institutions accessing to basic database of financial credit information

Type of institutional users	*Corporate credit information basic database*	*Individual credit information basic database*
City commercial bank	144	145
Foreign bank	108	17
Micro-loan company	90	12
Cooperative financial institution	88	
Financial company	77	5
Trust investment company	46	
Village bank	28	34
National bank	21	21
Automobile finance company	10	13
Leasing company	7	
Asset management company	1	1
Housing savings bank	1	1
Insurance company	1	1
Housing provident fund		310
Rural credit cooperative		61
Consumer finance company		4
Loan company		4

Data source Research report for credit investigation industry in China (2003–2013)

Generally speaking, the informatization degree of credit extension institutions is high and the data in their databases, which mainly refers to clients' credit information of commercial banks is good.

② Credit information produced by credit extension institutions which were not planned by CBRC: As it is supplementary data, the right of compulsory collection of it is also guaranteed through administrative laws and regulations. Due to small scale and varied informatization of these institutions, the quality of their data is not stable. Representative institutions include small-loan companies, small-sum guarantee companies and pawn shops.

③ Data with credit features provided by public institutions, such as telecom payment records of the public: this type of data is usually

Table 6 Overview of financial credit information basic database

Year	*Individual*			*Company*		
	Number of participants (hundred million)	*Credit history (hundred million)*	*Inquiry condition (ten thousand times)*	*Number of record (ten thousand households)*	*Credit card (ten thousand households)*	*Inquiry condition (ten thousand times)*
2007	5.95	1.03	8627	1331.2	612.4	2102
2008	6.36	1.41	15,205	1447.4	694.2	3229
2009	6.65	1.76	22,966	1575.9	741.5	3890
2010	7.77	2.25	29,004	1697	790.9	5200
2011	8.05	2.62	24,146	1809.2	844.3	6930
2012	8.23	2.89	27,427	1858.8	900	9733
2013	8.3	3.2	34,000	1920		10,000

Data source Research Report for Credit Investigation Industry in China (2003–2013), revised edition

collected through permission or negotiation and its quality depends on the informatization degree of public institutions.

④ Credit and legal-behavior information produced in the process of administrative enforcement of law by government sectors: this type of data has an important influence on credit reports on subjects of credit. With the gradual disclosure of government's administrative information, this type of information can be collected via public channels.

⑤ Information about case registration, litigation, judgment and execution produced in the course of case trial by court: this type of information also has important effects on credit reports on subjects of credit. Except in special cases, justice information will be disclosed in future and gradually gathered via public channels.

Data processing of the Credit Reference Center can be divided into six procedures, namely the data provision layer, the data exchange layer, the basic data layer, the data processing layer, the product processing layer and data migration. The data provision layer extracts data from the application system by means of files and databases, etc. On the data exchange layer, format and logic validation of data are conducted and loaded to the basic database. The basic data layer can store verified data and provides data sources for data and product processing. The data processing layer includes main data management to recognize and integrate credit subjects

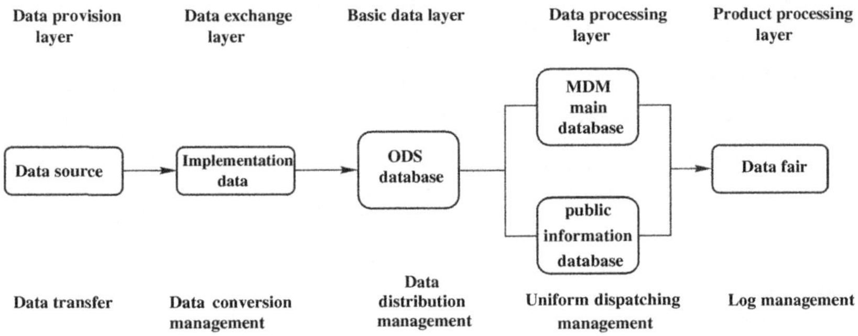

Fig. 7 Credit investigation center data processing framework (*Data source* The Internet Finance Report, 2014, modified)

and a shared information base to conduct crude processing of transaction data for data markets. On the product processing layer, products, including basic and value-added products, are processed. Data migration includes dispatch, data transfer and format conversion, etc.

According to different consumer scales and demands, the Credit Reference Center has planned five types of products: data products, tool products, solution products, outsourcing service products and credit subject service products. These five types of products provide different credit investigation services (Fig. 7 and Tables 7 and 8).

Credit Market

So far, China has basically established a multi-level comprehensive credit market with various types of credit investigation institutions and the Credit Reference Center as its core, where numerous basic and value-added services of credit information have been developed.

According to the classification of credit markets, there are different classification methods based on different standards. As shown in Table 8, credit markets can be divided in accordance with subjects of credit investigation information, business type and credit investigation service.

By the end of 2012, China has more than 150 credit investigation institutions and the income of the credit investigation industry was more than 2 billion yuan. China's credit investigation institutions mainly include about 20 credit information service organizations with government background, about 50 social credit investigation institutions, and more than

Table 7 Main products in credit investigation center

Product type	*Product content*
Data product	Credit report, instrument development, verification information service
Instrument product	All sorts of instruments for credit rating, molding, monitoring assessment, and asset management
Solution product	Loan application services, fraud detection services, customer life cycle management, receivable services, data management services, model representation tracking, and model performance monitoring services
Outsourcing service product	Provide IT technologies and business flow management trusteeship services for small, weak financial institutions and industry organizations
Subject of credit service product	Learn about users' credit record, assess credit risks and timely monitor personal credit changes and information services

Data source Xie Ping, The Internet Finance Report of 2014

Table 8 Classification of credit investigation market

Classification standards	*Type*
Credit investigation information subject	Corporate credit service market, individual credit service market
Business type	Credit registration market, credit survey market, credit rating market, other credit investigation markets
Credit investigation service area	Capital credit service market, credit service market, business credit service market, individual consumption credit service market

Data source Research Report for Credit Investigation Industry in China (2003–2013)

70 credit rating institutions, including 8 institutions engaged in rating of bond markets and other institutions engaged in rating of credit markets and involving rating of borrowing enterprises and guarantee companies, etc.

The present credit products are rich in types and cover enterprise credit reports, individual credit reports, credit investigation reports, credit subject rating reports, bond debt rating reports, borrowing enterprise rating reports, guarantee institution rating reports and continuous-tracking rating reports, etc.

The service scope of credit products covers markets, such as credit markets, bond markets, individual consumption credit markets and commercial credit markets, and multiple types of market subjects, such as individuals, enterprises, banks, non-bank financial institutions, professional service organizations and government sectors.

Enterprise Credit Investigation

Since the publication of Management Regulations of the Credit Investigation Industry and Management Methods of Credit Investigation Institutions in 2013, enterprise credit investigation conducted by credit investigation institutions should follow a filing system and the individual credit investigation should follow an examination system. Data of enterprise credit investigation is more complete than that of individual credit investigation with a mature credit investigation model and great market demands. Therefore, China's credit investigation industry gives priority to enterprise credit investigation.

On June 18, 2014, the central bank issued enterprise credit investigation operation registration certificates to eight institutions, including Zhima Credit Management Co., Ltd, Tencent Credit Co., Ltd, Shenzhen Qianhai Credit Center Limited Company, Pengyuan Credit Service Co., Ltd, CCX, Intellcredit Co., Ltd, Lakala Credit Management Co., Ltd and Beijing Sinoway Credit Co., Ltd, marking the openness of individual credit investigation. On July 25 of the same year, the central bank issued enterprise credit investigation licenses to thirteen institutions, including 3GOLDEN (Beijing), Zhongqi Pingxie (Beijing), Dongfang Anzhuo (Beijing), Chinadaas, Beijing Guofutai, Beijing Dongfang Jincheng, Beijing HRT, Quanlian (Beijing), Yuansu Zixun, Huaxia Xinrong, Beijing Lianxin, Lvcheng Xinhe (Beijing), Unicorn Credit (Beijing). On August 28, it issued enterprise credit investigation licenses to five institutions, including Shanghai Dongfang, Shanghai Jianke, Shanghai Huayuxin, Shanghai Jiesheng Business Consultation and Shanghai Yongcheng and on December 26, issued licenses to four institutions, including Houpu, Guochengxin (Beijing), Xinhe Huicheng (Beijing) and Bairong (Beijing). So far, the central bank has issued 25 and 5 credit investigation licenses to enterprises in Beijing and Shanghai, respectively, in four batches (Table 9).

Table 9 Licensed credit investigation enterprises

Time	*Batch/number*	*List*	*Area*
2014.6.18	8 in first batch	Zhongcheng Credit Investigation Co., Ltd, Lacarra (Beijing) Credit Investigation Service Co., Ltd, Beijing Yixinzhicheng Credit Assessment Co., Ltd, Network Credit Investigation Co., Ltd, Beijing Haizhi Jincheng Credit Management Co., Ltd, Zhongcheng Xinyuan Credit Investigation Co., Ltd, Beijing Guanjieshisu Credit Management Co., Ltd, Zhongpinzhixie (Beijing) Quality Credit Assessment Center Co., Ltd	Beijing
2014.7.25	13 in second batch	Jindianlianhang (Beijing) Information Technology Co., Ltd, Zhongqipingxie Credit Rating Center (Beijing) Co., Ltd, Dongfang Anzhuo (Beijing) International Credit Assessment Center Co., Ltd, Beijing Zhongshuzhihui Science and Technology Co., Ltd, Beijing Guofutai Credit Management Co., Ltd, Beijing Dongfangjincheng Credit Counseling Co., Ltd, Beijing and Rongtong Credit Service Co., Ltd, Quanlian (Beijing) Credit Investigation Co., Ltd, Yuansu Counseling Co.,Ltd, Huaxia Xinrong Science and Technology Co., Ltd, Beijing Lianxin Credit Investigation Counseling Co., Ltd, Lvchengxinhe (Beijing) Credit Management Co., Ltd, Unicorn Credit Assessment (Beijing) Co., Ltd	Beijing
2014.8.28	5 in third batch	Shanghai Dongfang Corporate Credit Investigation Co., Ltd, Shanghai Jianke Corporate Credit Investigation Co., Ltd, Shanghai Huayuxin Corporate Credit Investigation Co., Ltd, Shanghai Jiesheng Business Counseling Co., Ltd, Shanghai Yongcheng Corporate Credit Investigation Co., Ltd	Shanghai

(continued)

Table 9 (continued)

Time	*Batch/number*	*List*	*Area*
2014.12.26	4 in fourth batch	Houput Credit Investigation Co., Ltd, Guochengxin (Beijing) Credit Investigation Co., Ltd, Xinhehuicheng Credit Management (Beijing) Co., Ltd, Bairong (Beijing) Financial Information Co., Ltd	Beijing

Data source People's Bank of China

Individual Credit Investigation

Unlike enterprise credit investigation, the license of domestic individual credit investigation has not been opened yet. This is mainly because: 1. There are few demands of individual credit investigation in China. Unlike the consumer-oriented economy in the USA, China's demands of consumption credit are not abundant on the whole. Hence, individual credit service is limited. 2. Credit services of commercial banks meet most credit needs. As the credit investigation system with credit data of commercial banks as its core can meet loan demands of most consumers for housing, car buying and education, etc., there's no need of a third-party credit investigation institution. 3. Data of individual credit investigation is very limited. Most credit data are held by commercial banks and basic information of individuals and public information are held by government sectors. As commercial credit investigation institutions cannot assess to government sectors and banks, they cannot obtain basic and core data of consumers, let alone carrying out individual credit investigation. 4. The individual credit model is not mature. As there is no mature individual credit evaluation model in China, the development of the individual credit investigation industry is highly inadequate.

Due to various causes above, individual credit investigation developed slowly for a long time and was behind enterprise credit investigation. Even the credit investigation industry was opened to the public, the central bank still gave priority to enterprise credit investigation. However, with the development of information technology, especially search engine and cloud computing, some Internet giants started to discover individual characteristics of consumers from big data of consumers, including data of transactions, payment, behavior, credit, social contact, search and communication, etc. to evaluate loan repayment ability and repayment willingness of consumers and obtain the credit conditions of consumers. Therefore, network credit investigation based on big data started to develop rapidly. Though the gold content and applicability of big data are lower than those of credit data of banks, big data credit investigation can increase data dimensions of consumers to strengthen data correlations. Hence, big data credit investigation is a form of credit investigation and can be regarded as a rational supplement to traditional credit investigation. So far, there are only four institutions offering individual credit investigation service in China, namely the Credit Reference Center of PBOC (March 2006), Shanghai Credit Information Services Co., Ltd (July, 1999), Pengyuan Credit (April 2005), Anrong Huizhong (2012), where the Credit Reference Center with government background dominates. However, it cannot meet increasing credit investigation demands of consumers. Against this background, the central bank started to consider the openness of individual credit investigation.

On January 5, 2015, PBOC published the Notification on the Preparation for Individual Credit Investigation Business and asked eight institutions, including Zhima Credit Management Co., Ltd, Tencent Credit Co., Ltd, Shenzhen Qianhai Credit Center Limited Company, Pengyuan Credit Service Co., Ltd, CCX, Intellcredit Co., Ltd, Lakala Credit Management Co., Ltd and Beijing Sinoway Credit Co., Ltd, to prepare for individual credit investigation, marking the imminent openness of individual credit investigation. These eight institutions are on behalf of different types of data. Depending on Alibaba, Zhima Credit have huge payment data, transaction data and payment records of utilities from Alipay; Tencent Credit has mass social data; relying on the Ping An Group, Qianhai Credit has a large amount of financial data; Pengyuan Credit and CCX are typically old-brand credit enterprises; Intellcredit is a third-party credit enterprise founded in September 2013 and good at blacklist business; Lakala Credit depends on Lakala, a giant of offline payment; and Beijing Sinoway Credit is controlled by Shenzhen Yinzhijie, a listed GEM IT enterprise specializing in software products, software development, financial equipment and technology service for banks. Thus, it can be seen that these eight institutions have different backgrounds and advantages. Obviously, this is a pilot run. Of course, it is

Zhima Credit and Tencent Credit that attracted most attention, especially Zhima Credit.

Case 2: Zhima Credit

Unlike traditional credit investigation whose data mainly comes from the credit loan industry, Zhima Credit, originating from the Internet, has data from more sources and of more types and high timeliness. Its data covers repayment by credit cards, online shopping, transfer, money management, payment of utilities, renting information, address history and social relations, etc. As one of the eight institutions, Zhima Credit under Ant Financial has integrated payment and transaction data of more than 300 million individuals and more than 37 million small and micro businesses through Taobao, Tmall and Juhuasuan, etc. In addition, with the development of business, it also contains data relating to payment of utilities, taxi taking and medicine, etc. These data generated on the Internet are mainly characterized by real time and have traces that can be tracked easily. Collection and integration of these data are more comprehensive and accurate than those of traditional offline data (Table 10).

As the subsidiary brand of Ant Financial, Zhima Credit involves Zhima point, Zhima authentication, risk list base, Zhima Credit reports and Zhima rating, etc. On the basis of big data, Zhima Credit adopts five dimensions, namely user credit history, behavior preference, compliance capacity, identity traits and connections, to evaluate individual credit. These five dimensions corresponds to past credit account repayment records and credit account history; shopping and payment, transfer, money management; various types of credit service; ample and reliable basic personal information reflected in the process of using relevant services; the identity of friends and the degree of interaction with friends, respectively.[4] The basic calculation model of Zhima point conducts overall consideration of the five dimensions above, where there's no single item can directly or completely decide Zhima point.

Depending on businesses, such as e-commerce, payment, Internet finance, taxi taking and the future hospital plan, Alibaba has accumulated huge data. However, these data are not enough to realize full coverage. There are three main data sources of Zhima Credit, namely data owned by Alibaba, data of public service (including some government sectors)

[4] Data source: http://it.sohu.com/20150130/n408200740.shtml.

Table 10 Alibaba credit investigation system data source

System		*Alibaba credit investigation system*	*Credit investigation center in central bank*
Number of merchants/participants	Corporate credit investigation	Over 6 million households (Taobao.com only)	Over 10 million
	Individual credit investigation	145 million participants (Taobao.com only)	600 million
Credit investigation content	Corporate credit investigation	Sellers' identity information, commodity trading volume, shop vitality, user satisfaction, inventory, cash flow, water and electricity payment, and other data about shop operation	Corporate identity information, credit information, environmental protection information, payment of social maintenance cost, housing provident, quality testing information, unpaid wage information and payment of telecommunication information fee
	Individual credit investigation	Buyer information and corporate credit investigation system; buyer identity information, online shopping expenditures, living payment, social vitality	Individual bank credit information, identity information, payment of social security fee and housing fund
Data source		Automatic system recording	Commercial banks and government departments

Data source Xie Ping, The Internet Finance Report of 2014

and data submitted by users. Zhima Credit scores these data. As Zhima Credit constantly obtains external data through purchase, cooperation and replacement, data of Alibaba may only account for about 30% of total data of Zhima Credit in the future.

Case 3: Tencent Credit

Tencent Credit possesses 800 million QQ accounts, more than 500 million WeChat accounts and more than 300 million payment users as well as QQ space, Tencent website, QQ e-mail and Weibo, etc., leading to great advantages.

In 2013, Tenpay of Tencent started to attempt credit investigation and help users to create personal credit. It is reported that on the basis of active users of QQ and WeChat as well as SNS and Tencent website, Tencent Credit will predict individual risks and credit through mass data mining and analysis technology.

In addition to internal data of Tencent, Tencent Credit also introduces external data, including data of the central data and social economy, such as flight ticket transactions, education institutions and data of other information companies. Wang Xiaoxia, assistant general legal counsel of Tencent Group, points out that the data of the present credit investigation system cannot support the development of the Internet, which requires mass external data, such as data from dating websites, transportation websites and public departments, even data of social network and mobile locations as supplement. For instance, we can locate home and unit addresses of users according to their GPS locations.

Through comparison between Zhima Credit and Tencent Credit, it can be seen that they have both similarities and differences. They mainly have two similarities:

Their data have few relations with loan behavior and play a limited role in evaluating credit. In fact, this is not a specific deficiency for Zhima Credit and Tencent Credit, but a common problem in the big data credit investigation industry. As their data could not lead to effective credit investigation, they started to evaluate credit of borrowers with Internet big data. From this perspective, we should not judge big data credit investigation too harshly. This is the problem of this industry. Big data credit investigation is the supplement to central-bank credit investigation. Zhima Credit mainly possesses payment and transaction data and doesn't involve the credit industry. However, Alibaba Small-loan started to conduct credit evaluation with these data early with a bad debt rate of less than 1%, resulting in a good effect. Tencent mainly possesses social data, which is less related to credit loan and even has nothing to do with economic transactions. Therefore, big data credit investigation represented by Alibaba and Tencent has to face an awkward situation of limited data value.

In fact, the social data of Tencent can have good effects on network marketing and promotion. If it is used for credit investigation, it will make little sense. The application of social data to credit verification in the USA has proved this problem. As the largest P2P platform in the USA, Lending Club originally attempted to assess credit of users through their performance on Facebook, which eventually failed. Afterward Lending Club turned to obtain data from American Credit Bureau, leading to great reduction of its bad debt rate.

Though Alibaba possesses mass transaction data, these data are of certain value for individual credit investigation. As for non-mainstream data, such as browsing cookies, online length and active degree, their effect on individual credit investigation is quite limited. The primary defect of big data is that it has no loan record, leading to its limited credit model. The accuracy of big data credit investigation may be only 70% of that of the risk control model of ppai.com. In the model of ppai.com, repayment records and behavior of users account for 50% ~ 60% of the data, social data of users only accounts for 8% ~ 9% and the proportion of consumption data is less than 10%. Though Alibaba and JD have launched Ant Check Later and Baitiao, respectively, they cannot attract enough users in a short time, leading to limited data. Perhaps they can provide valuable personal information after a period of development.

In addition, it is still unknown that whether it can access to the Credit Reference Center of PBOC. Whether private credit investigation enterprises access to the core data of the Credit Reference Center (such as income, social security records, credit card records and loan records, etc.) directly determines the effectiveness of their credit investigation reports. At present, most P2P platforms have to spend lots of time and money in offline credit investigation because they cannot access to the data of the Credit Reference Center.

If Zhima Credit and Tencent Credit cannot access to the credit investigation system of PBOC, it means that the credit reports of third-party credit investigation may not be recognized by mainstream financial institutions. Due to lack of credit data, third-party credit investigation institutions have to keep trying to find out data dimensions that can reflect credit conditions of borrowers. Then they slowly replace traditional financial data with their internal data. It usually takes three to five years to complete this process. Taking P2P as an example, a credit cycle usually requires 1.5 ~ 3 years. That is to say, to understand the credit condition of a borrower, a credit investigation institution must wait until the termination of the credit cycle, which still requires repeated verification.

Furthermore, the data of the Credit Reference Center is not complete. In terms of the individual database, though it covers 850 million people, only 320 million people have credit records. Among these 320 million people, most of them are quality clients who have business contact with banks. However, people covered by the third-party credit investigation are grass-roots clients who have few credit records. Therefore, even they access to the central-bank system, it's still likely that the data is insufficient. It still needs exploration of third-party credit investigation companies.

However, there are still many differences between Zhima Credit and Tencent Credit:

First, Tencent has more data than Alibaba. The data of Zhima Credit mainly comes from Alipay and Taobao. Now Alipay has more than 300 million real-name users and its daily data processing capacity is more than 30 PB, amounting to the aggregate data of 5000 national libraries. Its data involves online shopping, repayment, transfer and personal information of users. In respect of user volume and use frequency, Tencent is even better than Alibaba. There are more than 500 million WeChat users and more than 800 million active QQ users. In addition, the big-data system of WeBank has gathered 40 trillion pieces of data information.

Second, in terms of data type, Alibaba mainly possesses data of payment and transactions, while Tencent mainly hold social data. It is determined by their platforms. As a senior e-commerce brand, Alibaba possesses huge data of payment and transactions. Starting with online dating software, Tencent has mass dating data from QQ and WeChat. Hence, their data types are different.

Third, their data values are different. Generally speaking, the data that is more related to capital has larger value. As a third-party payment tool, Alipay not only provides payment service for Taobao, but also enters the network PC payment market, maintaining a market share of 50%. In addition, its share of the mobile market is close to 70%. The more scenes an app involves, the more data it can possess, leading to clearer description of individuals' economic level. Therefore, Tencent's data is of a low gold content. However, as QQ and WeChat are of high use frequency, Tencent may catch up from behind in the future if they expand their application scenes (Table 11).

Fourth, their capacities of analytical application are different. Alibaba's capacity of analysis on Internet credit investigation data has been verified. For example, Ali Small-loan carries out credit evaluation and extension according to users' data on the platform and users can apply for loan without guarantee or pledge. From 2010 to March 2014, it provided loans worth 190 billion yuan for more than 700 thousand small and micro businesses. Its bad debt rate is less than 1%. However, Tencent has not launched similar credit investigation service yet. In this respect, Alibaba is far better than Tencent.

Fifth, recognition and application by external institutions: in fact, Alibaba has provided credit investigation service for banks. In July, 2014, Alibaba declared to cooperate with seven banks, such as Bank of China and China Merchants Bank, and launch a clean loan plan based on network commerce credit: a high version of network commerce loan, where the highest credit extension involves 10 million yuan. Banks

Table 11 Comparison of BAT data

Company	*Data*	*Technology*	*Talent*	*Direction*
Alibaba	E-commerce data Credit data	Bottom layer system Concurrent processing	System grading talent, such as Linux, Kernal, database, server	Improve bottom layer system Create a co-sharing platform
Tencent	Relation data Social contact data	Low-profile technology, strong executive force, closed development, collective overtime, reward incentive	Strong technical Executive force Focus on high-efficient cooperation	Complete product line, form a stable ecosphere, develop products
Baidu	Public data Demand data	Data aggregation Semantic understanding In-depth learning	Headhunting high-end talents in related fields	Combine research and practicability around search

Data source Xie Ping, The Internet Finance Report of 2014

provided capital, while Alibaba provided transaction data and business rules. It was Alibaba that evaluated borrowers and loan amounts. Banks took all risks of bad debts. As risk control is the lifeline of banks, banks should set the highest threshold of data accuracy. Banks endowed the lending right with Alibaba, because they trust its data and its capacity of analytical application. Hence, in this regard, Alibaba is also much better than Tencent.

5 Problems of Credit Investigation

The overall development plan of China's credit investigation industry is to establish a credit investigation system led by the Credit Reference Center and promoting common development of multi-level credit investigation institutions. The Credit Reference Center is responsible for building a nationally unified basic database of individual credit information, while multi-level credit investigation institutions play a supplementary role. However, there are still many problems relating to the present credit investigation system of China, restricting the further development of the credit investigation industry.

Low Coverage of Population

The credit rating system of the USA involves three major credit investigation institutions and FICO and covers 85% of the population. The rest 15% of the population are covered by ZestFinance, a rising credit investigation company. However, the credit investigation system of China is mainly built by the Credit Reference Center. Though the system covers 850 million people, among them, only 320 million people have credit records and the rest 530 million people only have basic information. Therefore, these 530 million people and people who are not covered by the system consist of a large market gap of the credit investigation industry.

Rare Types of Credit Investigation Data

The data of the Credit Reference Center mainly comes from banks and includes basic information, credit cards and bank cards, etc. of individuals. Though these data are the most important, they cannot fully reveal the credit condition of individuals.

Limited Collection of Credit Investigation Data

In January 2013, Management Regulations of Credit Investigation was issued to clearly stipulate collection of individual information. For instance, it prohibits credit investigation institutions from gathering individual information of religion, genes, fingerprints, blood types, diseases and medical history and other individual information that mustn't be gathered according to laws and administration regulations. Credit investigation institutions should not collect information of individuals' income, deposit, securities, commercial insurance, real estates and taxes. However, Credit investigation institutions should clearly inform credit subjects of possible negative consequences caused by providing the information, except they obtain their written consent. As the data that credit investigation institutions cannot gather reflect individuals' credit condition most, the Management Regulations shows a very obvious effect on restricting the development of the credit condition industry.

Different Data Formats

Data of institutions, such as banks, have a similar standard, format and definition. However, big data gathered by private institutions are of different formats, definitions, business operations and extension standards, so it's difficult to develop a unified data standard.

CHAPTER 10

Where is the Road: The Future of Internet Finance

Internet finance has attracted much attention in a short time which represents people's interest in it but calls for management of Internet finance in case of occurrence and spread of risks. Now people fail to come to any agreement on the future of Internet finance. As said at the beginning of this book, according to development experience, Internet finance can only be a supplement to traditional finance and cannot replace it, which should be assured. It can be predicted that various industries, including traditional finance, will be combined with the Internet in the near future. There will be enduring competition and cooperation between traditional finance and Internet finance. China hopes to accelerate financial reform through certain development of Internet finance. In the future, Internet finance may be integrated with the Internet of traditional finance.

Internet finance is a financial form which is formed in a short time and developed rapidly. Characterized by big data, low cost and convenient and fast user experience, Internet finance develops a complete ecosphere of Internet finance, including models of credit assessment, financial search, investment and financing and payment, and a complete financial closed loop. All of a sudden, a wave of Internet finance sweeps the whole nation and Bao-type products, P2P, crowdfunding and supply chain finance are quite popular among people. In addition, the regulatory authority changes its attitude toward Internet finance from cautious to salutatory. As Internet finance obtains tacit permission of regulatory authority and

Q. Guan and W. Gao, *Internet Finance*,
The Great Transformation of China,
https://doi.org/10.1007/978-981-16-4740-6_10

is supported by the common people, it seems that Internet finance has obtained favorable climatic, geographical and human conditions. As a result, it is obsessed with the idea of becoming the third type of financing mode, following indirect financing and direct financing, and even shows a trend of complete subversion of traditional finance. How on earth does the role of Internet finance play; how will the future of Internet finance be; and how do we develop Internet finance normatively?

1 The Role of Internet Finance

The appearance of Internet finance is passive behavior. Jack Ma once doughtily said, "if banks don't change, we will change banks". At first, you may feel how heroic it is. However, after tasting it carefully, it is full of helplessness. The most important thing for a business is to focus, professional and whole-hearted. However, nobody likes to not exert strengths but put his finger into another's pie. However, in an old economic model and a financing mode, the new Internet mode represented by Alibaba cannot find favor in traditional finance, which is determined by the environment of economic development. It is not so much competition between new and old financial modes as fighting between new and old financial modes. The factor-input economic model represented by traditional low-end manufacturing and the innovation-driven economic model represented by the high-end manufacturing industry must correspond to different investment and financing systems. The transformation from the former to the latter must be accompanied by the transformation of investment and financing modes.

In the economic model with the traditional manufacturing industry as its core, led by large enterprises, real estate enterprises and local investment and financing platforms, traditional finance pours massive funds into manufacturing and real estate, etc. to support economic growth driven by investment and export and obtain monopoly spreads. In the stage of commodity shortage featured by batch, homogenization and price, production relations tally with requirements of productivity growth. However, in the economic pattern with the service industry as its core, demands for commodities gradually be of individualization, intelligence, customization and the enterprise organization form gradually be of miniaturization. The primary cause for appearance of Internet finance is the contradiction between increasing financing demands of middle- and small-sized enterprises and the intrinsic mode of large enterprises of traditional financial services. In other words, the appearance of Internet finance is not active behavior but a new financial service mode appeared because the inherent financial system cannot provide financial service for middle- and small-sized enterprises.

It can be seen that now and even some time in the future Internet finance mainly covers middle- and small-sized enterprises, small and micro businesses, individual business and individuals, etc. This group is mainly characterized by lack of credit assurance, so that they cannot obtain adequate financial service from traditional financial institutions. However, their exuberant and huge financial needs generate a huge market. First, traditional finance needs to cover large enterprises. Second, they direct the eyes upon grass-roots economy and step back because of its high service cost. As a result, the Internet finance appeared to make up for the market space left by traditional finance. It determines that in the period of economic transition or an even longer period, Internet finance can only be a beneficial supplement to traditional finance, which won't change as a trend. Internet finance can conduct financial innovation, including modes, products and services. Internet finance contributes to improvement of efficiency of financial services, reduction of operating costs and optimization of resource allocation and also impacts the traditional financial system in many aspects. However, it cannot subvert the leading position of traditional finance, which should be clearly noted. Now many voices advocate the development of Internet finance, which is good, but we beg to differ with people who advocate subversion. Now Internet finance is still in the early stage of development. Though the ecosphere of Internet finance has been initially formed, many industries relating to Internet finance are not mature yet with nonstandard development and constant change. Hence, it is not realistic to entrust many responsibilities and obligations to Internet finance. The appearance of Internet finance is a passive process forced by low efficiency and low coverage of Internet finance. Internet finance is used to cover a field, instead of replacing the traditional field.

According to the scale of Internet finance, the current scale of Bao-type products, P2P, big data finance and crowdfunding, etc. cannot put on a par with that of traditional finance. Hence, Internet finance still has a long way to go. The most important task now is to for a sound development model, which is crucial for the development of Internet finance. Now the rapid development of Internet finance is also accompanied by much disorderly and uncultivated development, where many cases have offset the original track of Internet finance and become some legal coats of illegal finance. In this condition, it is ridiculous to blindly advocate the replacement of traditional finance by Internet finance. In fact, the reason for appearance of this point of view is that perspective is biased. Third-party payment, P2P, big-data finance, crowdfunding and Bao-type finance serve small businesses and individuals. Internet finance service is characterized by small scale, large amount and quick frequency, etc., verifying its service objects. These objects are in striking contrast with service objects of the traditional financial system. The market of Internet finance is determined by the scale of these groups, instead of by all groups. Internet finance cannot provide high-quality finance service that traditional financial institutions provide for large enterprises and institutions. Especially in respect of risk control and risk pricing, the present strength of Internet finance doesn't allow itself to shake the traditional finance. In other words, now Internet finance cannot offer high-level customized service for clients. In this condition, can Internet finance replace the traditional finance?

We should face the role and positioning of Internet finance squarely, which is of important significance for research on Internet finance. That's also why this book stated a brief description on positioning of Internet finance in the beginning. Perhaps readers have many questions in the process reading this book, maybe because they have no clear positioning of Internet finance. Now there are many studies on Internet finance and researchers include officials, scholars and financial practitioners, etc. After reviewing many related studies, people can have blurry understanding on Internet finance and may think that Internet finance can solve all problems appearing in traditional finance and then magnify the action of Internet finance. However, in fact, now Internet finance is still in a primary stage and only develops a narrow concept. The ecology of Internet finance is small and the real ecology of Internet finance of the whole society has not been formed yet. In this condition, the main part of the ecology of Internet finance can only be grass-roots economy in the society and the ecology of Internet finance has no ability or strength to provide effective financial service for all orders of society. However, it may have such ability and strength in the future.

2 The Development of Internet Finance

Now many people ask what the development of Internet finance is like. Though it's difficult to answer it, we can see the three future development stages: 1. the development of narrow-sense Internet finance; 2. the Internetization of the traditional finance industry; and 3. the Internetization of the whole financial industry.

Now the Internet finance that we discuss mainly refers to its narrow-sense concept. The ecology of Internet finance is in a stage of development and perfection. From the perspective of industry development, different financial models, products and services keep changing. In 2013, Bao-type products burst out; in 2014, P2P platforms rose sharply; and in 2015, equity-based crowdfunding grew up. Now each mode is growing up rapidly and also changing quickly without a mature business model, which will be an important characteristic in the future development of Internet finance. Another characteristic is constant perfection of the whole ecology of Internet finance, including credit investigation, search, money management, investment and financing and payment. Now money management, investment and financing and payment are developing rapidly and the development of payment and money management is relatively mature. However, credit investigation and search have not been developed yet, requiring certain time. It's worth noting that if Internet finance wants to become a type of business and form a type of strength, it must be manifested in the form of ecosphere. One or a few business models cannot be called Internet finance and only have limited influence. Now the embryonic form of the ecosphere of Internet finance has been basically formed with various functions. However, each part of the ecosphere is relatively independent with poor mutual coordination. For example, now the P2P business cries out for credit assessment of borrowers, but now there's no special credit assessment company yet. As a result, it cannot cover loan transactions, and lots of P2P companies have to pay much attention to conduct offline survey, increasing costs of P2P financing. Consequently, P2P companies are quite similar to private small-loan companies and lose the connotation of Internet finance. However, big-data finance solves this problem by using mass data accumulated by the platform in credit assessment. However, its limitation is relating to user applicability. Big-data finance cannot provide service for users outside the platform because of lack of data accumulation. In fact, it reflects the vulnerability of the present Internet finance. In the ecology of Internet finance, various functions develop unevenly and cannot coordinate with each other effectively to exert a synergistic effect. Thus, they have to rely on the offline part, which is the reason for the popularity of the Internet finance O2O mode. A perfect Internet finance requires no offline end, but now is not the right time yet. The current Internet finance only establishes a rough framework and a boundary, but various models are not mature or interconnected yet. Thus, the present ecology of Internet finance is not perfect yet and cannot fully exert its strength. After all, the Internet finance is only three years old and we cannot expect a perfect system developed in mere three years. In the coming years, its models and systems will be constantly perfected. This process may last long, but Internet finance is of high vitality on the whole.

Meanwhile, we should note that traditional finance also pays much attention to Internet finance. Though what Internet finance does is what traditional finance is not willing to do and worth doing and covers groups that traditional finance does not cover, traditional finance pays high attention to the spirit and thinking of Internet finance and related business, models, products and service. For example, Yu'e Bao have absorbed a large number of current deposits from commercial banks, leading to money shortage of banks, which is a great impact on these banks. Though Internet finance cannot impact the leading position of traditional finance in a short time, traditional finance should learn from the thinking of Internet finance. In fact, traditional finance is also coping with infiltration of Internet finance actively; Shanrong Business of China Construction Bank, Jiaobohui of Bank of Communications and Zhongyin Yishang of the Bank of China, for example. From the perspective of Internet finance, in fact, the big data advantage of traditional finance is far bigger than that of Internet enterprises. Among "1+7" types of big data, credit data is the most effective for credit assessment and it is owned by commercial banks. However, unfortunately, commercial banks have never taken full advantage of their big data. According to the thinking of Internet finance, the most important thing is to exert effects of big data. If traditional finance realizes this point, it will carry out quicker layout of Internet finance than Internet enterprises. However, as a "regular army", traditional finance can rely on the system advantage, where private enterprises cannot. Hence, it can be predicted that the future Internet finance will be a process of integration. Internet enterprises will enter into the financial field, while traditional finance will also come into contact with the Internet. Their core is to provide better service for clients through utilization of their relative advantages and Internet thinking. Finance is always the core of Internet finance. In the process of integration, both sides cooperate and compete with each other at the same time. The result of the business competition is Internetization of the industry, which is consistent with the "Internet Plus" action plan.

It can be imagined that in the future, the financial industry and even the whole society will be Internetized. At that time, the name of finance Internet may disappear and all industries will be related to the Internet. As the whole financial industry will be conducted online, there would be no difference between traditional finance and Internet finance. That is to say, the future financial industry will be dominated by the Internet. At that time, after competition and cooperation of the financial industry, three types of companies will remain: 1. finance companies led by large financial institutions; 2. finance companies led by large Internet companies; and 3. characteristic vertical finance companies. These three types of company will constitute the main body of the financial industry and can completely cover all market individuals.

3 The Supervision of Internet Finance

Since the appearance of Yu'e Bao in 2013, the supervision problem of Internet finance has entered into endless arguments. Some people think it should not be supervised prematurely, for it can throttle financial innovation. In other words, they disagree to supervise it with traditional finance together and traditional means of supervision are not suitable for Internet finance. However, some people hold that Internet finance must be supervised in case of financial risks and it can also lead to healthy development of Internet finance. In fact, some Western countries also don't have existing experience about supervision of Internet finance and they also need to feel their way. Now regulators have admitted that the model of Internet finance is important for removing financing constraints of small and micro enterprises, increasing investment channels of consumers and improving resource allocation efficiency. Hence, with the development of Internet finance, two matters should be considered: namely innovation and supervision.

The Internet itself is a result of innovation. Hence, the development of Internet finance must center on innovation. It has a positive effect on efficiency improvement of financial services and optimization of resource allocation, where people have reached an agreement on it. Regulators place great hopes on innovation of Internet finance and support innovation. However, from another angle, to avoid large-scale financial risks, supervision is necessary. However, how do relevant departments supervise and how do they grasp the degree of supervision? Once the degree of supervision is not grasped well, it's very likely that it will throttle the innovative property of Internet finance. This is because innovation needs to break through the original supervision limits. According to the existing thinking, the supervision of Internet finance should be led by the People's Bank of China, where CBRC, CSRC and China Insurance Regulatory Commission take concerted action. The government also feels conflicted about the supervision of Internet finance and it's difficult for it to balance between innovation and supervision. In an unguarded moment, it may impact the development of the whole industry.

As for supervision of Internet finance, we should pay attention to the following issues. The first issue is about qualification. Does Internet finance have a threshold? Though many Internet finance companies don't have strong strength in respect of capital, risk control and technology, etc., they can enter the field of Internet finance easily to engage into finance activity. For instance, many P2P platforms start accommodation of funds as long as they establish a website. The loose admittance in the early stage leads to high risks of platforms in the later stage. Therefore, risks should be controlled from the origin, namely the issue of admittance qualification. We tend to adopt license management. We can carry out qualification examination and verification of companies or platforms and issue licenses. We do not recommend the filing system. As finance is a special industry characterized by high risks, wide spread and large influence, etc., it is usually out of control. Therefore, the filing system goes against risk prevention. We should stick to license management and issue a license of Internet finance business to companies with certain qualification and operation capability. For example, the third-party payment is managed with the license system. Through license management, we can raise the requirement of platforms in respect of capital, technology and risk control, etc. We should put an end to companies without capacity of financial service and clearly define the business scope of platforms. Now many platforms carry out many financial businesses according to the idea that "no license stands for all licenses and no scope indicates a full scope", enhancing the business risk. Hence, we should try to solve problems relating to platform qualification and business scope through license management.

In addition, during the operation of platforms, we should adopt principles of moderate supervision, classified supervision, collaborative supervision and innovative supervision. Though now the development of Internet finance is like a raging fire, on the whole, Internet finance still requires supervision. However, its supervision methods remain to be discussed. The first principle is moderate supervision, which leaves enough space for some financial models. On the premise of an exact bottom line, Internet finance is allowed to go ahead of the rest and bring its innovation superiority into full play. It's inadvisable to supervise these new models in a traditional way and regulators can give them proper supervision bonus. The second principle is classified supervision. That is to say, businesses should be classified into different types and managed respectively. For example, third-party payment and P2P clearly belong to different financial businesses, where the former is payment business, while the latter is investment and financing business. It is obviously improper if both of them are supervised in the same way. Therefore, we must adopt different supervision means for different types of business. The third principle is collaborative supervision. The same business in both traditional finance and Internet finance should be supervised in the same way. For instance, if Yu'E Bao allows investors to draw in advance without interest penalty according to the original interest rate, it goes against the principle of collaborative supervision. Essentially, Yu'E Bao still belongs to deposit management, so it must accord with the measures for the administration of deposits of commercial banks. If a client draws in advance, the interest should be calculated according to the interest rate of current deposit. If Yu'E Bao allows investors to draw in advance without interest penalty, it will cause a defect of policy and lead to interest arbitrage of supervision, going against the industry development. As for this problem, regulators should strengthen function supervision and behavior supervision, analyze the essence of Internet finance business and compare it with traditional finance business. Businesses with similar function should be managed according to the traditional method in case of interest arbitrage of supervision. The fourth principle is innovative supervision. According to characteristics of Internet finance development, we should adopt means of Internetization and informatization to conduct supervision and analysis and innovate online supervision tools. A new type of business requires new tools and methods. We should not rigidly adhere to old ways and methods. All new technology and thinking can be applied to supervision of Internet finance.

In addition, Internet finance should persist in serving entity economy, serving the overall situation and protecting interests of consumers. The cause for appearance of Internet finance is the demand of entity economy for financial service, so to serve entity economy is the mission and destination of Internet finance. Internet finance is not a capital game, but a bridge connecting capital needs and capital supply. Therefore, Internet finance should base itself upon small and micro economy, serve entity economy and put an end to capital pool, illegal fundraising and illegal deposit attaching, etc. As a beneficial complement to China's financial system, Internet finance is a part of China's financial system, which means that Internet finance must serve the overall situation with the entire financial system, ensure smooth operation of economy and maintain financial stability. Moreover, Internet finance should protect lawful rights and interests of investors. Facing grass roots, we must ensure lawful rights and interests of the masses and carry out sufficient information disclosure and risk warning.

4 Conclusion

At present, people's life is combined with the Internet in every respect; Internet+agriculture, manufacturing industry, medicine, education and housing, etc., for example. Internet finance is the most leading and mature industry among them. Now it is an era of whole-people Internet finance. Throughout China's financial history, Internet finance may be the most influential except bank deposits. This is the times of the Internet and also that of Internet finance.

First, we should understand that Internet finance is not a simple term, behind which there's huge network ecology. If there's no ecology behind Internet finance, Internet finance is hollow and cannot show so many influences. If the ecology is not rich enough, its development must be very limited. So far, the ecology of Internet finance includes credit investigation, search, third-party payment, online money management, big data finance, P2P and crowdfunding, where credit investigation, search and third-party payment belong to basic business and online money management, big data finance, P2P and crowdfunding belong to core financial business. Credit investigation is the precondition and basis of all financial activity. Search is to increase efficiency of information matching. Payment is the basic express to realize fund movement. The development of Internet finance is based on such a complete and rich financial system. In other words, these seven models are integral for Internet finance, determining the future development of Internet finance. However, so far, the development of these seven models is not even. Some of them are developed; third-party payment, for example; some, such as P2P, are developing rapidly; and some, credit investigation, for example, have not started yet. The boundary of Internet finance is already clear and the ecosystem is already complete. However, the ecosystem is far from normal operation. In our opinion, Internet finance is an overall concept and each model cannot do without the overall ecology. The most obvious example is that in a condition of lack of credit investigation, P2P platforms have to carry out much offline field research. In fact, it is not Internet finance in the strict sense but online traditional finance at most. If it can be called Internet finance, we are unworthy of the concept of big data. Hence, if Internet finance wants to achieve long-term development, each model in the ecology must be mature. If Internet finance is a bucket, each model is like its slab, which cannot be short. Otherwise, the whole ecology of Internet finance will be impacted. The ecology is of synergetic existence. Some models of rapid development also gradually realize that if other models are not developed, it will severely restrict its development. Thus, credit investigation has been put on the agenda.

In fact, besides the research, we often ask us what the future of Internet finance will be like; and will the term of Internet finance disappear five years later, which are difficult to answer. However, if we think carefully, there are some answers. The future world will be an Internet world of complete Internetization. The present concept of "Internet Plus" is the first to drive a reform of world Internetization. The essence of Internetization is digitization, changing all previous materialized thinking sets. In future, we can digitize everything and analyze digits and data through information technology and network technology and its application to production will become the core of a new industrial revolution. The core of Internet finance is big data thinking. Hence, they lead to the same destination. Since everything will be digitized, what will happen to the future Internet finance? We think the future finance industry will be completely online. Of course, there will be offline physical networks, which are essential. However, the physical networks will be small, intelligentized and community based. Online transformation will be the key point of future business to deal with all financial needs online. In this condition, can we simply call it Internet finance? At that time, Internet finance has included traditional finance. As a result, Internet finance has lost its original meaning and its concept may disappear. In addition, online transformation of traditional finance can also cover clients who were covered by Internet finance. Digital resources of traditional finance are far more than those of Internet finance, but the former has not been fully developed yet. It indicates that Internet finance cannot replace traditional finance. At that time, traditional finance and Internet finance have been integrated into a whole and we can no longer distinguish traditional finance from Internet finance.

Postscript

Each creation is like an adventure full of challenges. Exploration of the mysterious unknown and the idea of keep surmounting myself constitute my motivation to advance. In this process, loneliness, depression and vexation are the price that I should pay for exploration, creation and surmounting. However, when I finished this book, I felt slightly melancholy because of seemingly incomplete expression and thirst for starting again.

From creation to publication, this book experienced ups and downs. If I didn't cherish research results, readers may never see this book. Originally, this book intended to include appearance, models, impacts and future of Internet finance. However, due to limited time of writing and repeated prompting messages from China Institute for Reform and Development, I had no mood to finish additional contents, although I understood the feelings of the publisher. Consequently, I adjusted the outline of the book to highlight ecology and models of Internet finance. In my opinion, as these two directions are important development and breakthrough points of reform during the period of the "13th Five-Year Plan" or an even longer period, highlighting of them accord with the theme of this book. However, it also leads to many regrets. For example, the impact of Internet finance on traditional finance is increasingly obvious and the reform of financial institutions is also quickened, which is a respect of cooperation and competition between Internet finance and traditional finance. However, due to limited time and length,

Q. Guan and W. Gao, *Internet Finance*,
The Great Transformation of China,
https://doi.org/10.1007/978-981-16-4740-6

these contents cannot be expressed in this book. In this condition, it arouses my enthusiasm to write another book, which is already under conception.

Regardless of my hardships, I'd like to express my thanks to people who helped me. First, I'd like to express my thanks to Yu Zheng, chairman of Minsheng Securities, for his support. After Mr. Yu learned that I was creating this book, he highly supported me and encouraged me to study carefully for fruitful results. I remembered that when I first met Mr. Yu, he directly told me that though my study is important, how to combine theory with practice is more important, which should be the starting point and the foothold of this study. Mr. Yu also told me that we must consider the future trend of finance industry development comprehensively. For example, as for discussion on effects of Industry 4.0 on the financial industry, if we only focus on papers about Industry 4.0 without in-depth research, we may have no idea to deal with it. Mr. Yu's erudition, diligent thinking and practical style of work impressed me very much.

Second, I'd like to thank Zhang Dejiang, vice president of Minsheng Securities. When I first entered Minsheng Securities, Mr. Zhang explained the work direction to me and repeatedly advised me to pay attention to matters needing attention in work. For the sake of my study, he also gave me relevant books. Mr. Zhang's care and encouragement motivated my work and allowed me to integrate into work smoothly and quickly. Therefore, I feel deeply grateful for him.

Third, I'd like to express my thanks to Xin Shengli, general manager of Minsheng Securities. Mr. Xin is rich in work experience and has special understanding on Internet finance and Internet securities traders. When he introduced the blueprint of future development of Internet business of securities companies to me, I admired his calm and confident bearing.

Last but not least, I'd like to thank friends who helped me during creation of this book. I could not finish the enormous work without their help.

In addition, as I consulted lots of research results of experts and scholars, I'd like to show my thanks to them as well.

Qingyou Guan
Weigang Gao
April, 2015

References

Analysys. Enterprise analysis report: Alibaba [R]. 2014.
Analysys. A special research report on China's Internet financial finance market [R]. 2014.
ASKCI. In-depth analysis on market development of Yu'E Bao in 2013 [R].
AliResearch. A research report of Internet Plus [R]. 2015.
Chen Yanyan. SUNING and JD launch the "supply chain" service war by trying "small-loan" e-commerce [N]. *Securities Daily*, 12 December 2012.
Chengdu Shexin Caifu Equity Investment Fund Center. An in-depth research report on 2014 Internet Finance Industry in China [R].
CBN New Financial Research Center. *White paper of P2P online loan service industry in China 2013* [M]. Beijing: China Economic Publishing House, 2013.
Financial World of Xinhua News Agency, Internet Society of China, iResearch Group, Internet Laboratory and the Research Center of Internet Society of China [R]. 2014.
Hong Hao. A research report on the development trend of 2015—2018 Internet finance in China [R]. 2015.
Hu. *2014: The first year of online supply chain finance* [N]. Posts and Telecommunications Press, 21 April 2014.
iiMedia Research. A research report on P2P platform Market in China in the first half of 2014 [R].
iResearch and Haitong Securities. A research report on Internet of Securities Industry [R]. 2014.
iResearch. A case study report on the typical model of P2P microcredit [R]. 2014.

Q. Guan and W. Gao, *Internet Finance*,
The Great Transformation of China,
https://doi.org/10.1007/978-981-16-4740-6

iResearch. Research on the financial model of internet innovation [R]. 2013.
iResearch. A report on the trend of China's Internet consumption and finance industry [R]. 2014.
iResearch. A report on the annual Inspection of Internet payment Industry in China [R]. 2011.
iResearch. A report of the research on Chinese equity crowdfunding market [R]. 2015.
iResearch. A report of the research on offline receipt market in China [R]. 2011–2012.
iResearch. A report of the research on the China's mobile payment market [R]. 2012–2013.
ITJUZI and AngelCrunch . A report of Internet equity-based crowdfunding [R]. 2014.
Jiang Rong. Ecommerce giants scramble to launch supply chain finance [N]. *China Business Journal*, 24 December 2012.
Li Bing. DJ Finance appears in Gold Expo with Jingxiaodai and puts securitization of small-loan assets aside [N]. *Securities Daily*, 1 November 2014.
Li Keqiang. A government work report in 2015 [Z].
Li Wenlong. Supply-chain finance: fresh troops supporting small and micro businesses [N]. *Financial Times*, 16 August 2014.
Luo Mingxiong, Tang Ying and Liu Yong. *Internet Finance* [M]. Beijing: Chinese Financial & Economic Publishing House, 2013.
Nong Cheng. An analysis report on vertical search Industry of Internet finance [R]. 2014.
Ping An Bank. Peking University HSBC Business School, Internet Finance Work Committee of Internet Society of China, Chuangfuzhi and Shenzhen Yuanzhi Business Model Research Institute. A research report on internet financial business model [R]. 2014.
Rong 360. A report of China's Internet crowdfunding in 2014 [R].
Sheng Songcheng and Zhang Xuan. Management of Yu'E Bao and the Deposit Reserve [N]. *Financial Times*, 19 March 2014.
Sohu. A research report on the Top 16 enterprises of Internet finance in China [R]. 2014.
Sohu Finance and Economics and Rong 360. An annual report on Internet financial management 2014 [R].
SWS Research. Research on the present situation and future development trend of equity crowdfunding in China [R]. 2015.
Tang Xunfang . Transfer in three minutes, JD takes a further step for supply-chain finance [N]. 21 Century Economic Report, 10 December 2013.

The writing group of the Development Report of China Credit Investigation Industry of People's Bank of China. The Development Report of China Credit Investigation Industry (2003–2013) [R].

The financial stability analysis group of the People's Bank of China. *A report on China financial stability in 2014* [R]. Beijing: China Finance Publishing House, 2014.

Wang Rong. Jingbaobei upgrade supply-chain finance of JD [N]. *China Securities Journal*, 10 December 2013.

WDZJ. A brief report on P2P online loan industry in China in 2014 [R].

Xieping, Zou Chuanwei and Liu Haier. *Internet Finance Manual* [N]. Beijing: China Renmin University Press, 2014.

Xieping. 2014 Internet financial report: Lead to rational prosperity [R].

Xue Juan. Dunhuang network does supply chain financial service first [N]. *China Economic Times*, 22 August 2013.

Yang Dong and Su Lunga. Operation mode and risk prevention of equity crowdfunding platform [J]. *Journal of the National Public Prosecutor College*, 2014(7).

Yingcan Zixun and China Center for Financial Research. Annual report of China's online lending industry in 2014 [R].

Zhang Modong. Internet financial game upgrade supply chain financial innovation is expected to break through [N]. *Financial Times*, 8 February 2014.

Zero2IPO Group and Zhongchou.com. A statistical analysis report on the operation of crowdfunding model in China [R]. 2014.

Zero2IPO Research. A research report on 2015 investment in internet finance industry in China [R].

Zero2IPO Research. Savage growth of Internet finance: Bubbles or subverter? [Z]. 2014.

The manufacturer's authorised representative in the EU is Springer Nature Customer Service Centre GmbH, Europaplatz 3, 69115 Heidelberg, Germany. If you have any concerns regarding our products, please contact ProductSafety@springernature.com

Printed and bound by CPI Group (UK) Ltd, Croydon, CR0 4YY

30/09/2026

02225457-0018